W9-BSN-561

# YOU'RE SO COOL ②

YOUNGHEE LEE

**Translation: Jackie Oh**

**Lettering: Terri Delgado**

YOU'RE SO COOL, Vol. 2 © 2003 YOUNGHEE LEE. All rights reserved. First published in Korea in 2003 by Seoul Cultural Publishers, Inc. English translation rights arranged by Seoul Cultural Publishers, Inc.

English translation © 2008 Hachette Book Group USA, Inc.

Yen Press
Hachette Book Group USA
237 Park Avenue, New York, NY 10017

Visit our Web sites at www.HachetteBookGroupUSA.com and www.YenPress.com.

Yen Press is an imprint of Hachette Book Group USA, Inc. The Yen Press name and logo are trademarks of Hachette Book Group USA, Inc.

First Yen Press Edition: September 2008

ISBN-10: 0-7595-2863-2
ISBN-13: 978-0-7595-2863-5

10 9 8 7 6 5 4 3 2 1

BVG

Printed in the United States of America

# Sometimes, just being a teenager is hard enough.

**D**a-Eh, an aspiring manhwa artist who lives with her father and her little brother, comes across Sun-Nam, a softie whose ultimate goal is simply to become a "Tough guy." Whenever these two meet, trouble follows. Meanwhile, Ta-Jun, the hottest guy in town, finds himself drawn to the one girl that his killer smile does not work on–Da-Eh. With their complicated family history hanging on their shoulders, watch how these three teenagers find their way out into the world!

Available at bookstores near you!

# HISSING 1~4

**Kang EunYoung**

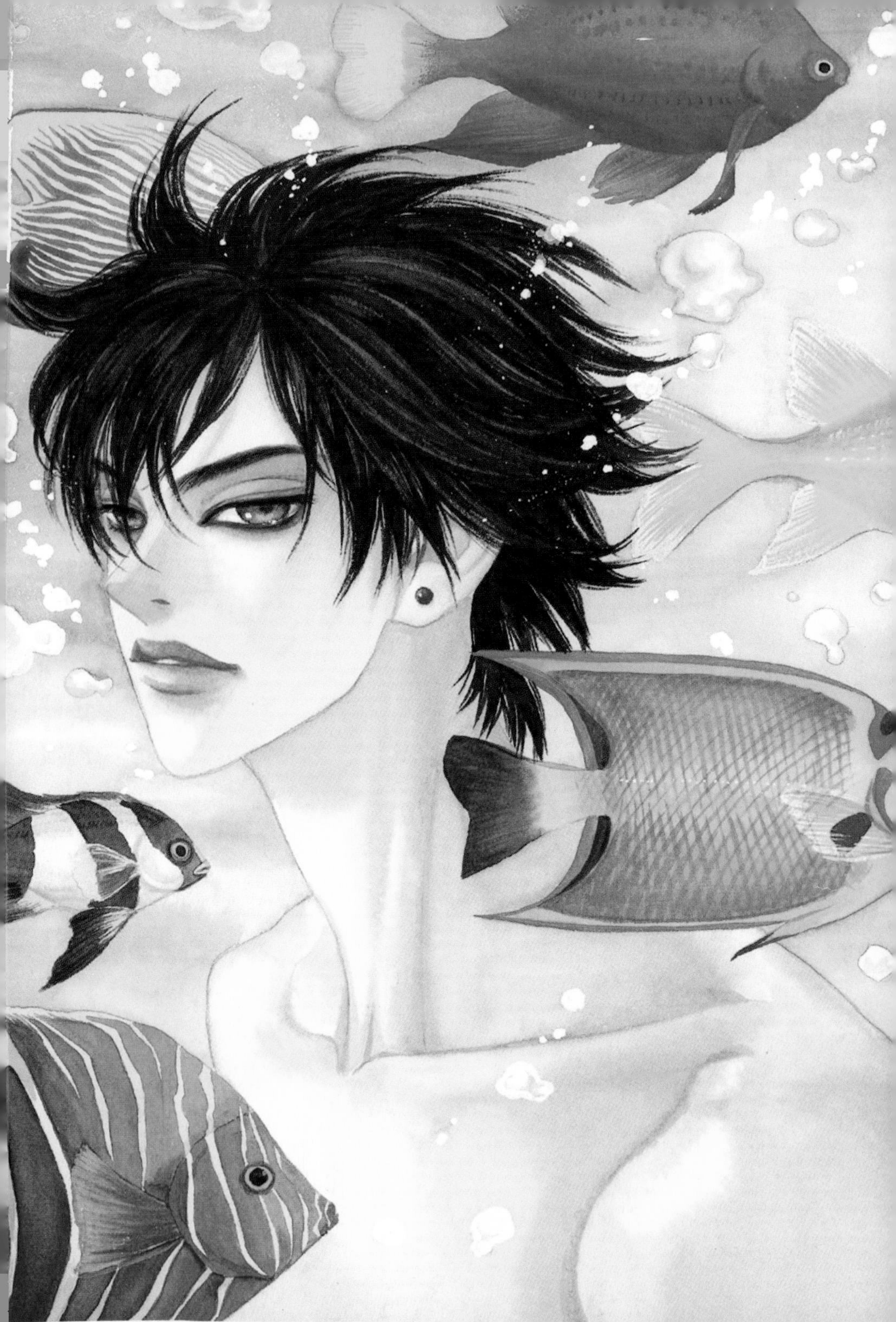

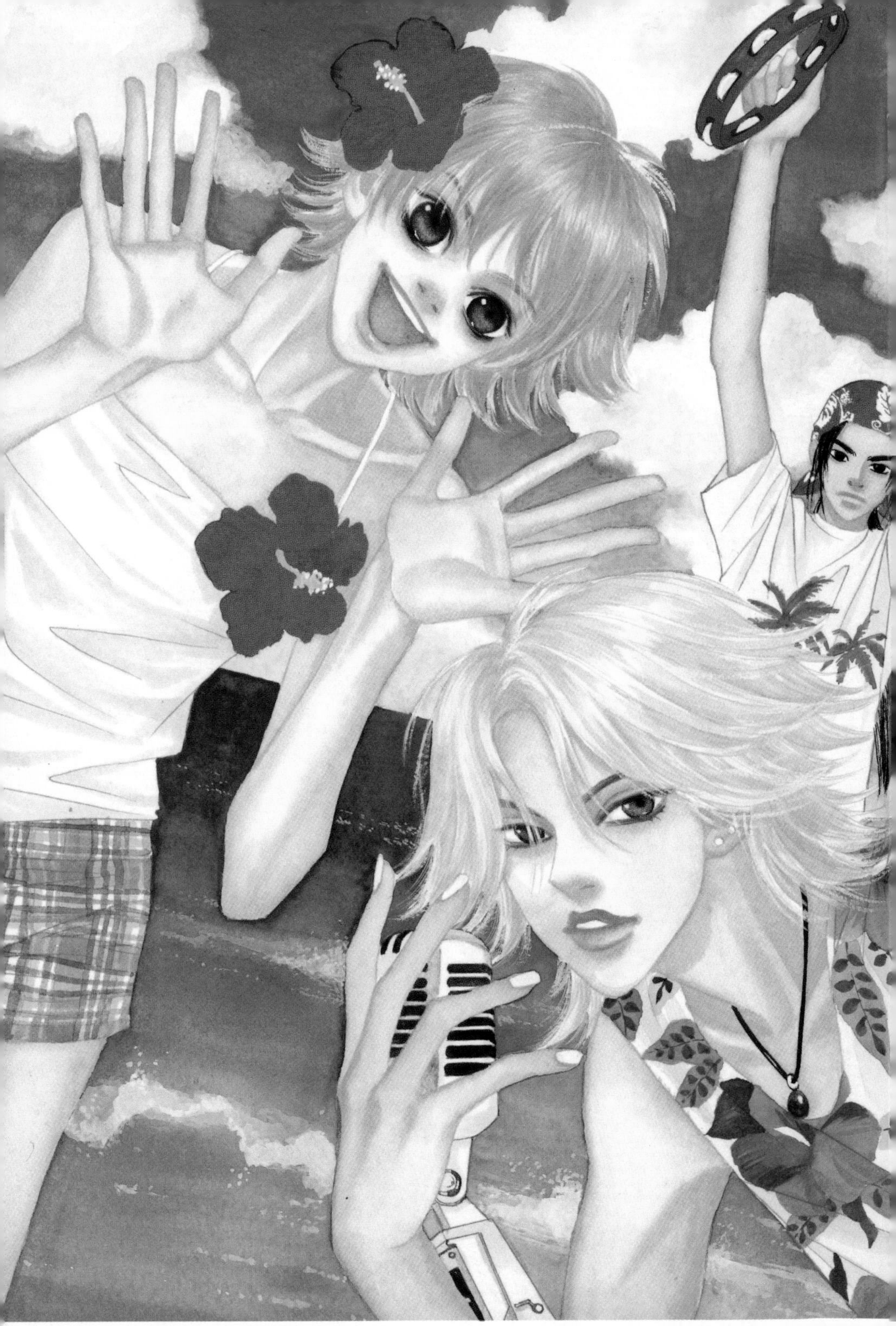

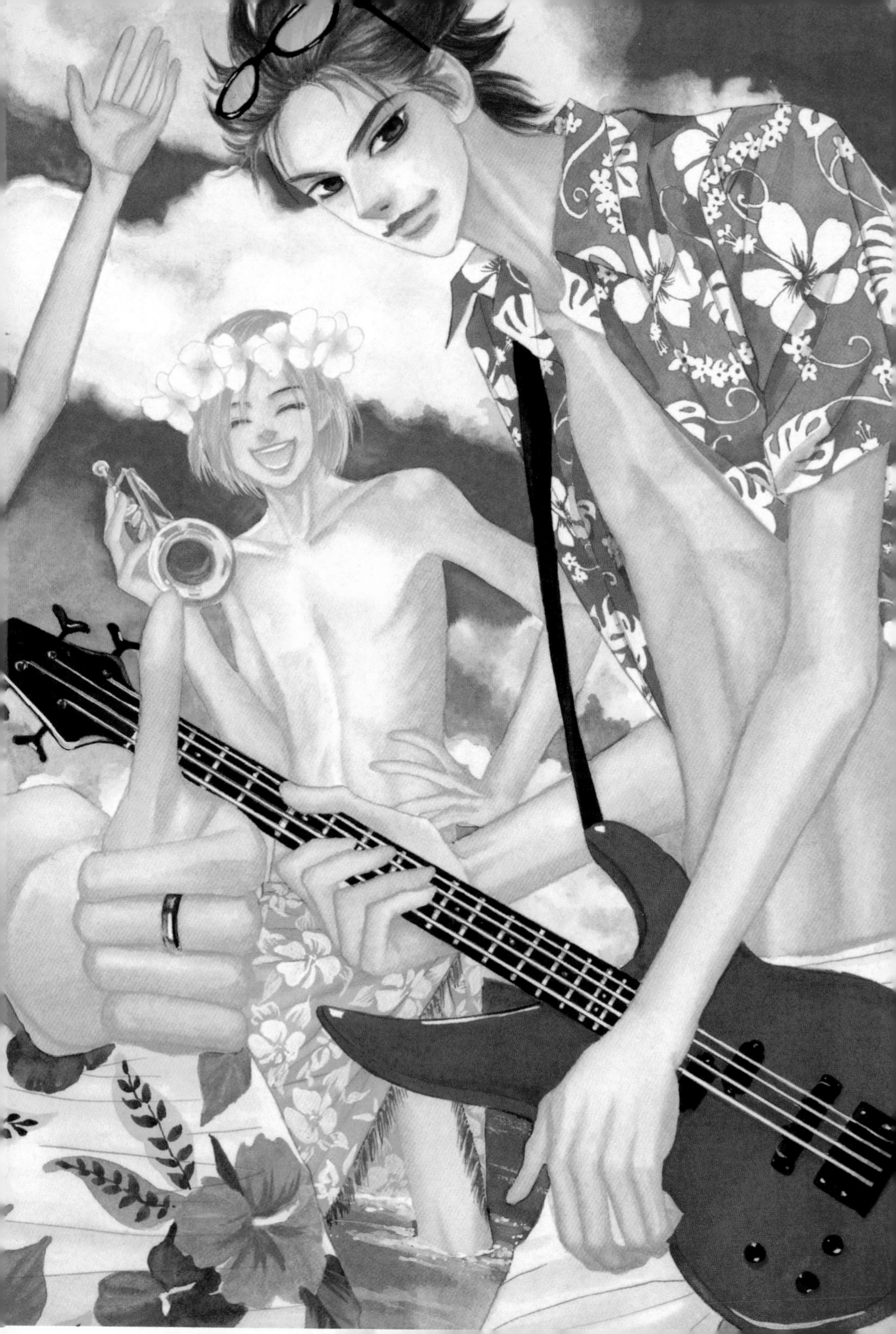

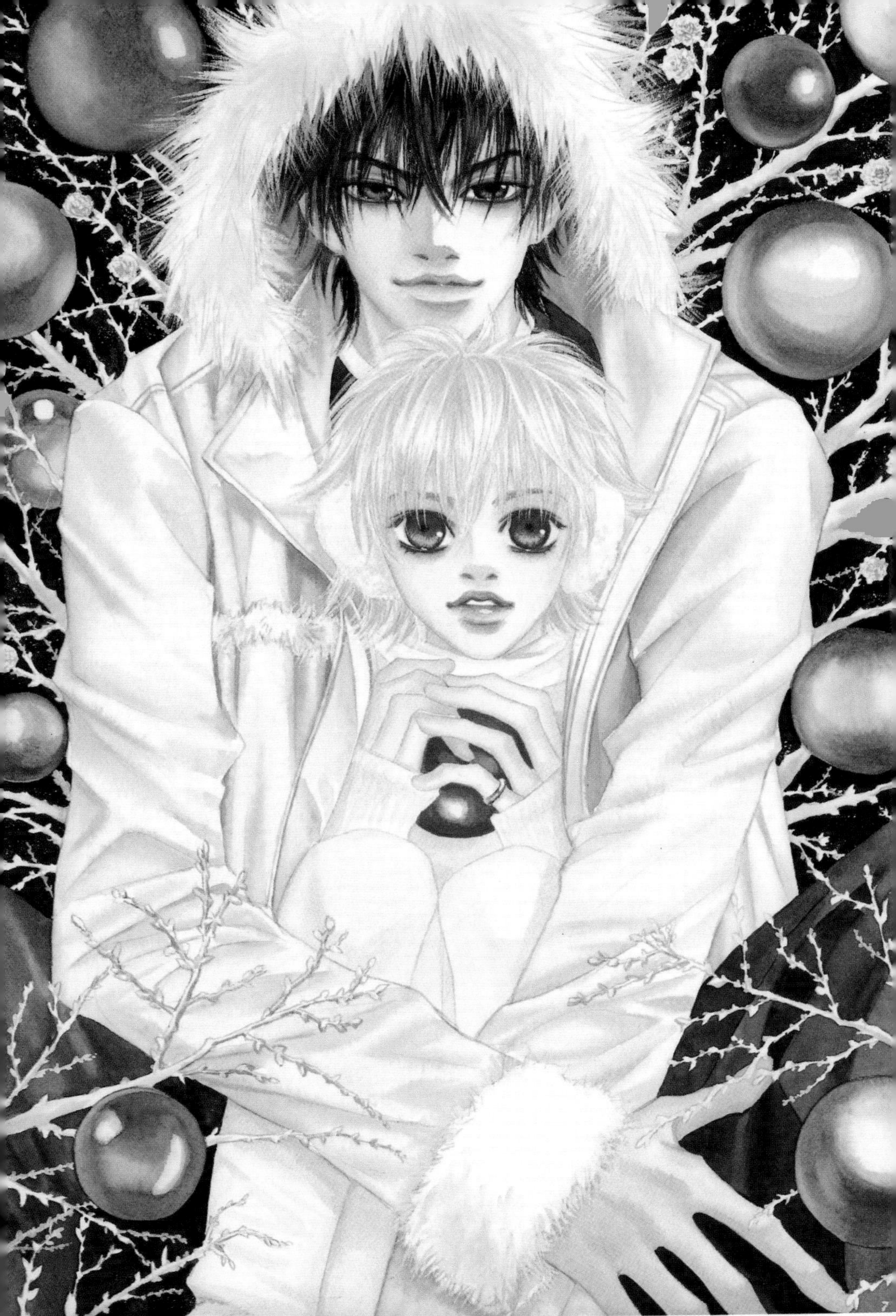

# You're So Cool

## vol. 2

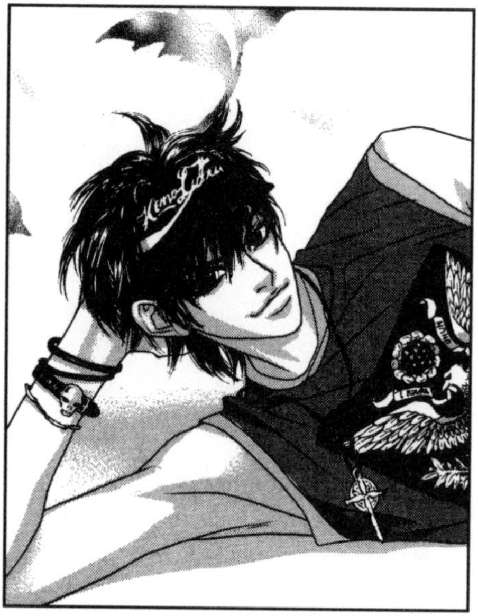

Hano Life


YoungHee Lee

Yen Press

## *THE STORY SO FAR...*

EVERYONE WANTS TO DO WELL ONCE THEY START HIGH SCHOOL, AND OUR HEROINE, NAN-WOO JUNG, HAD SUCH NORMAL DREAMS TOO. THOUGH A SHORT, KLUTZY KID WHO'D RUN INTO ALL SORTS OF TROUBLE, SHE WAS FREE TO HAPPILY DREAM THAT THE HOT SEUNG-HA RYU MIGHT ASK HER OUT SOMEDAY. SO WHEN HE SAID TO HER IN A LONELY VOICE, "I WONDER IF SOMEONE CAN LOVE ME AS I AM," NAN-WOO IMMEDIATELY SHOUTED, "ME! ME! ME!"

UNFORTUNATELY, SEUNG-HA'S TRUE NATURE REVEALED ITSELF ON THEIR FIRST DATE. HE TURNED OUT TO BE A JERK AND A PUNK WHO LIVES A DOUBLE LIFE — ONE AS A DILIGENT STUDENT, THE OTHER AS A GANGSTER. BUT NOW, IT'S TOO LATE FOR REGRETS...

POOR NAN-WOO.
WHAT KIND OF FATE
AWAITS HER?

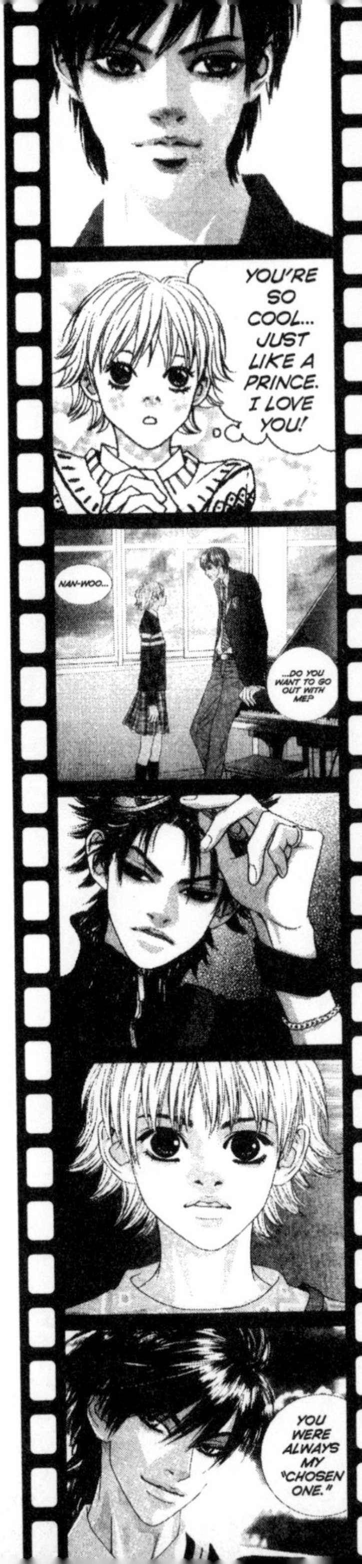
YOU'RE SO COOL... JUST LIKE A PRINCE. I LOVE YOU!
NAN-WOO...
...DO YOU WANT TO GO OUT WITH ME?
YOU WERE ALWAYS MY "CHOSEN ONE."

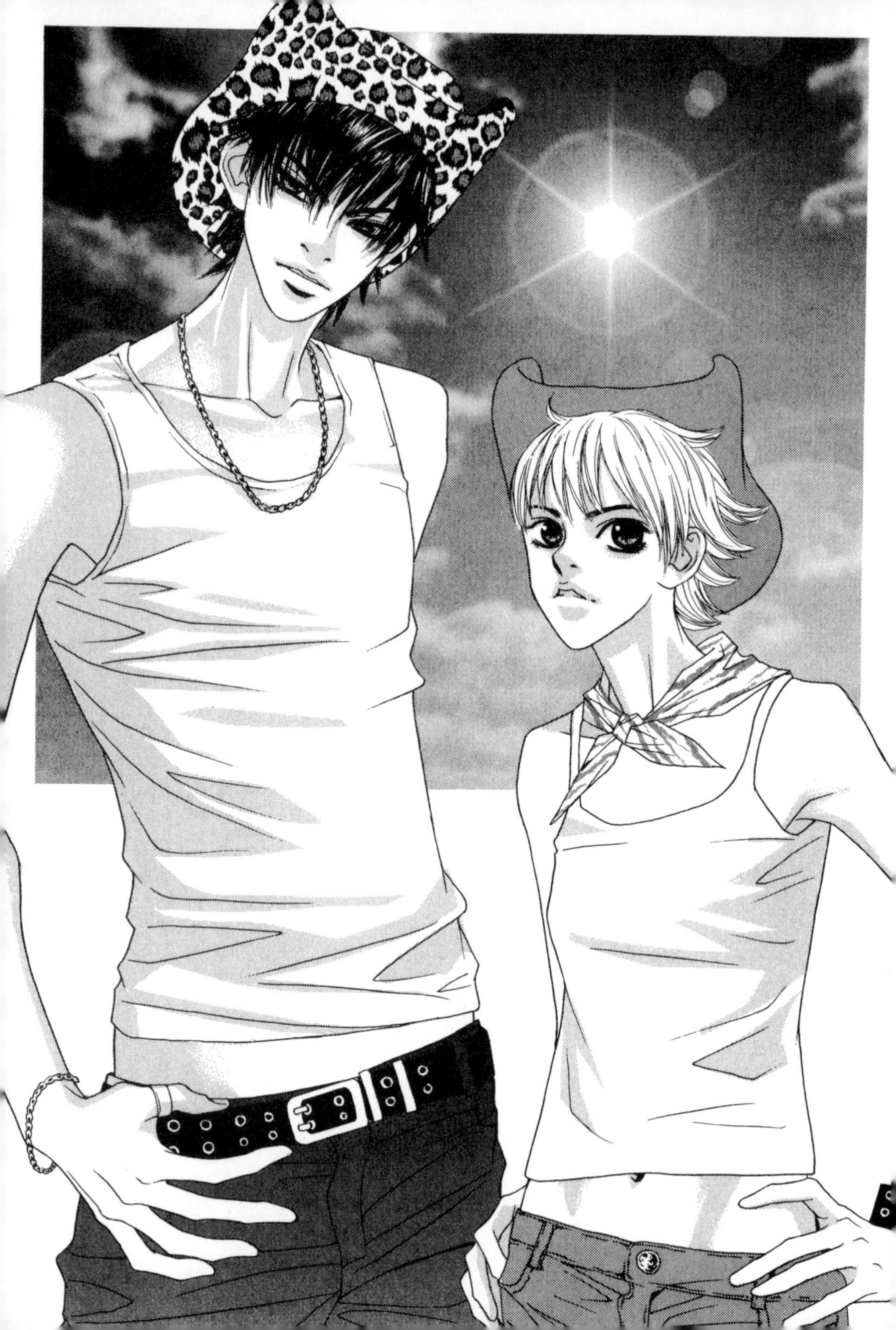

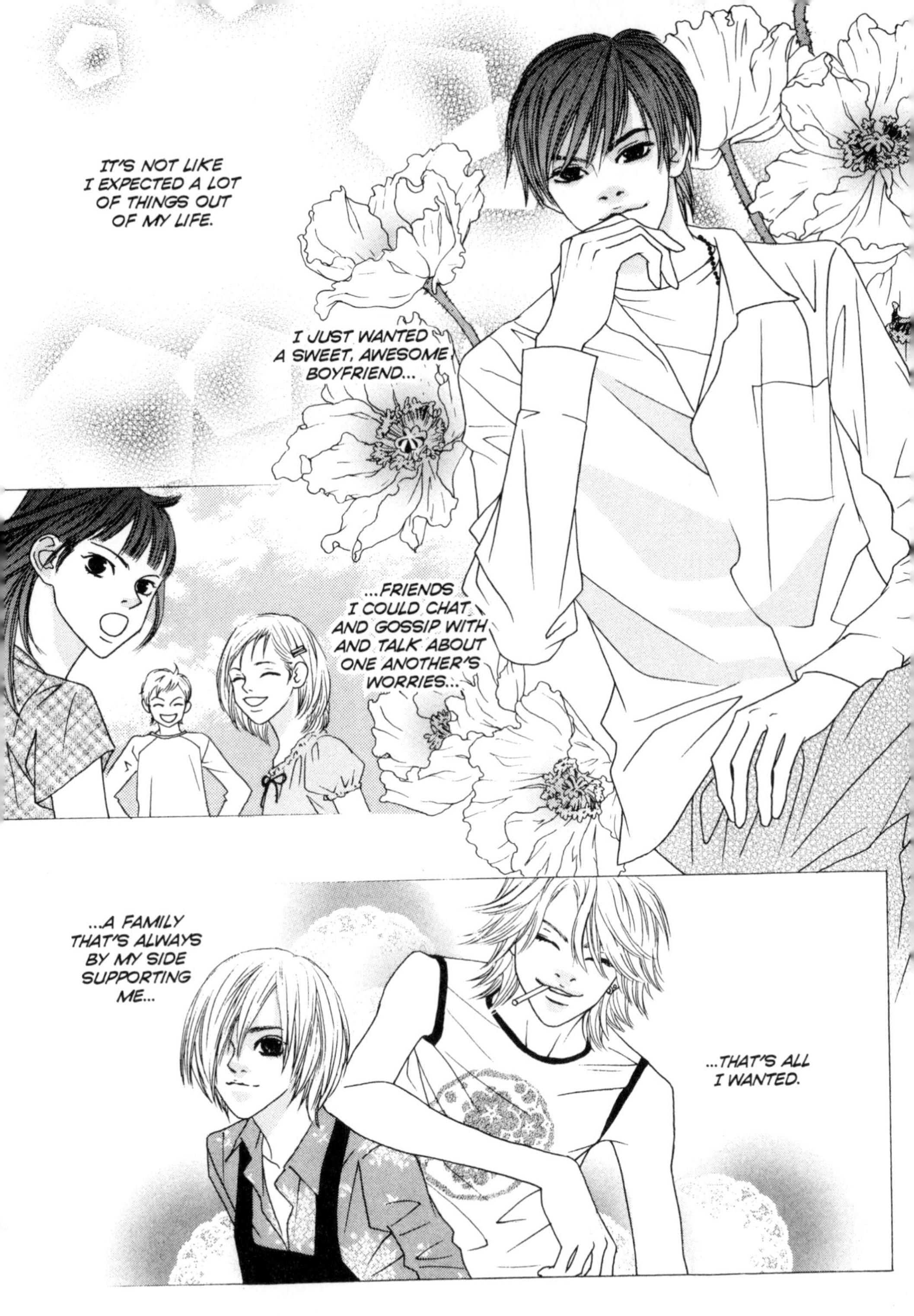
IT'S NOT LIKE I EXPECTED A LOT OF THINGS OUT OF MY LIFE.
I JUST WANTED A SWEET, AWESOME BOYFRIEND...
...FRIENDS I COULD CHAT AND GOSSIP WITH AND TALK ABOUT ONE ANOTHER'S WORRIES...
...A FAMILY THAT'S ALWAYS BY MY SIDE SUPPORTING ME...
...THAT'S ALL I WANTED.

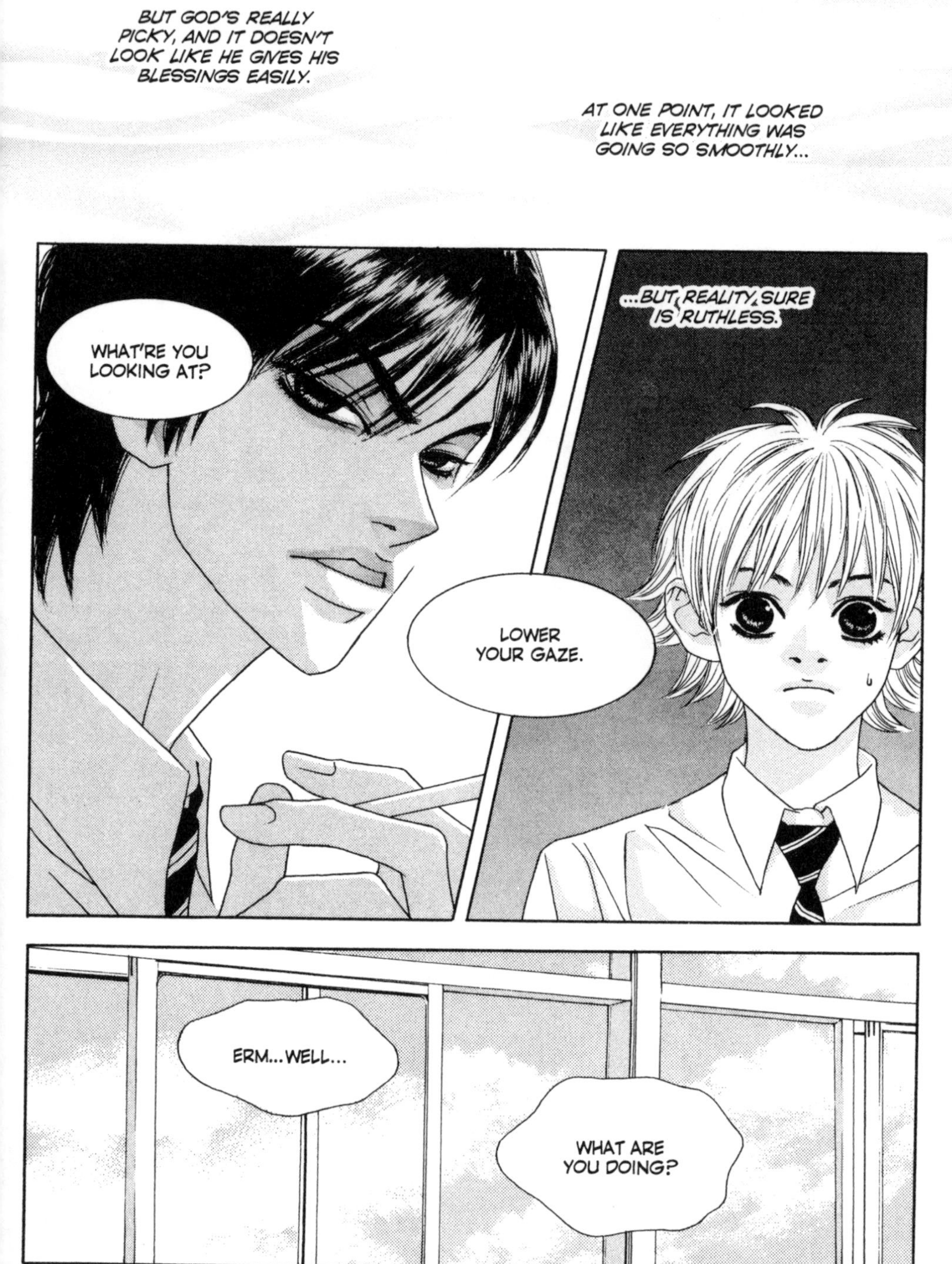
BUT GOD'S REALLY PICKY, AND IT DOESN'T LOOK LIKE HE GIVES HIS BLESSINGS EASILY.
AT ONE POINT, IT LOOKED LIKE EVERYTHING WAS GOING SO SMOOTHLY...
WHAT'RE YOU LOOKING AT?
LOWER YOUR GAZE.
...BUT REALITY SURE IS RUTHLESS.
ERM...WELL...
WHAT ARE YOU DOING?

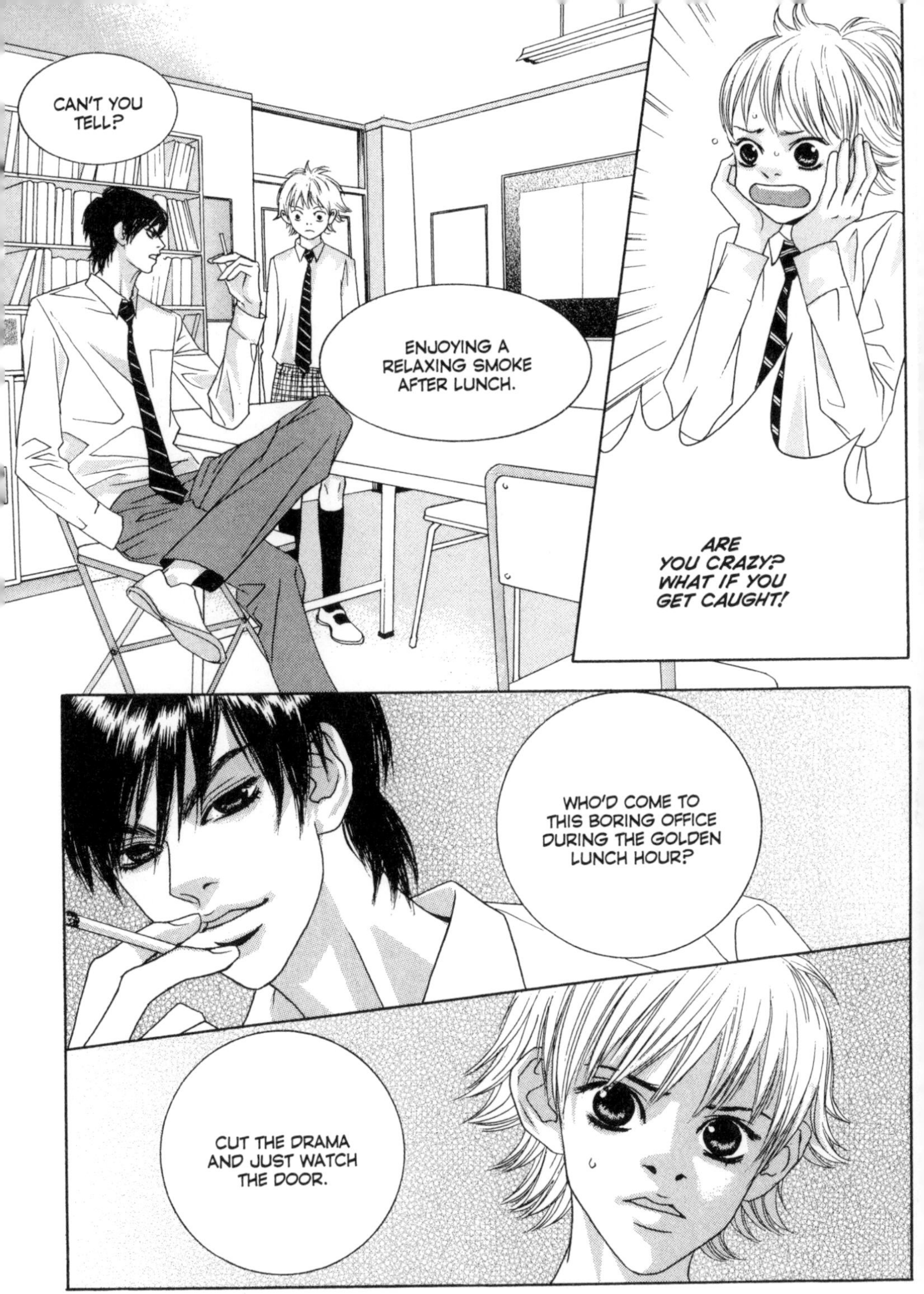
CAN'T YOU TELL?
ENJOYING A RELAXING SMOKE AFTER LUNCH.
ARE YOU CRAZY? WHAT IF YOU GET CAUGHT!
WHO'D COME TO THIS BORING OFFICE DURING THE GOLDEN LUNCH HOUR?
CUT THE DRAMA AND JUST WATCH THE DOOR.

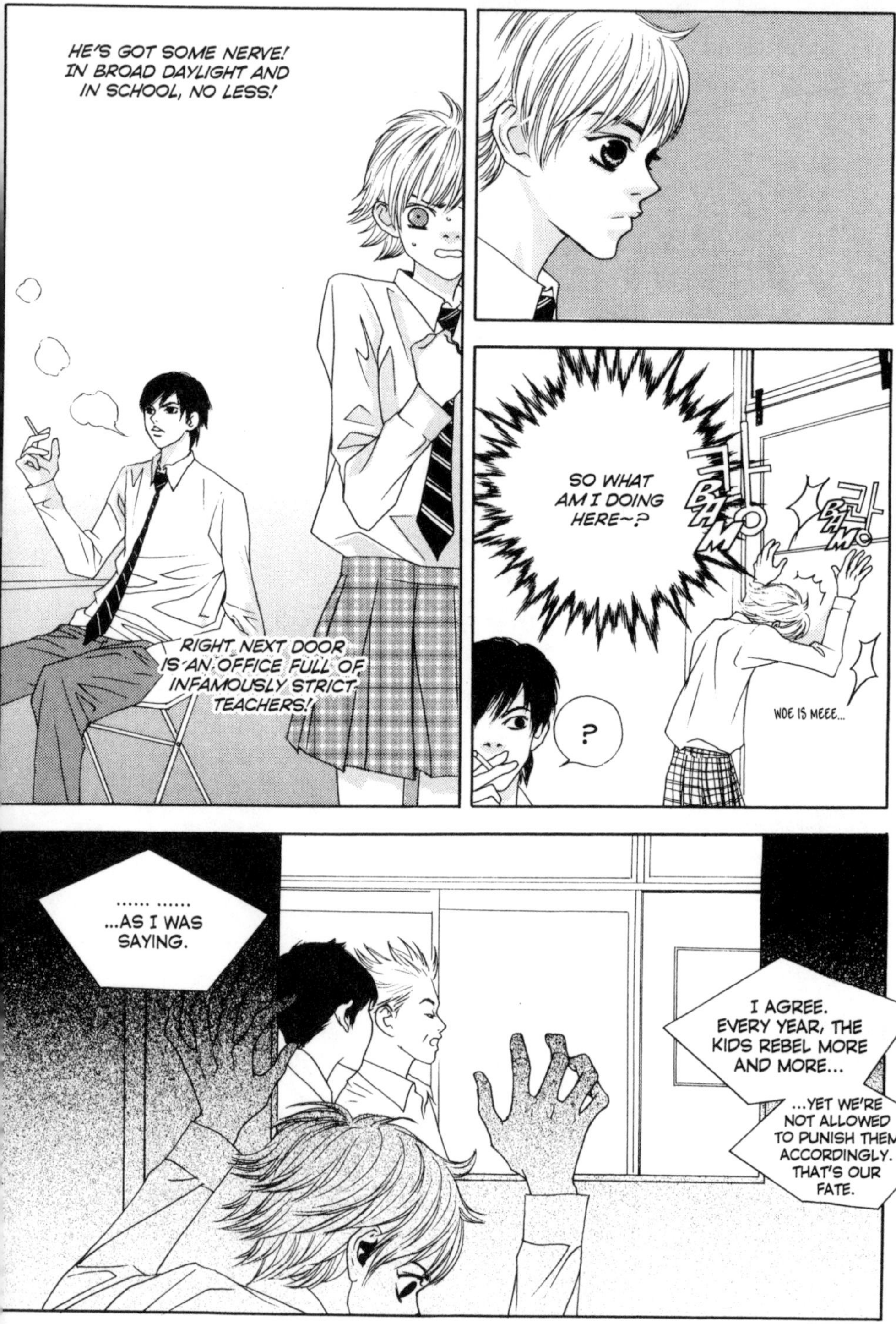
HE'S GOT SOME NERVE! IN BROAD DAYLIGHT AND IN SCHOOL, NO LESS!
RIGHT NEXT DOOR IS AN OFFICE FULL OF INFAMOUSLY STRICT TEACHERS!
SO WHAT AM I DOING HERE~?
쾅
BAM
쾅
BAM
?
WOE IS MEEE...
...... ......
...AS I WAS SAYING.
I AGREE. EVERY YEAR, THE KIDS REBEL MORE AND MORE...
...YET WE'RE NOT ALLOWED TO PUNISH THEM ACCORDINGLY. THAT'S OUR FATE.

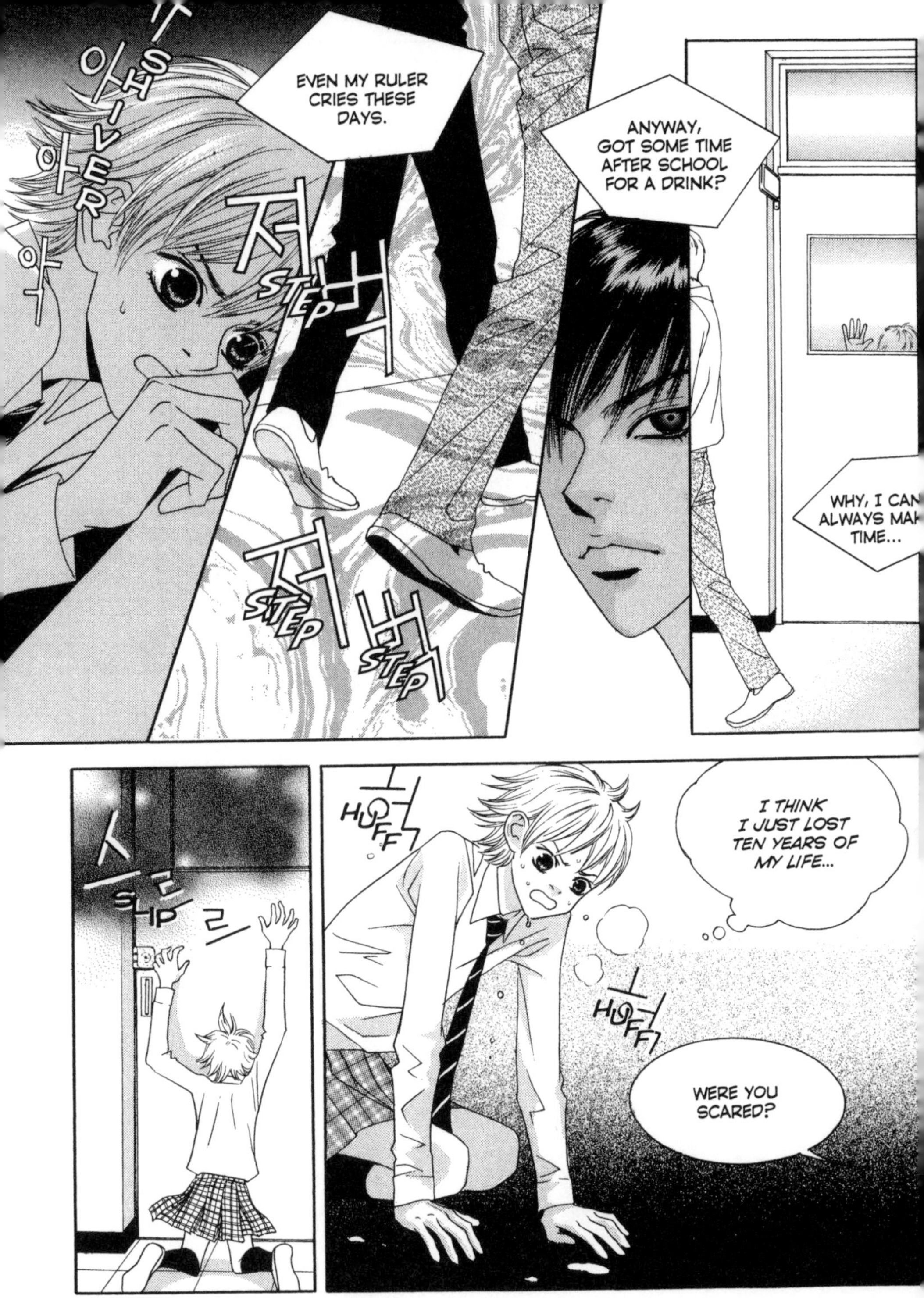
SHIVER
EVEN MY RULER CRIES THESE DAYS.
STEP
STEP
STEP
ANYWAY, GOT SOME TIME AFTER SCHOOL FOR A DRINK?
WHY, I CAN ALWAYS MAK TIME...
SHP
HUFF
I THINK I JUST LOST TEN YEARS OF MY LIFE...
HUFF
WERE YOU SCARED?

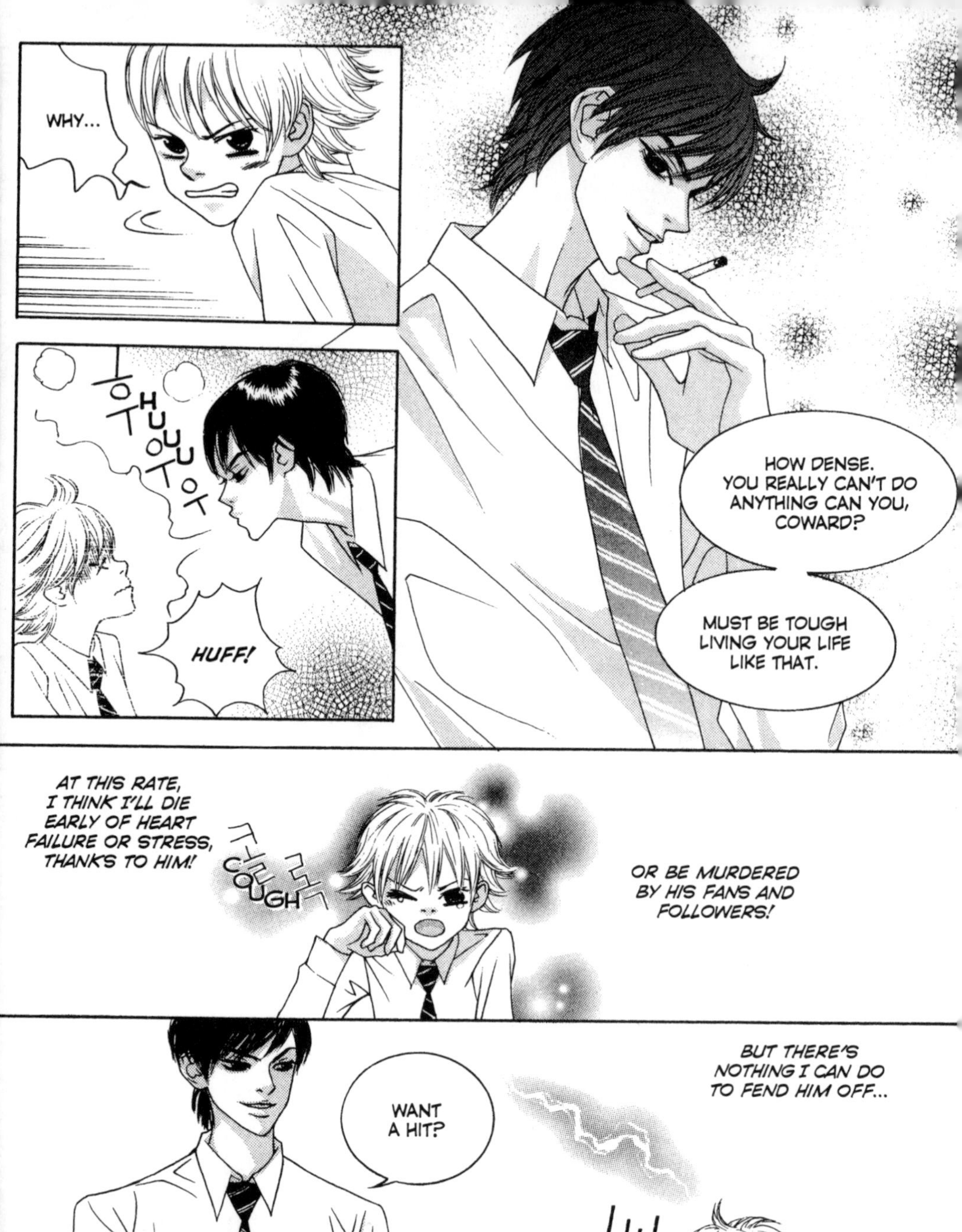
WHY...
HUUUT
HUFF!
HOW DENSE. YOU REALLY CAN'T DO ANYTHING CAN YOU, COWARD?
MUST BE TOUGH LIVING YOUR LIFE LIKE THAT.
AT THIS RATE, I THINK I'LL DIE EARLY OF HEART FAILURE OR STRESS, THANKS TO HIM!
COUGH
OR BE MURDERED BY HIS FANS AND FOLLOWERS!
WANT A HIT?
BUT THERE'S NOTHING I CAN DO TO FEND HIM OFF...
GRI-
-ND

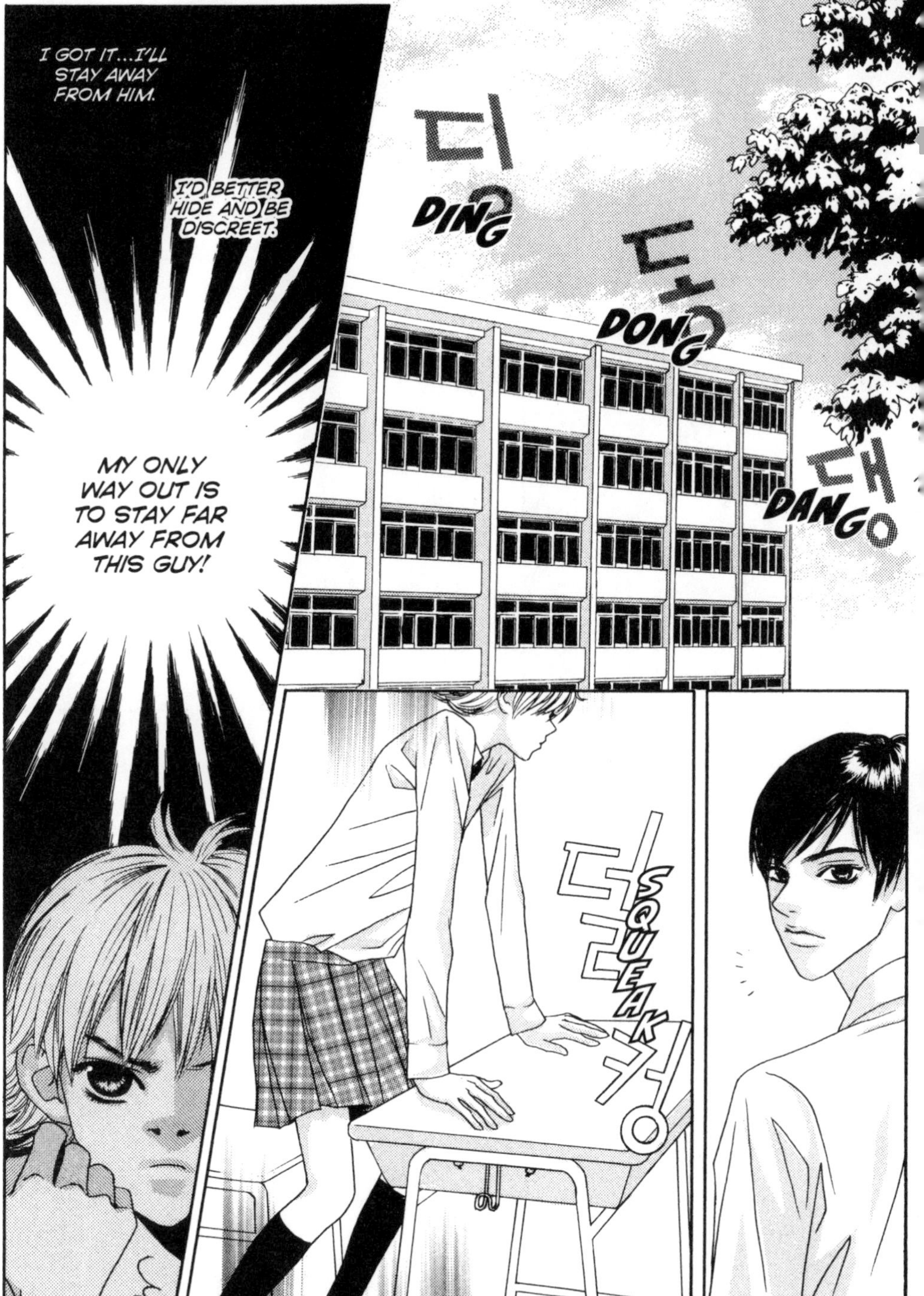
I GOT IT...I'LL STAY AWAY FROM HIM.
I'D BETTER HIDE AND BE DISCREET.
MY ONLY WAY OUT IS TO STAY FAR AWAY FROM THIS GUY!
DING
DONG
DANG
SQUEAK

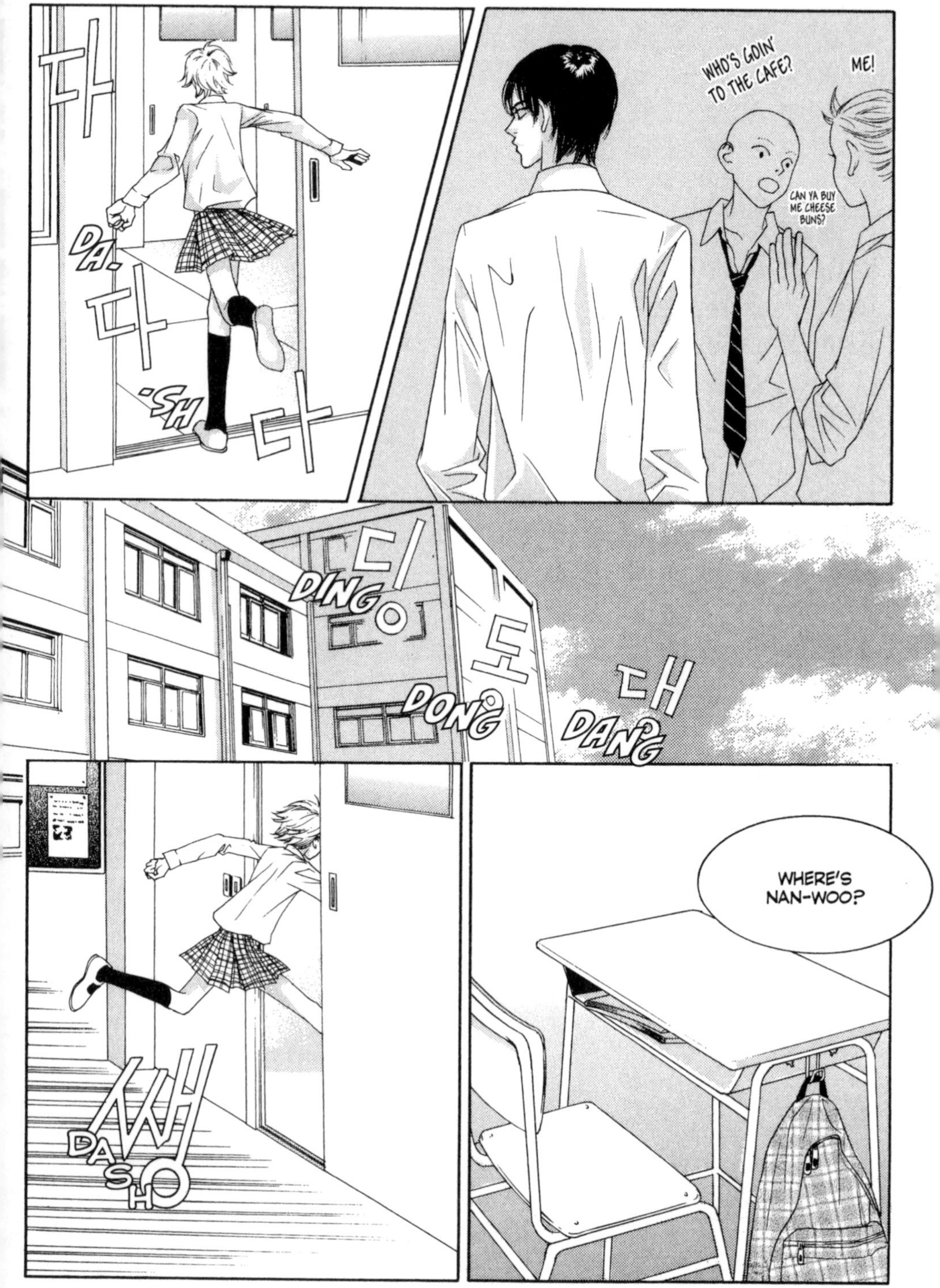
다
DA-
다
-SH
다
WHO'S GOIN' TO THE CAFE?
ME!
CAN YA BUY ME CHEESE BUNS?
딩
DING
동
DONG
댕
DANG
DASH
WHERE'S NAN-WOO?

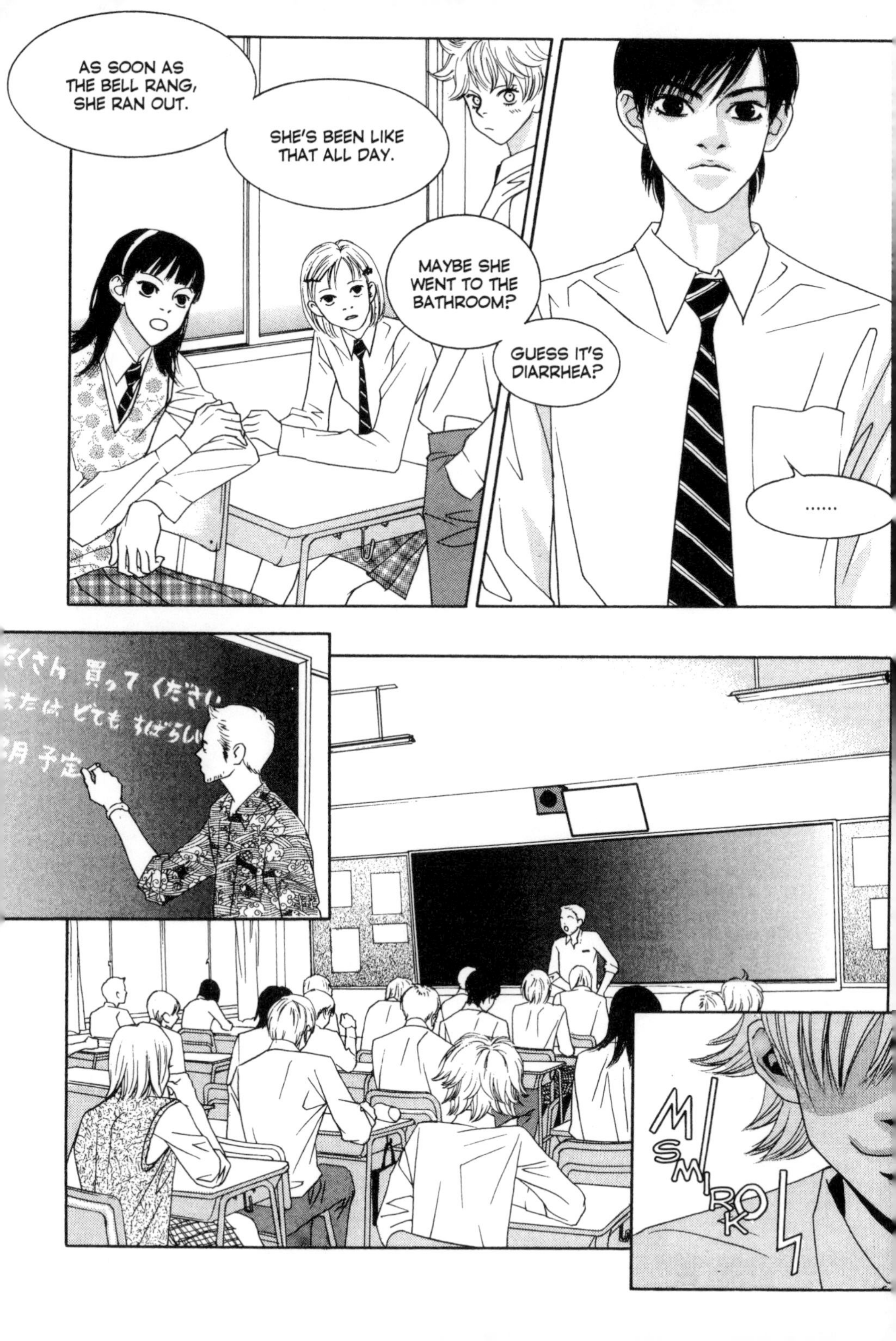
AS SOON AS THE BELL RANG, SHE RAN OUT.
SHE'S BEEN LIKE THAT ALL DAY.
MAYBE SHE WENT TO THE BATHROOM?
GUESS IT'S DIARRHEA?
......
SMIRK

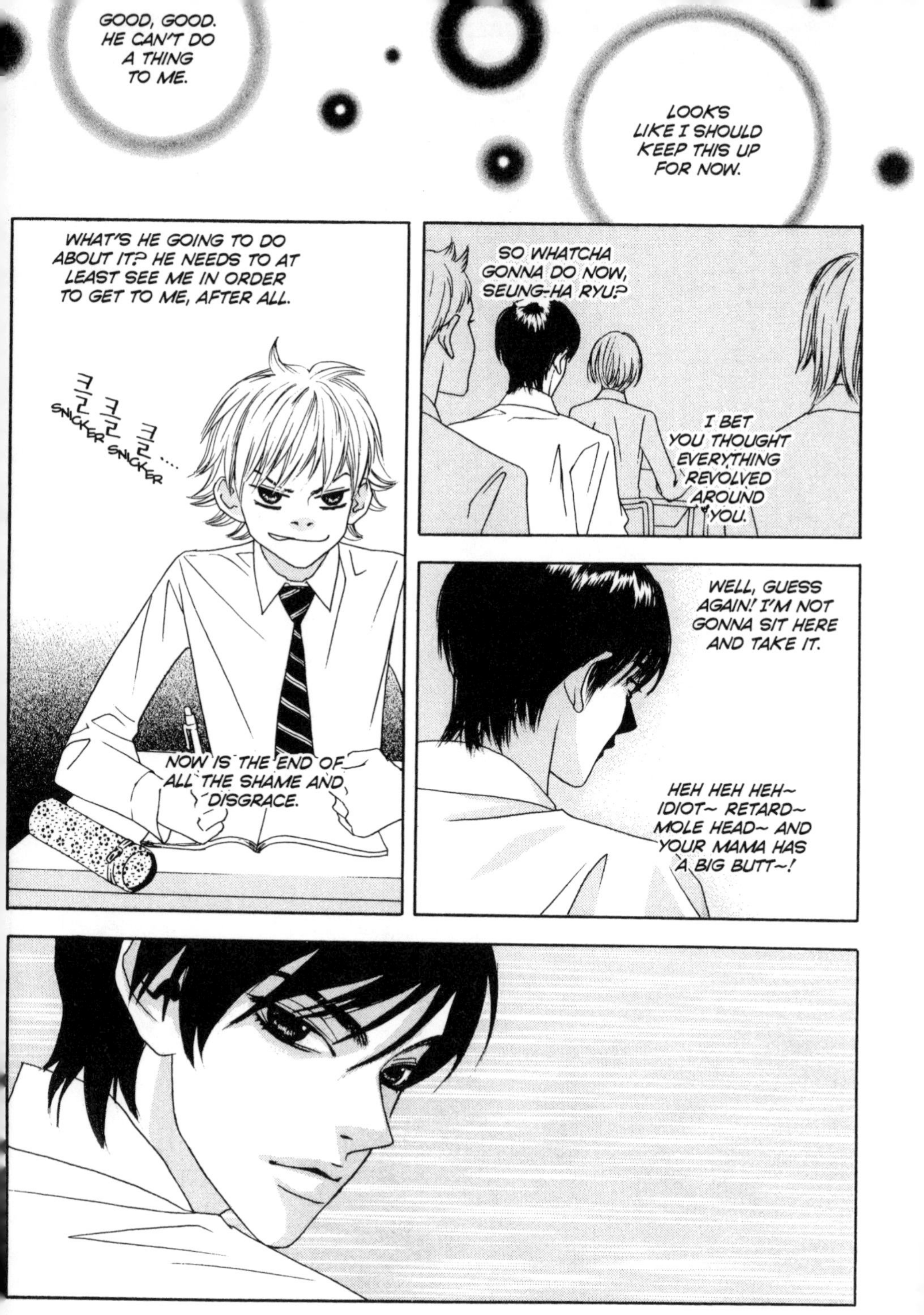
GOOD, GOOD. HE CAN'T DO A THING TO ME.
LOOKS LIKE I SHOULD KEEP THIS UP FOR NOW.
WHAT'S HE GOING TO DO ABOUT IT? HE NEEDS TO AT LEAST SEE ME IN ORDER TO GET TO ME, AFTER ALL.
크 크 크...
SNICKER SNICKER
NOW IS THE END OF ALL THE SHAME AND DISGRACE.
SO WHATCHA GONNA DO NOW, SEUNG-HA RYU?
I BET YOU THOUGHT EVERYTHING REVOLVED AROUND YOU.
WELL, GUESS AGAIN! I'M NOT GONNA SIT HERE AND TAKE IT.
HEH HEH HEH~ IDIOT~ RETARD~ MOLE HEAD~ AND YOUR MAMA HAS A BIG BUTT~!

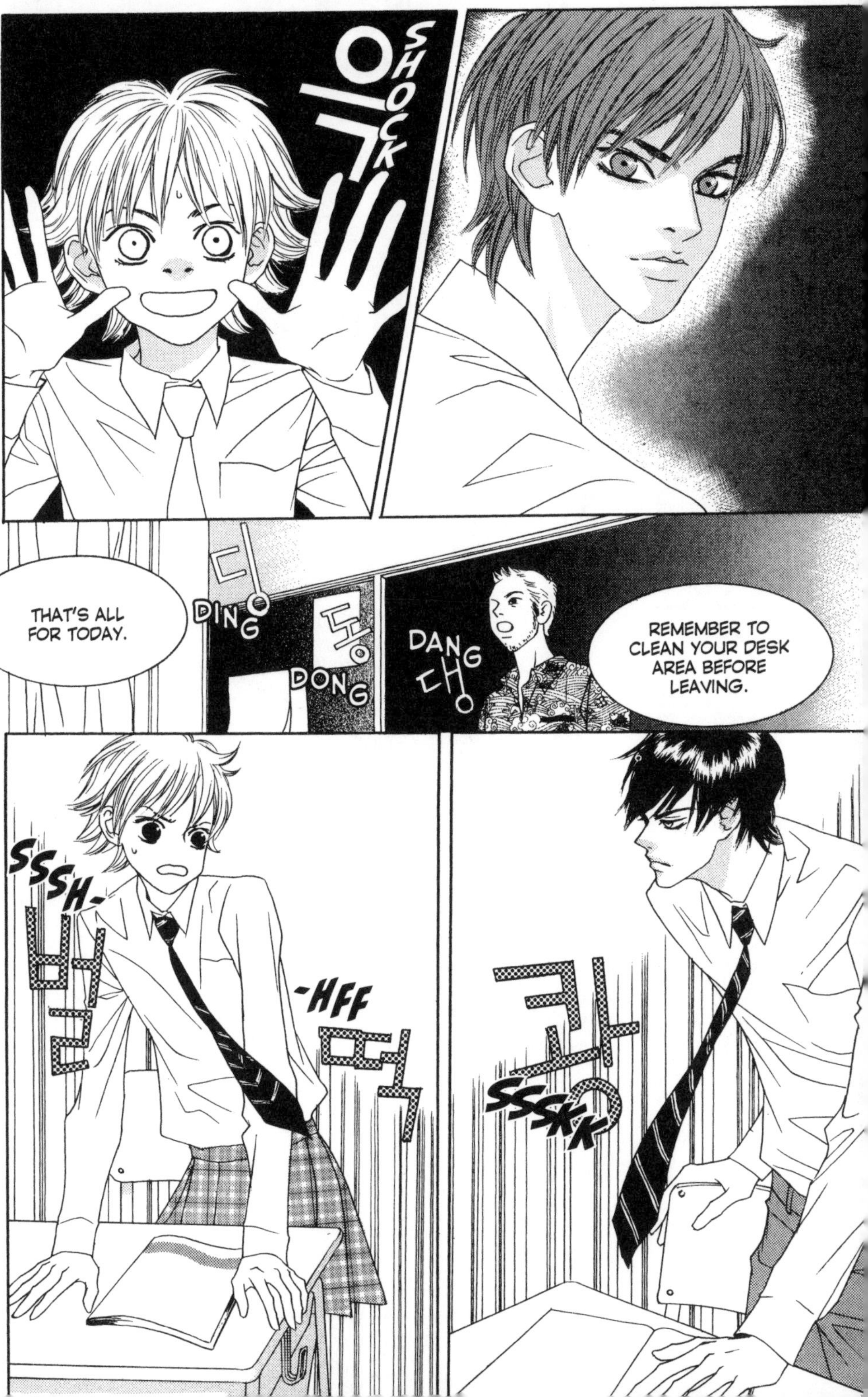
SHOCK
THAT'S ALL FOR TODAY.
DING
DONG
DANG
REMEMBER TO CLEAN YOUR DESK AREA BEFORE LEAVING.
SSSH-
-HFF
SSSKK

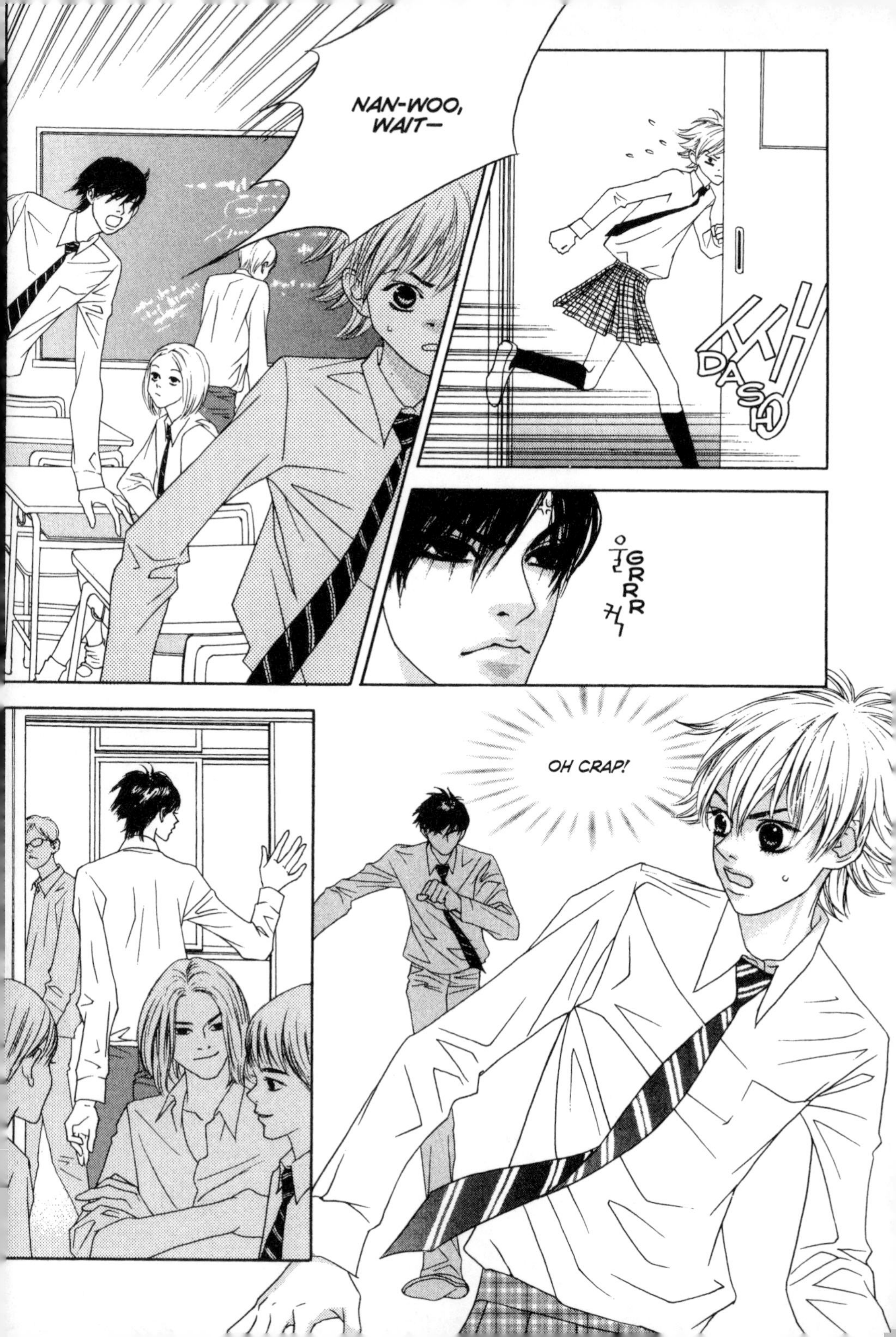
NAN-WOO, WAIT—
DASH
GRRR
OH CRAP!

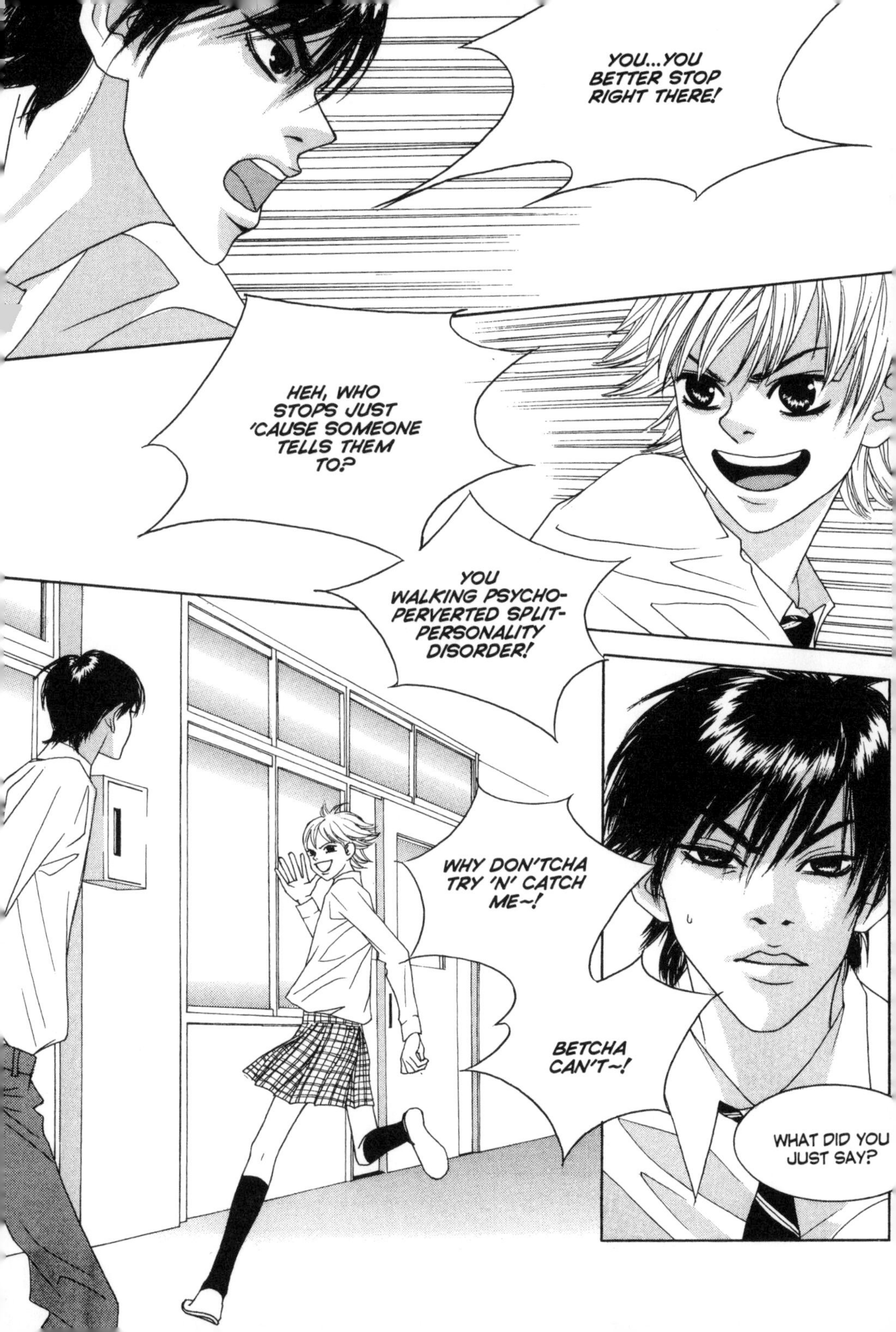
YOU...YOU BETTER STOP RIGHT THERE!
HEH, WHO STOPS JUST 'CAUSE SOMEONE TELLS THEM TO?
YOU WALKING PSYCHO-PERVERTED SPLIT-PERSONALITY DISORDER!
WHY DON'TCHA TRY 'N' CATCH ME~!
BETCHA CAN'T~!
WHAT DID YOU JUST SAY?

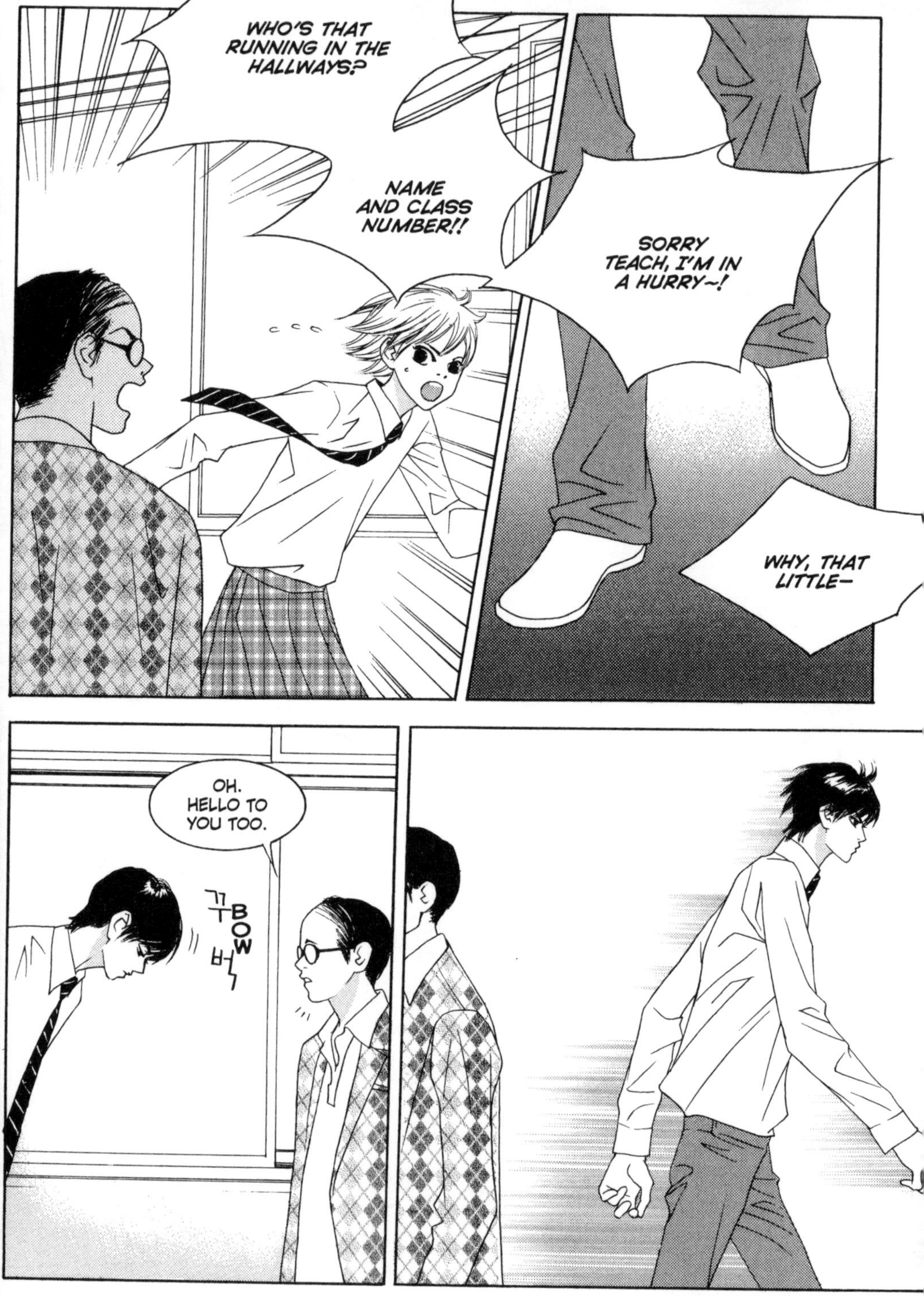
WHO'S THAT RUNNING IN THE HALLWAYS?
NAME AND CLASS NUMBER!!
SORRY TEACH, I'M IN A HURRY~!
WHY, THAT LITTLE—
OH. HELLO TO YOU TOO.
꾸벅
BOW

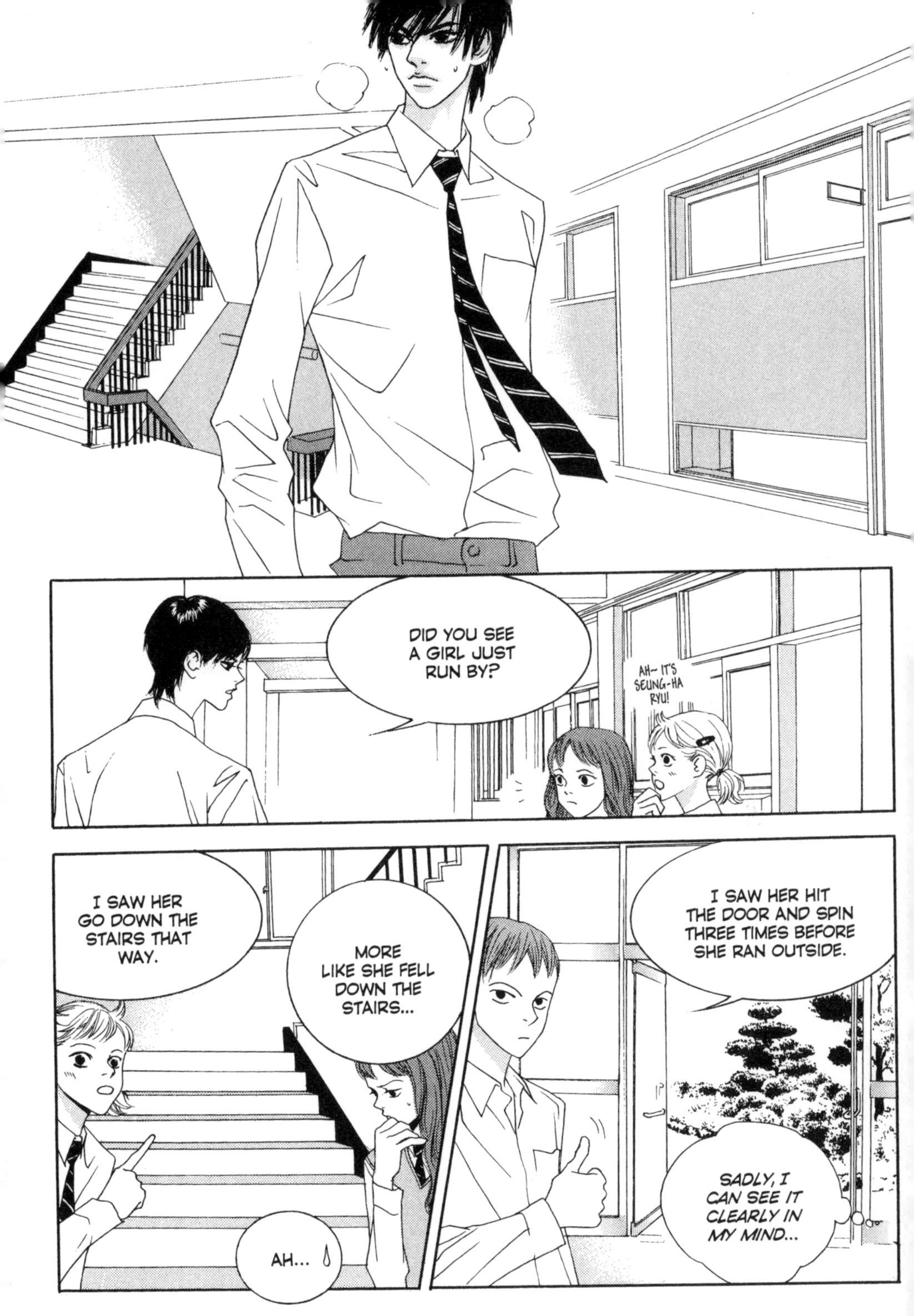
DID YOU SEE A GIRL JUST RUN BY?
AH~ IT'S SEUNG-HA RYU!
I SAW HER GO DOWN THE STAIRS THAT WAY.
MORE LIKE SHE FELL DOWN THE STAIRS...
AH...
I SAW HER HIT THE DOOR AND SPIN THREE TIMES BEFORE SHE RAN OUTSIDE.
SADLY, I CAN SEE IT CLEARLY IN MY MIND...

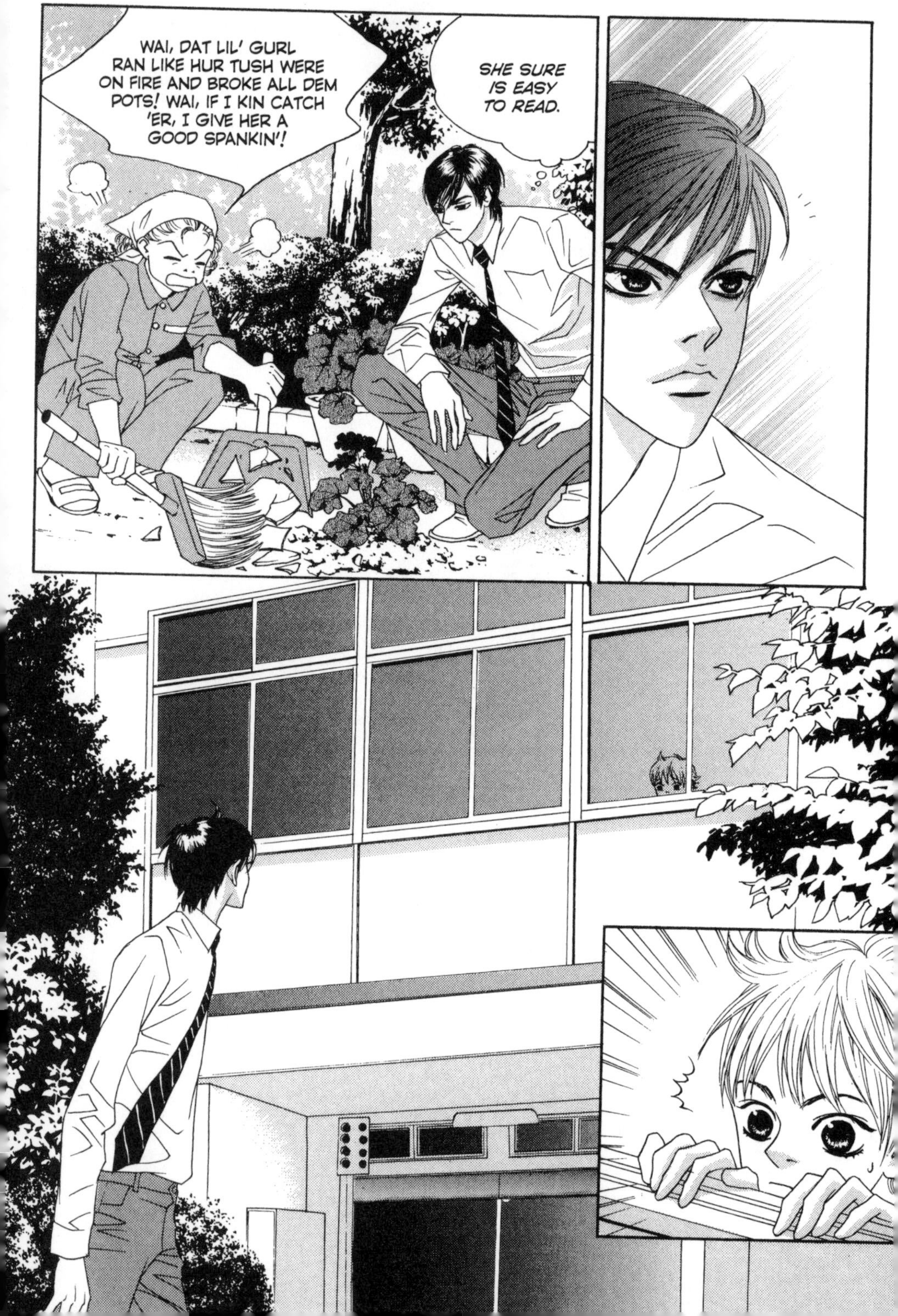
WAI, DAT LIL' GURL RAN LIKE HUR TUSH WERE ON FIRE AND BROKE ALL DEM POTS! WAI, IF I KIN CATCH 'ER, I GIVE HER A GOOD SPANKIN'!
SHE SURE IS EASY TO READ.

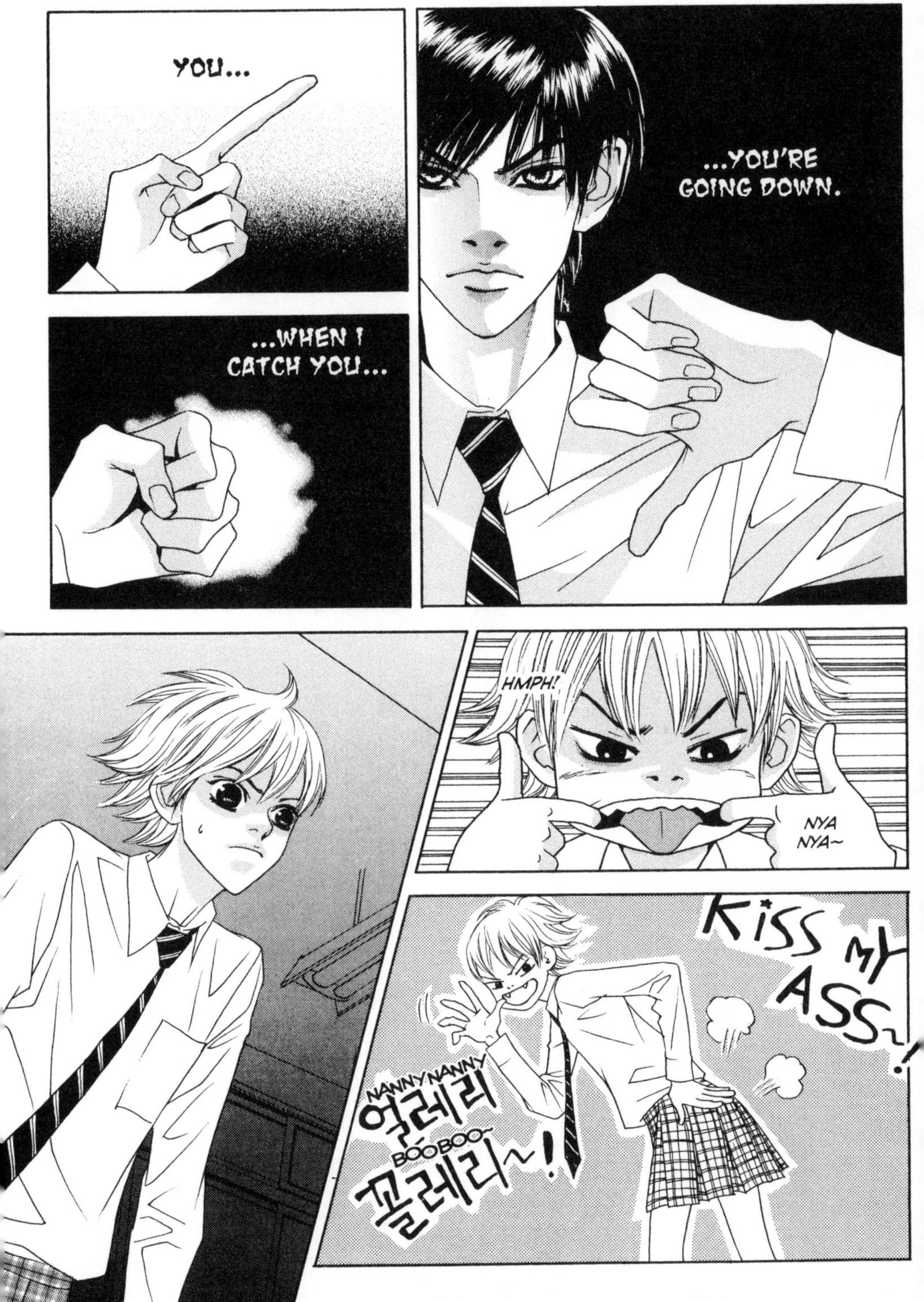
YOU...
...WHEN I CATCH YOU...
...YOU'RE GOING DOWN.
HMPH!
NYA NYA~
KISS MY ASS~!
NANNY NANNY 얼레리
BOO BOO~ 꼴레리~!

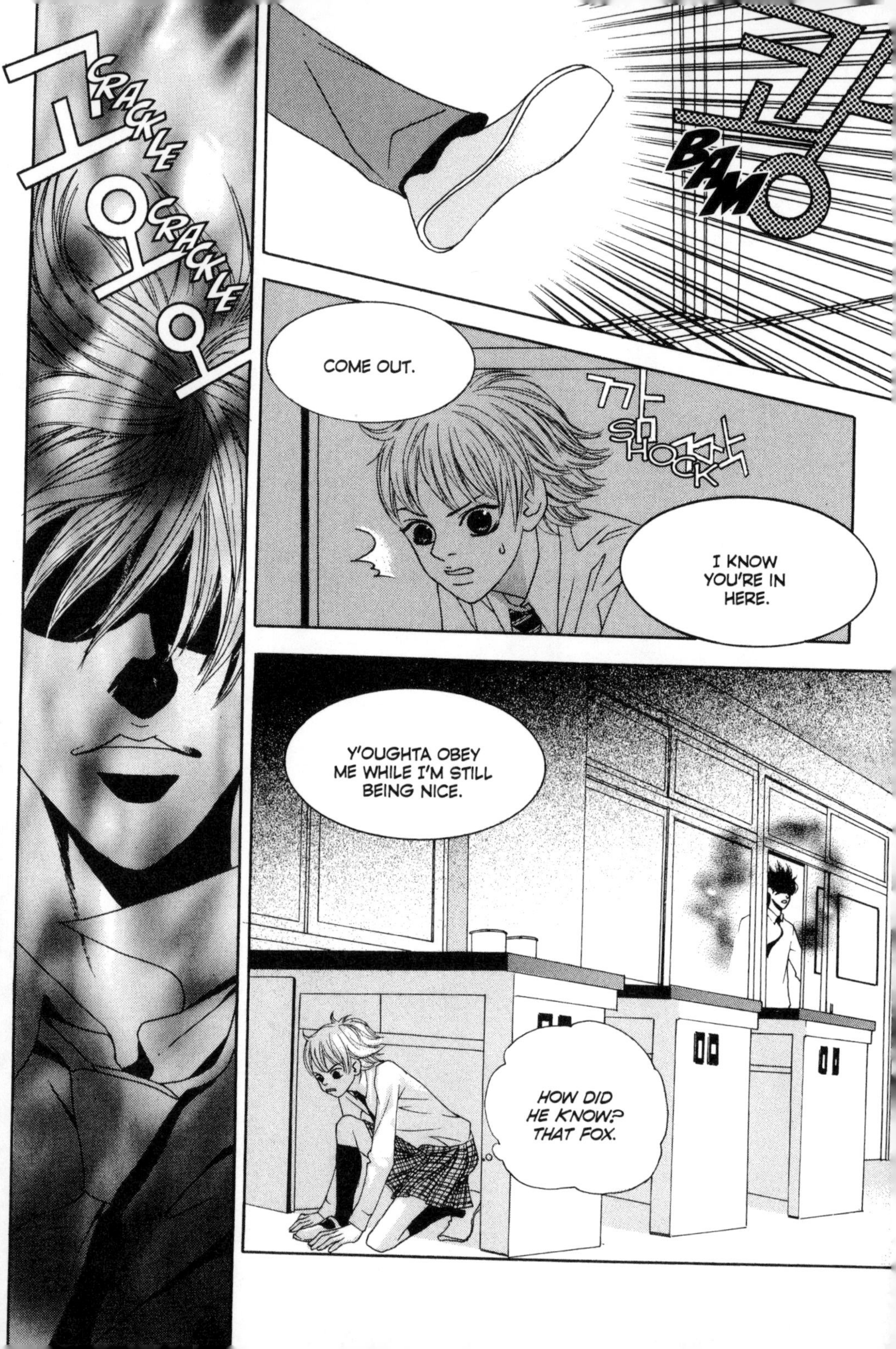

CRACKLE
CRACKLE
BAM
COME OUT.
SHOCK
I KNOW YOU'RE IN HERE.
Y'OUGHTA OBEY ME WHILE I'M STILL BEING NICE.
HOW DID HE KNOW? THAT FOX.

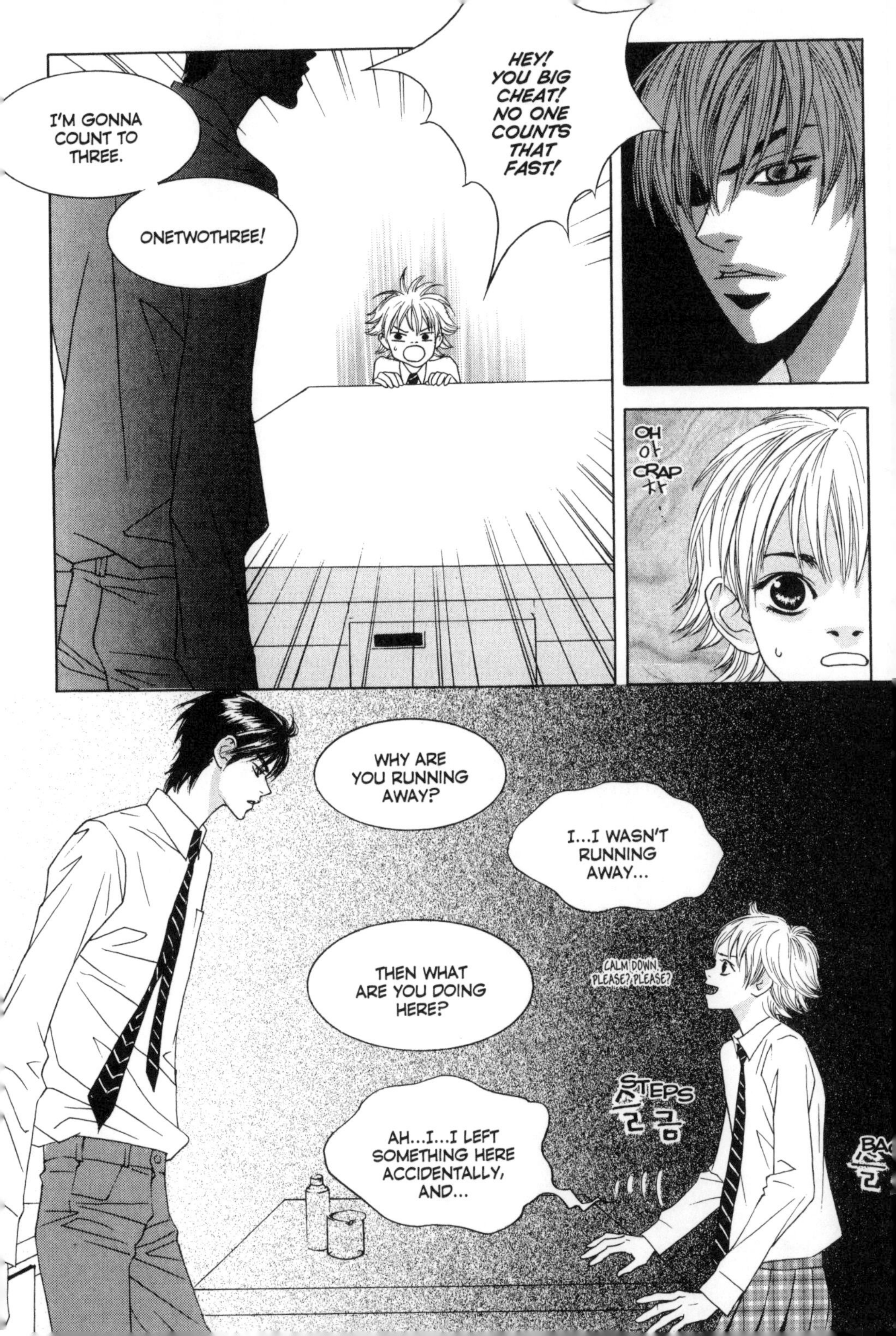
I'M GONNA COUNT TO THREE.
ONETWOTHREE!
HEY! YOU BIG CHEAT! NO ONE COUNTS THAT FAST!
OH 아 CRAP 차
WHY ARE YOU RUNNING AWAY?
I...I WASN'T RUNNING AWAY...
THEN WHAT ARE YOU DOING HERE?
CALM DOWN, PLEASE? PLEASE?
STEPS
AH...I...I LEFT SOMETHING HERE ACCIDENTALLY, AND...

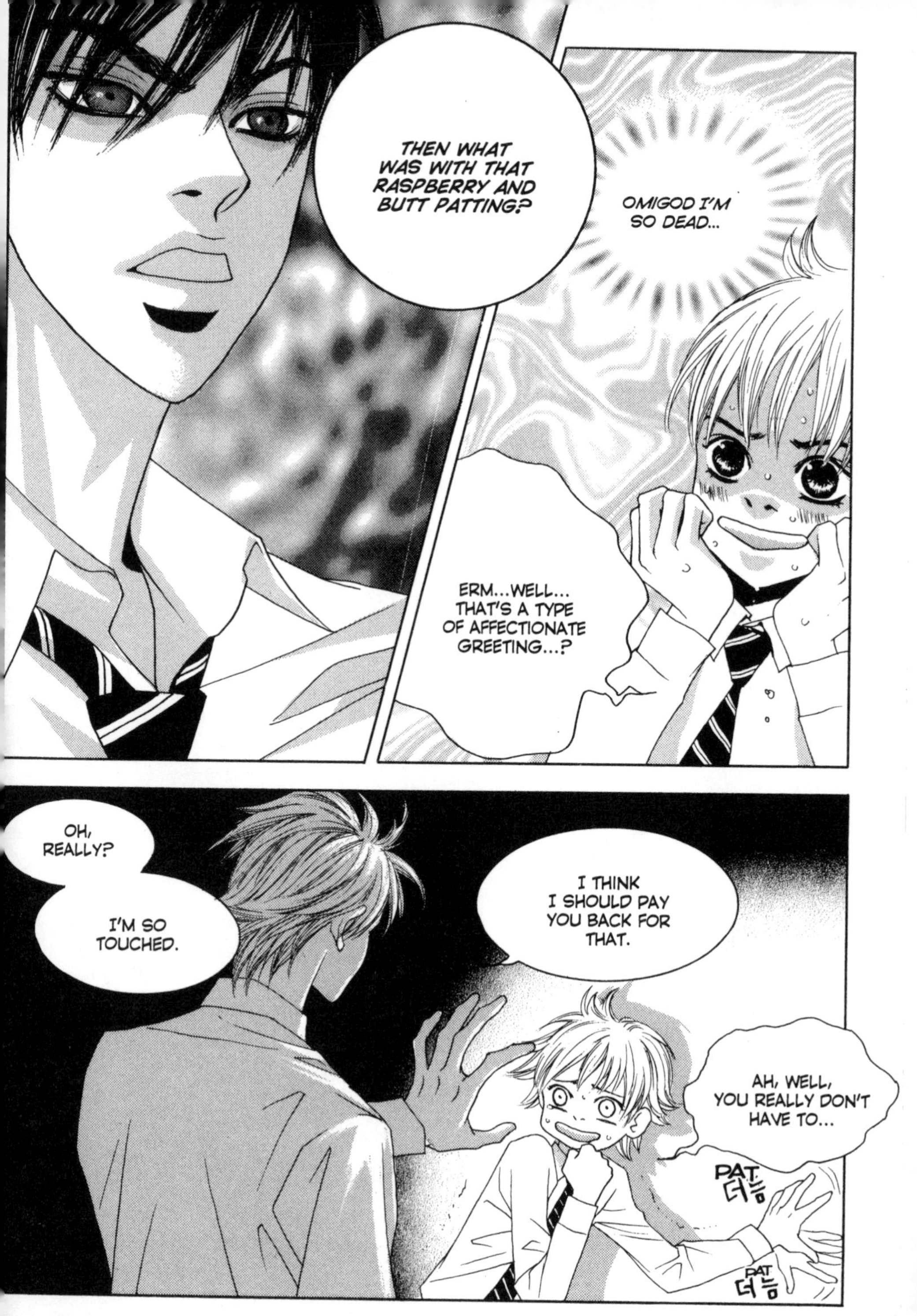
THEN WHAT WAS WITH THAT RASPBERRY AND BUTT PATTING?
OMIGOD I'M SO DEAD...
ERM...WELL... THAT'S A TYPE OF AFFECTIONATE GREETING...?
OH, REALLY?
I'M SO TOUCHED.
I THINK I SHOULD PAY YOU BACK FOR THAT.
AH, WELL, YOU REALLY DON'T HAVE TO...
PAT
더듬
PAT
더듬

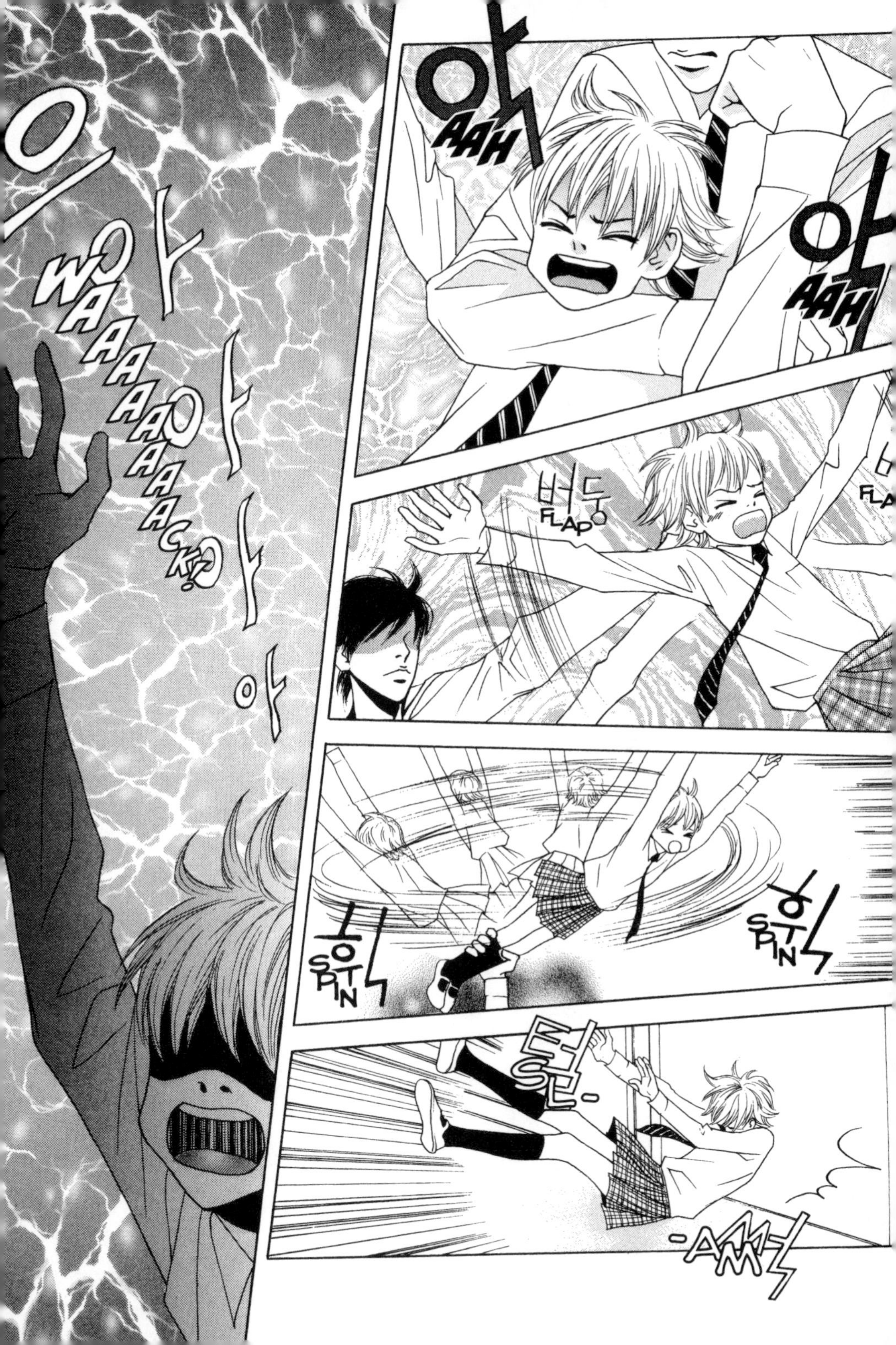

으아아아아
WAAAAAAAAAACK!!
악
AAH
악
AAH
버둥
FLAP
FLA
SPIN
SPIN
SL-
-AM

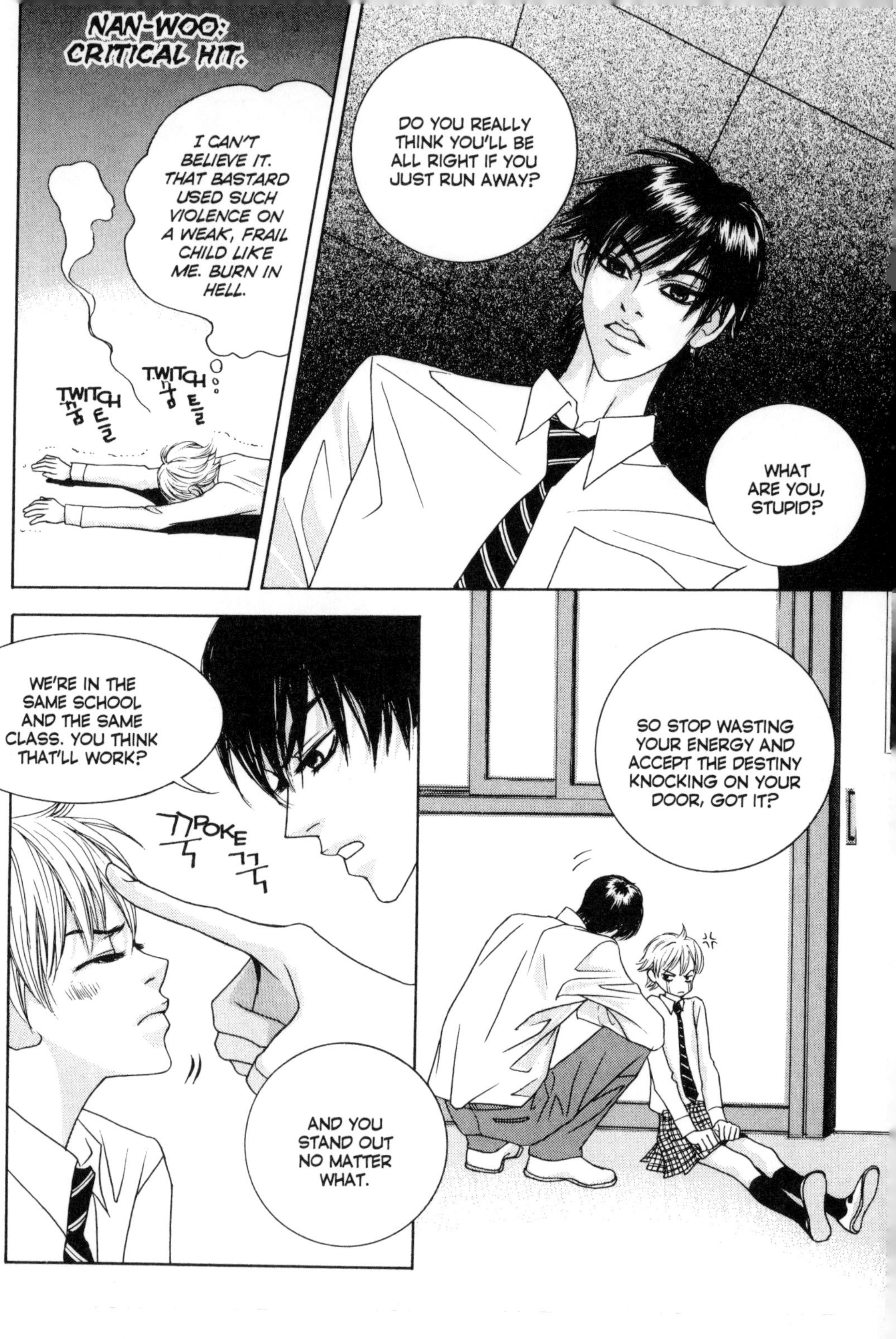
NAN-WOO: CRITICAL HIT.
I CAN'T BELIEVE IT. THAT BASTARD USED SUCH VIOLENCE ON A WEAK, FRAIL CHILD LIKE ME. BURN IN HELL.
TWITCH
TWITCH
DO YOU REALLY THINK YOU'LL BE ALL RIGHT IF YOU JUST RUN AWAY?
WHAT ARE YOU, STUPID?
WE'RE IN THE SAME SCHOOL AND THE SAME CLASS. YOU THINK THAT'LL WORK?
POKE
AND YOU STAND OUT NO MATTER WHAT.
SO STOP WASTING YOUR ENERGY AND ACCEPT THE DESTINY KNOCKING ON YOUR DOOR, GOT IT?

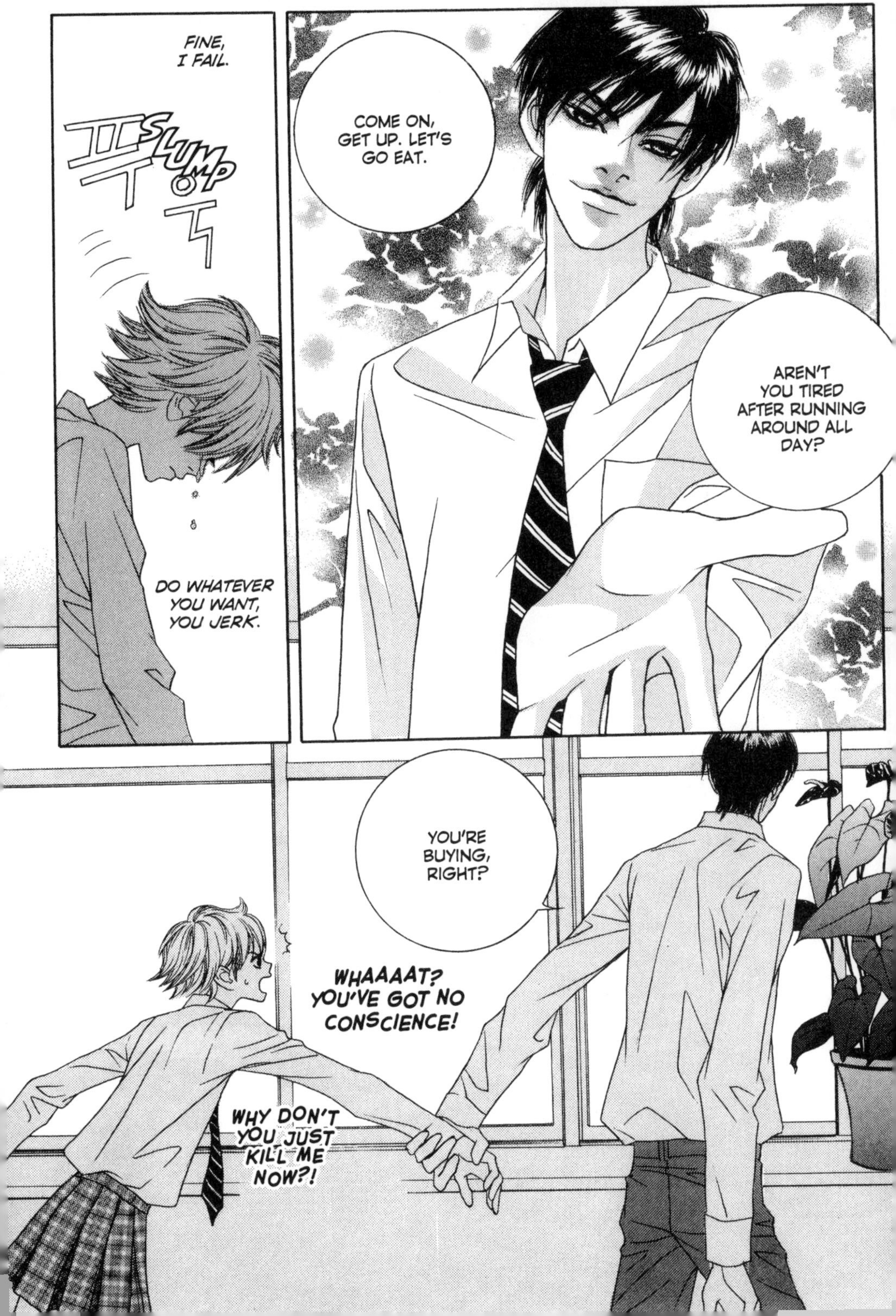
FINE, I FAIL.
SLUMP
DO WHATEVER YOU WANT, YOU JERK.
COME ON, GET UP. LET'S GO EAT.
AREN'T YOU TIRED AFTER RUNNING AROUND ALL DAY?
YOU'RE BUYING, RIGHT?
WHAAAAT? YOU'VE GOT NO CONSCIENCE!
WHY DON'T YOU JUST KILL ME NOW?!

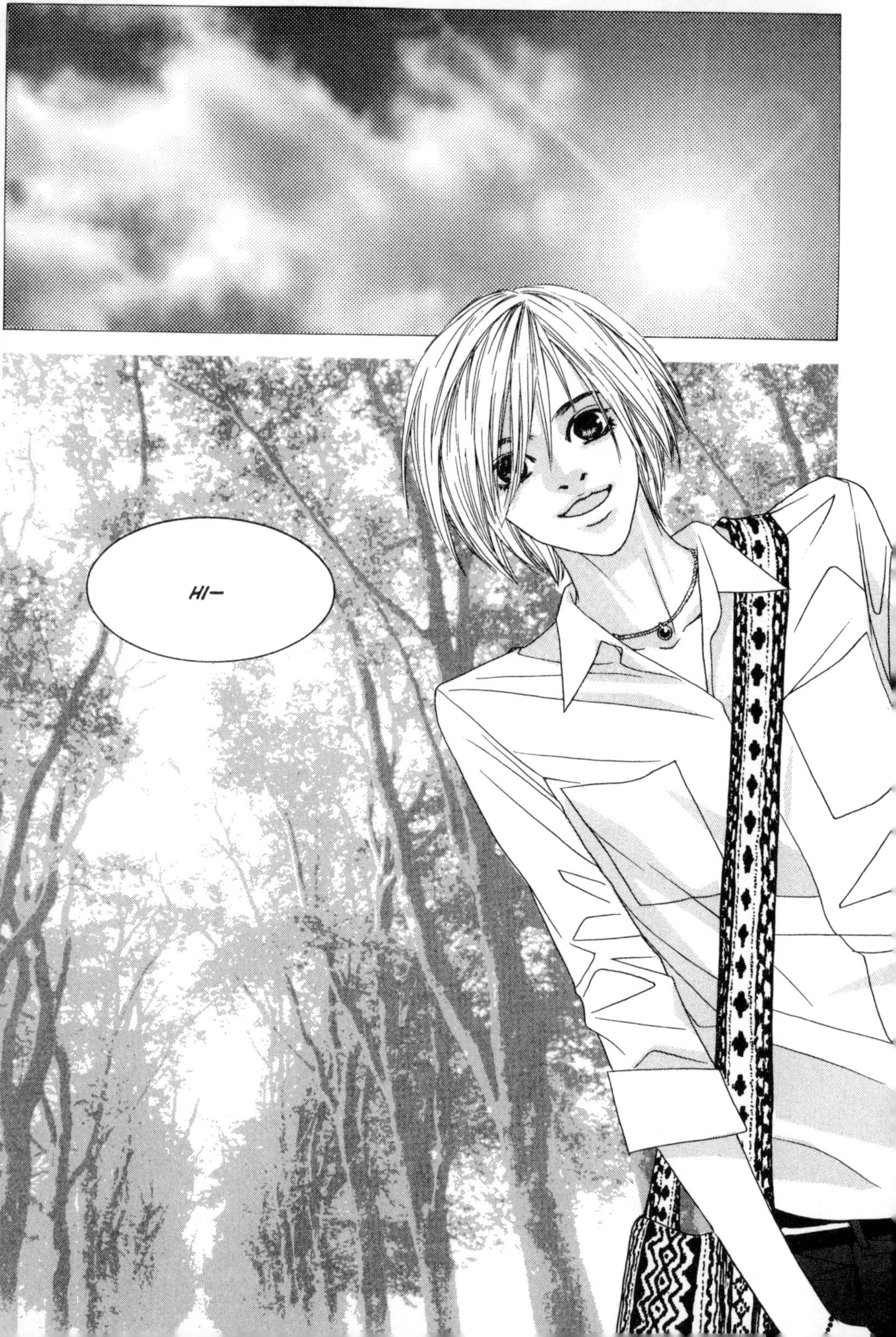
HI—

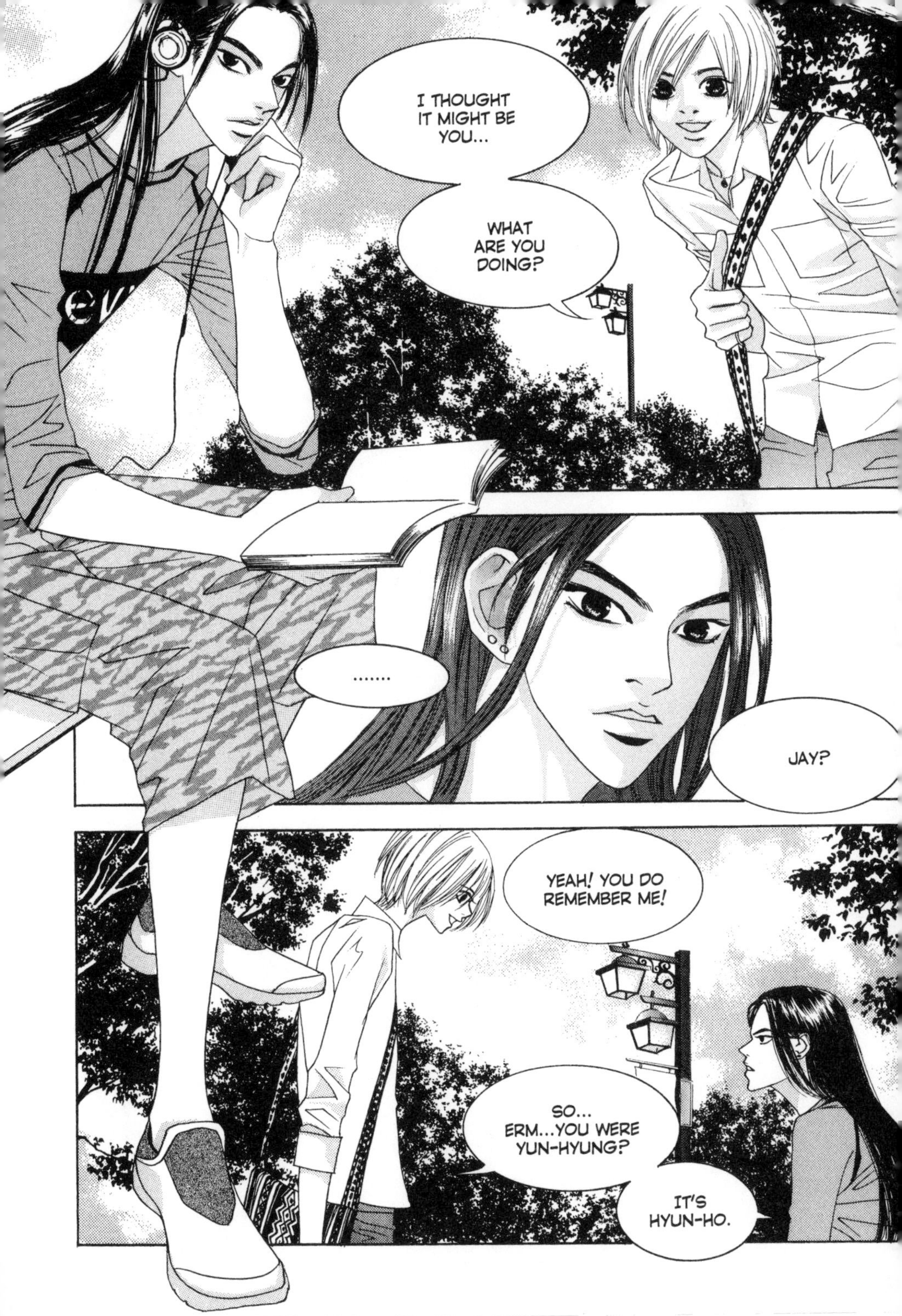
I THOUGHT IT MIGHT BE YOU...
WHAT ARE YOU DOING?
.......
JAY?
YEAH! YOU DO REMEMBER ME!
SO... ERM...YOU WERE YUN-HYUNG?
IT'S HYUN-HO.

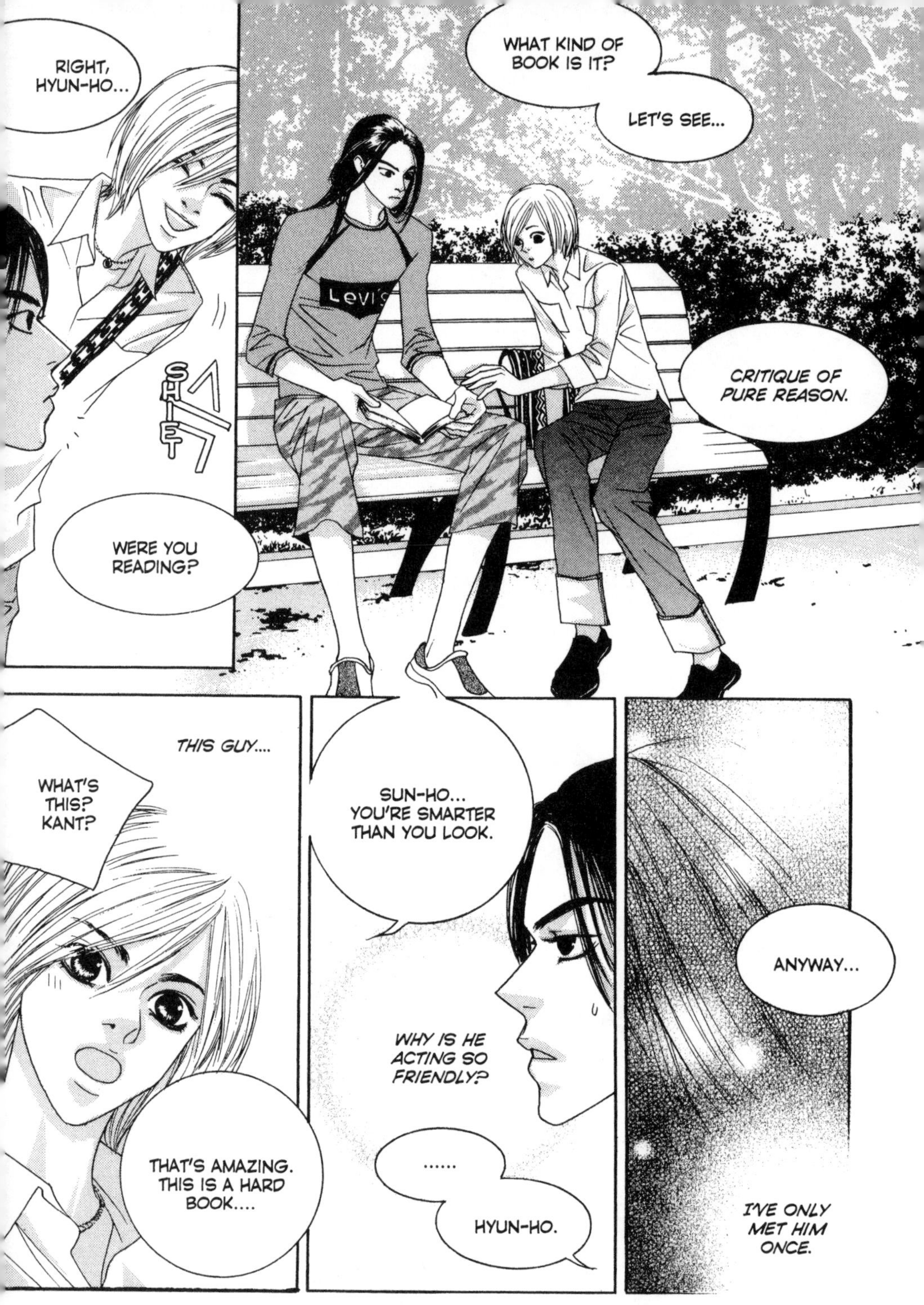
RIGHT, HYUN-HO...
SHIFT
WERE YOU READING?
WHAT KIND OF BOOK IS IT?
LET'S SEE...
CRITIQUE OF PURE REASON.
THIS GUY....
WHAT'S THIS? KANT?
THAT'S AMAZING. THIS IS A HARD BOOK....
SUN-HO... YOU'RE SMARTER THAN YOU LOOK.
WHY IS HE ACTING SO FRIENDLY?
......
HYUN-HO.
ANYWAY...
I'VE ONLY MET HIM ONCE.

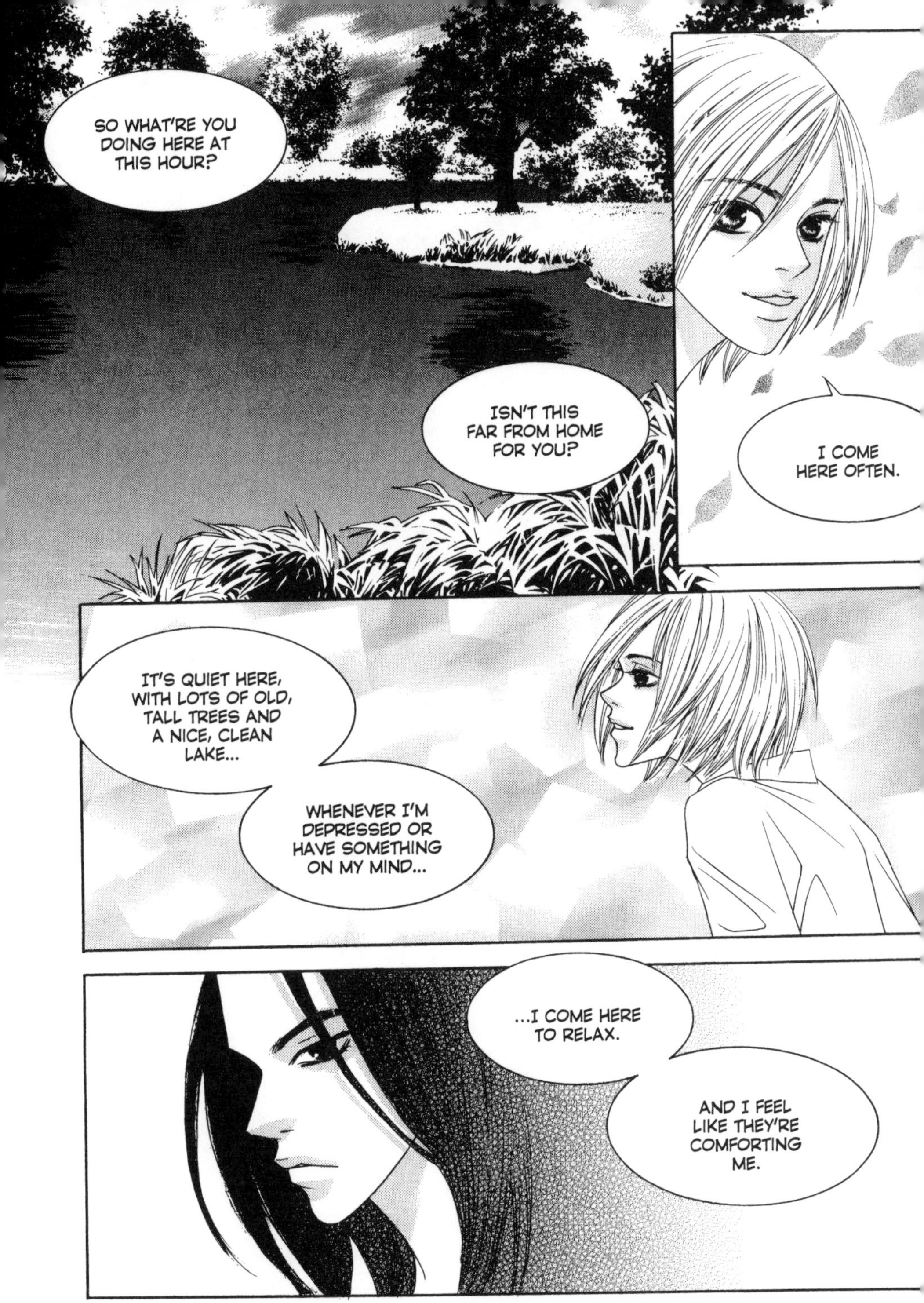
SO WHAT'RE YOU DOING HERE AT THIS HOUR?
ISN'T THIS FAR FROM HOME FOR YOU?
I COME HERE OFTEN.
IT'S QUIET HERE, WITH LOTS OF OLD, TALL TREES AND A NICE, CLEAN LAKE...
WHENEVER I'M DEPRESSED OR HAVE SOMETHING ON MY MIND...
...I COME HERE TO RELAX.
AND I FEEL LIKE THEY'RE COMFORTING ME.

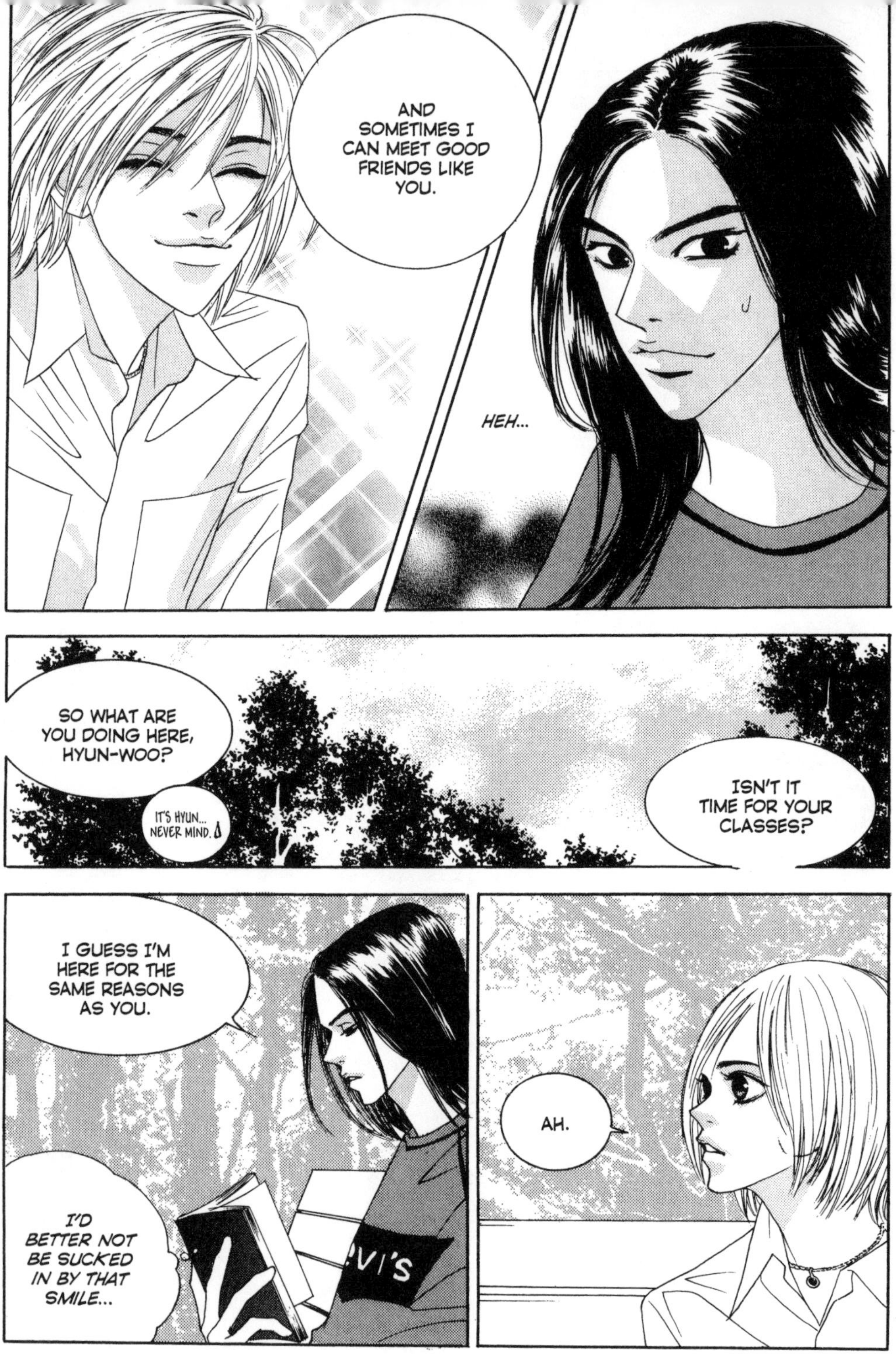
AND SOMETIMES I CAN MEET GOOD FRIENDS LIKE YOU.
HEH...
SO WHAT ARE YOU DOING HERE, HYUN-WOO?
IT'S HYUN... NEVER MIND.
ISN'T IT TIME FOR YOUR CLASSES?
I GUESS I'M HERE FOR THE SAME REASONS AS YOU.
I'D BETTER NOT BE SUCKED IN BY THAT SMILE...
AH.

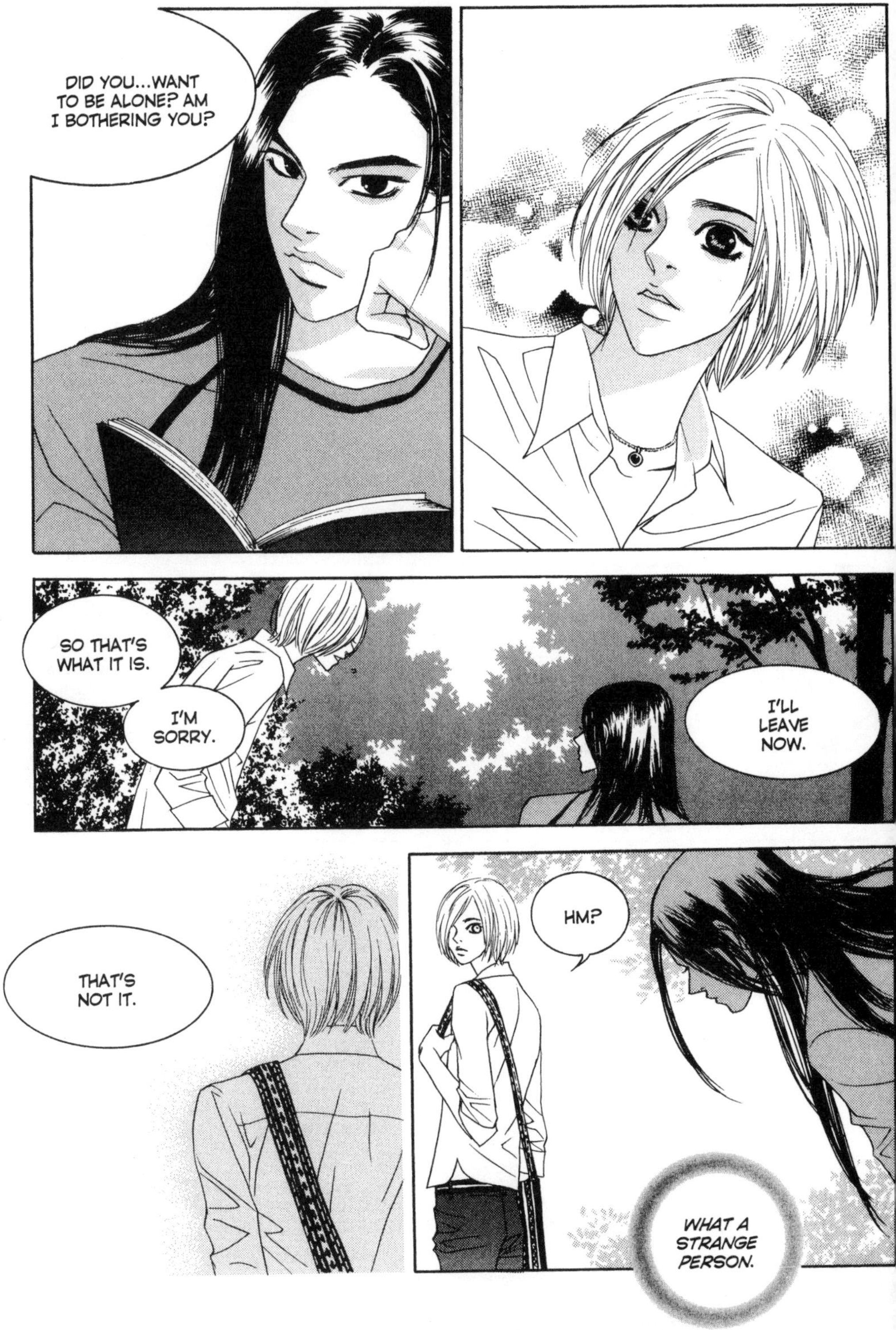
DID YOU...WANT TO BE ALONE? AM I BOTHERING YOU?
SO THAT'S WHAT IT IS.
I'M SORRY.
I'LL LEAVE NOW.
THAT'S NOT IT.
HM?
WHAT A STRANGE PERSON.

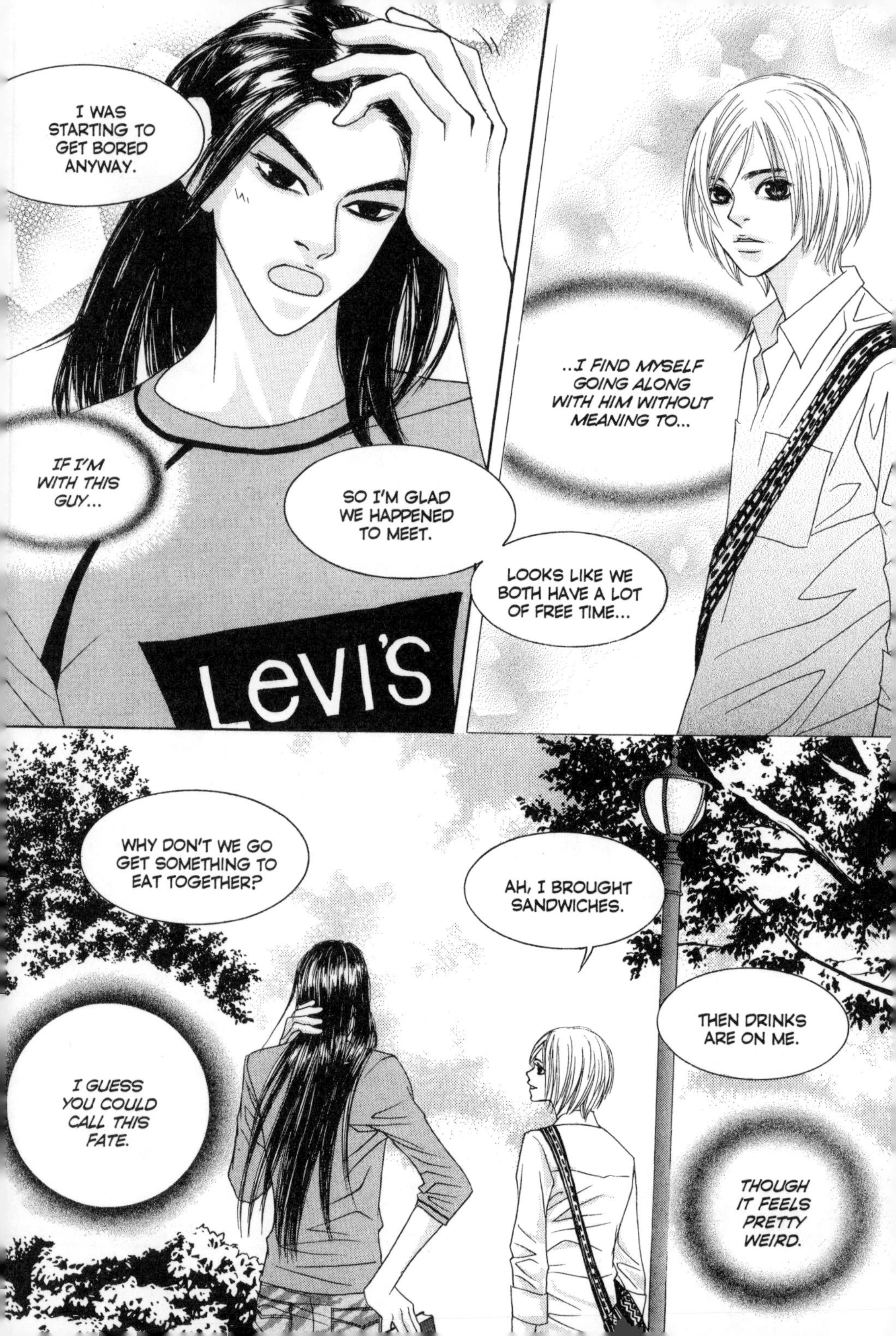
I WAS STARTING TO GET BORED ANYWAY.
SO I'M GLAD WE HAPPENED TO MEET.
LOOKS LIKE WE BOTH HAVE A LOT OF FREE TIME...
IF I'M WITH THIS GUY...
...I FIND MYSELF GOING ALONG WITH HIM WITHOUT MEANING TO...
LEVI'S
WHY DON'T WE GO GET SOMETHING TO EAT TOGETHER?
AH, I BROUGHT SANDWICHES.
THEN DRINKS ARE ON ME.
I GUESS YOU COULD CALL THIS FATE.
THOUGH IT FEELS PRETTY WEIRD.

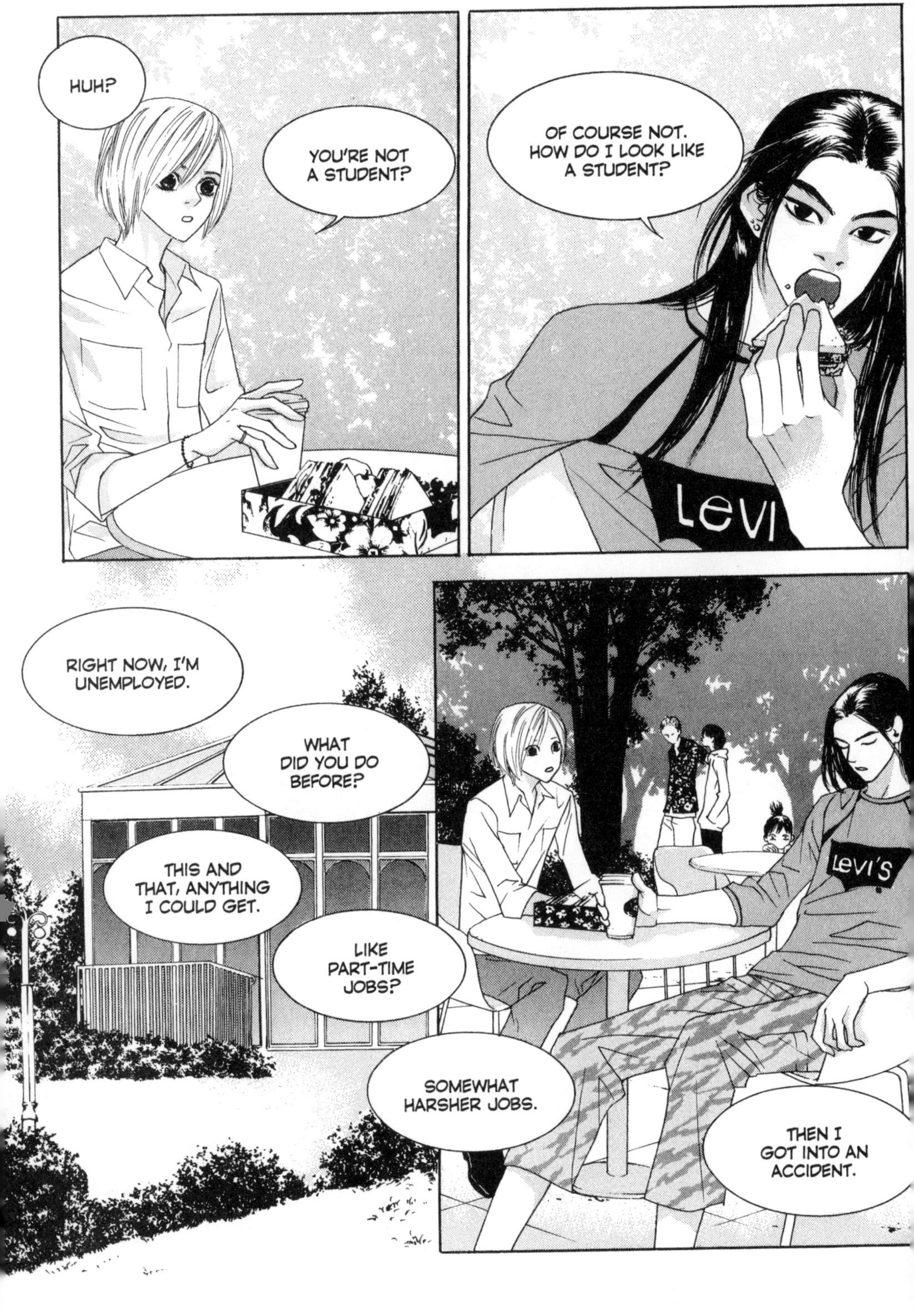
HUH?
YOU'RE NOT A STUDENT?
OF COURSE NOT. HOW DO I LOOK LIKE A STUDENT?
LEVI
RIGHT NOW, I'M UNEMPLOYED.
WHAT DID YOU DO BEFORE?
THIS AND THAT, ANYTHING I COULD GET.
LIKE PART-TIME JOBS?
SOMEWHAT HARSHER JOBS.
THEN I GOT INTO AN ACCIDENT.
LEVI'S

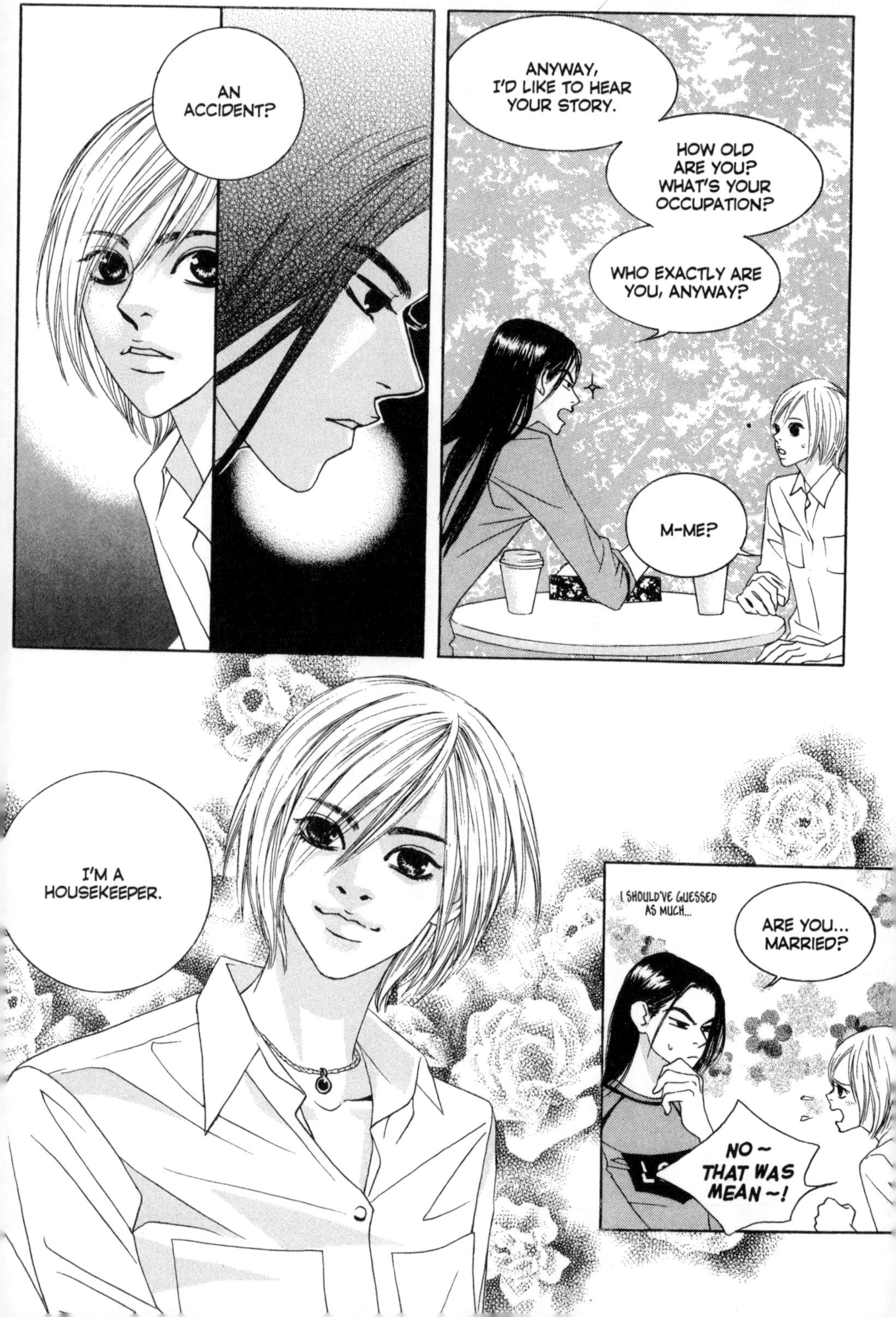
AN ACCIDENT?
ANYWAY, I'D LIKE TO HEAR YOUR STORY.
HOW OLD ARE YOU? WHAT'S YOUR OCCUPATION?
WHO EXACTLY ARE YOU, ANYWAY?
M-ME?
I'M A HOUSEKEEPER.
I SHOULD'VE GUESSED AS MUCH...
ARE YOU... MARRIED?
NO ~ THAT WAS MEAN ~!

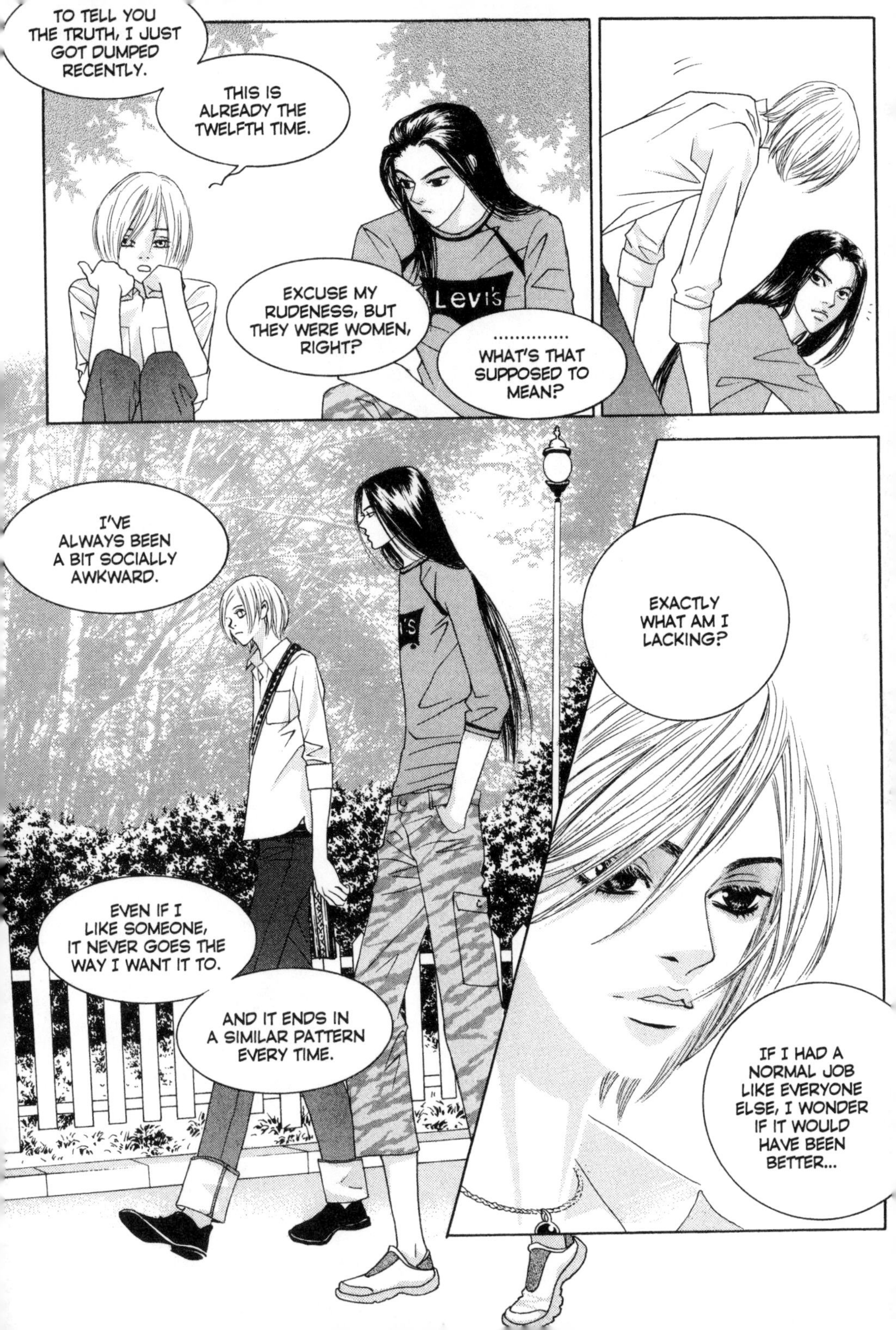
TO TELL YOU THE TRUTH, I JUST GOT DUMPED RECENTLY.
THIS IS ALREADY THE TWELFTH TIME.
EXCUSE MY RUDENESS, BUT THEY WERE WOMEN, RIGHT?
Levi's
..............
WHAT'S THAT SUPPOSED TO MEAN?
I'VE ALWAYS BEEN A BIT SOCIALLY AWKWARD.
EVEN IF I LIKE SOMEONE, IT NEVER GOES THE WAY I WANT IT TO.
AND IT ENDS IN A SIMILAR PATTERN EVERY TIME.
EXACTLY WHAT AM I LACKING?
IF I HAD A NORMAL JOB LIKE EVERYONE ELSE, I WONDER IF IT WOULD HAVE BEEN BETTER...

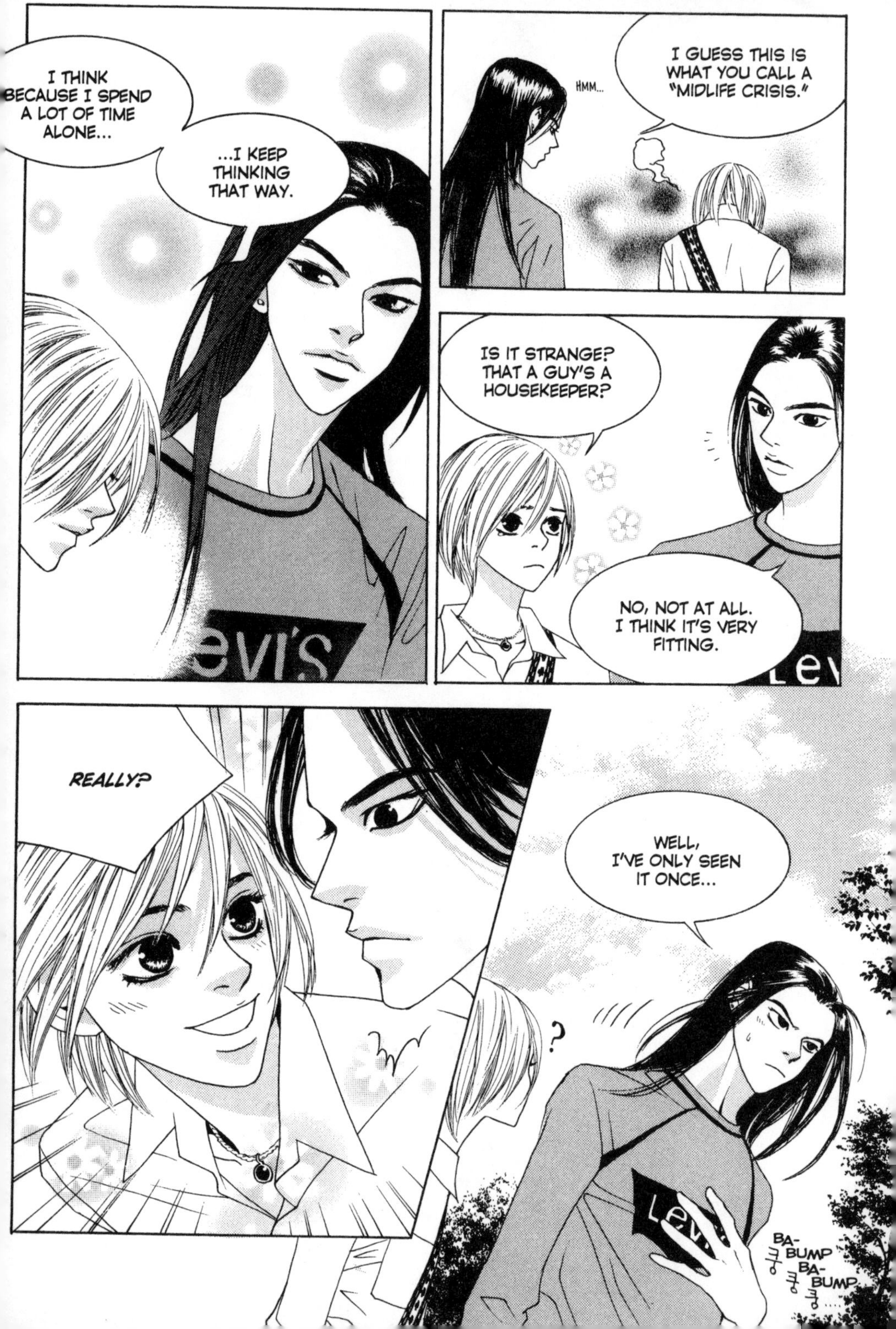
I THINK BECAUSE I SPEND A LOT OF TIME ALONE...
...I KEEP THINKING THAT WAY.
HMM...
I GUESS THIS IS WHAT YOU CALL A "MIDLIFE CRISIS."
IS IT STRANGE? THAT A GUY'S A HOUSEKEEPER?
NO, NOT AT ALL. I THINK IT'S VERY FITTING.
REALLY?
WELL, I'VE ONLY SEEN IT ONCE...
?
BA-BUMP BA-BUMP

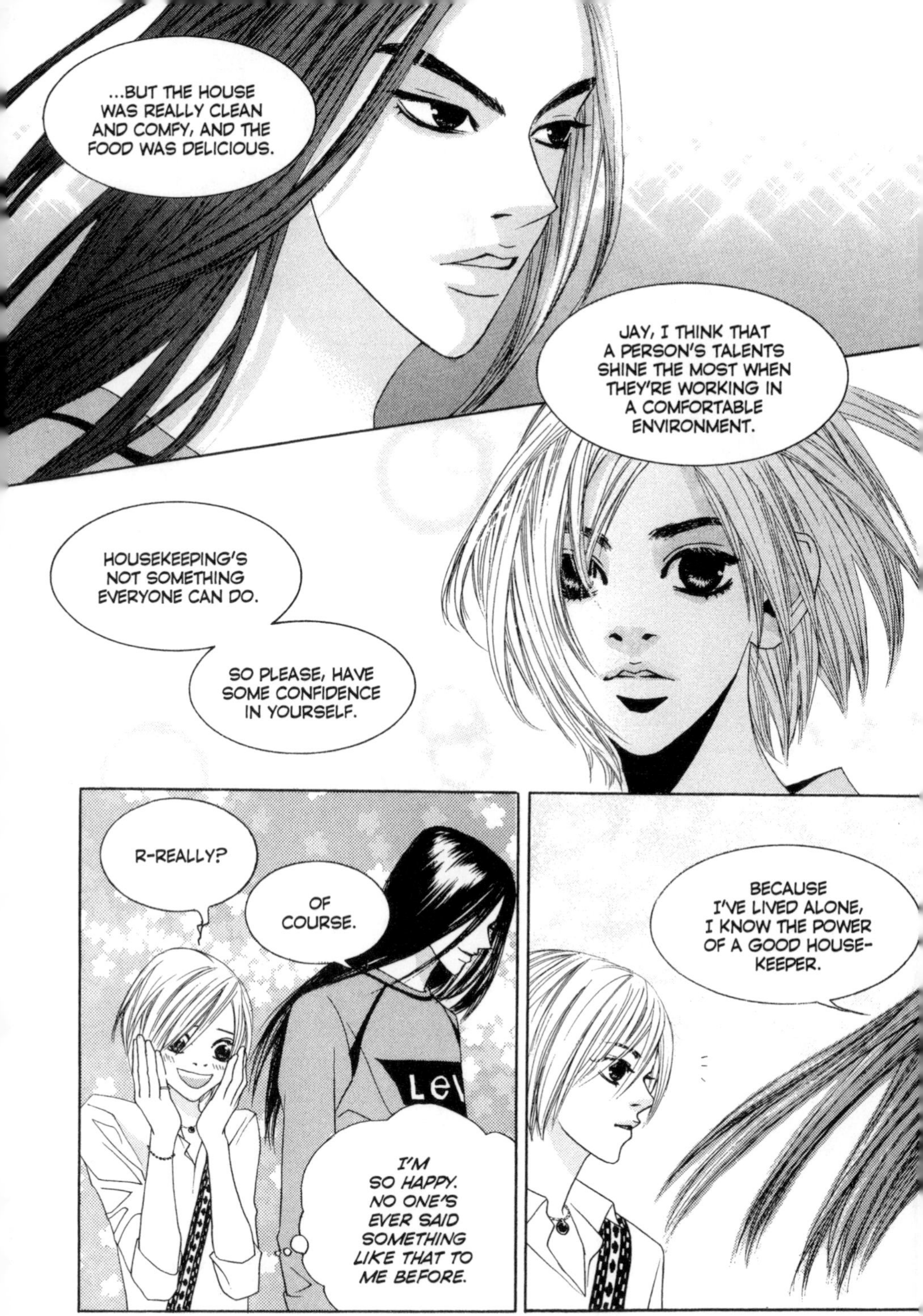
...BUT THE HOUSE WAS REALLY CLEAN AND COMFY, AND THE FOOD WAS DELICIOUS.
JAY, I THINK THAT A PERSON'S TALENTS SHINE THE MOST WHEN THEY'RE WORKING IN A COMFORTABLE ENVIRONMENT.
HOUSEKEEPING'S NOT SOMETHING EVERYONE CAN DO.
SO PLEASE, HAVE SOME CONFIDENCE IN YOURSELF.
R-REALLY?
OF COURSE.
I'M SO HAPPY. NO ONE'S EVER SAID SOMETHING LIKE THAT TO ME BEFORE.
BECAUSE I'VE LIVED ALONE, I KNOW THE POWER OF A GOOD HOUSE-KEEPER.

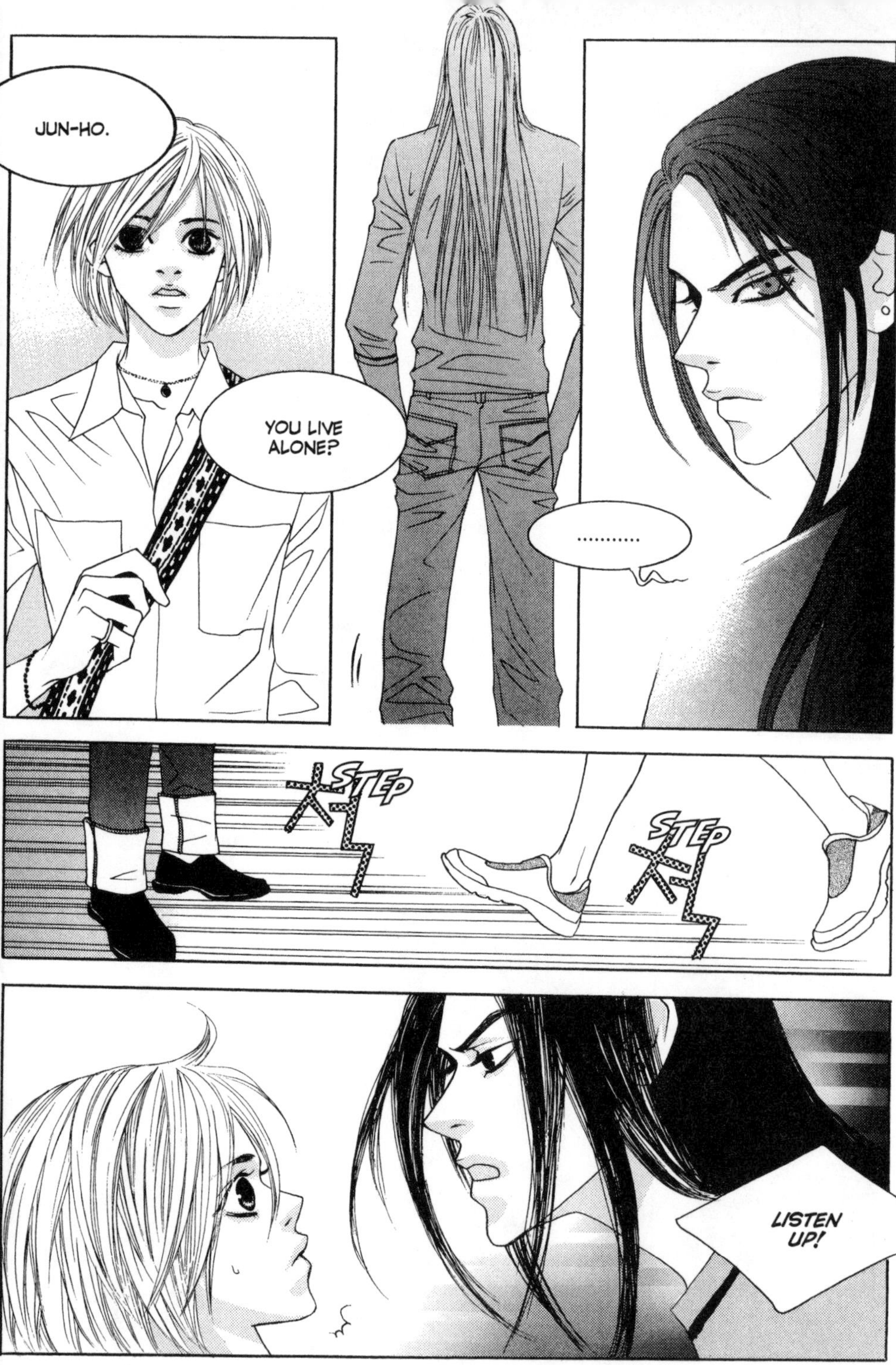
JUN-HO.
YOU LIVE ALONE?
............
STEP
STEP
LISTEN UP!

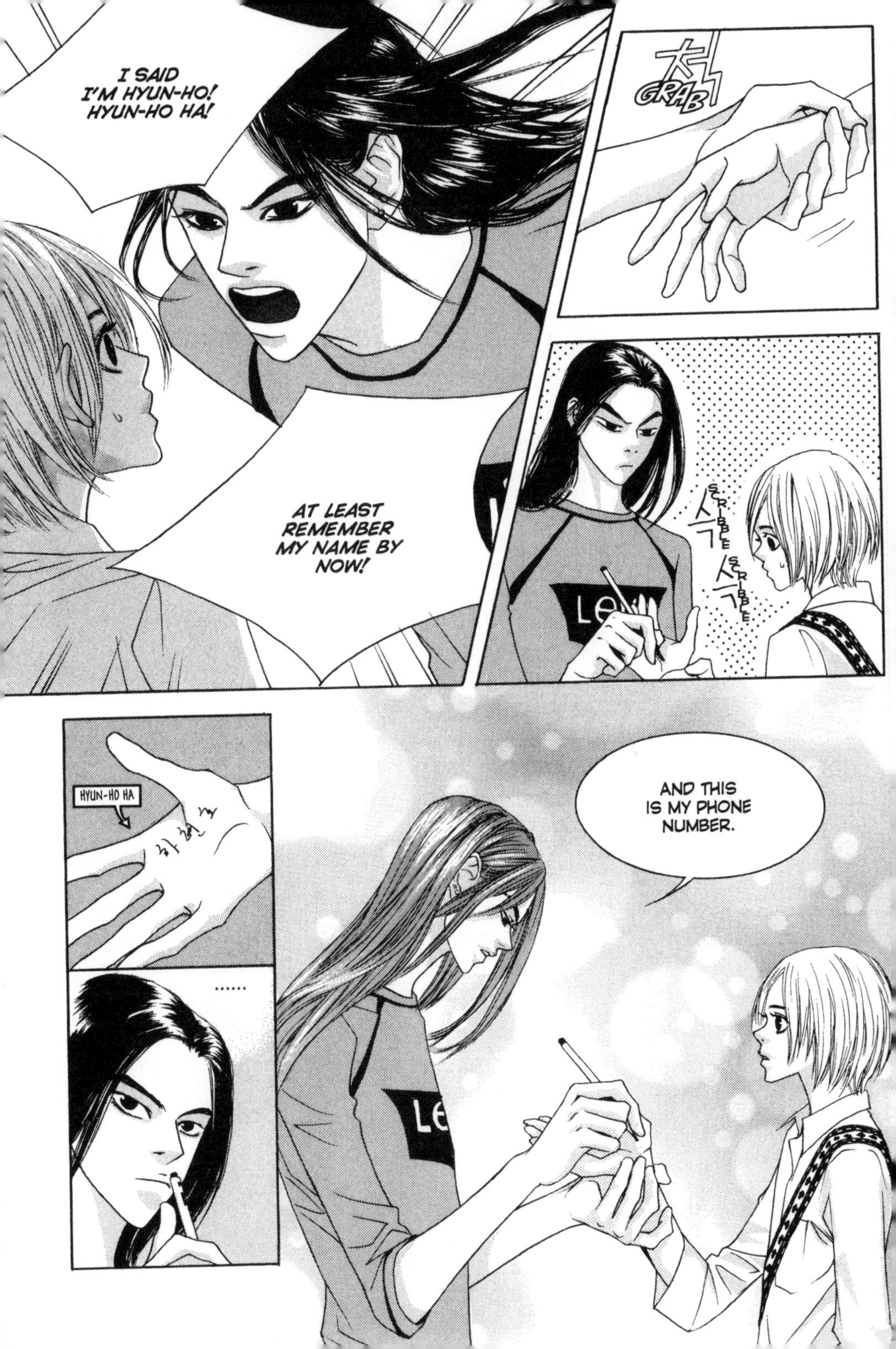
I SAID I'M HYUN-HO! HYUN-HO HA!
AT LEAST REMEMBER MY NAME BY NOW!
GRAB
SCRIBBLE
SCRIBBLE
HYUN-HO HA
......
AND THIS IS MY PHONE NUMBER.

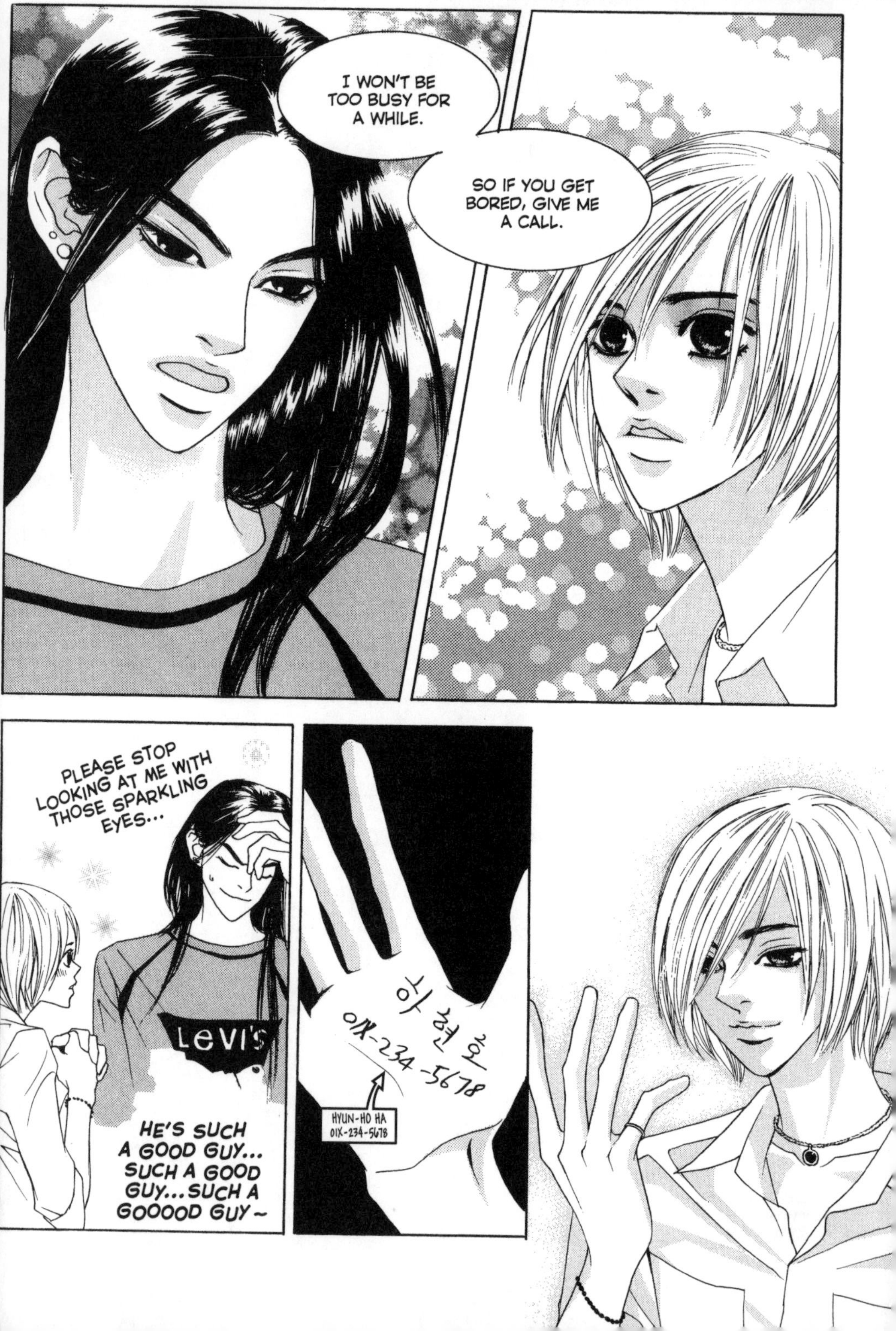
I WON'T BE TOO BUSY FOR A WHILE.
SO IF YOU GET BORED, GIVE ME A CALL.
PLEASE STOP LOOKING AT ME WITH THOSE SPARKLING EYES...
LEVI'S
HE'S SUCH A GOOD GUY... SUCH A GOOD GUY... SUCH A GOOOOD GUY~
HYUN-HO HA 01X-234-5678

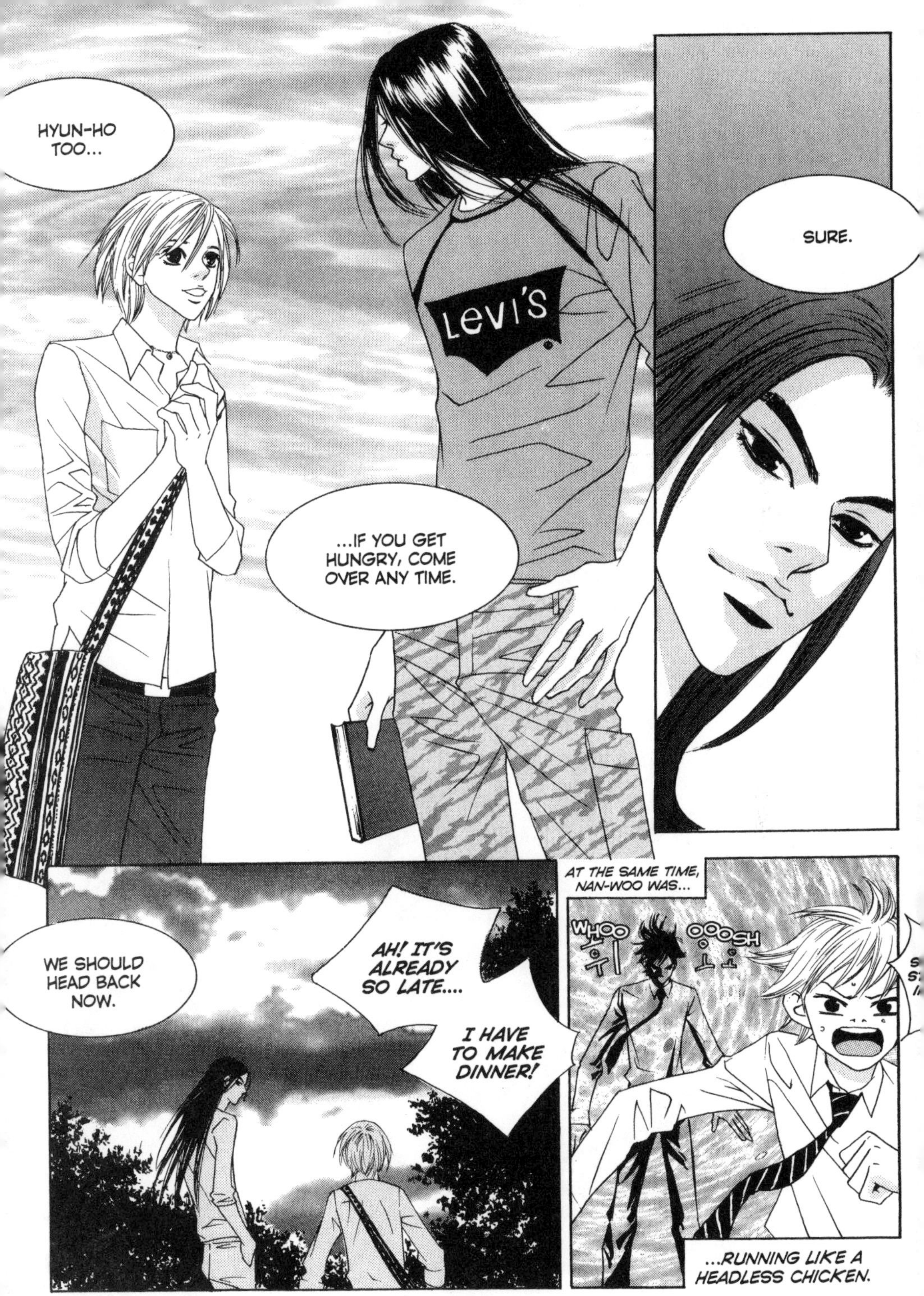
HYUN-HO TOO...
...IF YOU GET HUNGRY, COME OVER ANY TIME.
SURE.
WE SHOULD HEAD BACK NOW.
AH! IT'S ALREADY SO LATE....
I HAVE TO MAKE DINNER!
AT THE SAME TIME, NAN-WOO WAS...
WHOO
OOOSH
...RUNNING LIKE A HEADLESS CHICKEN.

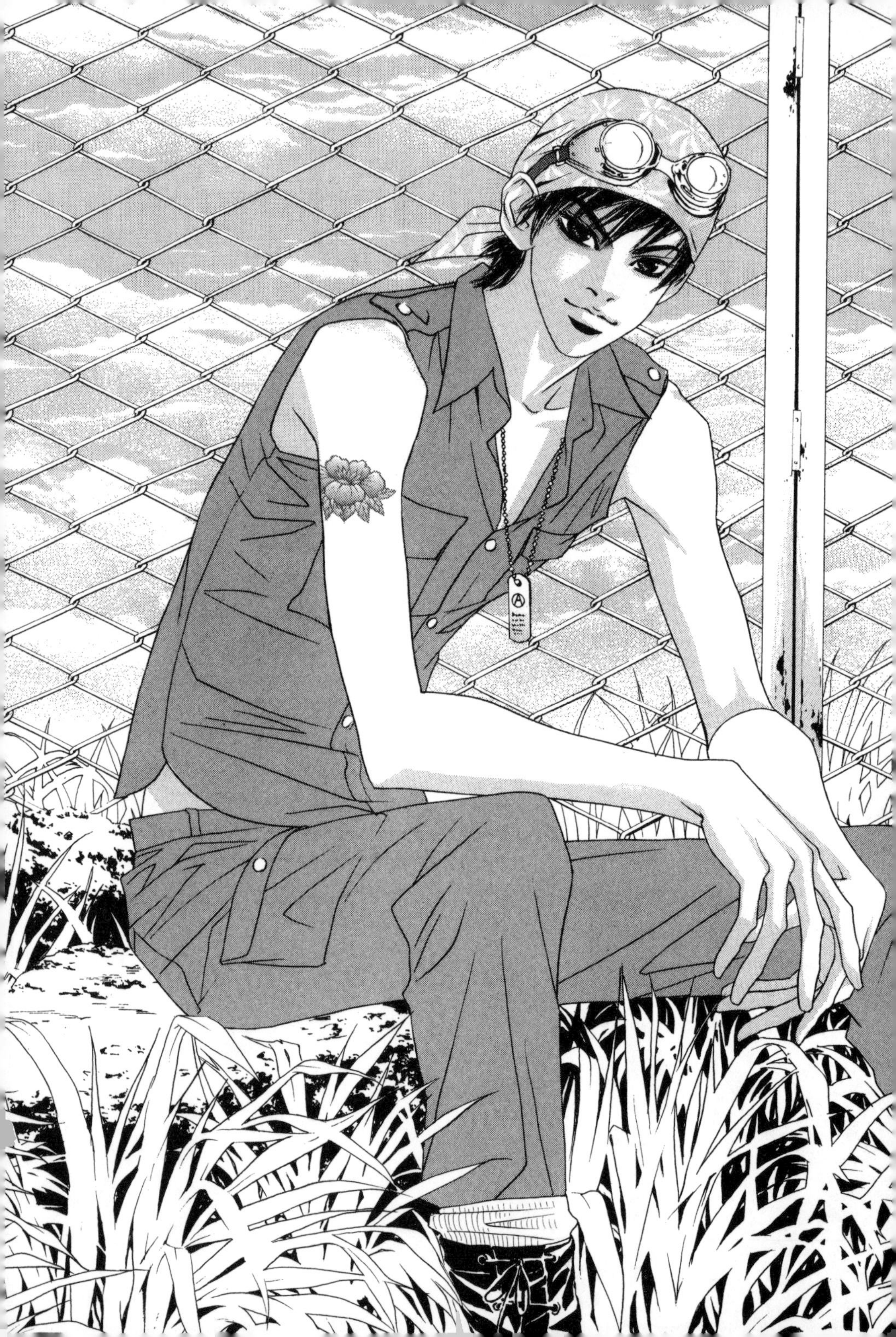

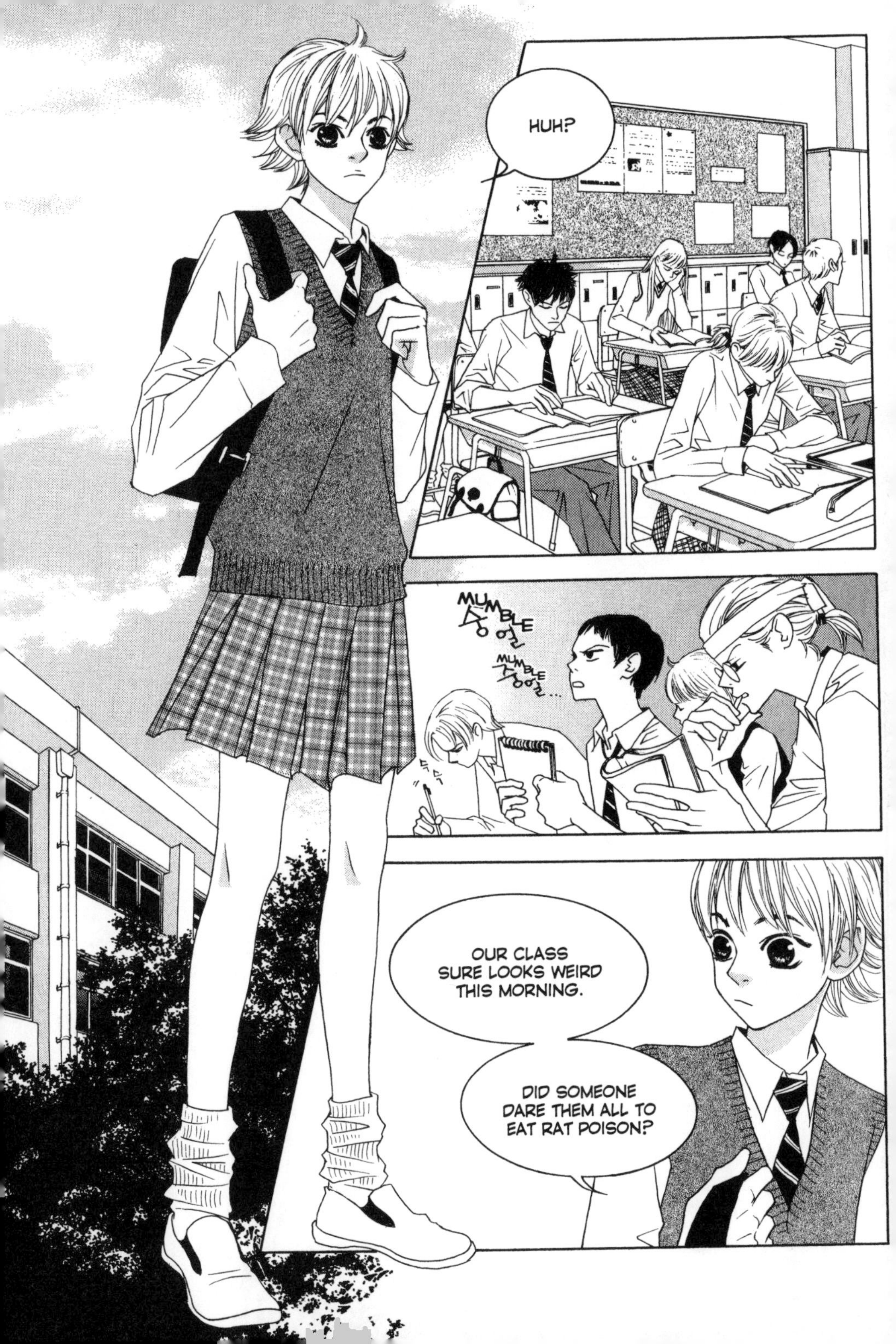
HUH?
MUMBLE
MUMBLE...
OUR CLASS SURE LOOKS WEIRD THIS MORNING.
DID SOMEONE DARE THEM ALL TO EAT RAT POISON?

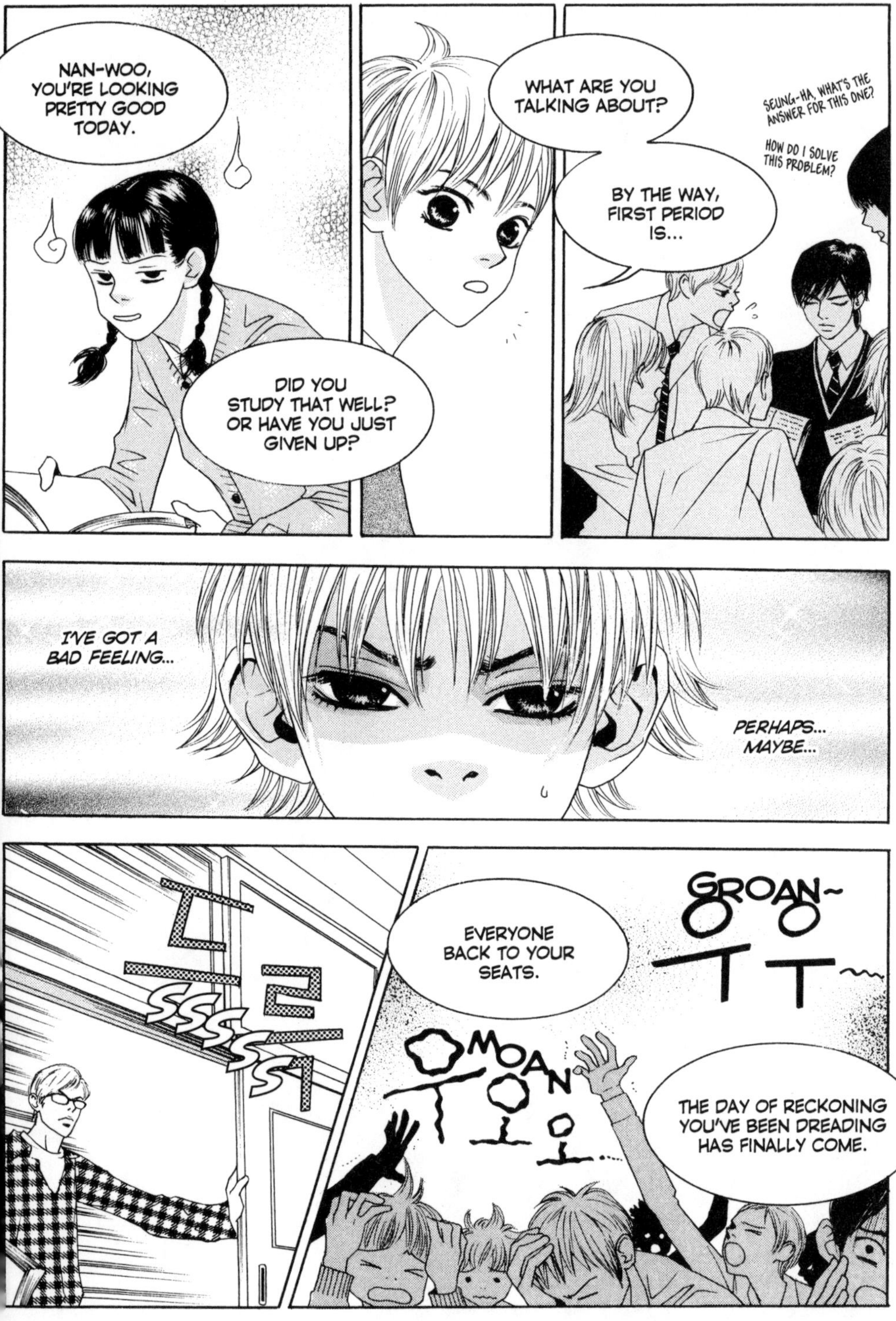

NAN-WOO, YOU'RE LOOKING PRETTY GOOD TODAY.
WHAT ARE YOU TALKING ABOUT?
BY THE WAY, FIRST PERIOD IS...
DID YOU STUDY THAT WELL? OR HAVE YOU JUST GIVEN UP?
SEUNG-HA, WHAT'S THE ANSWER FOR THIS ONE?
HOW DO I SOLVE THIS PROBLEM?
I'VE GOT A BAD FEELING...
PERHAPS... MAYBE...
SSSSS
EVERYONE BACK TO YOUR SEATS.
GROAN~
MOAN
THE DAY OF RECKONING YOU'VE BEEN DREADING HAS FINALLY COME.

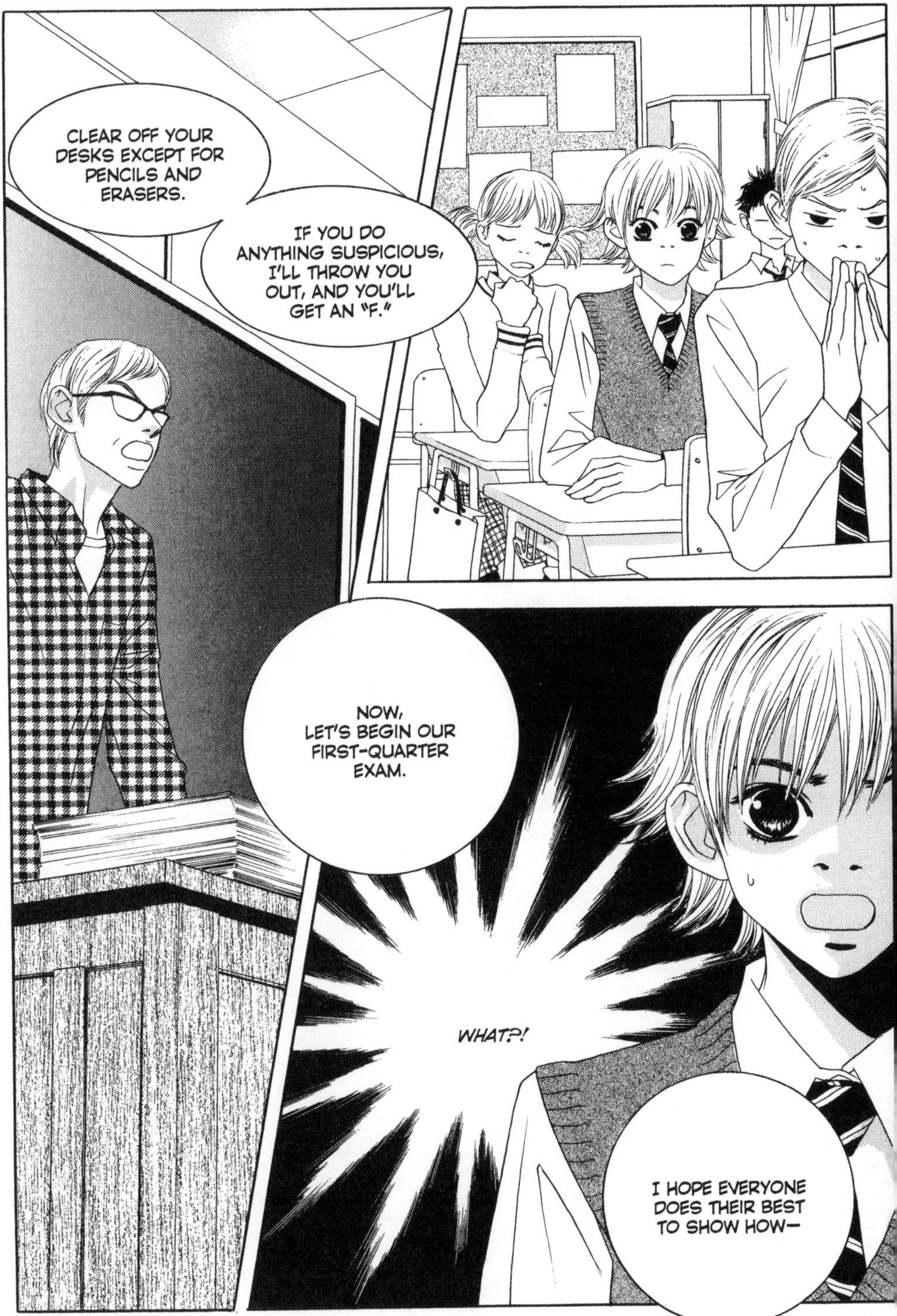
CLEAR OFF YOUR DESKS EXCEPT FOR PENCILS AND ERASERS.
IF YOU DO ANYTHING SUSPICIOUS, I'LL THROW YOU OUT, AND YOU'LL GET AN "F."
NOW, LET'S BEGIN OUR FIRST-QUARTER EXAM.
WHAT?!
I HOPE EVERYONE DOES THEIR BEST TO SHOW HOW—

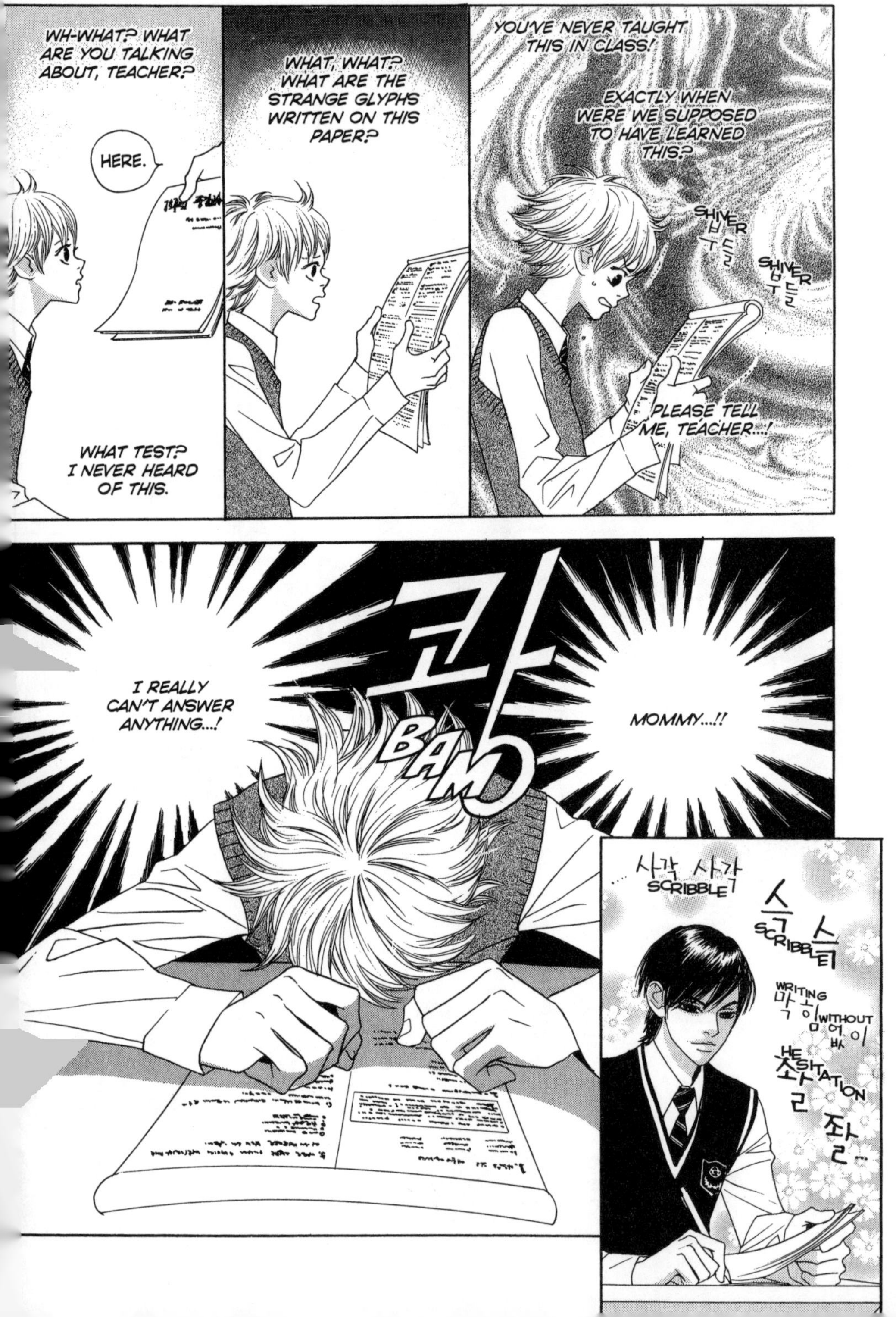
WH-WHAT? WHAT ARE YOU TALKING ABOUT, TEACHER?
HERE.
WHAT TEST? I NEVER HEARD OF THIS.
WHAT, WHAT? WHAT ARE THE STRANGE GLYPHS WRITTEN ON THIS PAPER?
YOU'VE NEVER TAUGHT THIS IN CLASS!
EXACTLY WHEN WERE WE SUPPOSED TO HAVE LEARNED THIS?
SHIVER
부들
SHIVER
부들
PLEASE TELL ME, TEACHER...!
I REALLY CAN'T ANSWER ANYTHING...!
쾅
BAM
MOMMY...!!
사각 사각
SCRIBBLE
SCRIBBLE
WRITING
WITHOUT
HESITATION

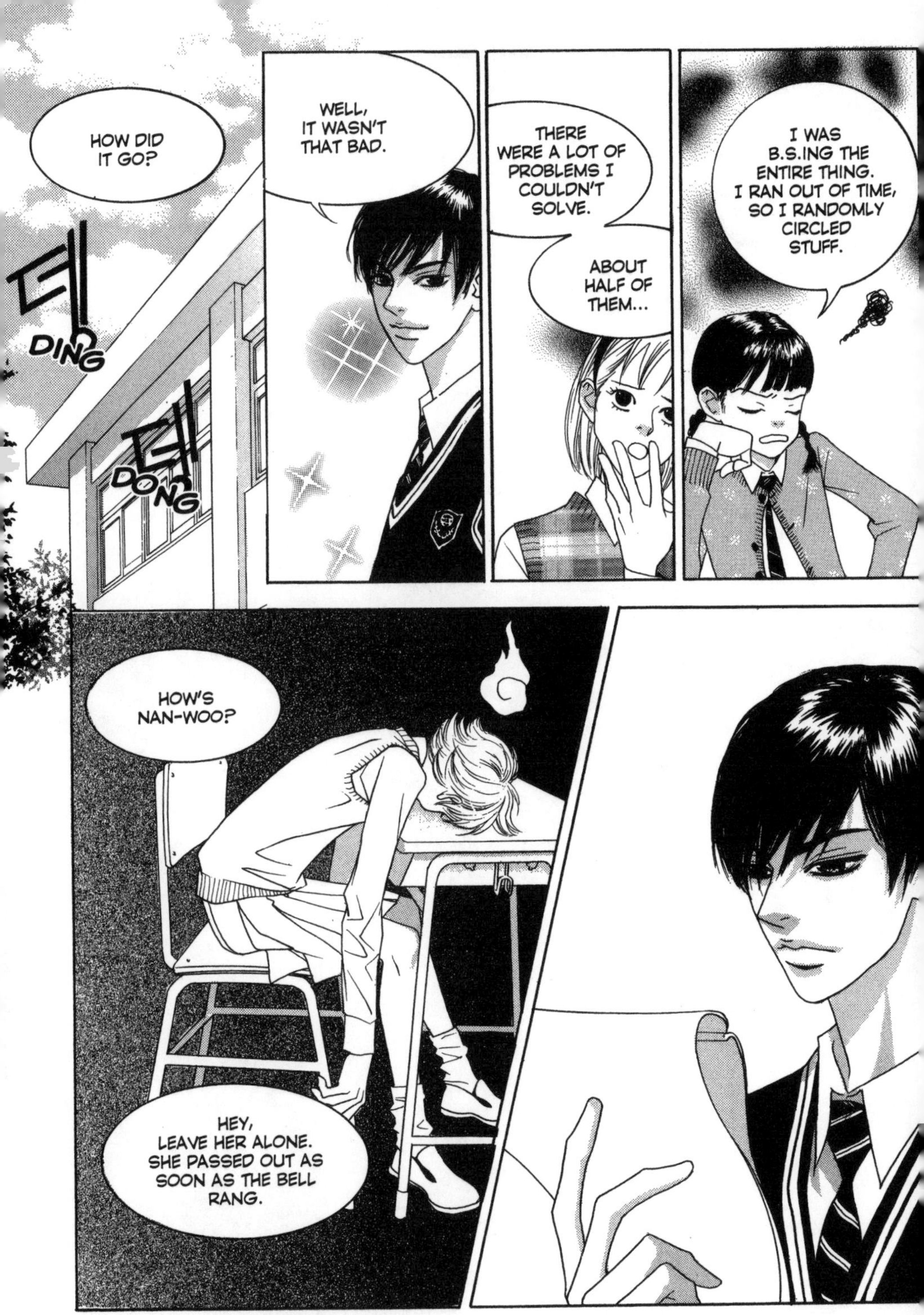
HOW DID IT GO?
DING
DONG
WELL, IT WASN'T THAT BAD.
THERE WERE A LOT OF PROBLEMS I COULDN'T SOLVE.
ABOUT HALF OF THEM...
I WAS B.S.ING THE ENTIRE THING. I RAN OUT OF TIME, SO I RANDOMLY CIRCLED STUFF.
HOW'S NAN-WOO?
HEY, LEAVE HER ALONE. SHE PASSED OUT AS SOON AS THE BELL RANG.

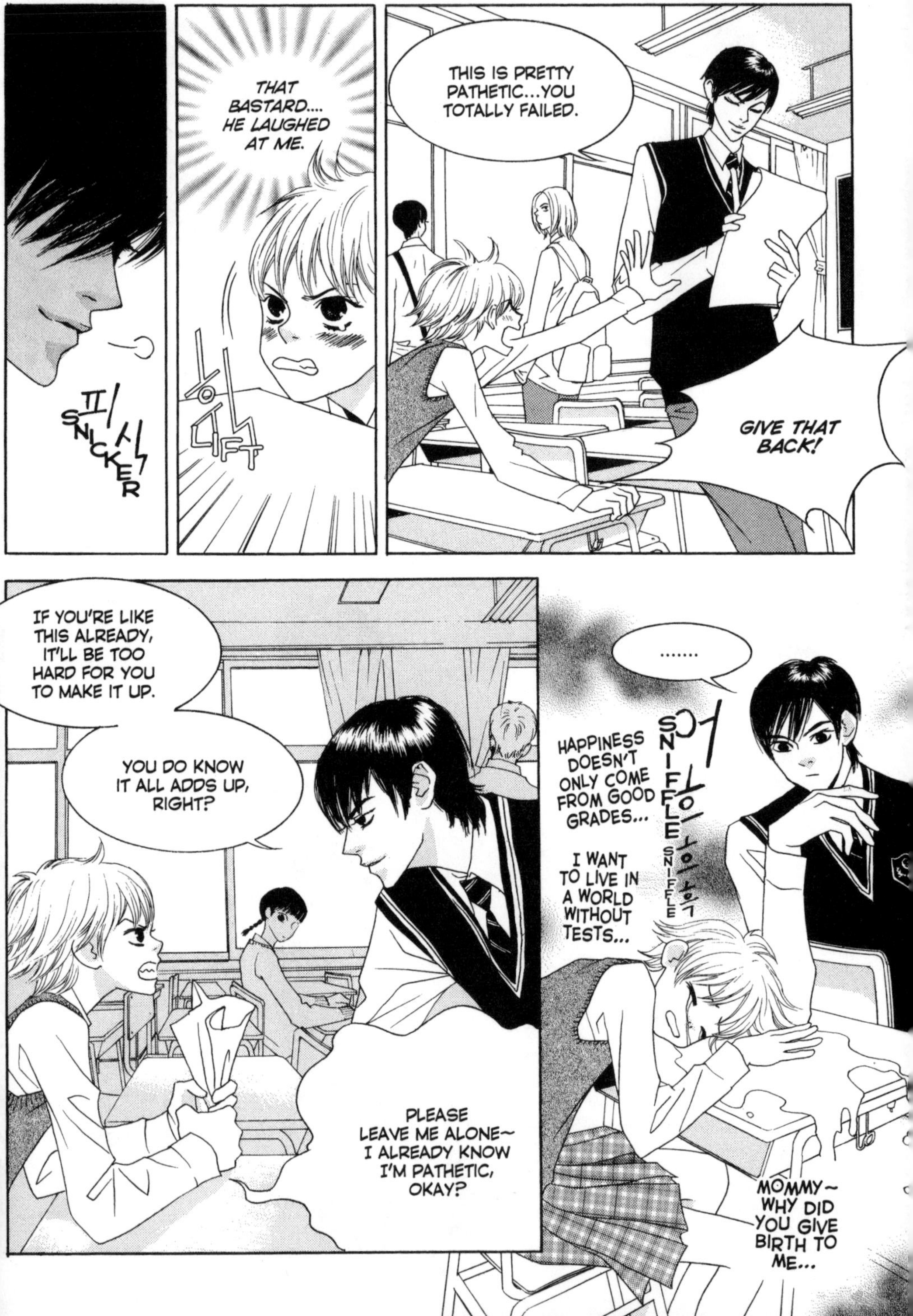
SNICKER
THAT BASTARD.... HE LAUGHED AT ME.
LIFT
THIS IS PRETTY PATHETIC...YOU TOTALLY FAILED.
GIVE THAT BACK!
IF YOU'RE LIKE THIS ALREADY, IT'LL BE TOO HARD FOR YOU TO MAKE IT UP.
YOU DO KNOW IT ALL ADDS UP, RIGHT?
PLEASE LEAVE ME ALONE~ I ALREADY KNOW I'M PATHETIC, OKAY?
.......
HAPPINESS DOESN'T ONLY COME FROM GOOD GRADES...
SNIFFLE
SNIFFLE
I WANT TO LIVE IN A WORLD WITHOUT TESTS...
MOMMY~ WHY DID YOU GIVE BIRTH TO ME...

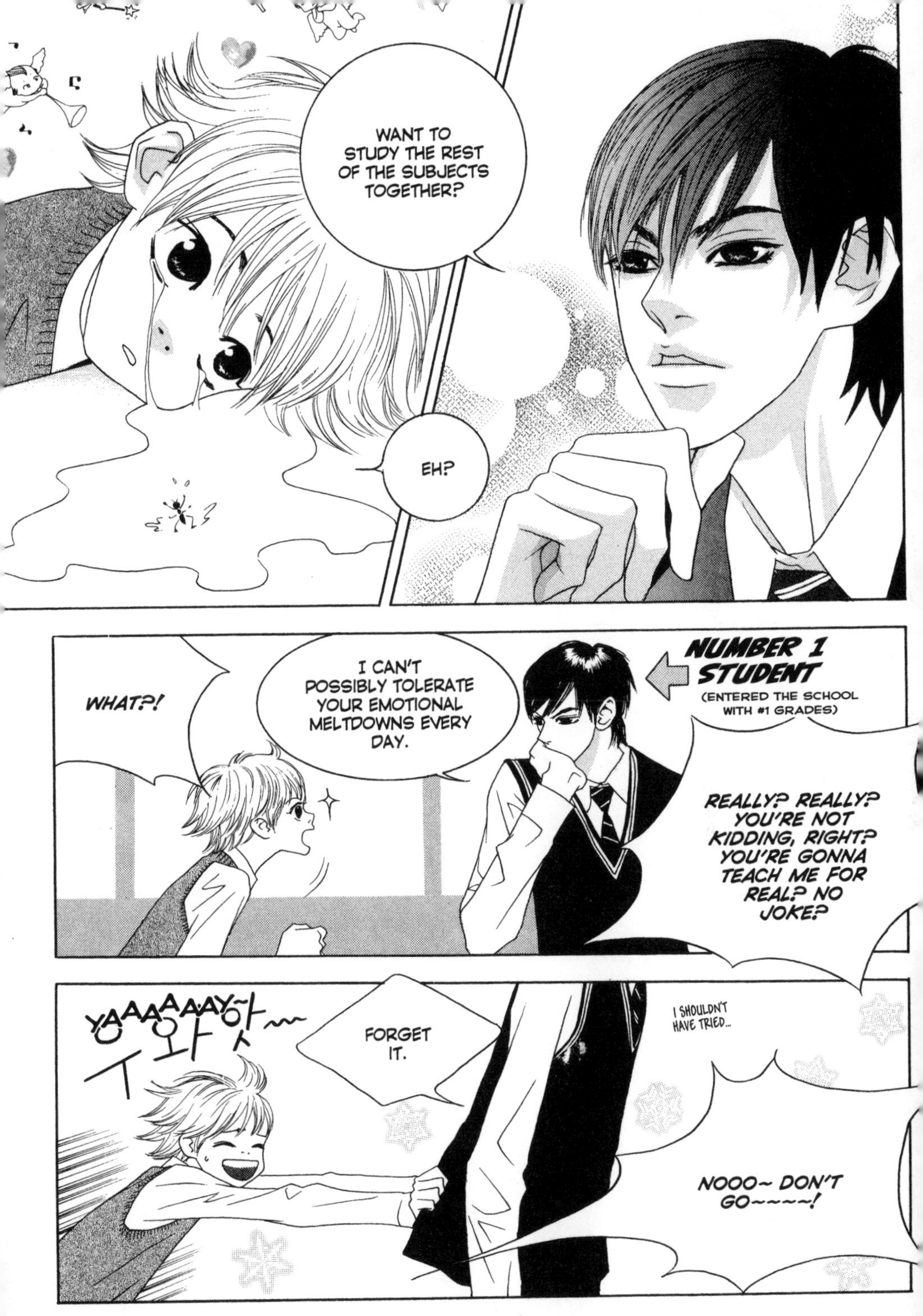
WANT TO STUDY THE REST OF THE SUBJECTS TOGETHER?
EH?
WHAT?!
I CAN'T POSSIBLY TOLERATE YOUR EMOTIONAL MELTDOWNS EVERY DAY.
NUMBER 1 STUDENT
(ENTERED THE SCHOOL WITH #1 GRADES)
REALLY? REALLY? YOU'RE NOT KIDDING, RIGHT? YOU'RE GONNA TEACH ME FOR REAL? NO JOKE?
YAAAAAY~
FORGET IT.
I SHOULDN'T HAVE TRIED...
NOOO~ DON'T GO~~~~!

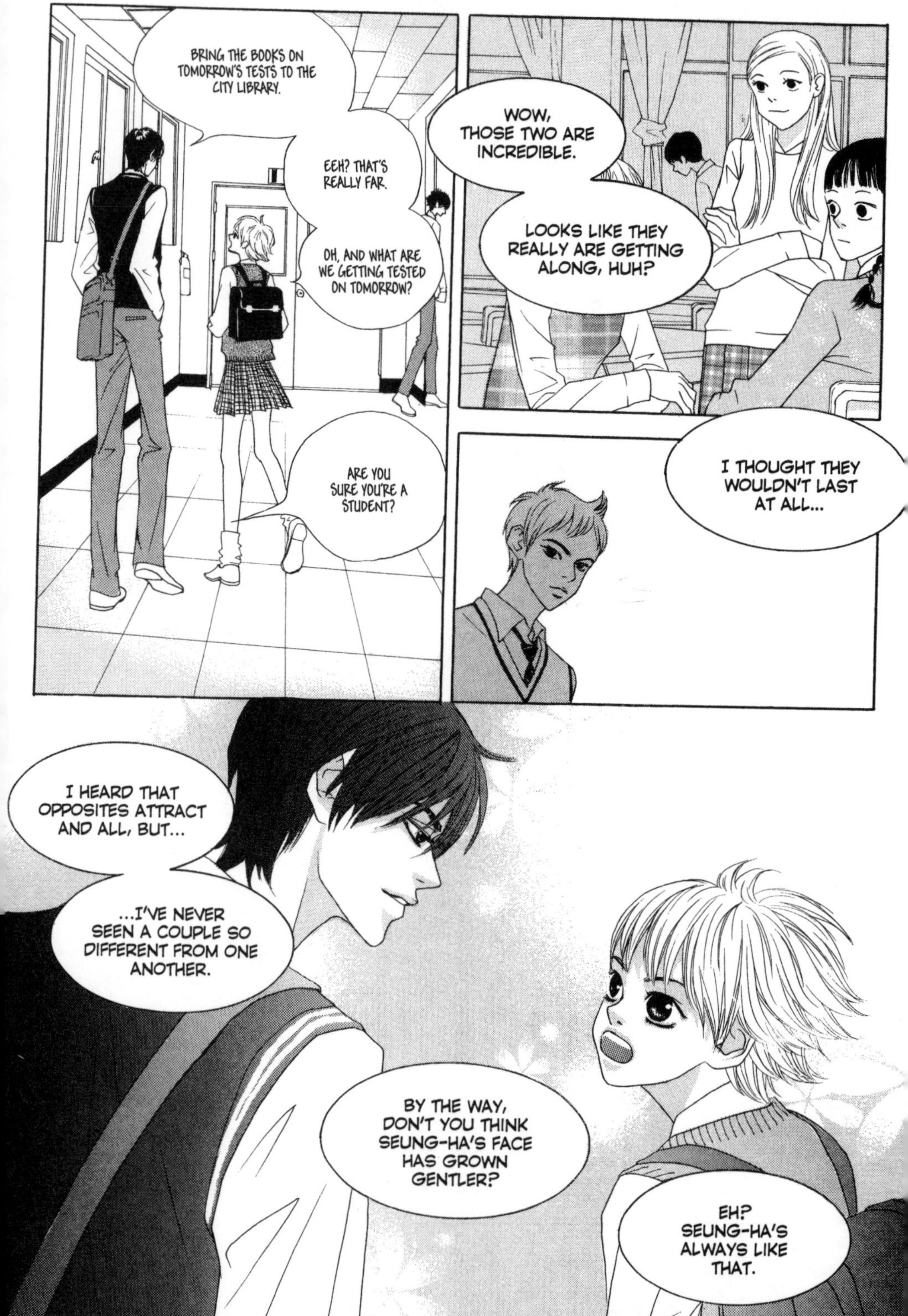
BRING THE BOOKS ON TOMORROW'S TESTS TO THE CITY LIBRARY.
EEH? THAT'S REALLY FAR.
OH, AND WHAT ARE WE GETTING TESTED ON TOMORROW?
ARE YOU SURE YOU'RE A STUDENT?
WOW, THOSE TWO ARE INCREDIBLE.
LOOKS LIKE THEY REALLY ARE GETTING ALONG, HUH?
I THOUGHT THEY WOULDN'T LAST AT ALL...
I HEARD THAT OPPOSITES ATTRACT AND ALL, BUT...
...I'VE NEVER SEEN A COUPLE SO DIFFERENT FROM ONE ANOTHER.
BY THE WAY, DON'T YOU THINK SEUNG-HA'S FACE HAS GROWN GENTLER?
EH? SEUNG-HA'S ALWAYS LIKE THAT.

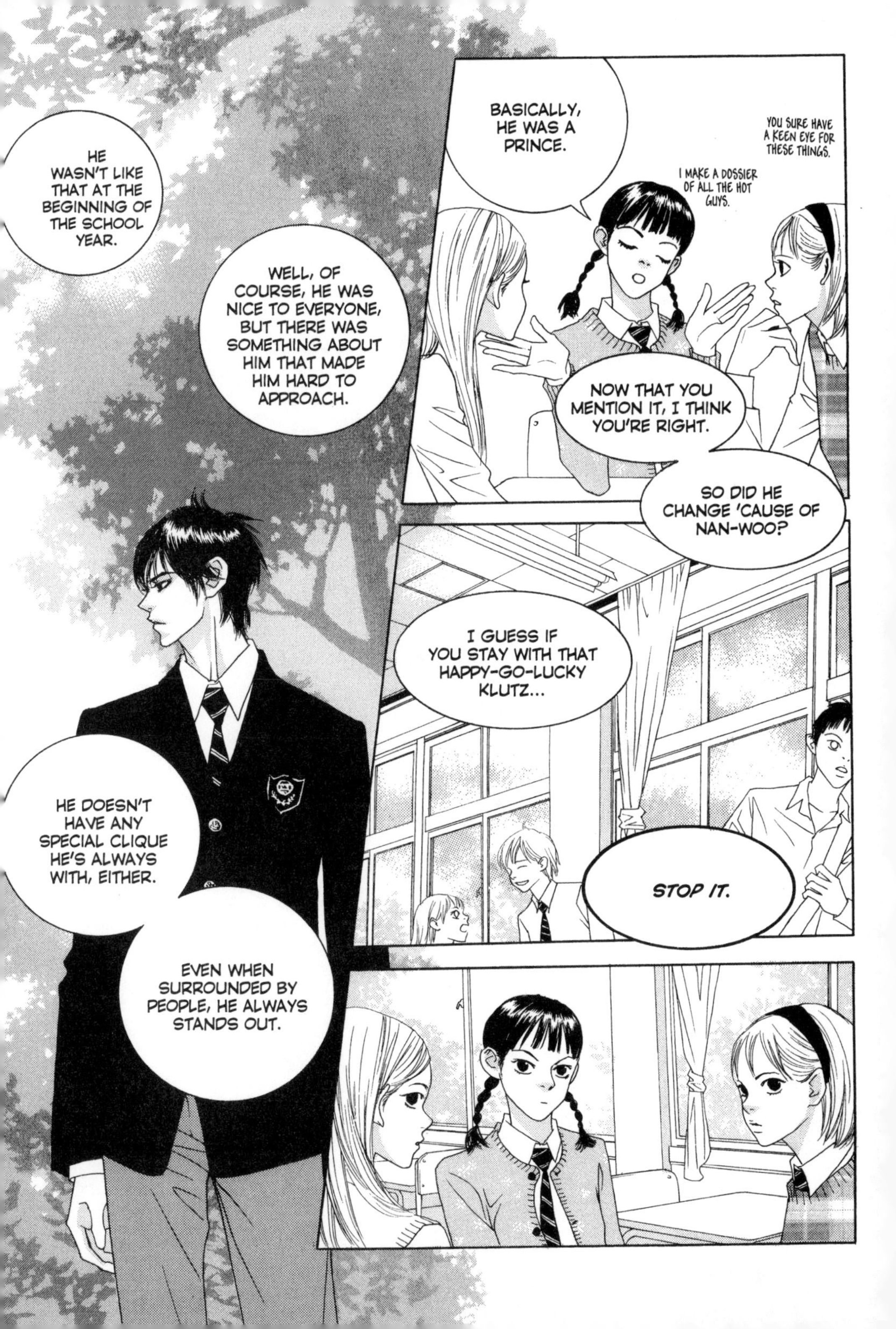
HE WASN'T LIKE THAT AT THE BEGINNING OF THE SCHOOL YEAR.
WELL, OF COURSE, HE WAS NICE TO EVERYONE, BUT THERE WAS SOMETHING ABOUT HIM THAT MADE HIM HARD TO APPROACH.
HE DOESN'T HAVE ANY SPECIAL CLIQUE HE'S ALWAYS WITH, EITHER.
EVEN WHEN SURROUNDED BY PEOPLE, HE ALWAYS STANDS OUT.
BASICALLY, HE WAS A PRINCE.
YOU SURE HAVE A KEEN EYE FOR THESE THINGS.
I MAKE A DOSSIER OF ALL THE HOT GUYS.
NOW THAT YOU MENTION IT, I THINK YOU'RE RIGHT.
SO DID HE CHANGE 'CAUSE OF NAN-WOO?
I GUESS IF YOU STAY WITH THAT HAPPY-GO-LUCKY KLUTZ...
STOP IT.

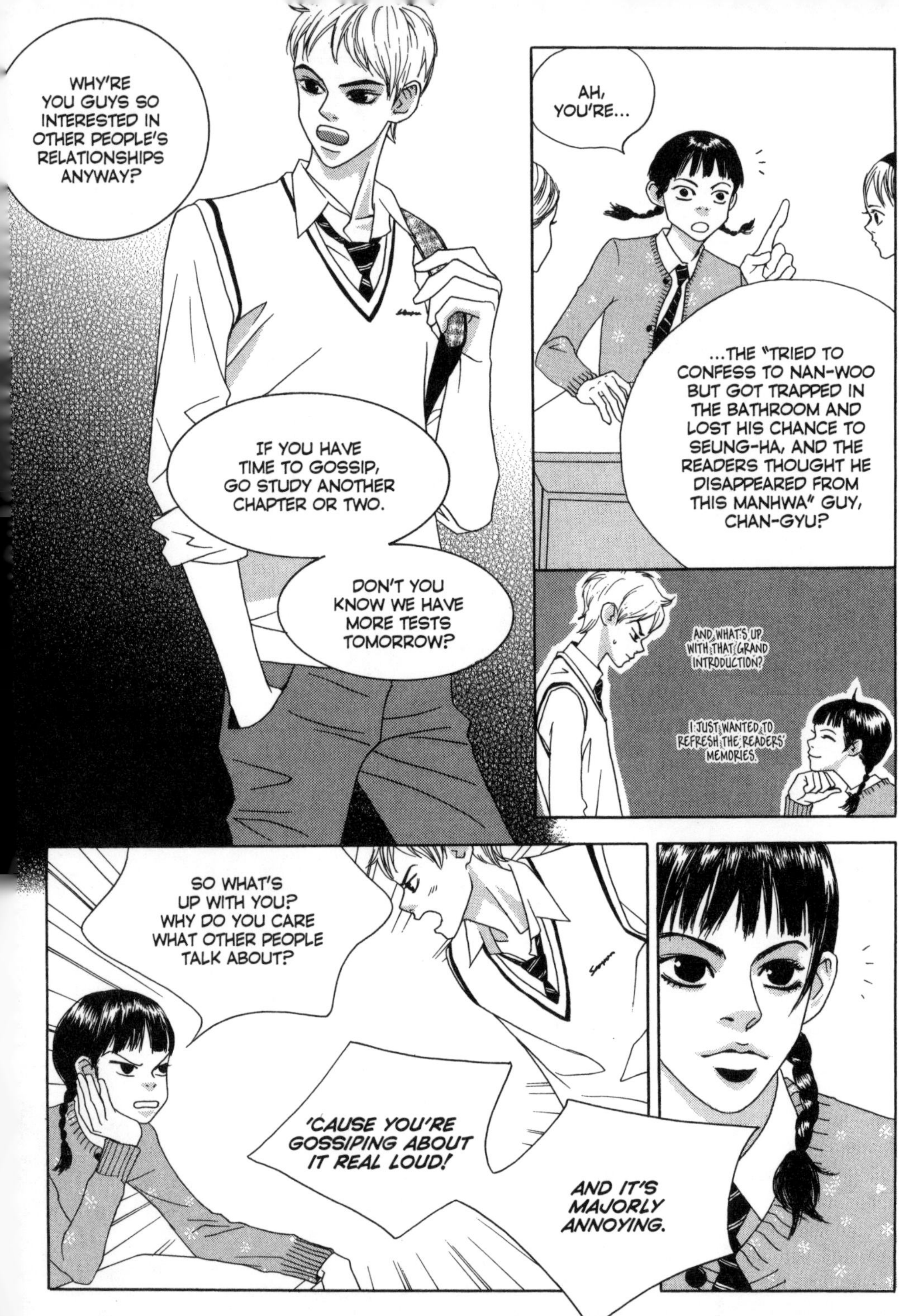
WHY'RE YOU GUYS SO INTERESTED IN OTHER PEOPLE'S RELATIONSHIPS ANYWAY?
IF YOU HAVE TIME TO GOSSIP, GO STUDY ANOTHER CHAPTER OR TWO.
DON'T YOU KNOW WE HAVE MORE TESTS TOMORROW?
AH, YOU'RE...
...THE "TRIED TO CONFESS TO NAN-WOO BUT GOT TRAPPED IN THE BATHROOM AND LOST HIS CHANCE TO SEUNG-HA, AND THE READERS THOUGHT HE DISAPPEARED FROM THIS MANHWA" GUY, CHAN-GYU?
AND WHAT'S UP WITH THAT GRAND INTRODUCTION?
I JUST WANTED TO REFRESH THE READERS' MEMORIES.
SO WHAT'S UP WITH YOU? WHY DO YOU CARE WHAT OTHER PEOPLE TALK ABOUT?
'CAUSE YOU'RE GOSSIPING ABOUT IT REAL LOUD!
AND IT'S MAJORLY ANNOYING.

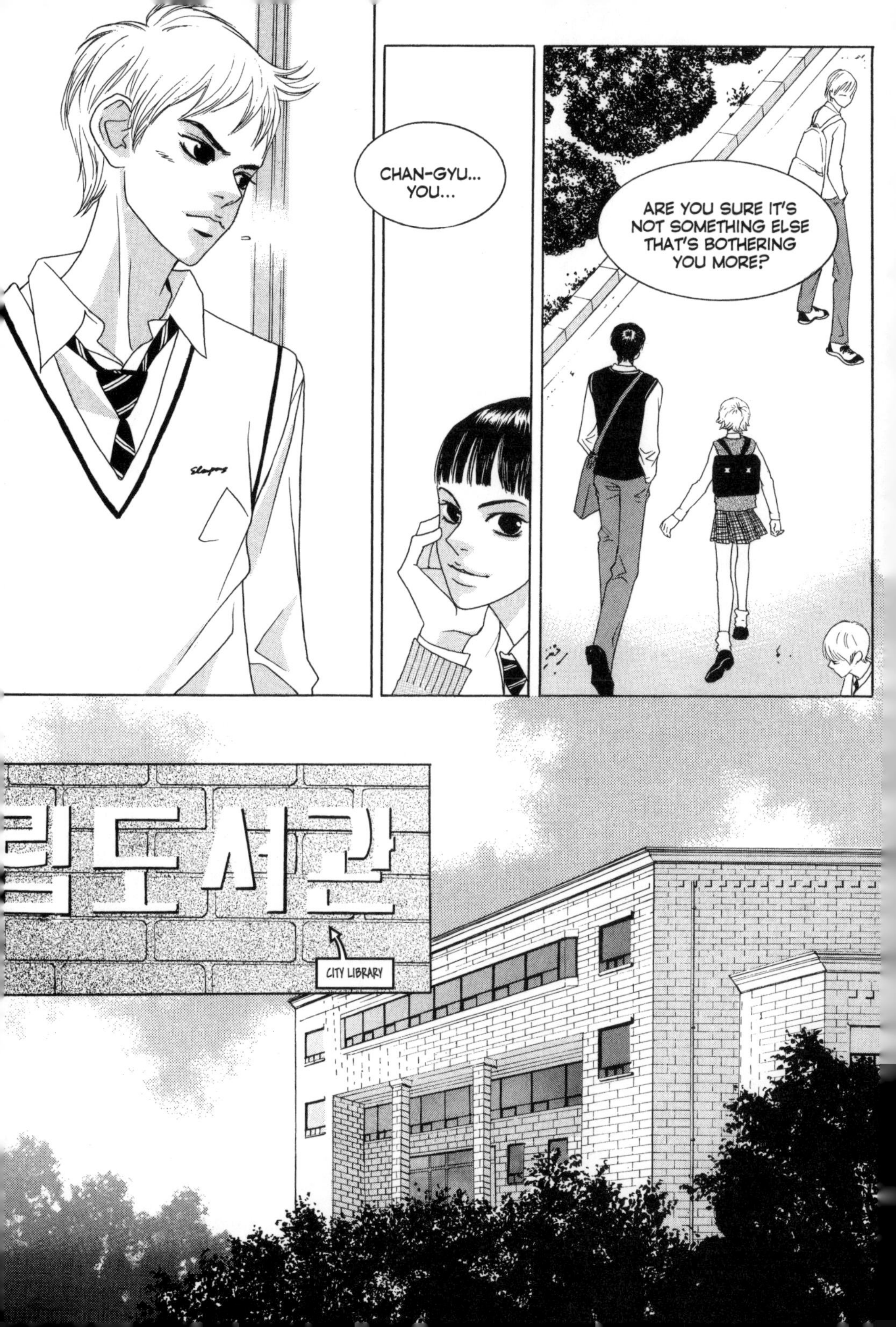
CHAN-GYU... YOU...
ARE YOU SURE IT'S NOT SOMETHING ELSE THAT'S BOTHERING YOU MORE?
립도서관
CITY LIBRARY

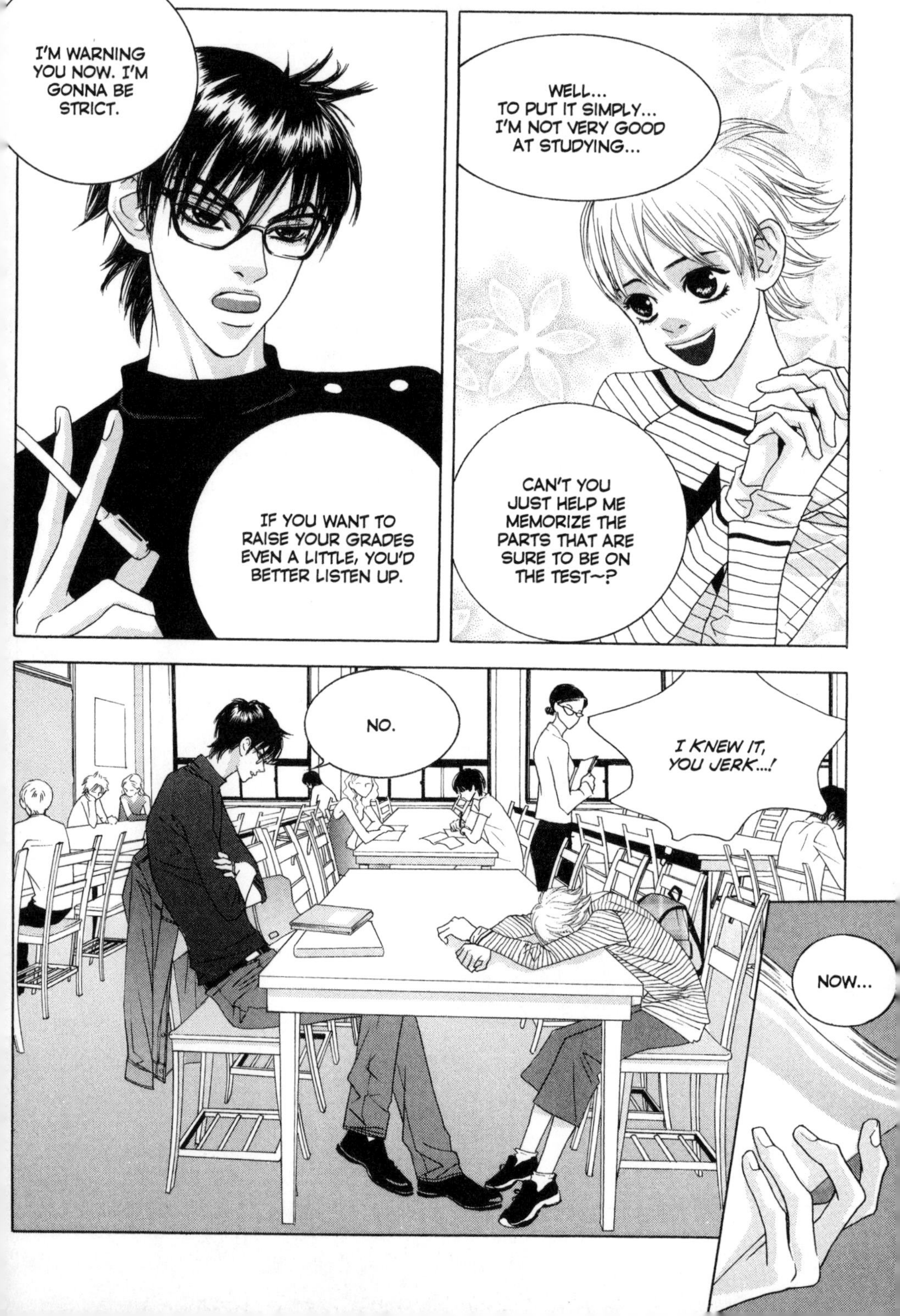
I'M WARNING YOU NOW. I'M GONNA BE STRICT.
IF YOU WANT TO RAISE YOUR GRADES EVEN A LITTLE, YOU'D BETTER LISTEN UP.
WELL... TO PUT IT SIMPLY... I'M NOT VERY GOOD AT STUDYING...
CAN'T YOU JUST HELP ME MEMORIZE THE PARTS THAT ARE SURE TO BE ON THE TEST~?
NO.
I KNEW IT, YOU JERK...!
NOW...

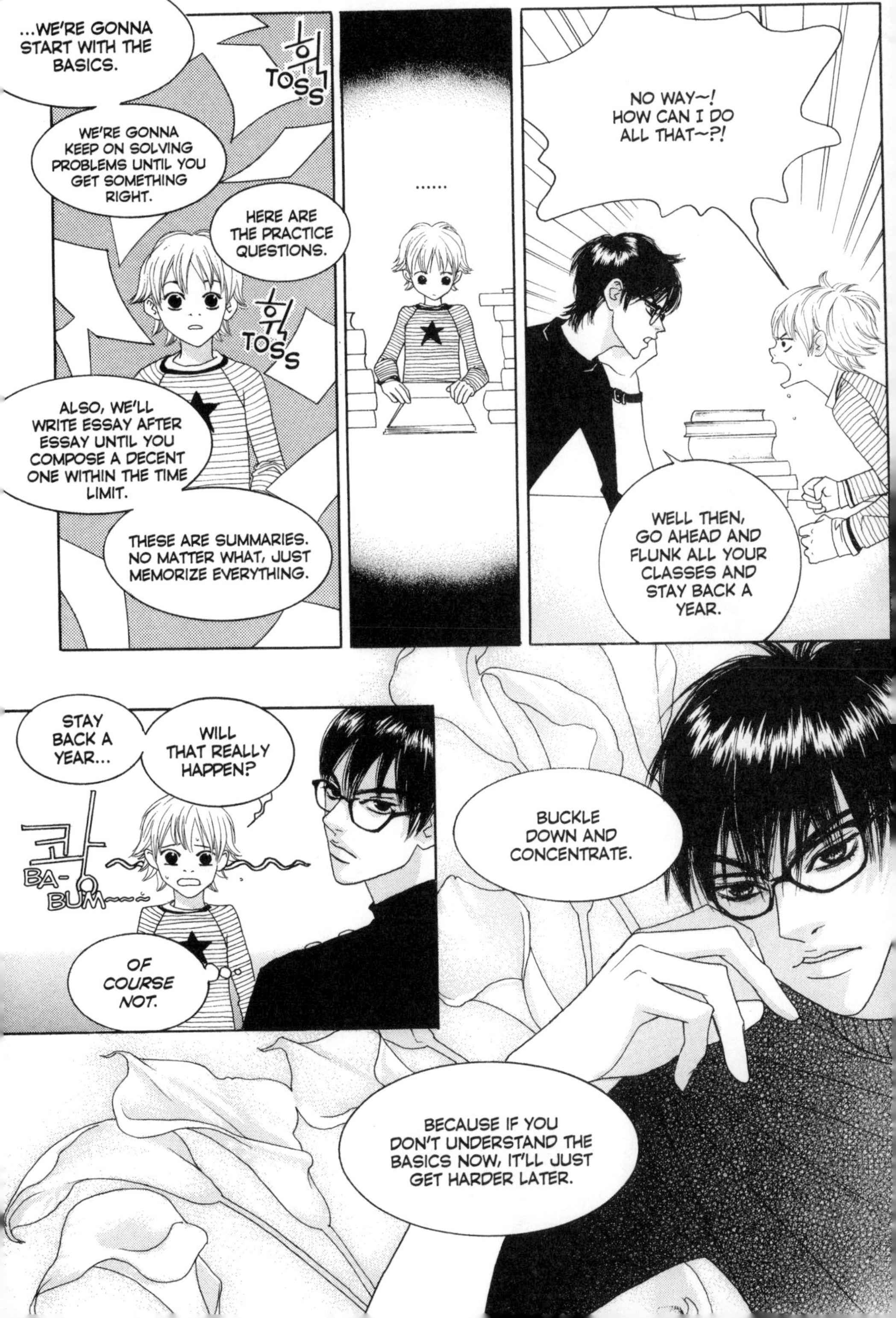
...WE'RE GONNA START WITH THE BASICS.
휙 TOSS
WE'RE GONNA KEEP ON SOLVING PROBLEMS UNTIL YOU GET SOMETHING RIGHT.
HERE ARE THE PRACTICE QUESTIONS.
휙 TOSS
ALSO, WE'LL WRITE ESSAY AFTER ESSAY UNTIL YOU COMPOSE A DECENT ONE WITHIN THE TIME LIMIT.
THESE ARE SUMMARIES. NO MATTER WHAT, JUST MEMORIZE EVERYTHING.
......
NO WAY~! HOW CAN I DO ALL THAT~?!
WELL THEN, GO AHEAD AND FLUNK ALL YOUR CLASSES AND STAY BACK A YEAR.
STAY BACK A YEAR...
WILL THAT REALLY HAPPEN?
쾅 BA-BUM~~
OF COURSE NOT.
BUCKLE DOWN AND CONCENTRATE.
BECAUSE IF YOU DON'T UNDERSTAND THE BASICS NOW, IT'LL JUST GET HARDER LATER.

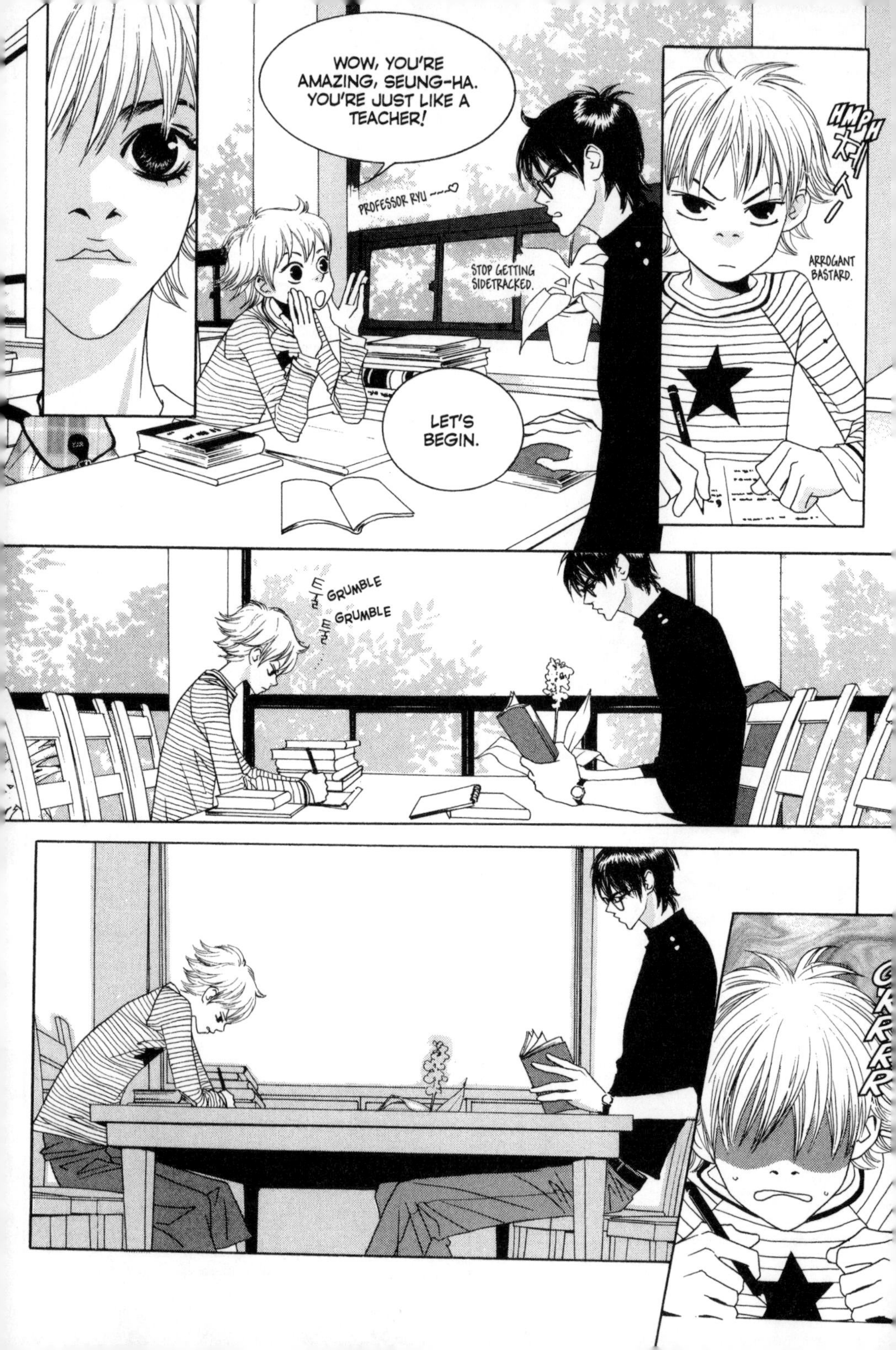

WOW, YOU'RE AMAZING, SEUNG-HA. YOU'RE JUST LIKE A TEACHER!
PROFESSOR RYU ~~~♡
STOP GETTING SIDETRACKED.
LET'S BEGIN.
HMPH
ARROGANT BASTARD.
GRUMBLE
GRUMBLE
GRRRR

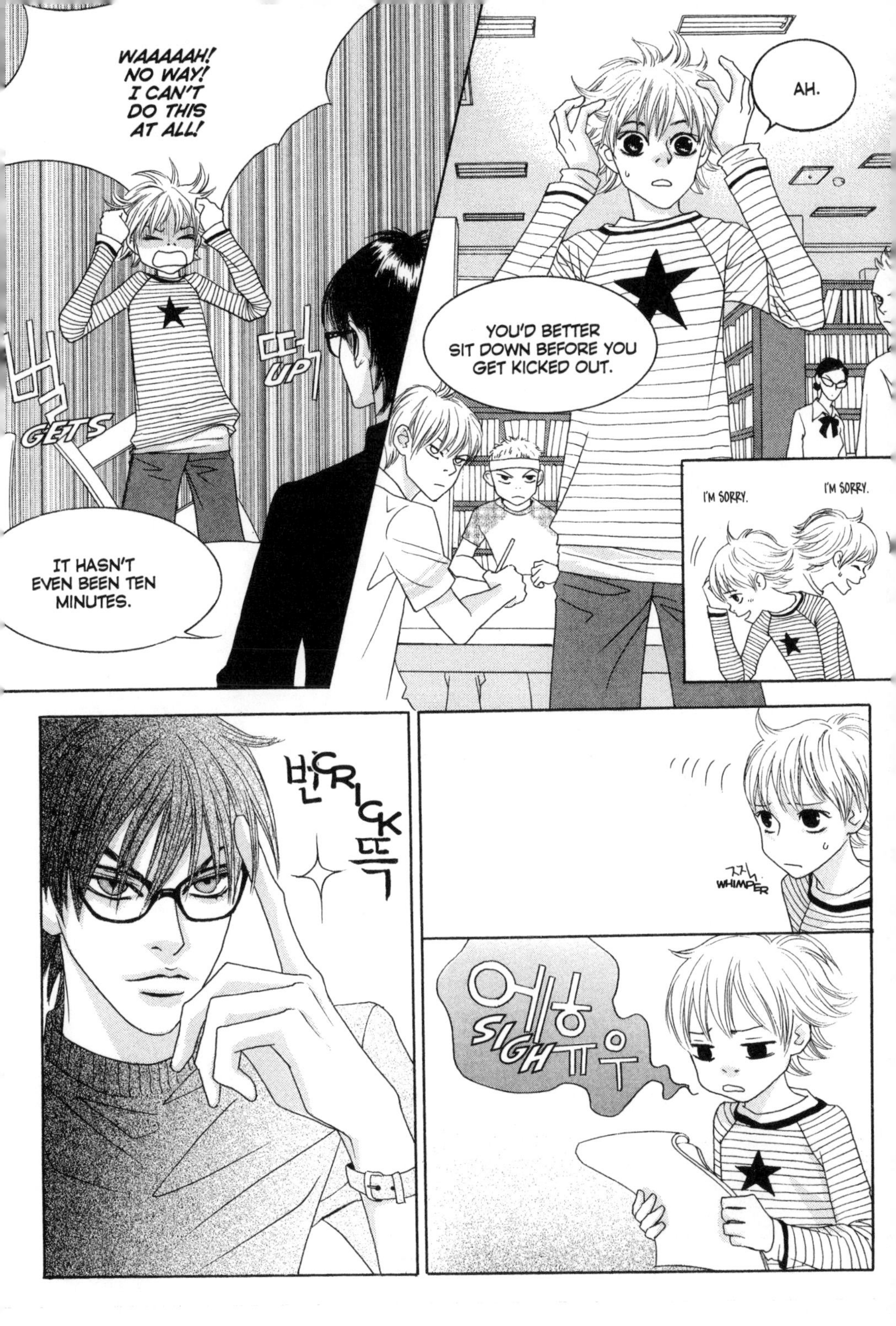
WAAAAAH! NO WAY! I CAN'T DO THIS AT ALL!
벌떡 GETS UP
IT HASN'T EVEN BEEN TEN MINUTES.
AH.
YOU'D BETTER SIT DOWN BEFORE YOU GET KICKED OUT.
I'M SORRY.
I'M SORRY.
빈CRICK뜨득
WHIMPER
에휴 SIGH 끄우

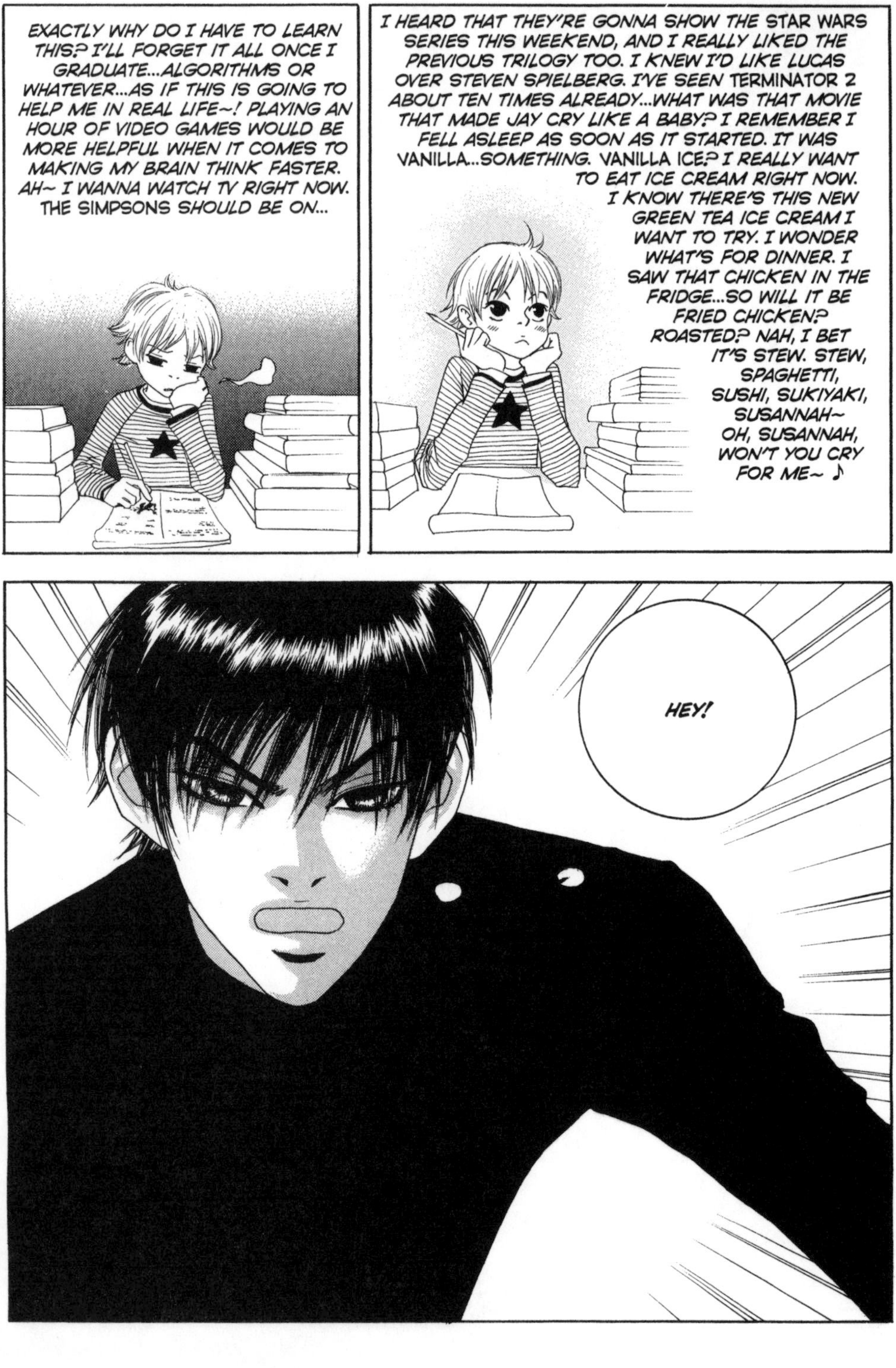
EXACTLY WHY DO I HAVE TO LEARN THIS? I'LL FORGET IT ALL ONCE I GRADUATE...ALGORITHMS OR WHATEVER...AS IF THIS IS GOING TO HELP ME IN REAL LIFE~! PLAYING AN HOUR OF VIDEO GAMES WOULD BE MORE HELPFUL WHEN IT COMES TO MAKING MY BRAIN THINK FASTER. AH~ I WANNA WATCH TV RIGHT NOW. THE SIMPSONS SHOULD BE ON...
I HEARD THAT THEY'RE GONNA SHOW THE STAR WARS SERIES THIS WEEKEND, AND I REALLY LIKED THE PREVIOUS TRILOGY TOO. I KNEW I'D LIKE LUCAS OVER STEVEN SPIELBERG. I'VE SEEN TERMINATOR 2 ABOUT TEN TIMES ALREADY...WHAT WAS THAT MOVIE THAT MADE JAY CRY LIKE A BABY? I REMEMBER I FELL ASLEEP AS SOON AS IT STARTED. IT WAS VANILLA...SOMETHING. VANILLA ICE? I REALLY WANT TO EAT ICE CREAM RIGHT NOW. I KNOW THERE'S THIS NEW GREEN TEA ICE CREAM I WANT TO TRY. I WONDER WHAT'S FOR DINNER. I SAW THAT CHICKEN IN THE FRIDGE...SO WILL IT BE FRIED CHICKEN? ROASTED? NAH, I BET IT'S STEW. STEW, SPAGHETTI, SUSHI, SUKIYAKI, SUSANNAH~ OH, SUSANNAH, WON'T YOU CRY FOR ME~ ♪
HEY!

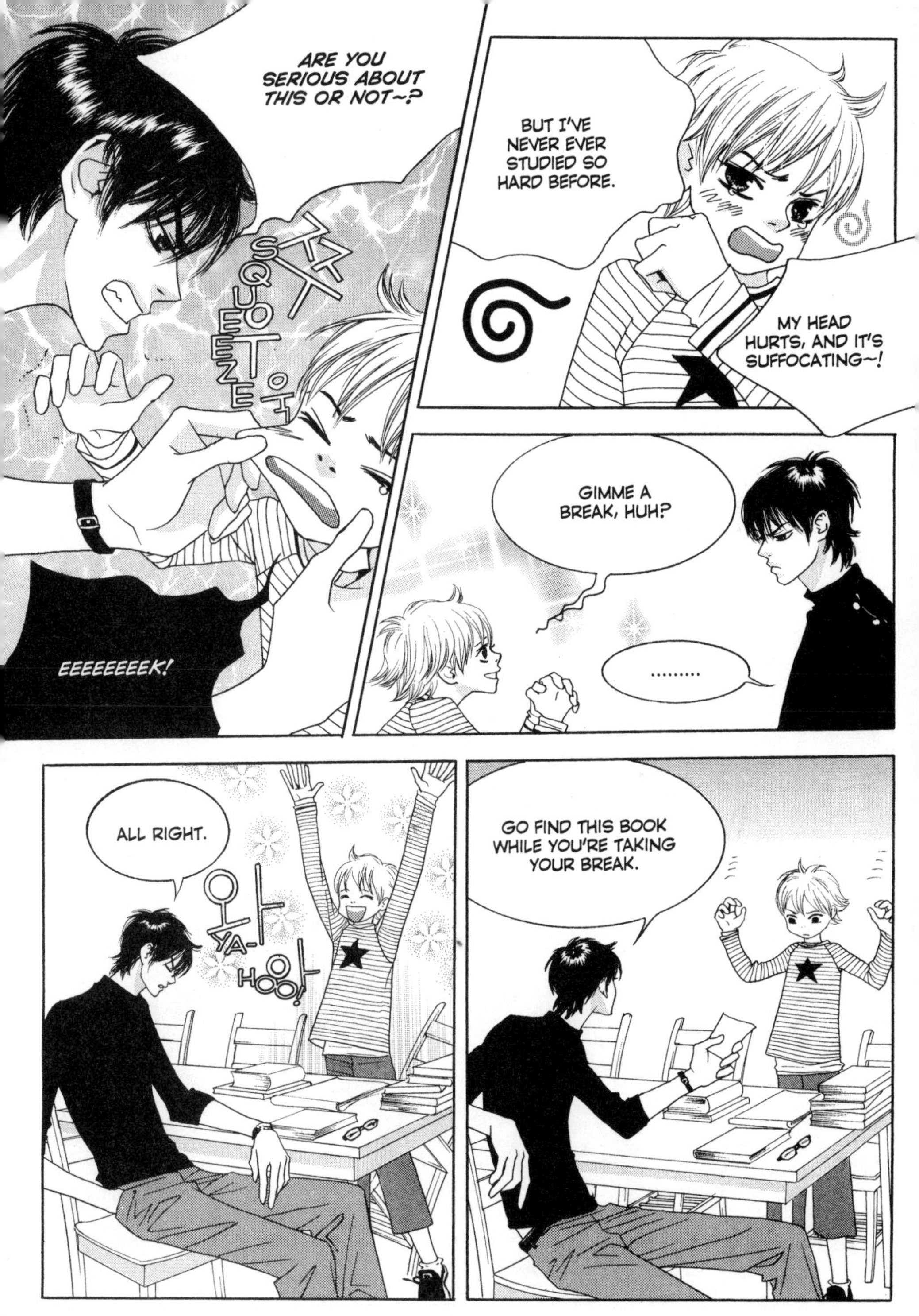
ARE YOU SERIOUS ABOUT THIS OR NOT~?
SQUEEZE
EEEEEEEEK!
BUT I'VE NEVER EVER STUDIED SO HARD BEFORE.
MY HEAD HURTS, AND IT'S SUFFOCATING~!
GIMME A BREAK, HUH?
..........
ALL RIGHT.
YA-HOO!
GO FIND THIS BOOK WHILE YOU'RE TAKING YOUR BREAK.

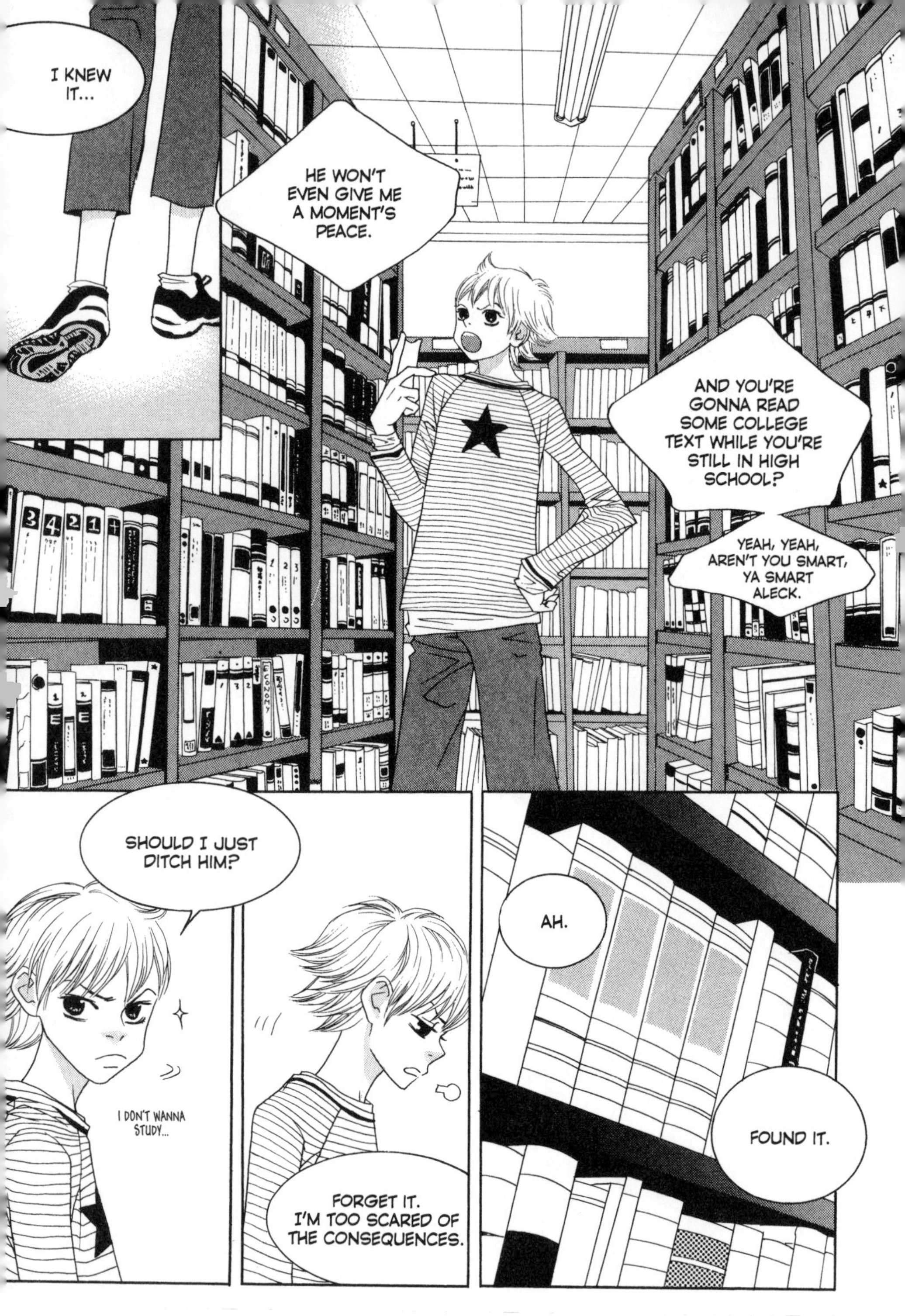
I KNEW IT...
HE WON'T EVEN GIVE ME A MOMENT'S PEACE.
AND YOU'RE GONNA READ SOME COLLEGE TEXT WHILE YOU'RE STILL IN HIGH SCHOOL?
YEAH, YEAH, AREN'T YOU SMART, YA SMART ALECK.
SHOULD I JUST DITCH HIM?
I DON'T WANNA STUDY...
FORGET IT. I'M TOO SCARED OF THE CONSEQUENCES.
AH.
FOUND IT.

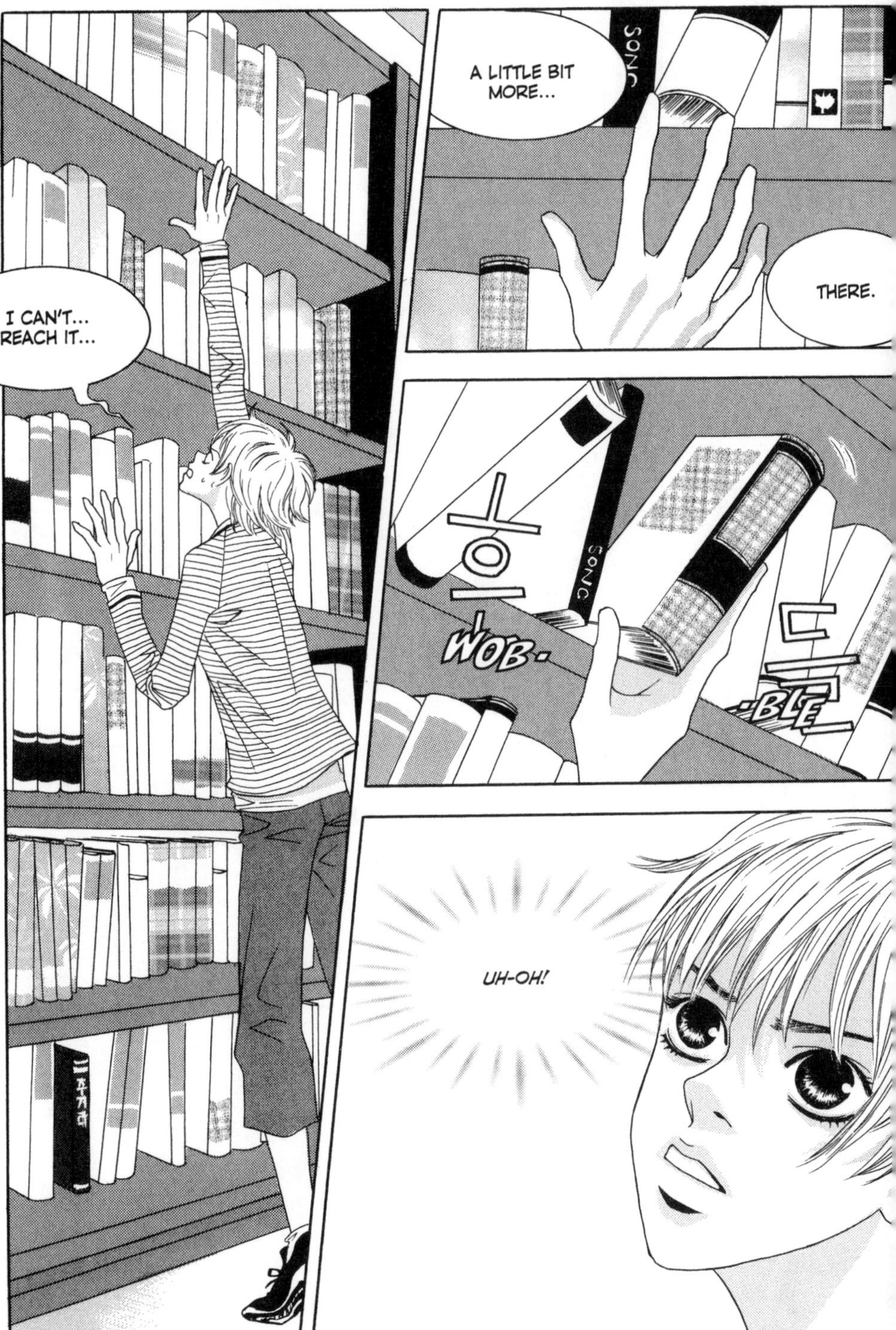

I CAN'T... REACH IT...
A LITTLE BIT MORE...
THERE.
WOB-
-BLE
UH-OH!

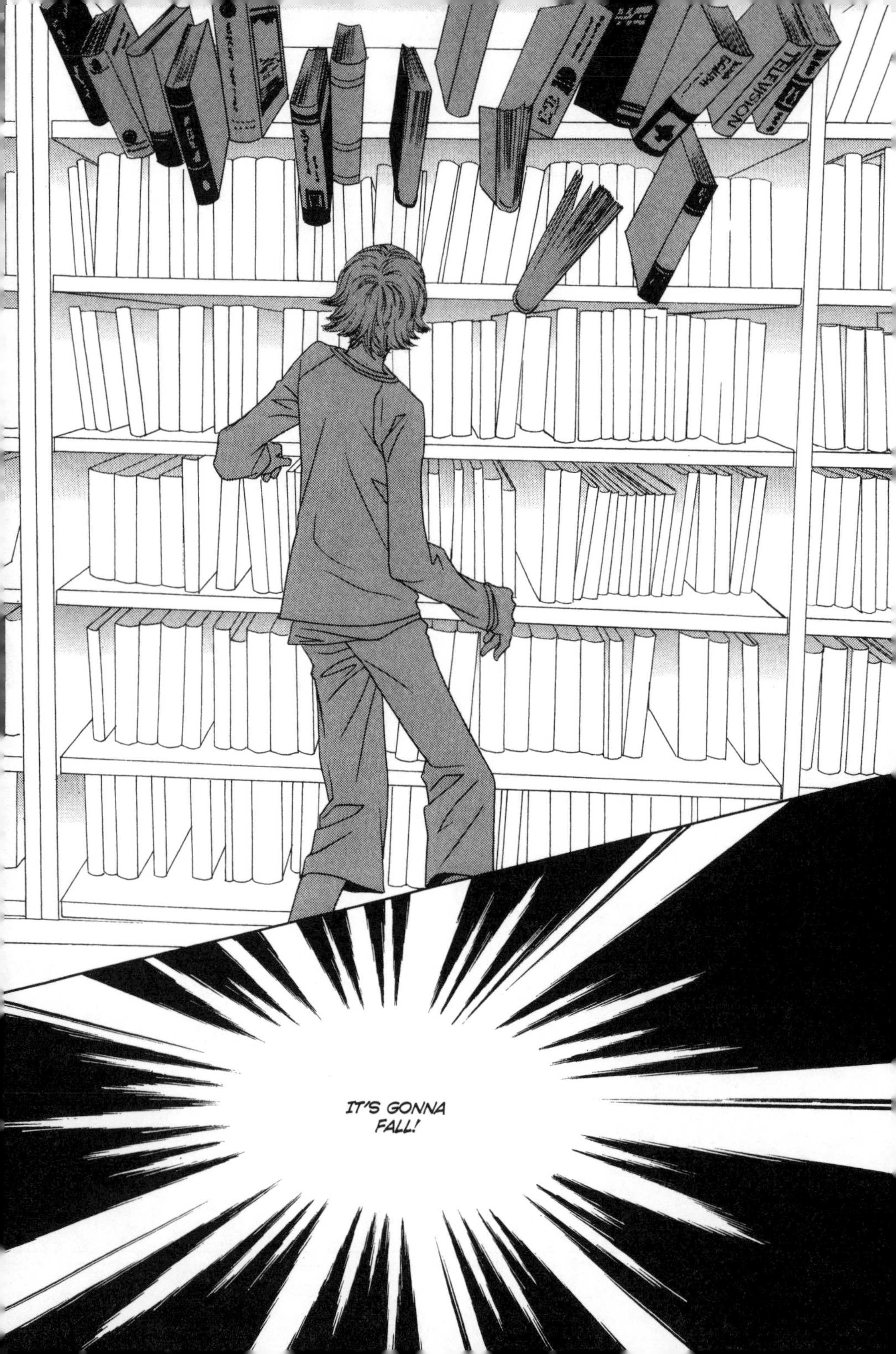
TELEVISION
IT'S GONNA FALL!

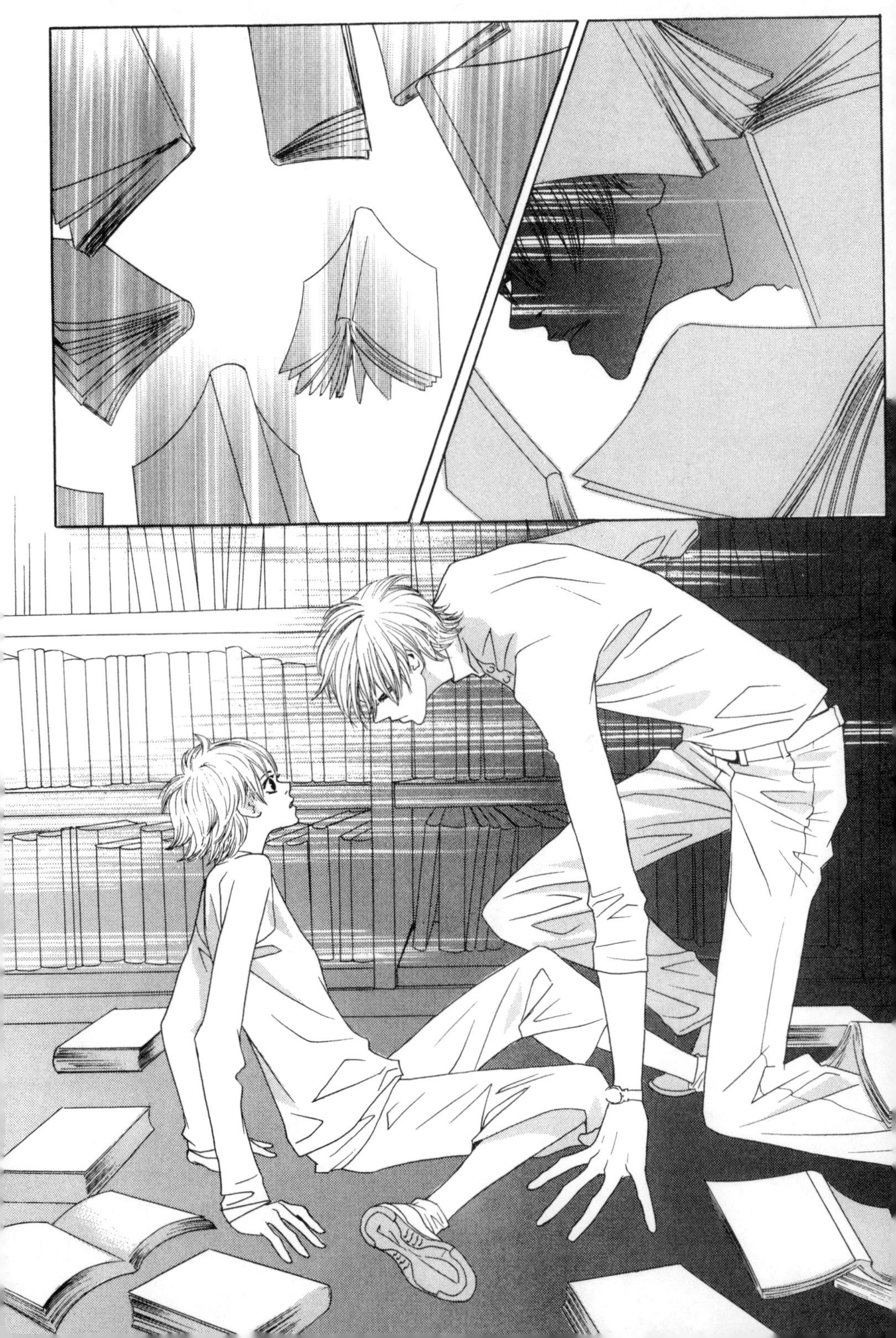

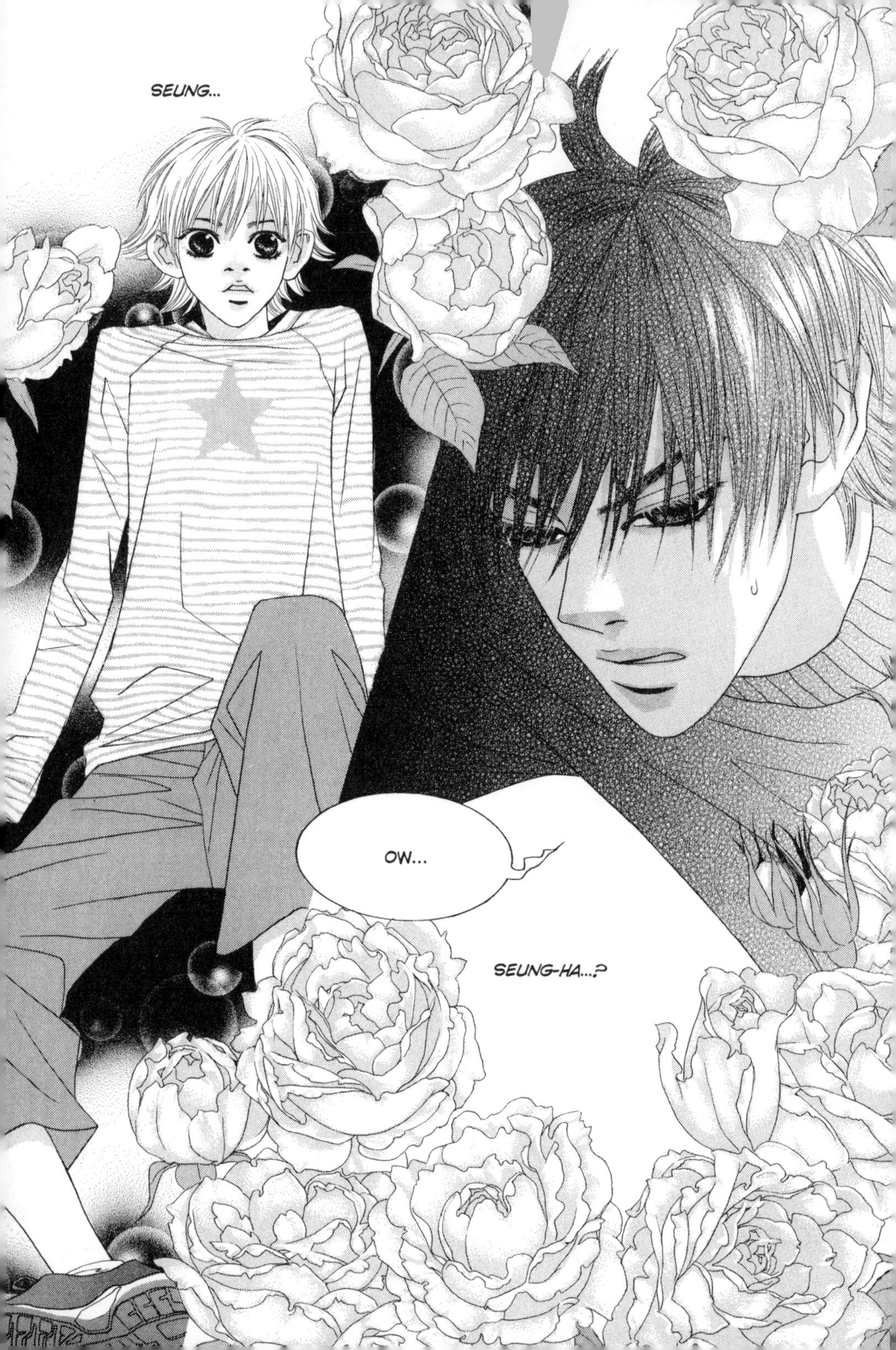
SEUNG...
OW...
SEUNG-HA...?

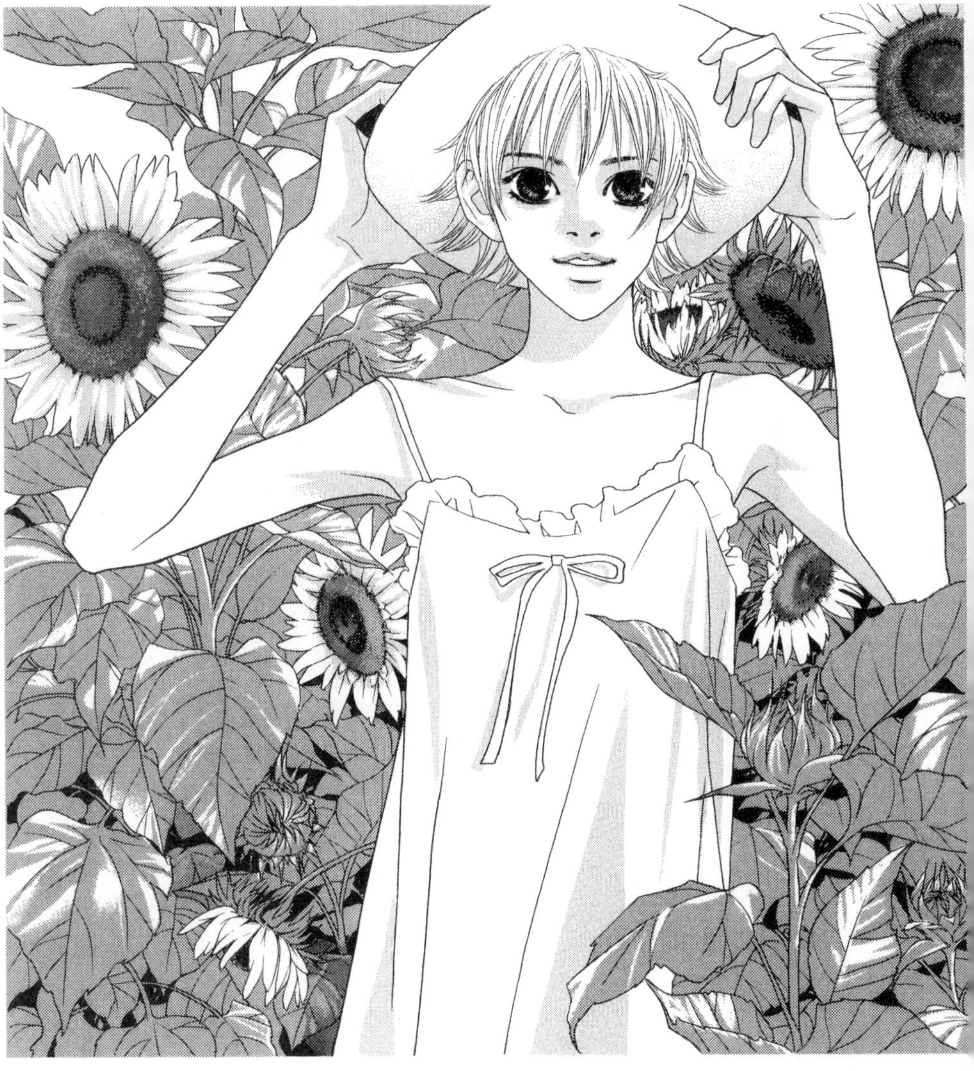

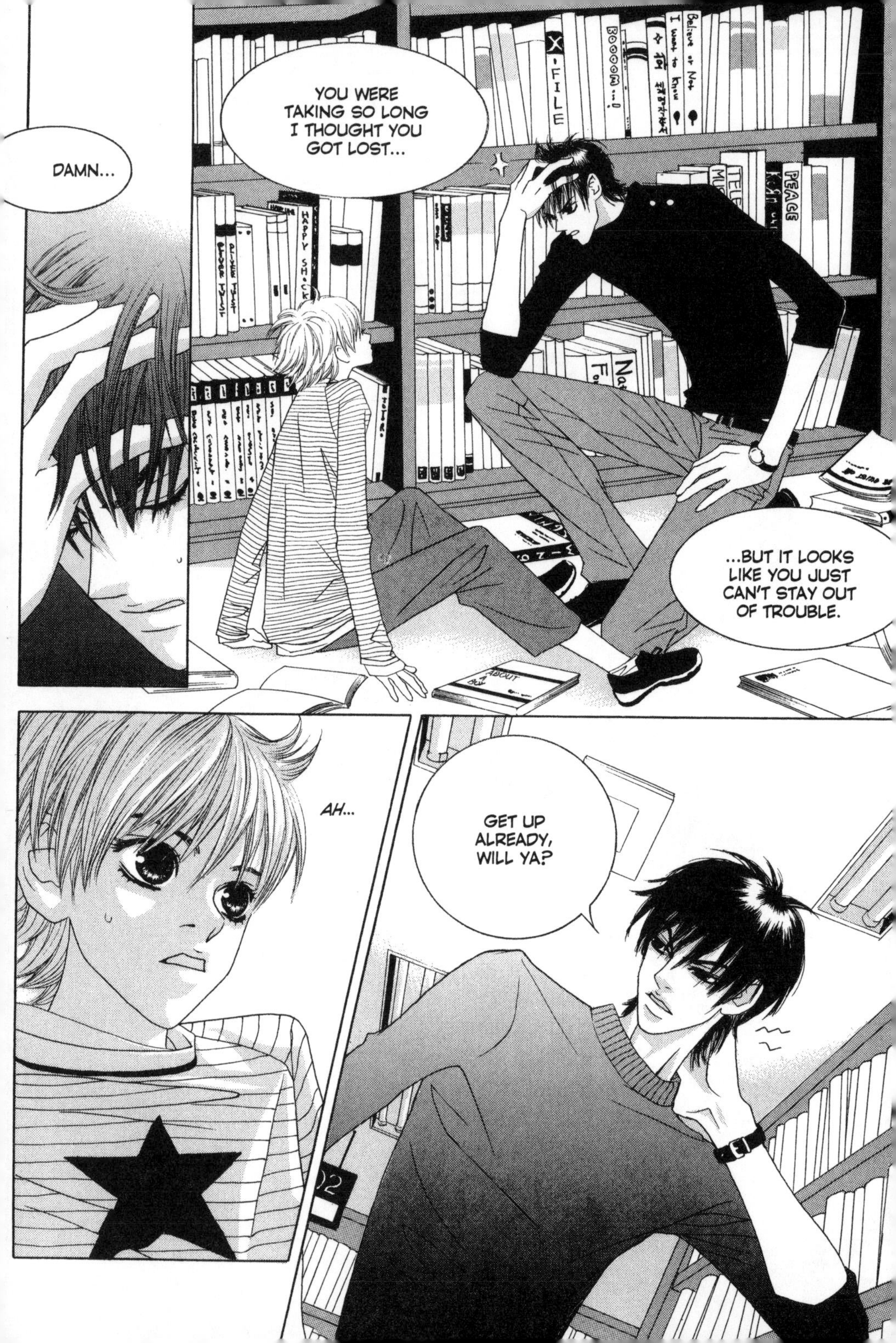
DAMN...
YOU WERE TAKING SO LONG I THOUGHT YOU GOT LOST...
...BUT IT LOOKS LIKE YOU JUST CAN'T STAY OUT OF TROUBLE.
AH...
GET UP ALREADY, WILL YA?

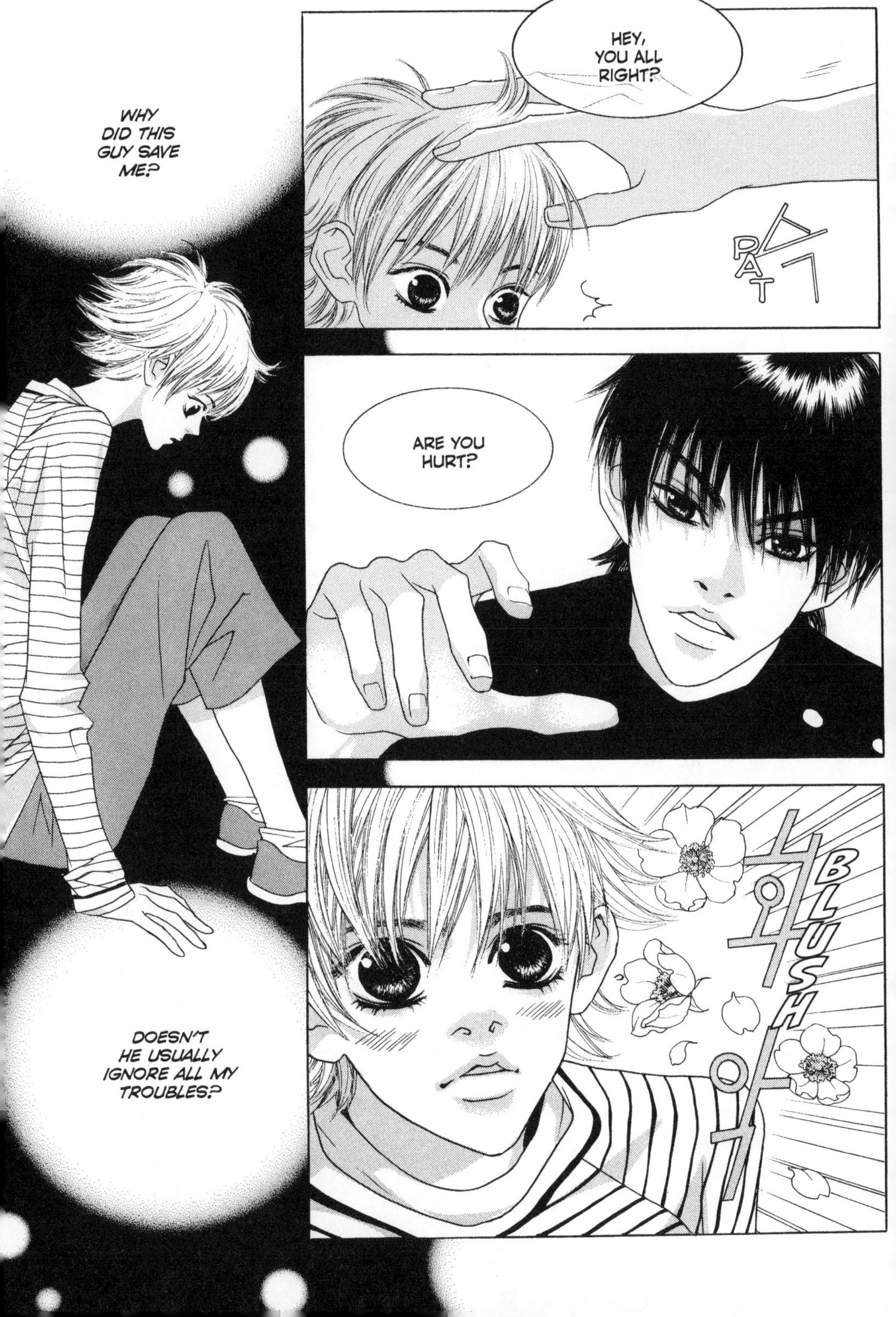
WHY DID THIS GUY SAVE ME?
DOESN'T HE USUALLY IGNORE ALL MY TROUBLES?
HEY, YOU ALL RIGHT?
PAT
ARE YOU HURT?
BLUSH

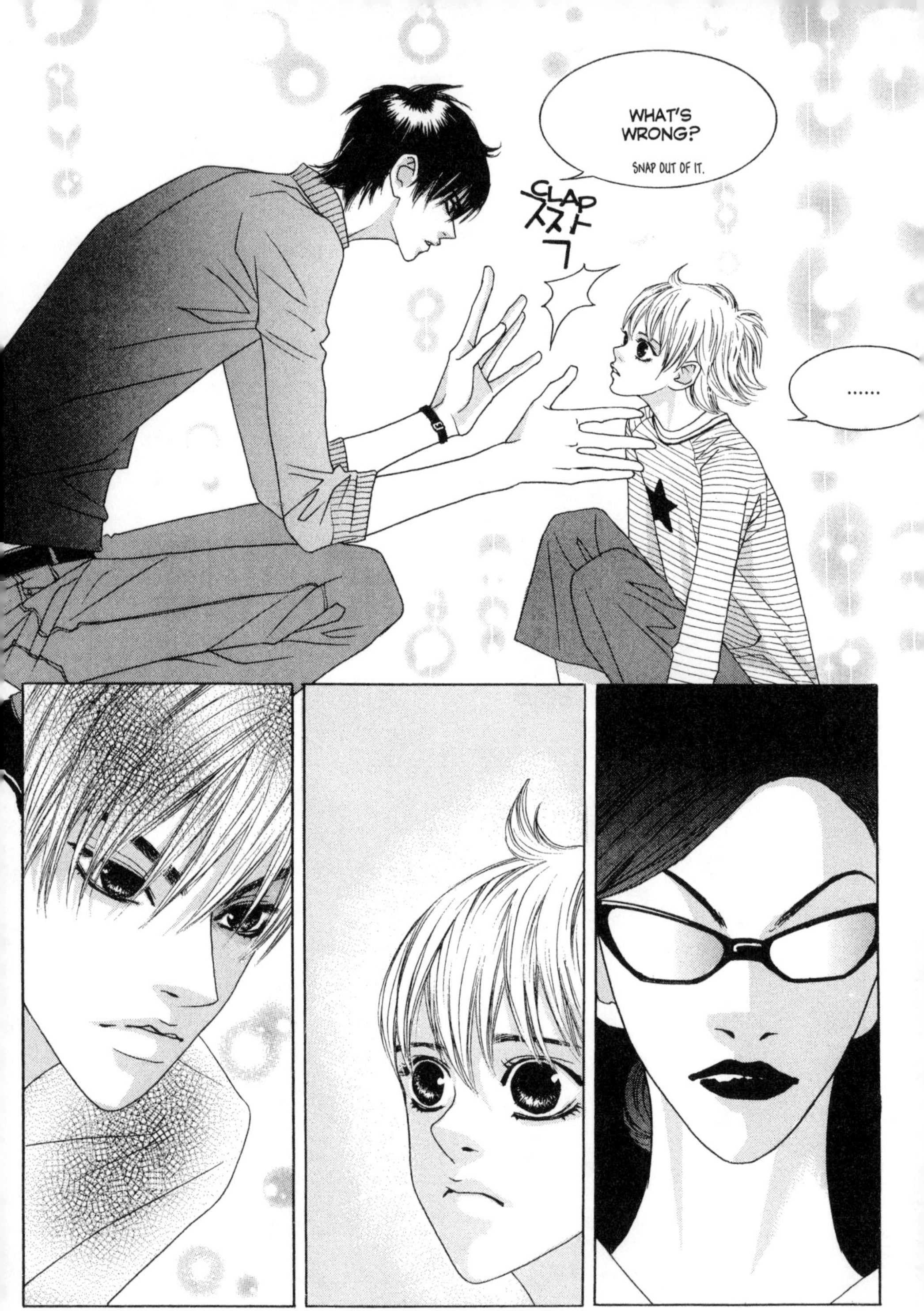
WHAT'S WRONG?
SNAP OUT OF IT.
CLAP
......

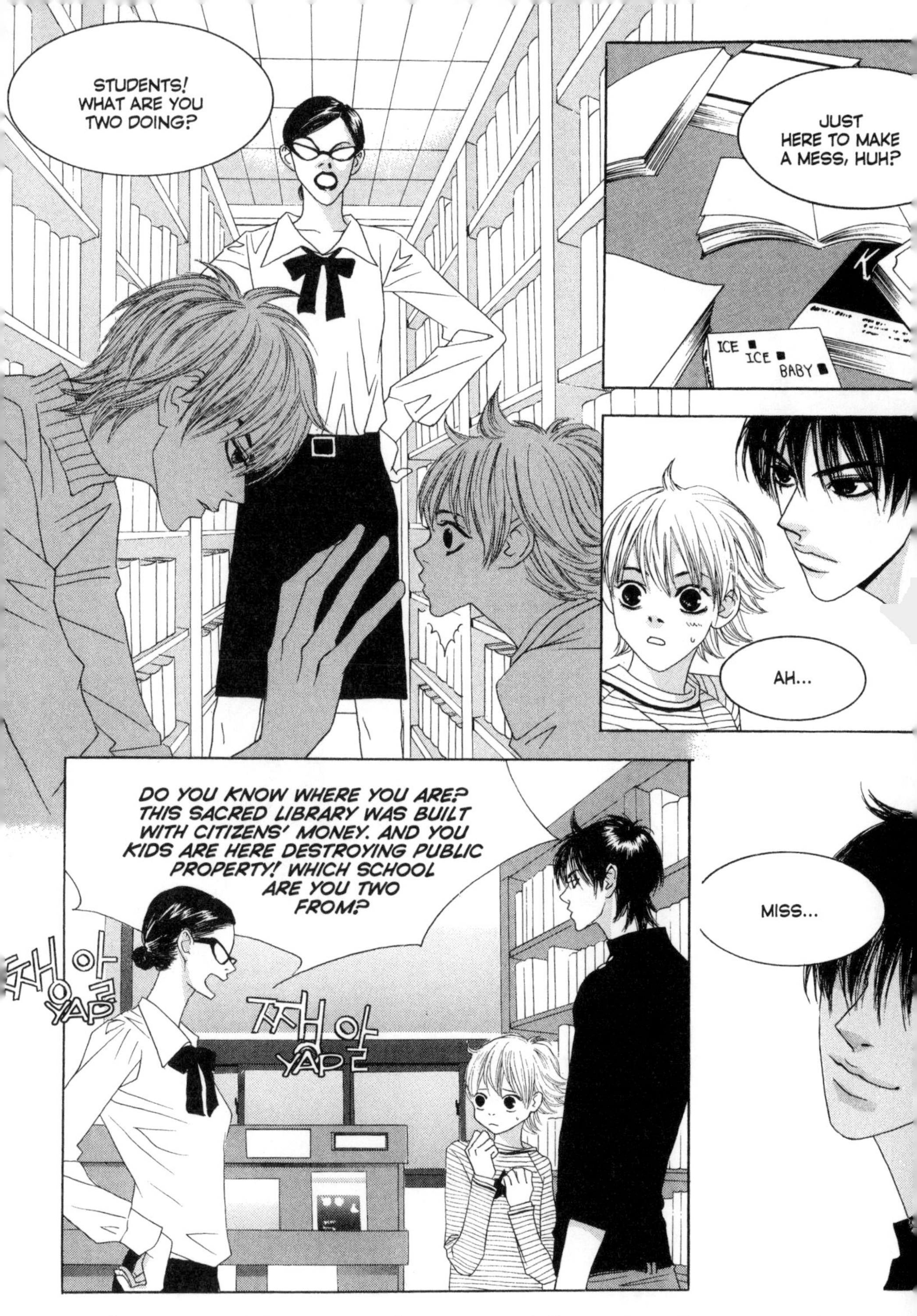
STUDENTS! WHAT ARE YOU TWO DOING?
JUST HERE TO MAKE A MESS, HUH?
ICE ICE BABY
AH...
DO YOU KNOW WHERE YOU ARE? THIS SACRED LIBRARY WAS BUILT WITH CITIZENS' MONEY. AND YOU KIDS ARE HERE DESTROYING PUBLIC PROPERTY! WHICH SCHOOL ARE YOU TWO FROM?
YAP
YAP
MISS...

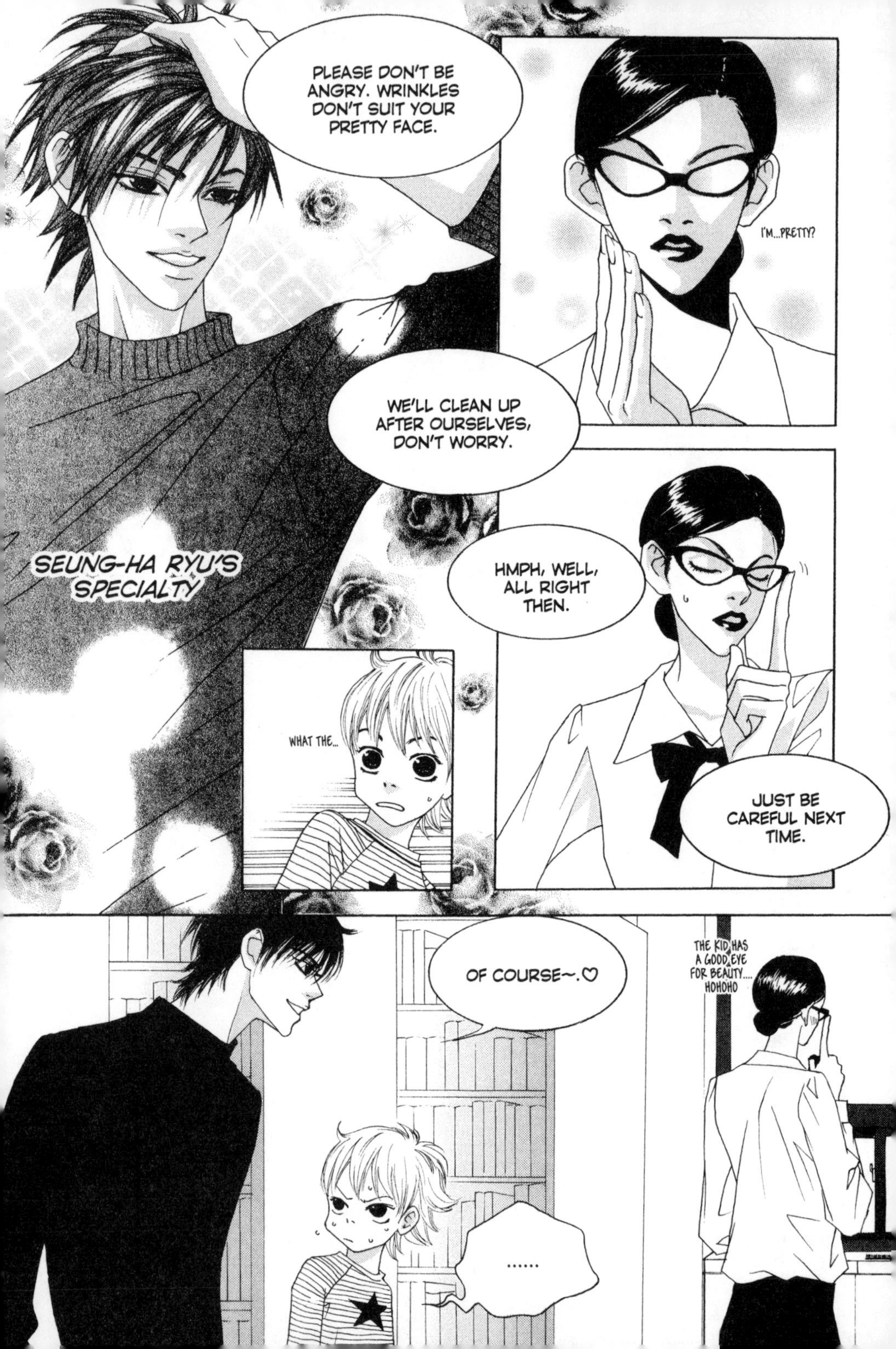
PLEASE DON'T BE ANGRY. WRINKLES DON'T SUIT YOUR PRETTY FACE.
WE'LL CLEAN UP AFTER OURSELVES, DON'T WORRY.
SEUNG-HA RYU'S SPECIALTY
WHAT THE...
I'M...PRETTY?
HMPH, WELL, ALL RIGHT THEN.
JUST BE CAREFUL NEXT TIME.
OF COURSE~.♡
......
THE KID HAS A GOOD EYE FOR BEAUTY.... HOHOHO

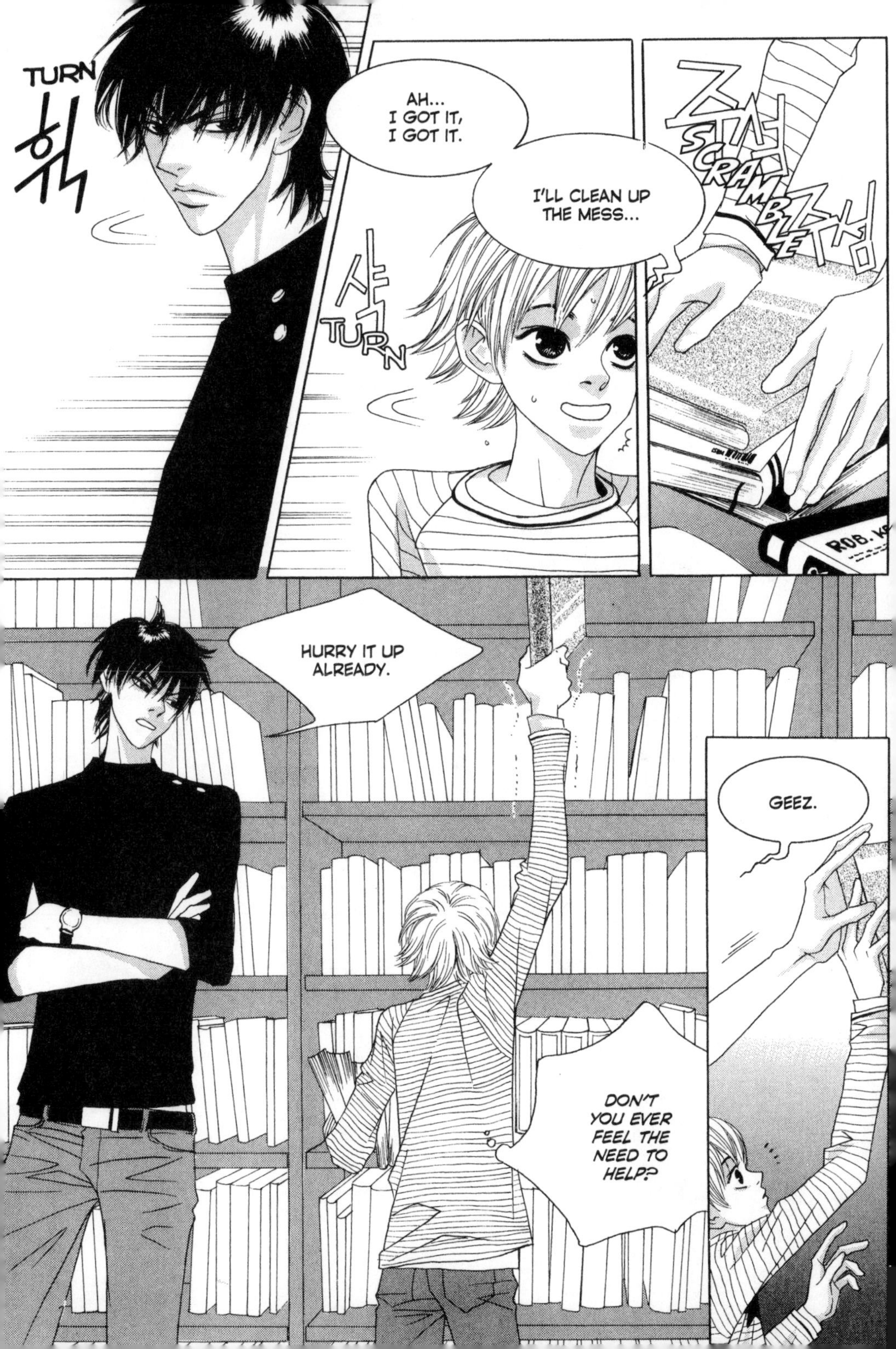
TURN
AH... I GOT IT, I GOT IT.
I'LL CLEAN UP THE MESS...
샥
TURN
SCRAMBLE
HURRY IT UP ALREADY.
GEEZ.
DON'T YOU EVER FEEL THE NEED TO HELP?
...

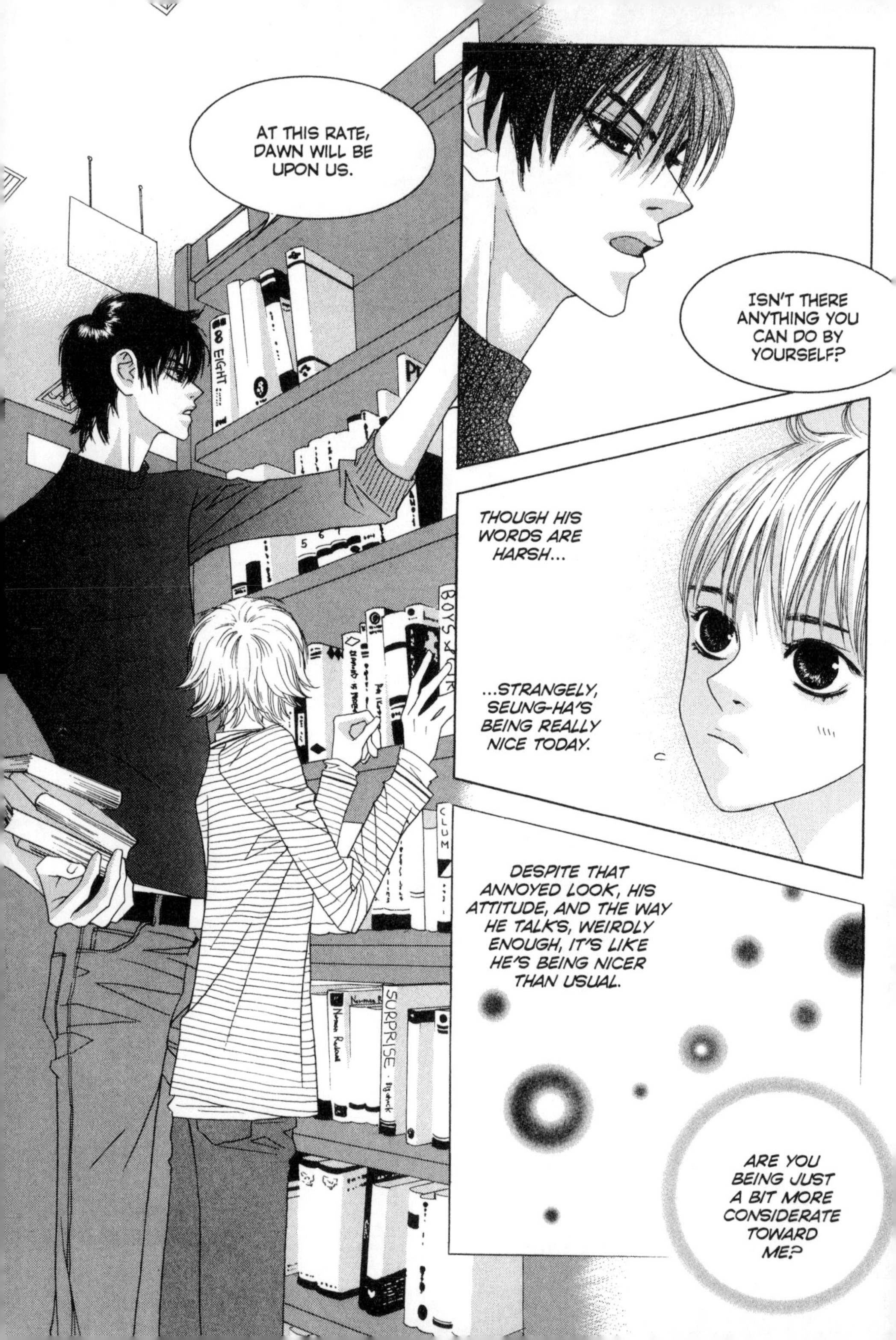
AT THIS RATE, DAWN WILL BE UPON US.
ISN'T THERE ANYTHING YOU CAN DO BY YOURSELF?
THOUGH HIS WORDS ARE HARSH...
...STRANGELY, SEUNG-HA'S BEING REALLY NICE TODAY.
DESPITE THAT ANNOYED LOOK, HIS ATTITUDE, AND THE WAY HE TALKS, WEIRDLY ENOUGH, IT'S LIKE HE'S BEING NICER THAN USUAL.
ARE YOU BEING JUST A BIT MORE CONSIDERATE TOWARD ME?

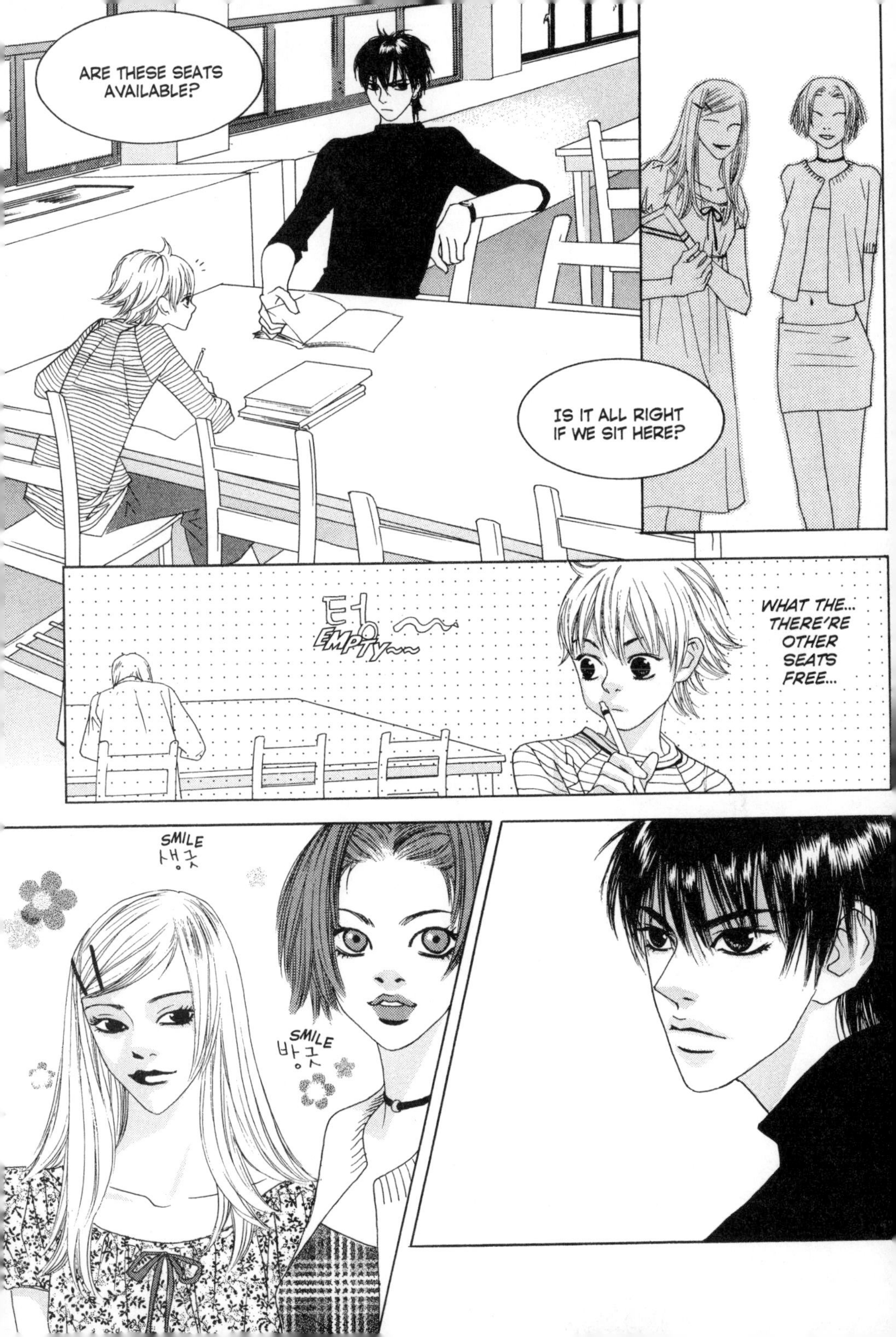
ARE THESE SEATS AVAILABLE?
IS IT ALL RIGHT IF WE SIT HERE?
텅~
EMPTY~~
WHAT THE... THERE'RE OTHER SEATS FREE...
SMILE
생긋
SMILE
방긋

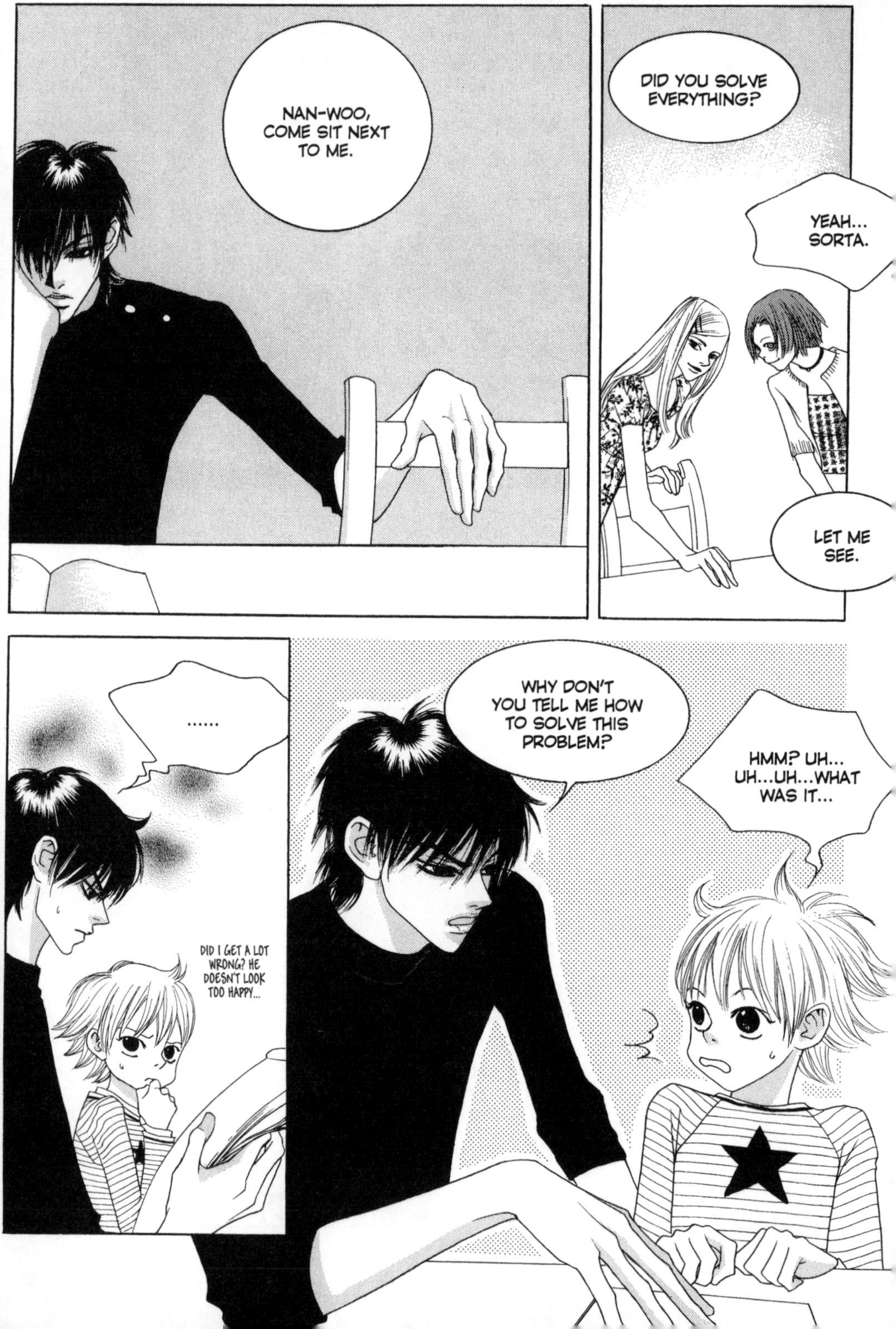
NAN-WOO, COME SIT NEXT TO ME.
DID YOU SOLVE EVERYTHING?
YEAH... SORTA.
LET ME SEE.
......
DID I GET A LOT WRONG? HE DOESN'T LOOK TOO HAPPY...
WHY DON'T YOU TELL ME HOW TO SOLVE THIS PROBLEM?
HMM? UH... UH...UH...WHAT WAS IT...

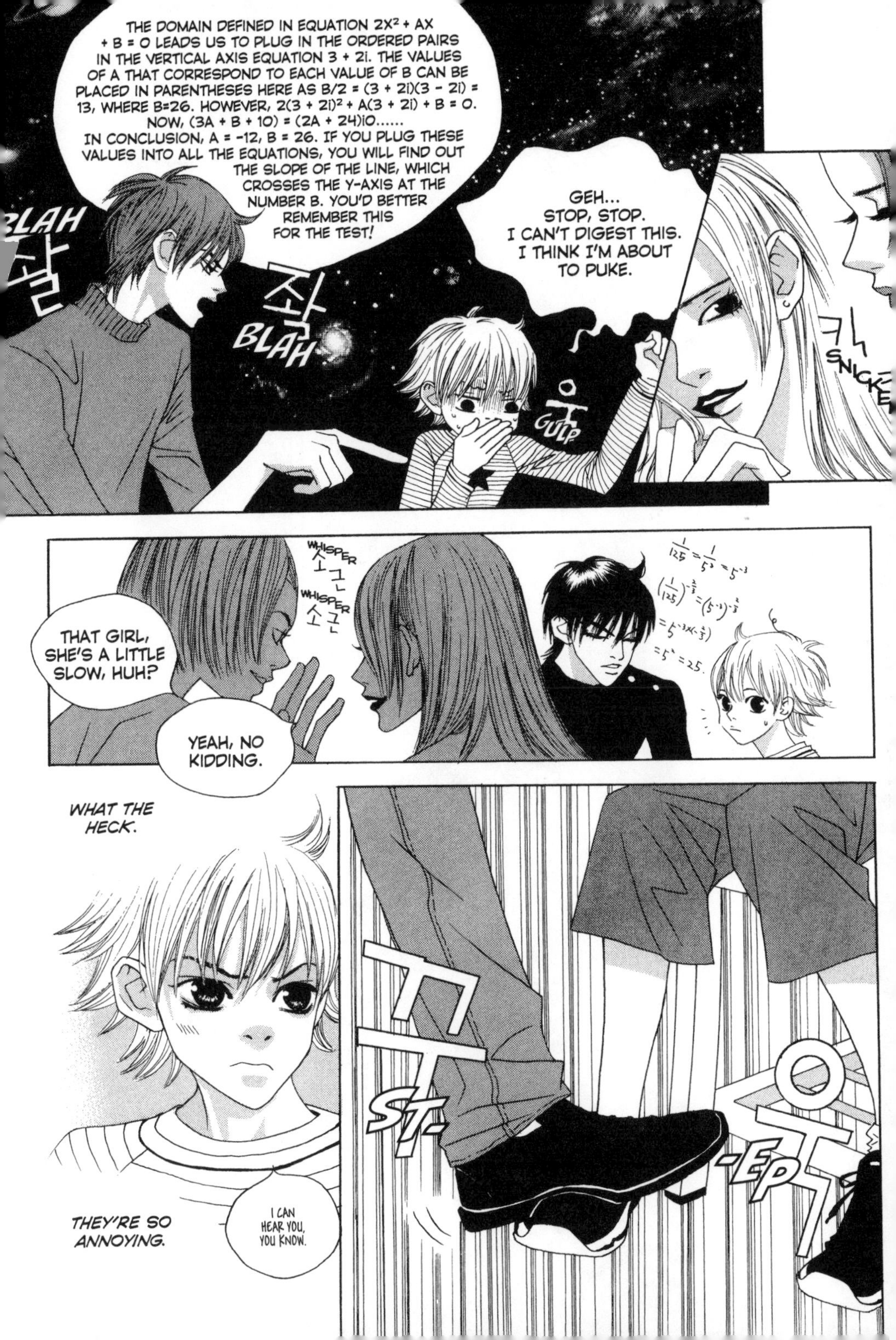

THE DOMAIN DEFINED IN EQUATION $2X^2$ + AX + B = O LEADS US TO PLUG IN THE ORDERED PAIRS IN THE VERTICAL AXIS EQUATION 3 + 2i. THE VALUES OF A THAT CORRESPOND TO EACH VALUE OF B CAN BE PLACED IN PARENTHESES HERE AS B/2 = (3 + 2i)(3 - 2i) = 13, WHERE B=26. HOWEVER, $2(3 + 2i)^2$ + A(3 + 2i) + B = O. NOW, (3A + B + 10) = (2A + 24)iO...... IN CONCLUSION, A = -12, B = 26. IF YOU PLUG THESE VALUES INTO ALL THE EQUATIONS, YOU WILL FIND OUT THE SLOPE OF THE LINE, WHICH CROSSES THE Y-AXIS AT THE NUMBER B. YOU'D BETTER REMEMBER THIS FOR THE TEST!
BLAH
BLAH
GULP
GEH... STOP, STOP. I CAN'T DIGEST THIS. I THINK I'M ABOUT TO PUKE.
SNICKER
WHISPER 소곤
WHISPER 소곤
THAT GIRL, SHE'S A LITTLE SLOW, HUH?
YEAH, NO KIDDING.
$\frac{1}{125} = \frac{1}{5^3} = 5^{-3}$
$\left(\frac{1}{125}\right)^{-\frac{2}{3}} = (5^{-3})^{-\frac{2}{3}}$
$= 5^{-3\times(-\frac{2}{3})}$
$= 5^2 = 25.$
WHAT THE HECK.
THEY'RE SO ANNOYING.
I CAN HEAR YOU, YOU KNOW.
ST-
-EP

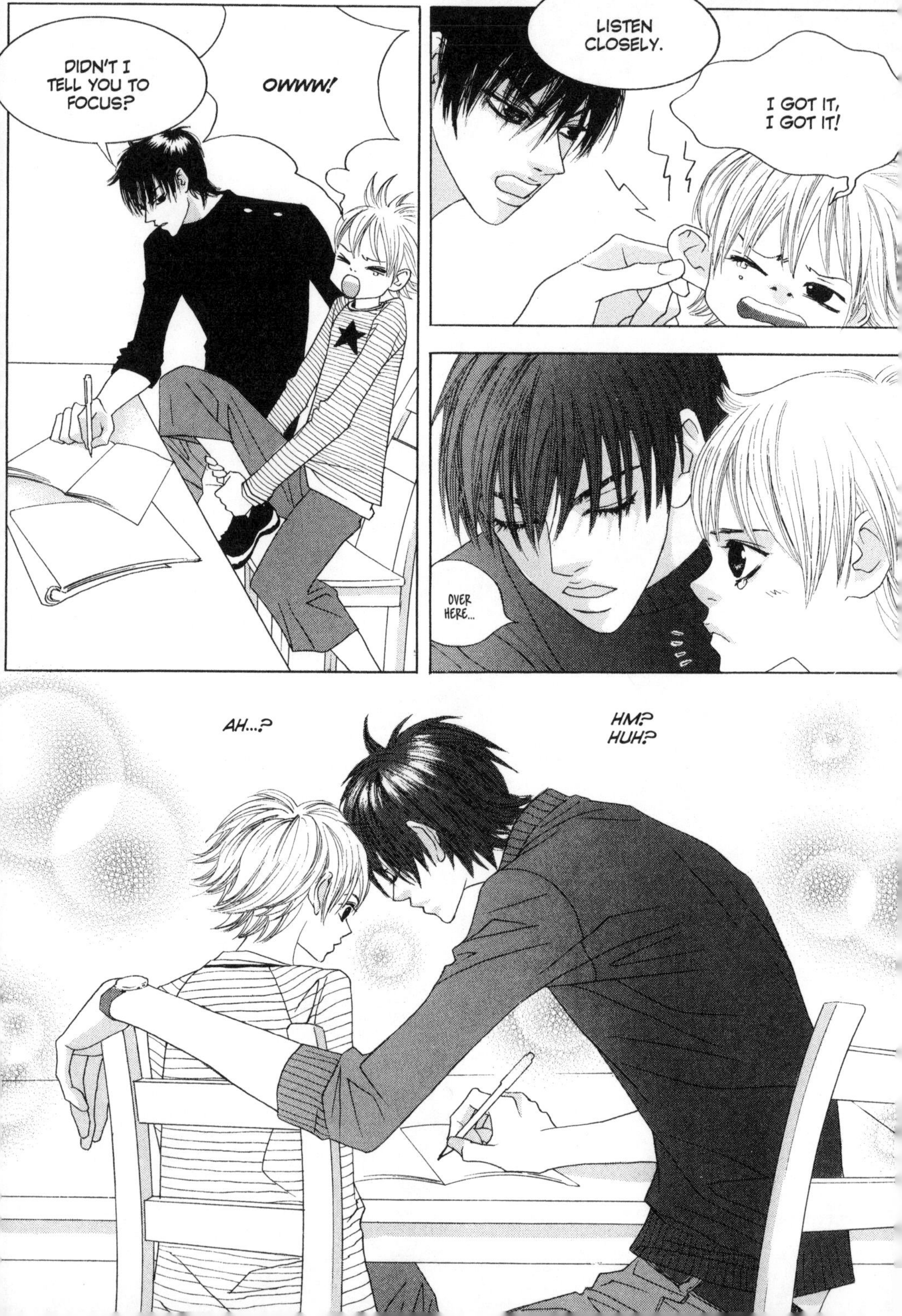
DIDN'T I TELL YOU TO FOCUS?
OWWW!
LISTEN CLOSELY.
I GOT IT, I GOT IT!
OVER HERE...
AH...?
HM? HUH?

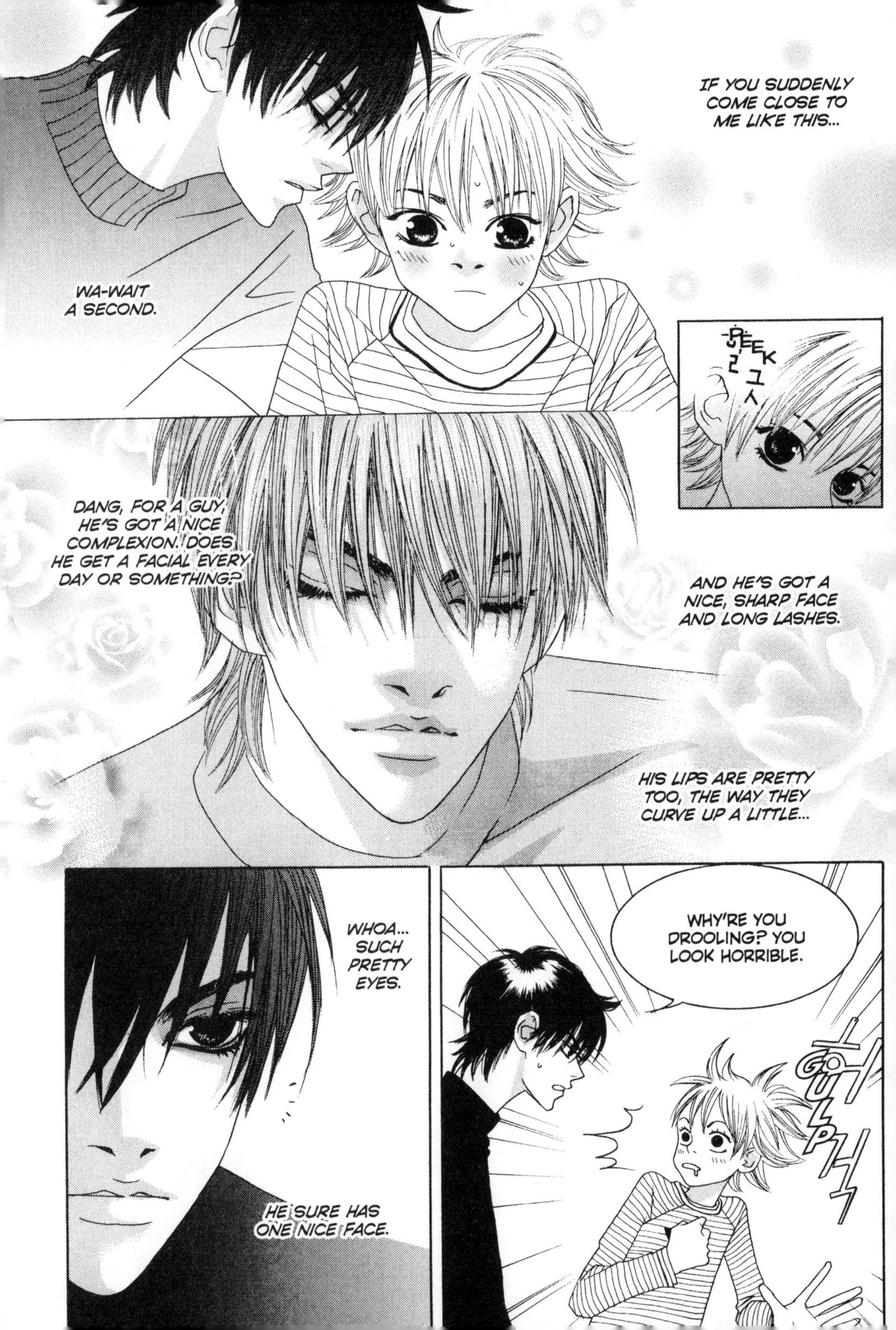
IF YOU SUDDENLY COME CLOSE TO ME LIKE THIS...
WA-WAIT A SECOND.
PEEK
DANG, FOR A GUY, HE'S GOT A NICE COMPLEXION. DOES HE GET A FACIAL EVERY DAY OR SOMETHING?
AND HE'S GOT A NICE, SHARP FACE AND LONG LASHES.
HIS LIPS ARE PRETTY TOO, THE WAY THEY CURVE UP A LITTLE...
WHOA... SUCH PRETTY EYES.
HE SURE HAS ONE NICE FACE.
WHY'RE YOU DROOLING? YOU LOOK HORRIBLE.
GULP

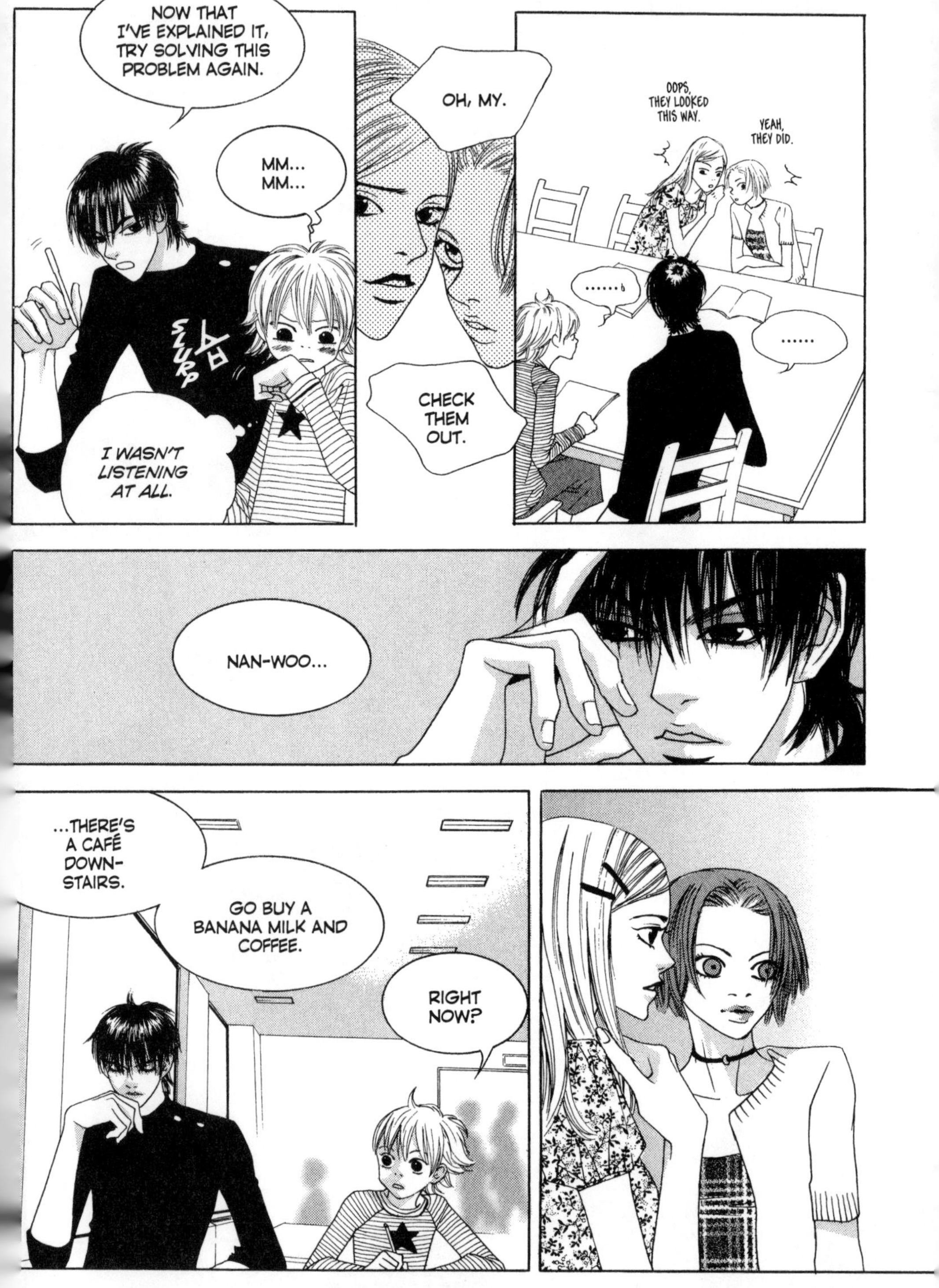

NOW THAT I'VE EXPLAINED IT, TRY SOLVING THIS PROBLEM AGAIN.
MM... MM...
I WASN'T LISTENING AT ALL.
OH, MY.
CHECK THEM OUT.
OOPS, THEY LOOKED THIS WAY.
YEAH, THEY DID.
......
......
NAN-WOO...
...THERE'S A CAFÉ DOWN-STAIRS.
GO BUY A BANANA MILK AND COFFEE.
RIGHT NOW?

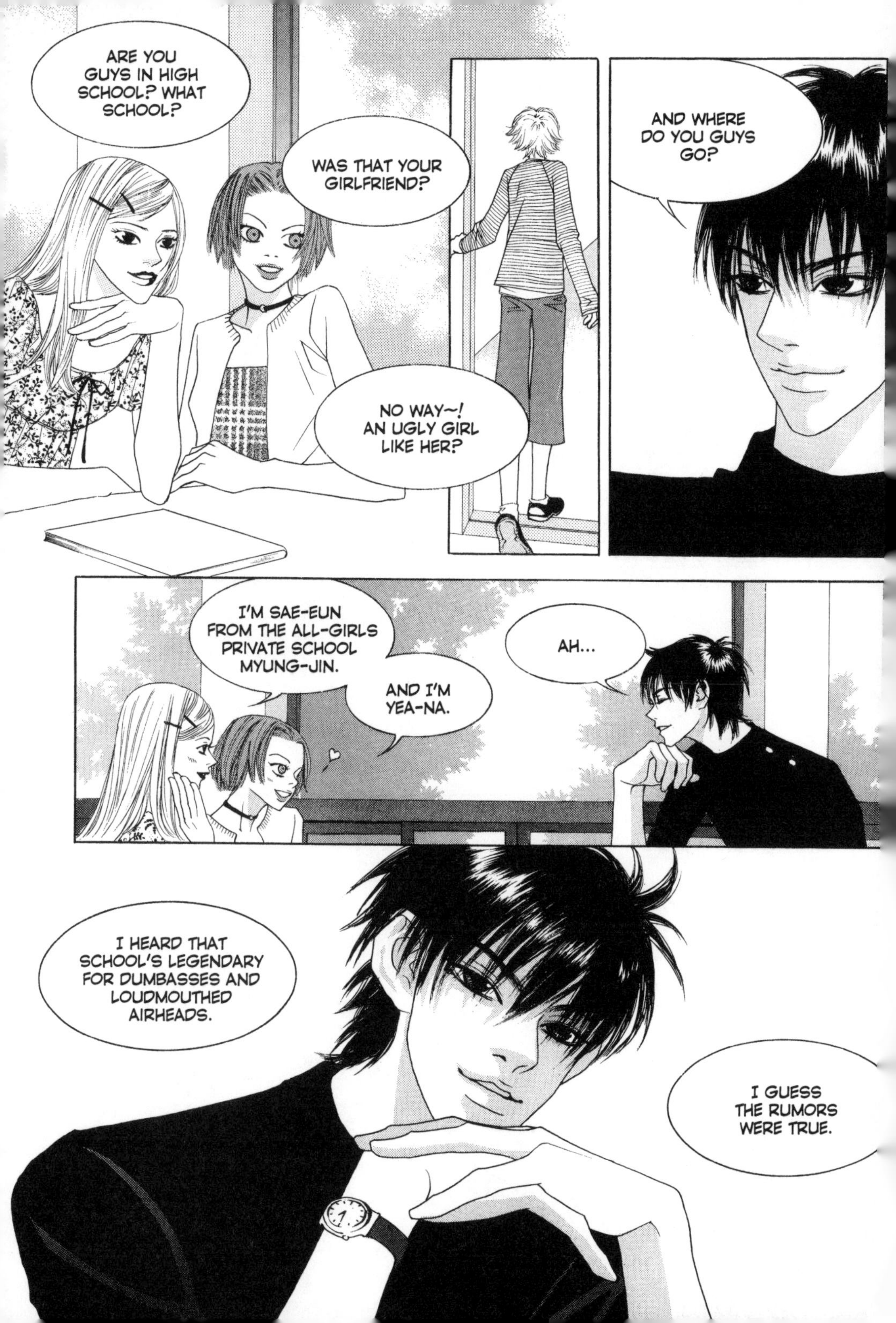
ARE YOU GUYS IN HIGH SCHOOL? WHAT SCHOOL?
WAS THAT YOUR GIRLFRIEND?
NO WAY~! AN UGLY GIRL LIKE HER?
AND WHERE DO YOU GUYS GO?
I'M SAE-EUN FROM THE ALL-GIRLS PRIVATE SCHOOL MYUNG-JIN.
AND I'M YEA-NA.
AH...
I HEARD THAT SCHOOL'S LEGENDARY FOR DUMBASSES AND LOUDMOUTHED AIRHEADS.
I GUESS THE RUMORS WERE TRUE.

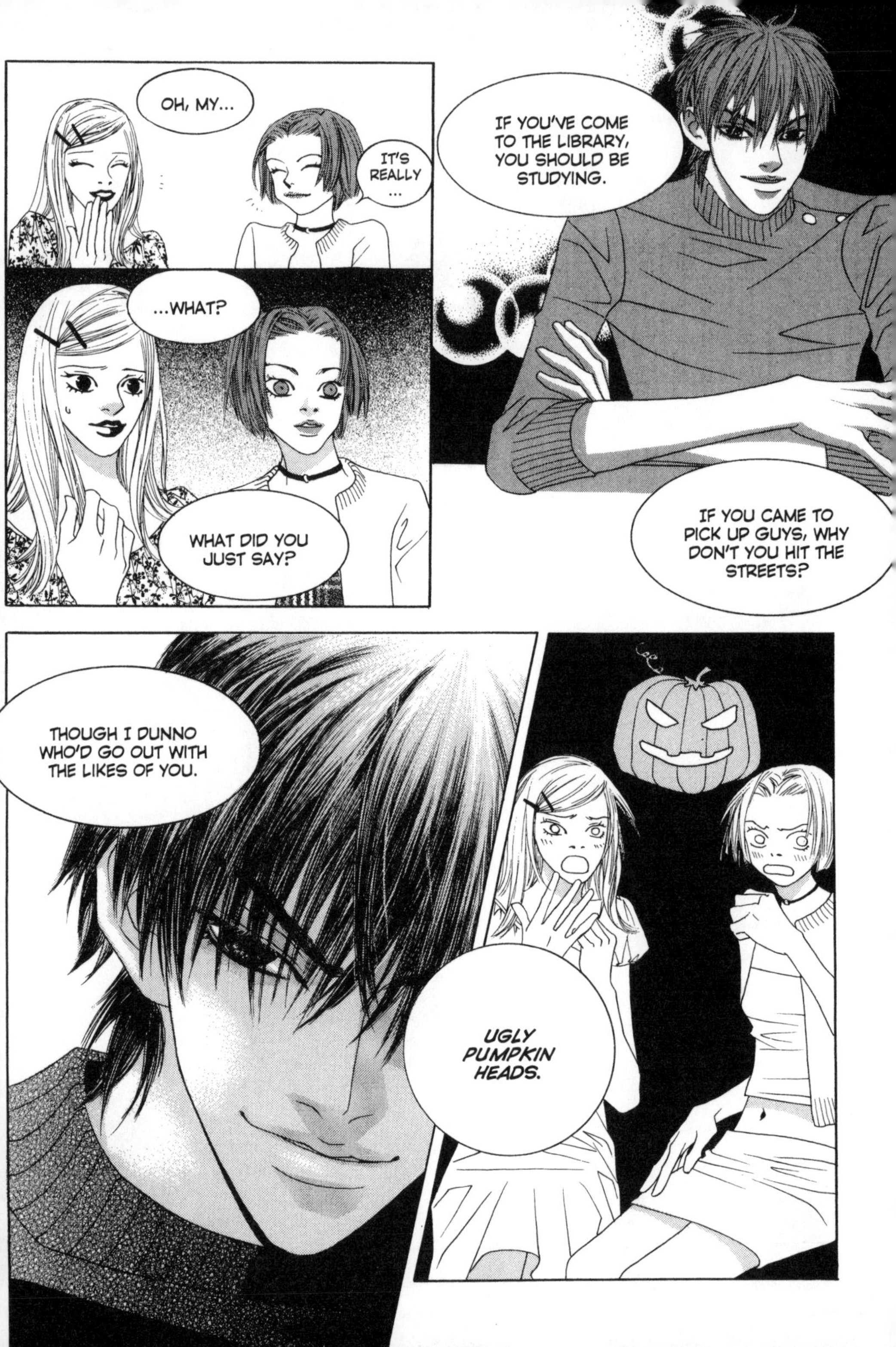
OH, MY...
IT'S REALLY ...
...WHAT?
WHAT DID YOU JUST SAY?
IF YOU'VE COME TO THE LIBRARY, YOU SHOULD BE STUDYING.
IF YOU CAME TO PICK UP GUYS, WHY DON'T YOU HIT THE STREETS?
THOUGH I DUNNO WHO'D GO OUT WITH THE LIKES OF YOU.
UGLY PUMPKIN HEADS.

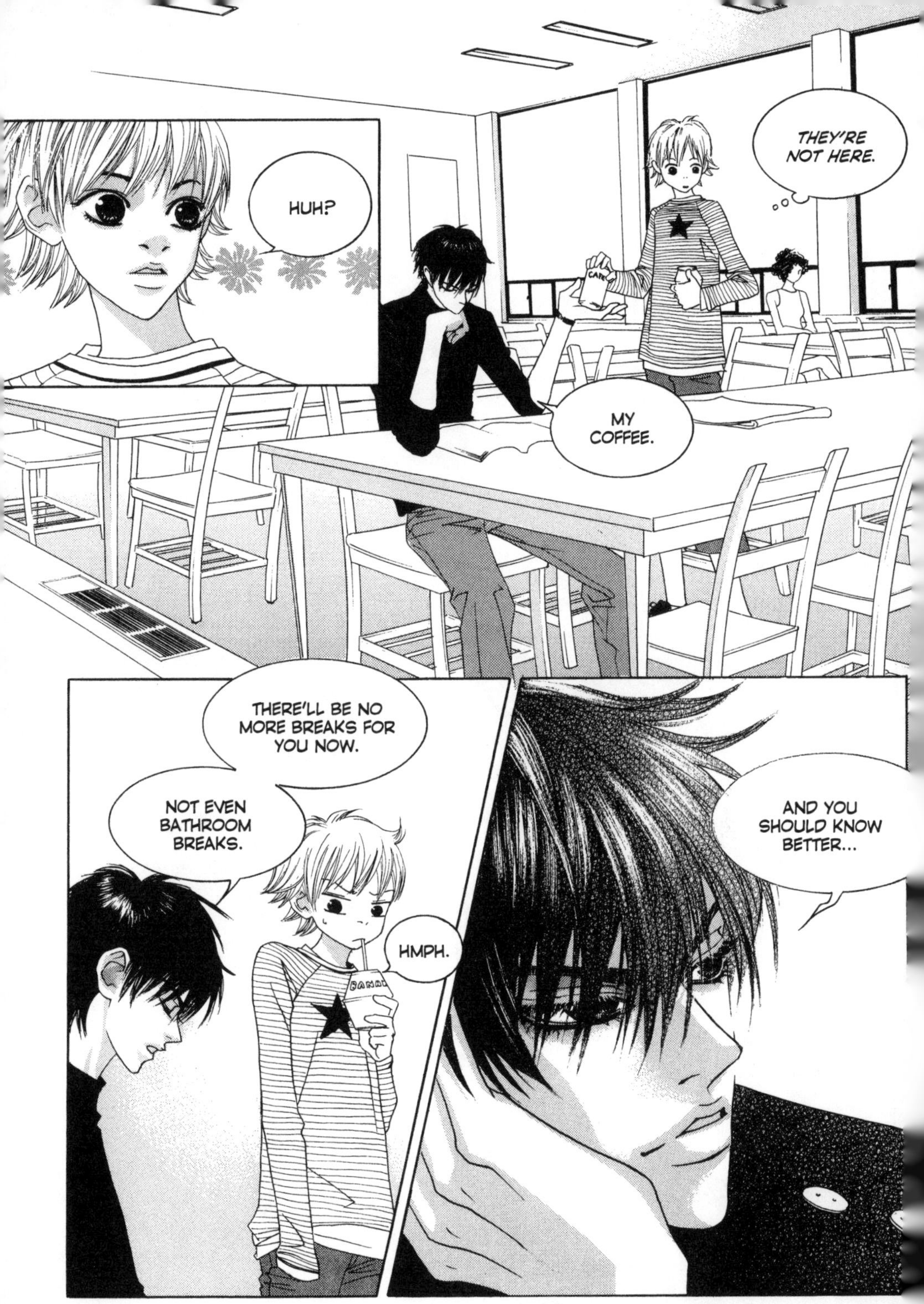
HUH?
THEY'RE NOT HERE.
MY COFFEE.
THERE'LL BE NO MORE BREAKS FOR YOU NOW.
NOT EVEN BATHROOM BREAKS.
HMPH.
AND YOU SHOULD KNOW BETTER...

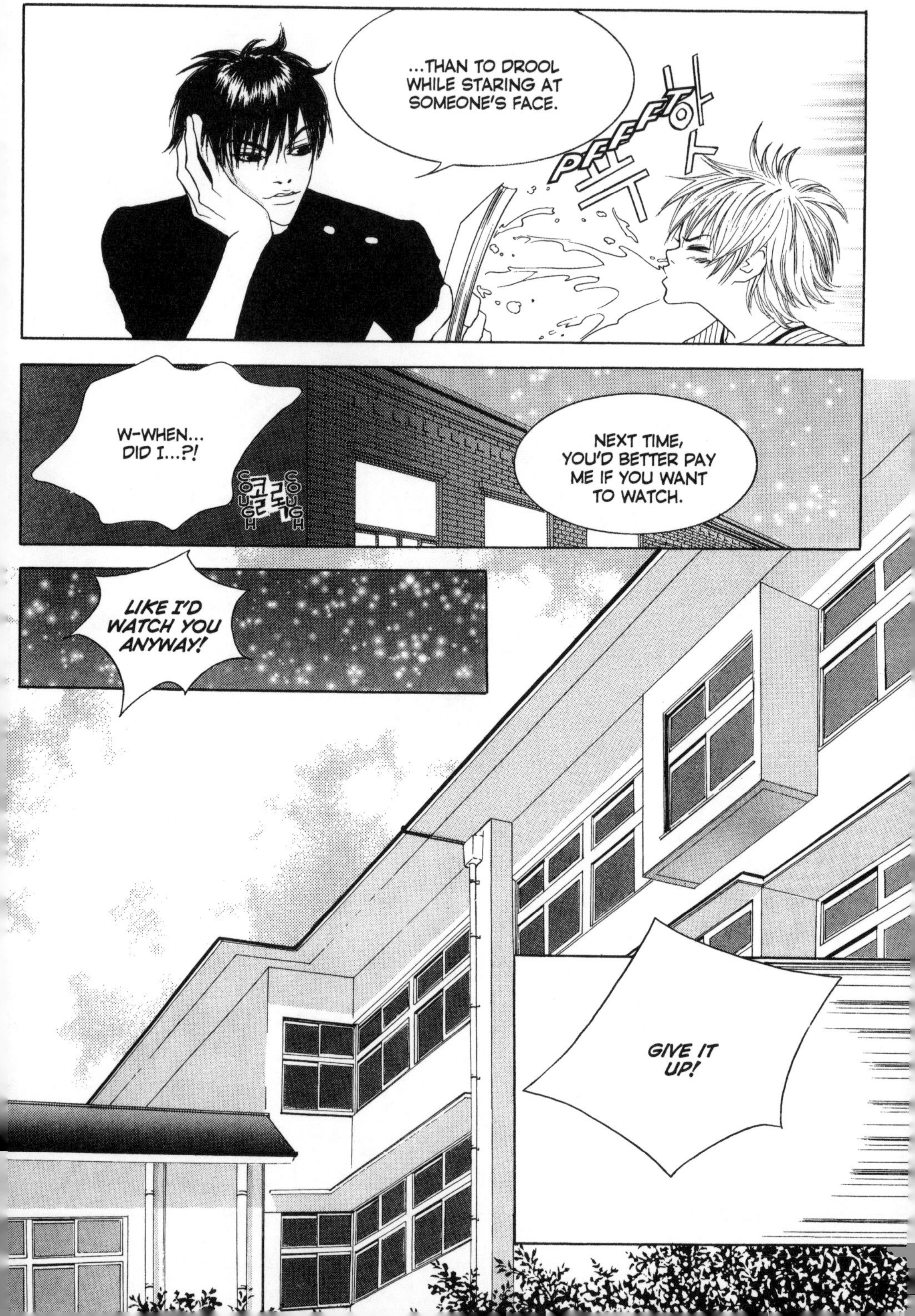
...THAN TO DROOL WHILE STARING AT SOMEONE'S FACE.
PFFFFT
W-WHEN... DID I...?!
COUGH COUGH
NEXT TIME, YOU'D BETTER PAY ME IF YOU WANT TO WATCH.
LIKE I'D WATCH YOU ANYWAY!
GIVE IT UP!

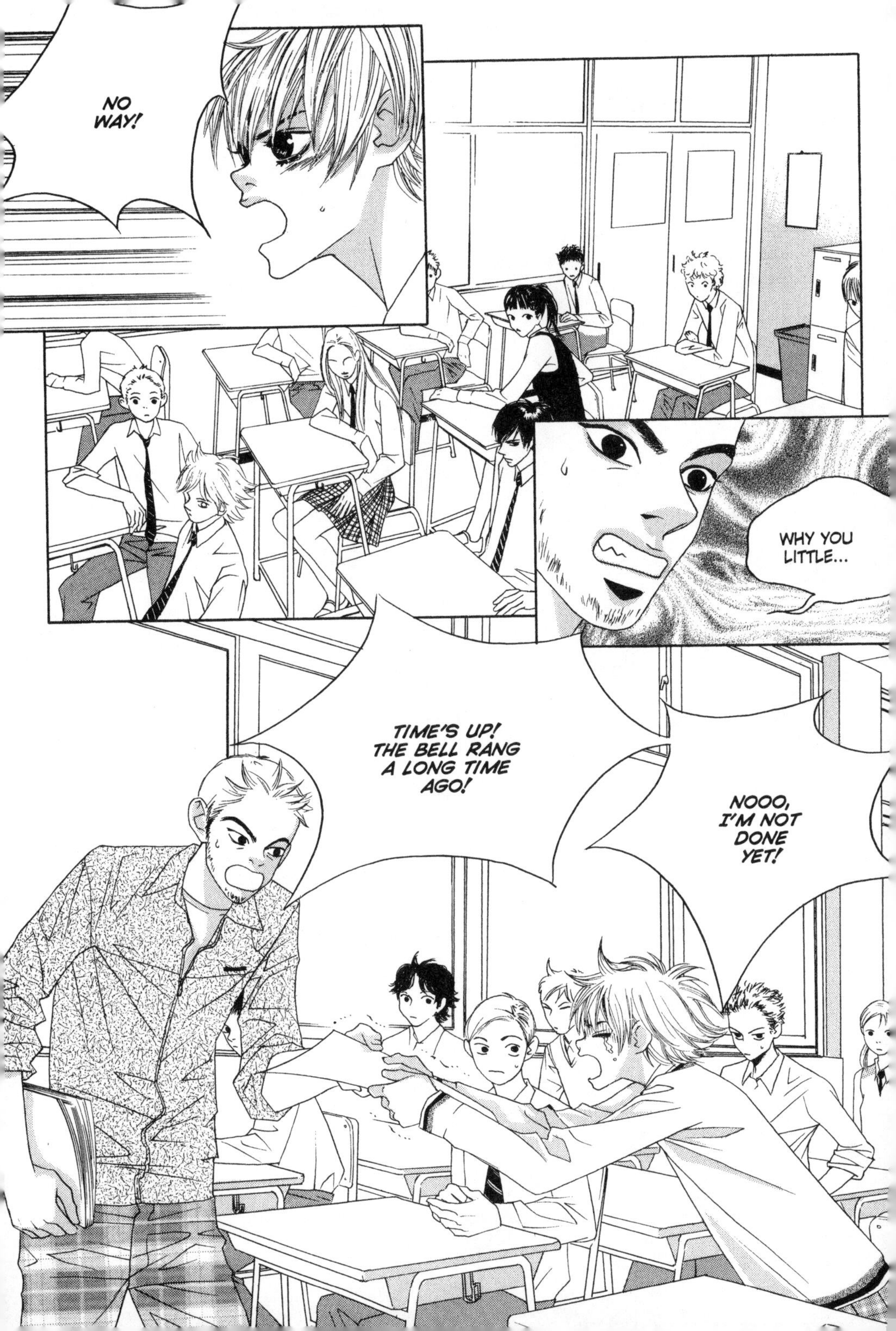
NO WAY!
WHY YOU LITTLE...
TIME'S UP! THE BELL RANG A LONG TIME AGO!
NOOO, I'M NOT DONE YET!

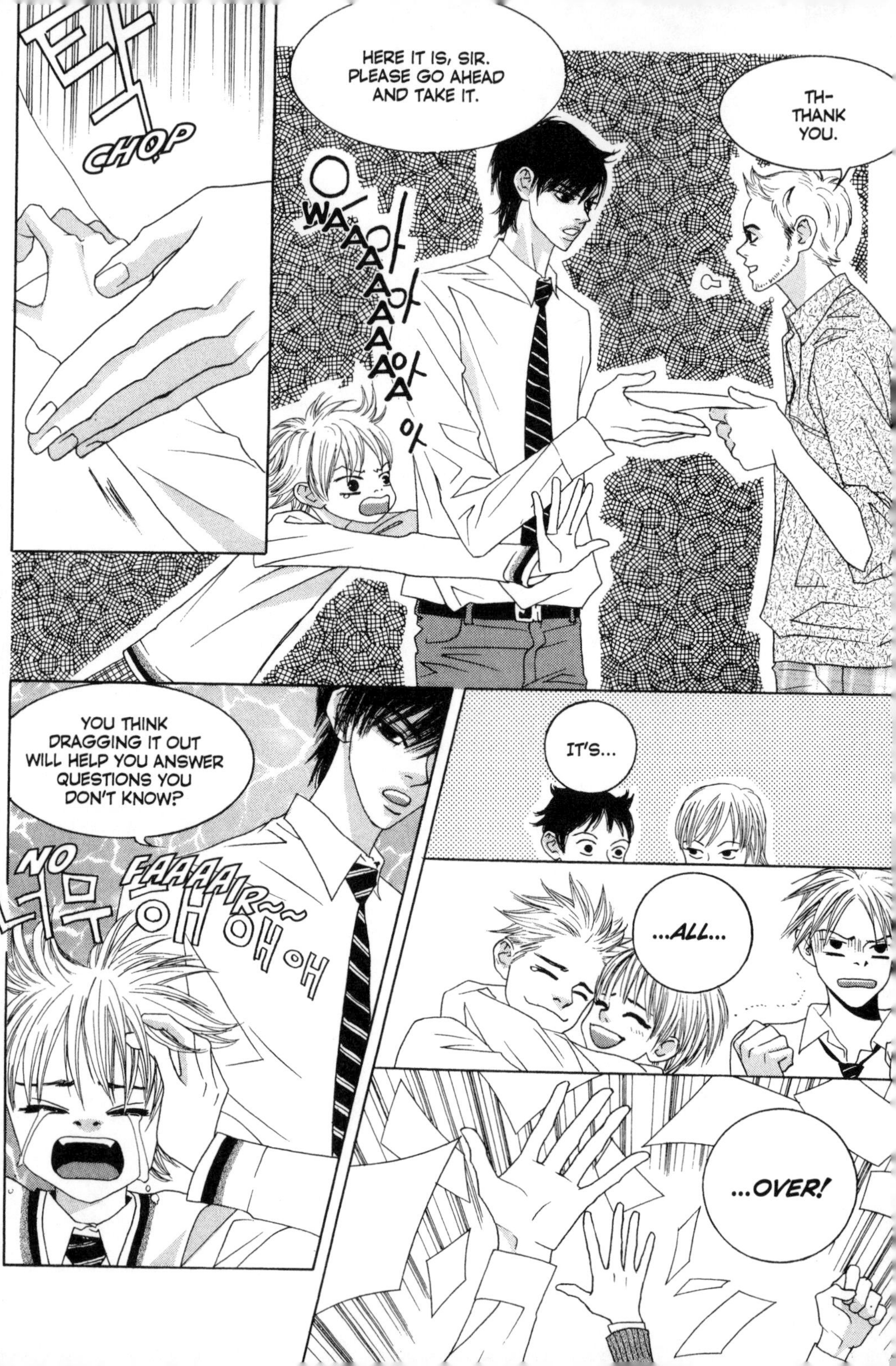
CHOP
HERE IT IS, SIR. PLEASE GO AHEAD AND TAKE IT.
WAAAAAAAA
TH-THANK YOU.
YOU THINK DRAGGING IT OUT WILL HELP YOU ANSWER QUESTIONS YOU DON'T KNOW?
NO FAAAAIR~~
IT'S...
...ALL...
...OVER!

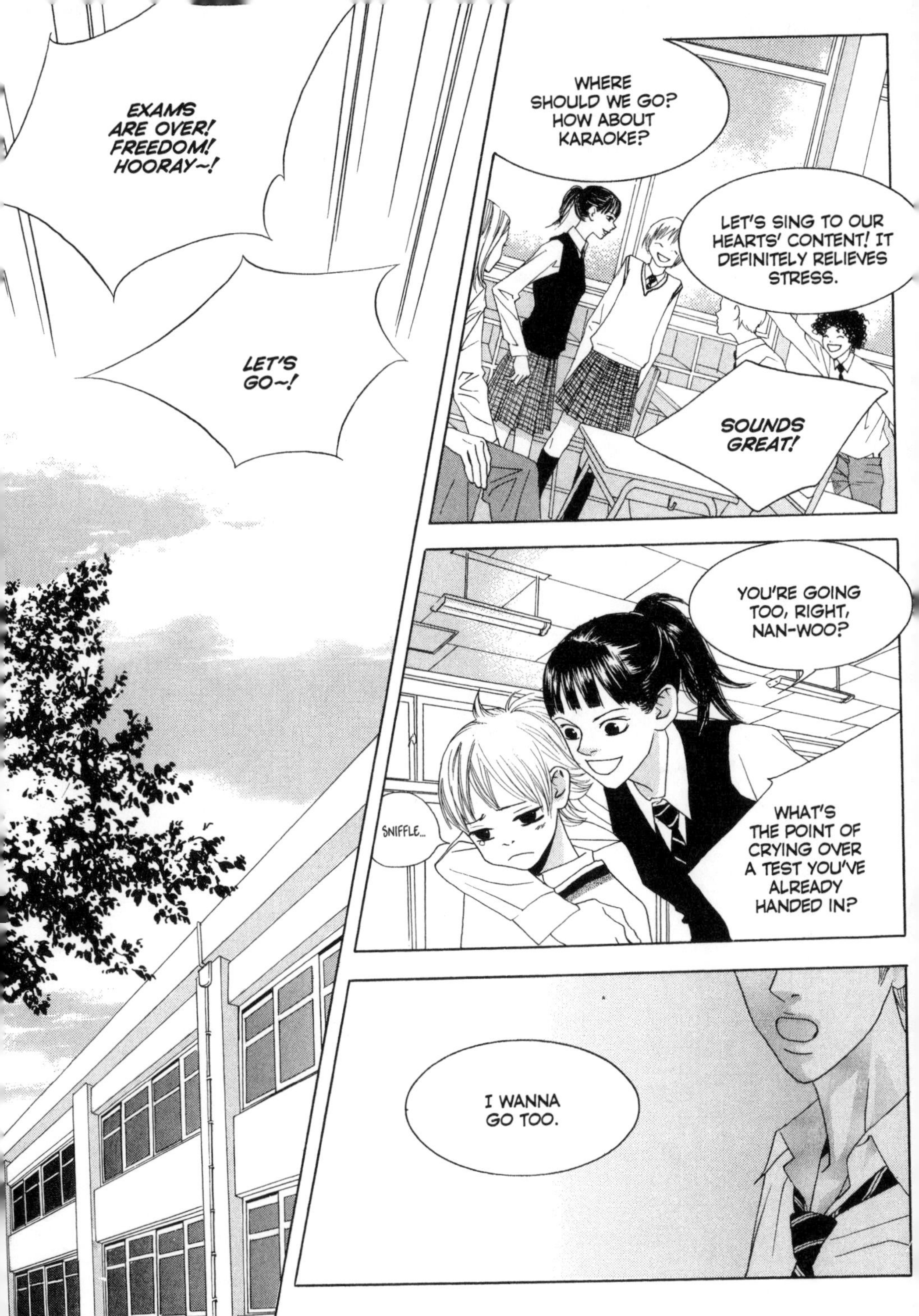
EXAMS ARE OVER! FREEDOM! HOORAY~!
LET'S GO~!
WHERE SHOULD WE GO? HOW ABOUT KARAOKE?
LET'S SING TO OUR HEARTS' CONTENT! IT DEFINITELY RELIEVES STRESS.
SOUNDS GREAT!
YOU'RE GOING TOO, RIGHT, NAN-WOO?
SNIFFLE...
WHAT'S THE POINT OF CRYING OVER A TEST YOU'VE ALREADY HANDED IN?
I WANNA GO TOO.

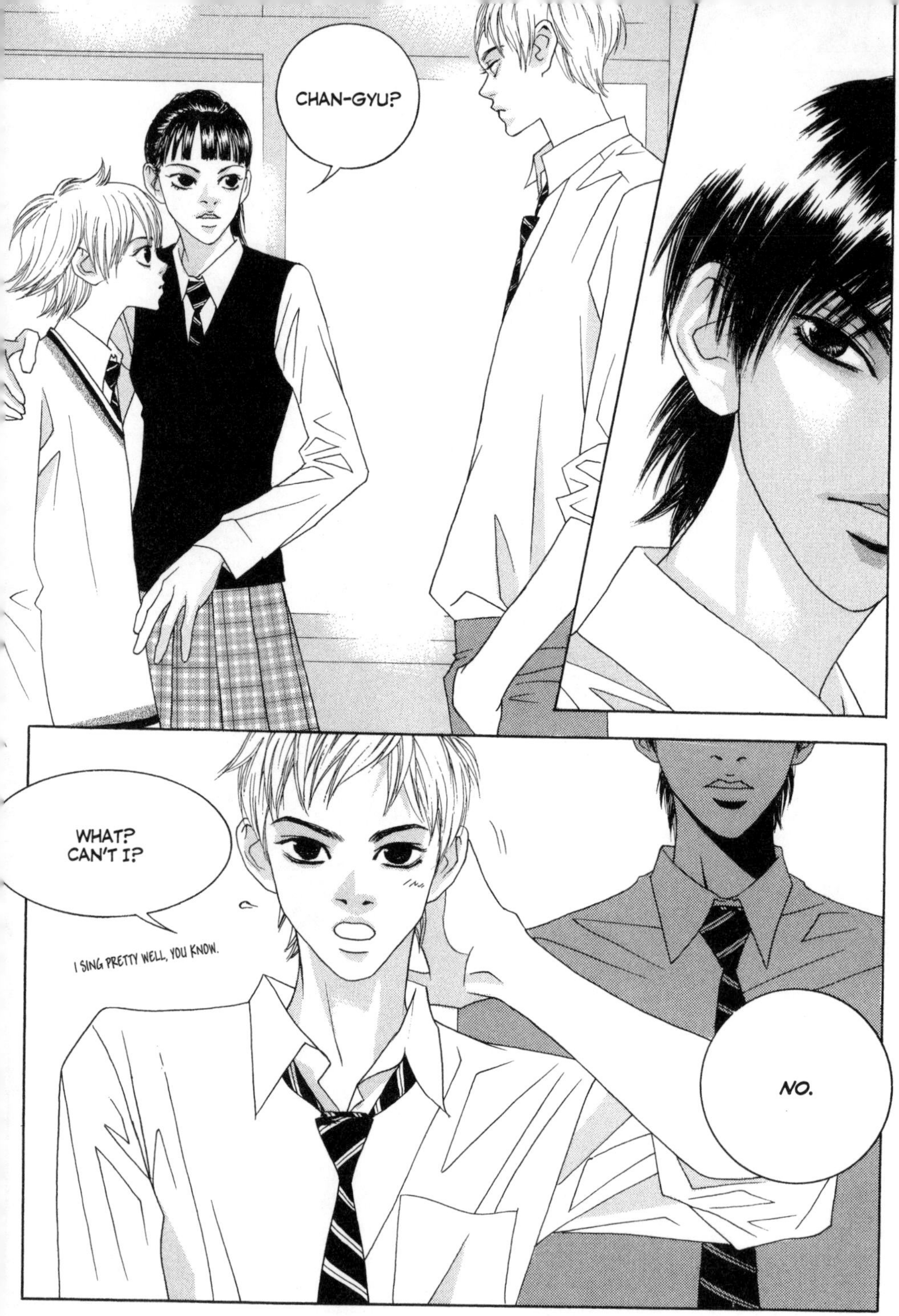
CHAN-GYU?
WHAT? CAN'T I?
I SING PRETTY WELL, YOU KNOW.
NO.

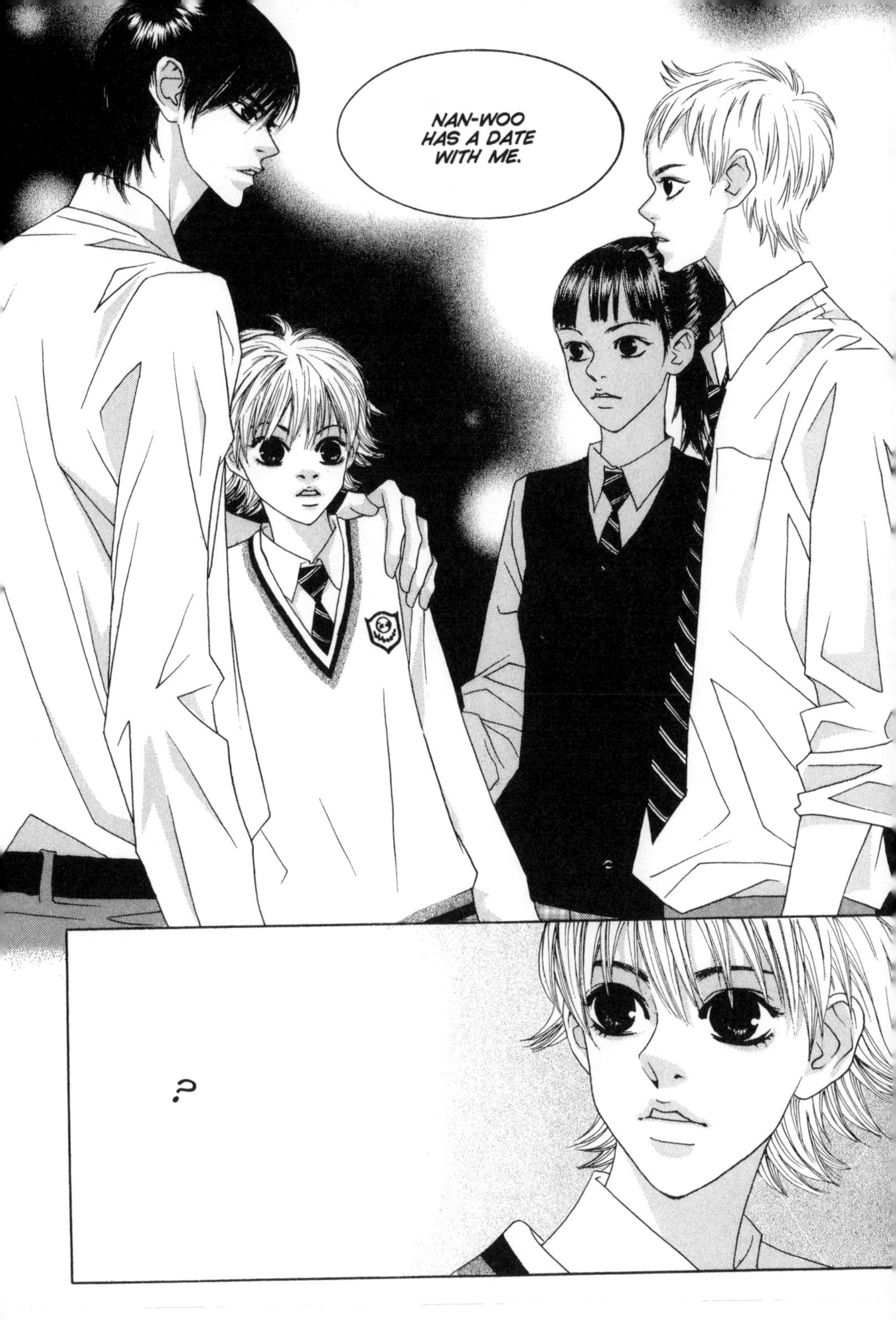
NAN-WOO HAS A DATE WITH ME.
?

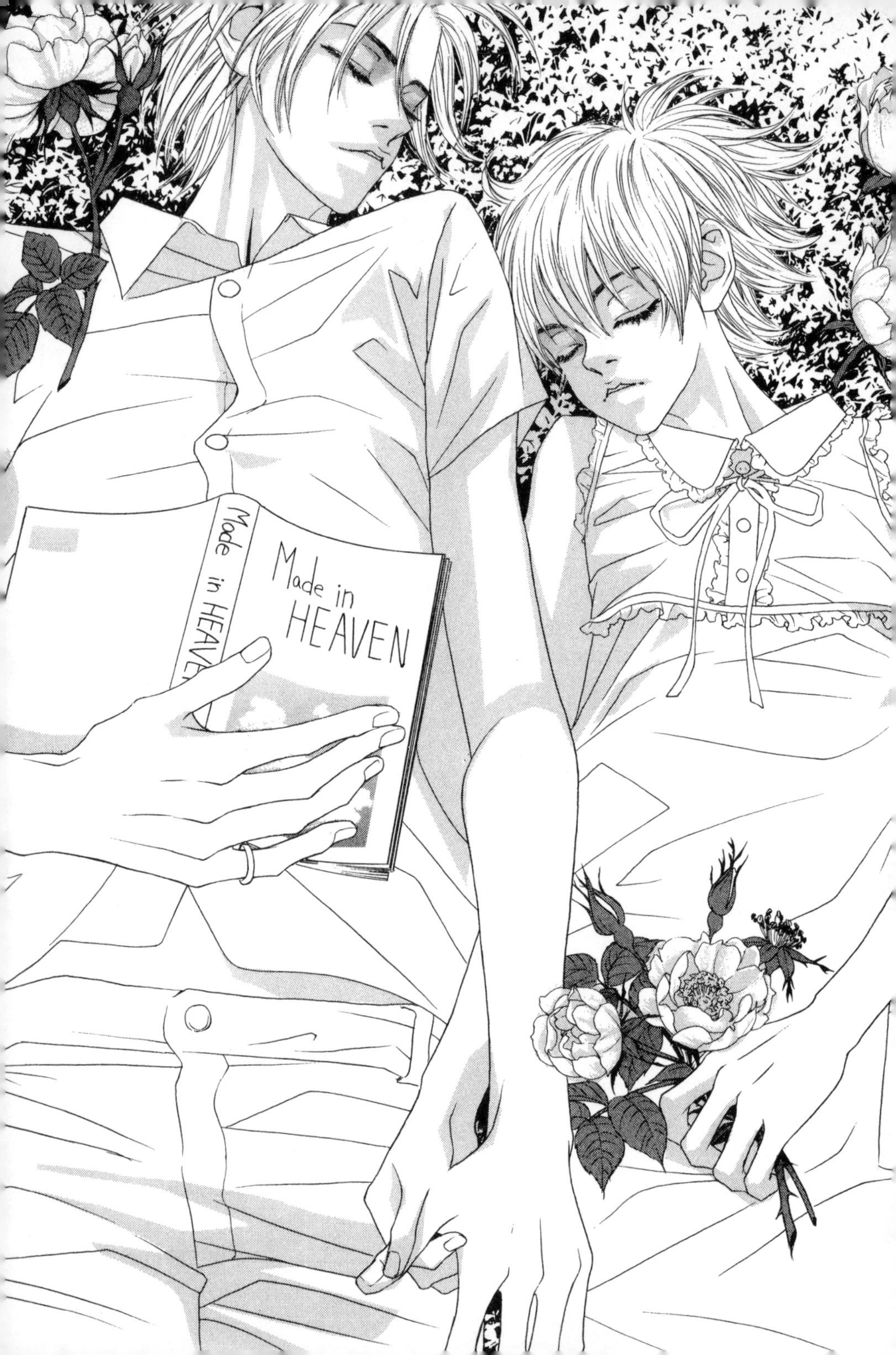
Made in HEAVEN
Made in HEAVEN

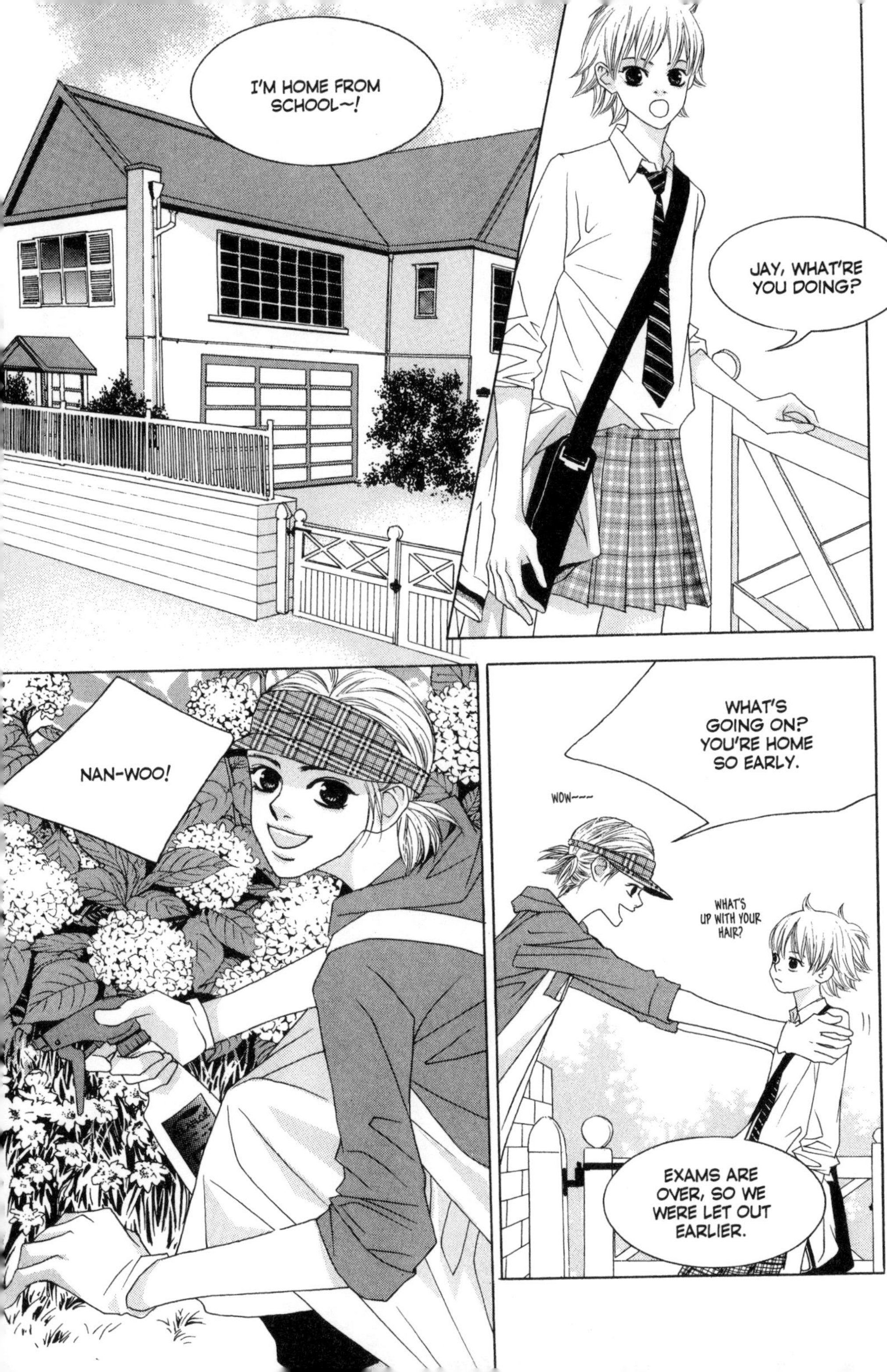
I'M HOME FROM SCHOOL~!
JAY, WHAT'RE YOU DOING?
NAN-WOO!
WHAT'S GOING ON? YOU'RE HOME SO EARLY.
WOW---
WHAT'S UP WITH YOUR HAIR?
EXAMS ARE OVER, SO WE WERE LET OUT EARLIER.

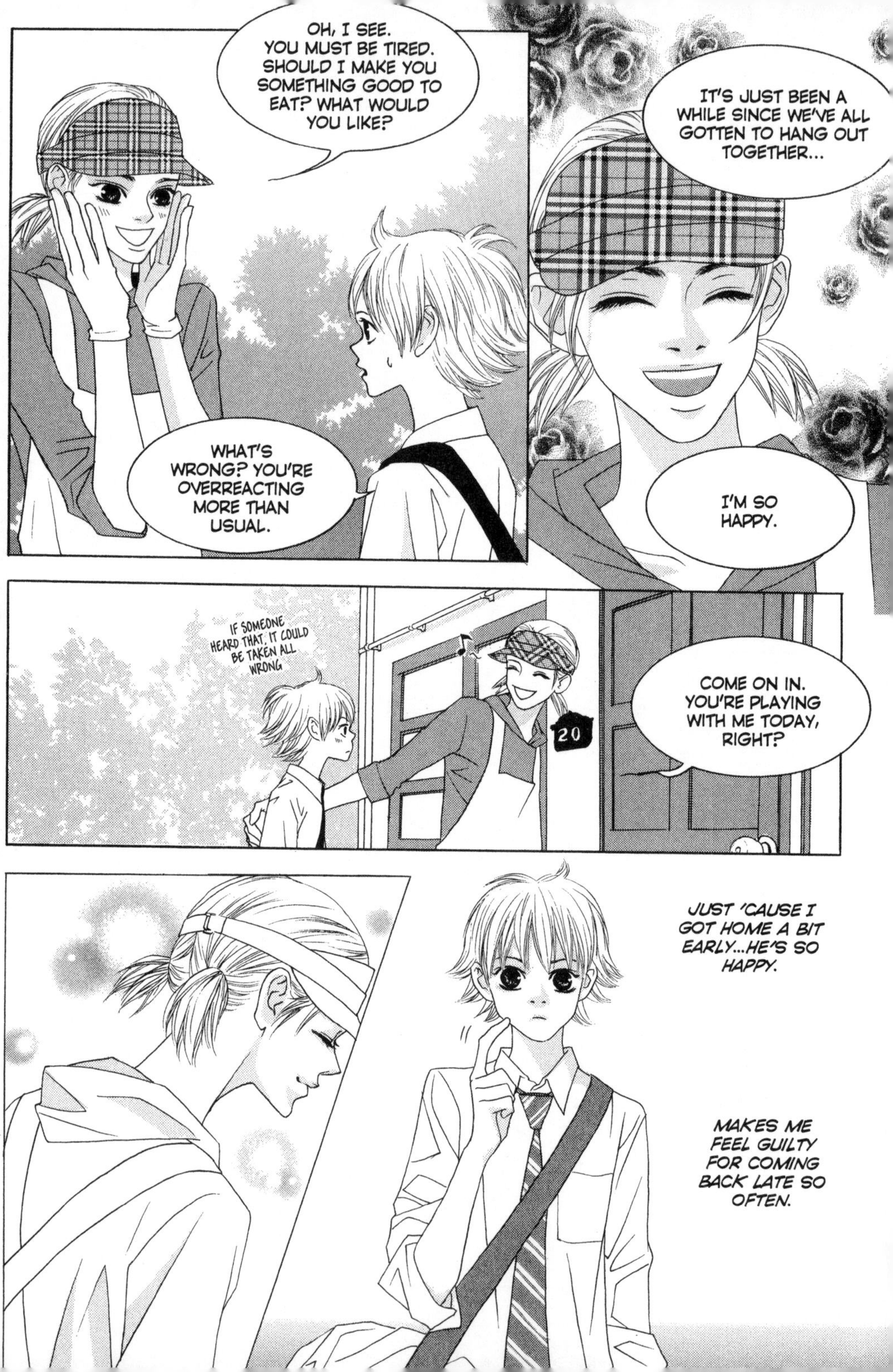
OH, I SEE. YOU MUST BE TIRED. SHOULD I MAKE YOU SOMETHING GOOD TO EAT? WHAT WOULD YOU LIKE?
WHAT'S WRONG? YOU'RE OVERREACTING MORE THAN USUAL.
IT'S JUST BEEN A WHILE SINCE WE'VE ALL GOTTEN TO HANG OUT TOGETHER...
I'M SO HAPPY.
IF SOMEONE HEARD THAT, IT COULD BE TAKEN ALL WRONG
20
COME ON IN. YOU'RE PLAYING WITH ME TODAY, RIGHT?
JUST 'CAUSE I GOT HOME A BIT EARLY...HE'S SO HAPPY.
MAKES ME FEEL GUILTY FOR COMING BACK LATE SO OFTEN.

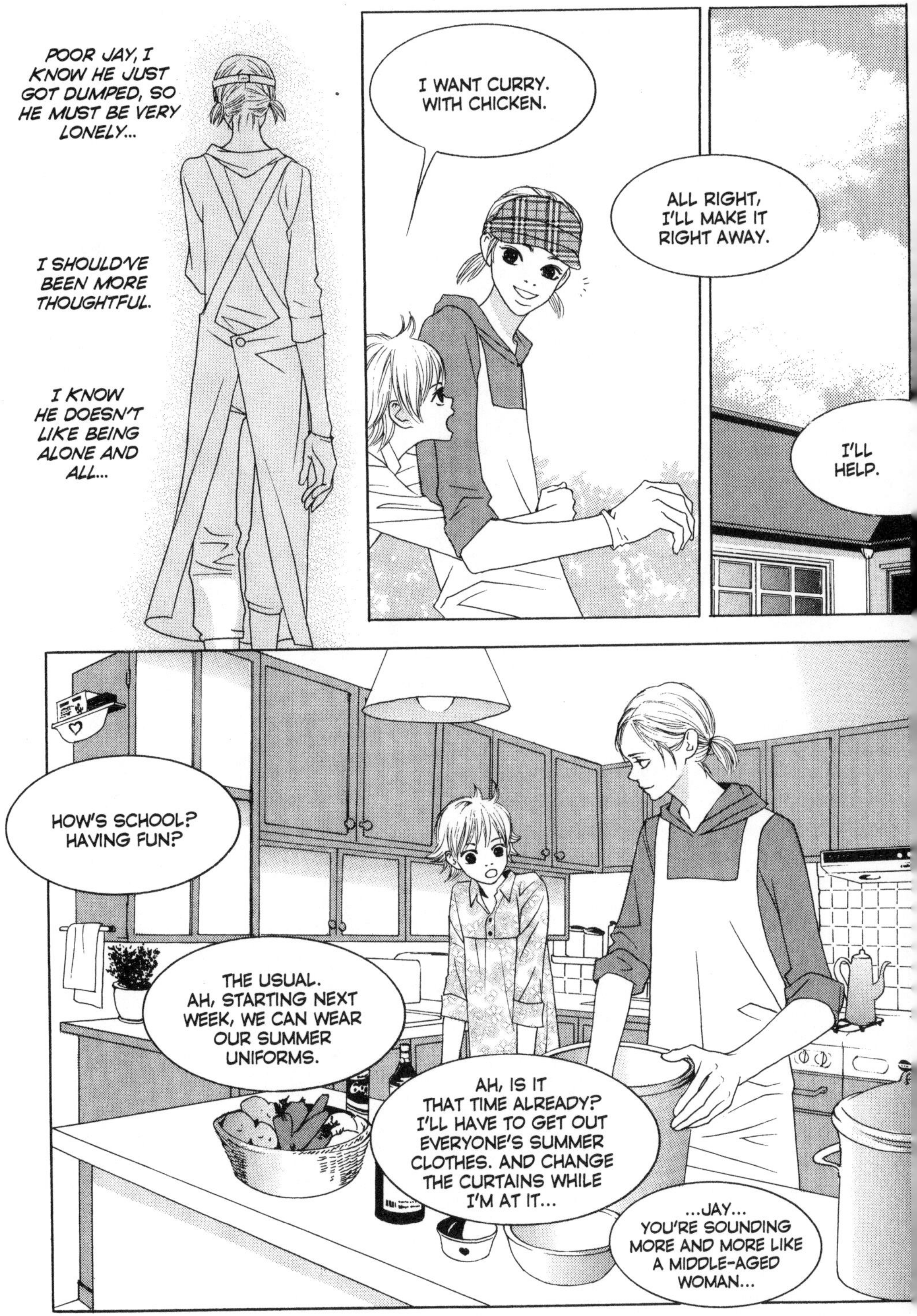
POOR JAY, I KNOW HE JUST GOT DUMPED, SO HE MUST BE VERY LONELY...
I SHOULD'VE BEEN MORE THOUGHTFUL.
I KNOW HE DOESN'T LIKE BEING ALONE AND ALL...
I WANT CURRY. WITH CHICKEN.
ALL RIGHT, I'LL MAKE IT RIGHT AWAY.
I'LL HELP.
HOW'S SCHOOL? HAVING FUN?
THE USUAL. AH, STARTING NEXT WEEK, WE CAN WEAR OUR SUMMER UNIFORMS.
AH, IS IT THAT TIME ALREADY? I'LL HAVE TO GET OUT EVERYONE'S SUMMER CLOTHES. AND CHANGE THE CURTAINS WHILE I'M AT IT...
...JAY... YOU'RE SOUNDING MORE AND MORE LIKE A MIDDLE-AGED WOMAN...

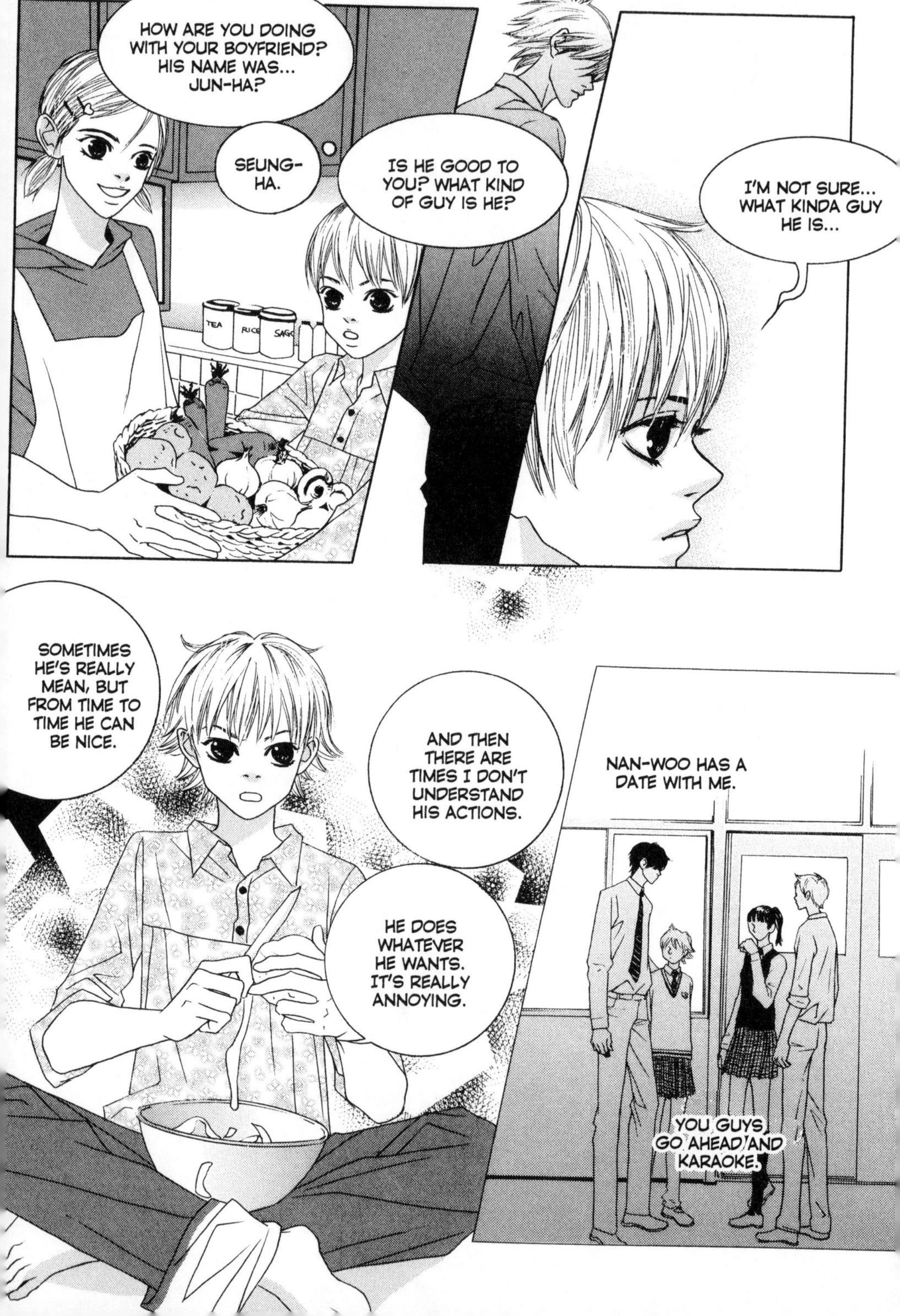
HOW ARE YOU DOING WITH YOUR BOYFRIEND? HIS NAME WAS... JUN-HA?
SEUNG-HA.
IS HE GOOD TO YOU? WHAT KIND OF GUY IS HE?
I'M NOT SURE... WHAT KINDA GUY HE IS...
TEA
RICE
SAGO
SOMETIMES HE'S REALLY MEAN, BUT FROM TIME TO TIME HE CAN BE NICE.
AND THEN THERE ARE TIMES I DON'T UNDERSTAND HIS ACTIONS.
HE DOES WHATEVER HE WANTS. IT'S REALLY ANNOYING.
NAN-WOO HAS A DATE WITH ME.
YOU GUYS GO AHEAD AND KARAOKE.

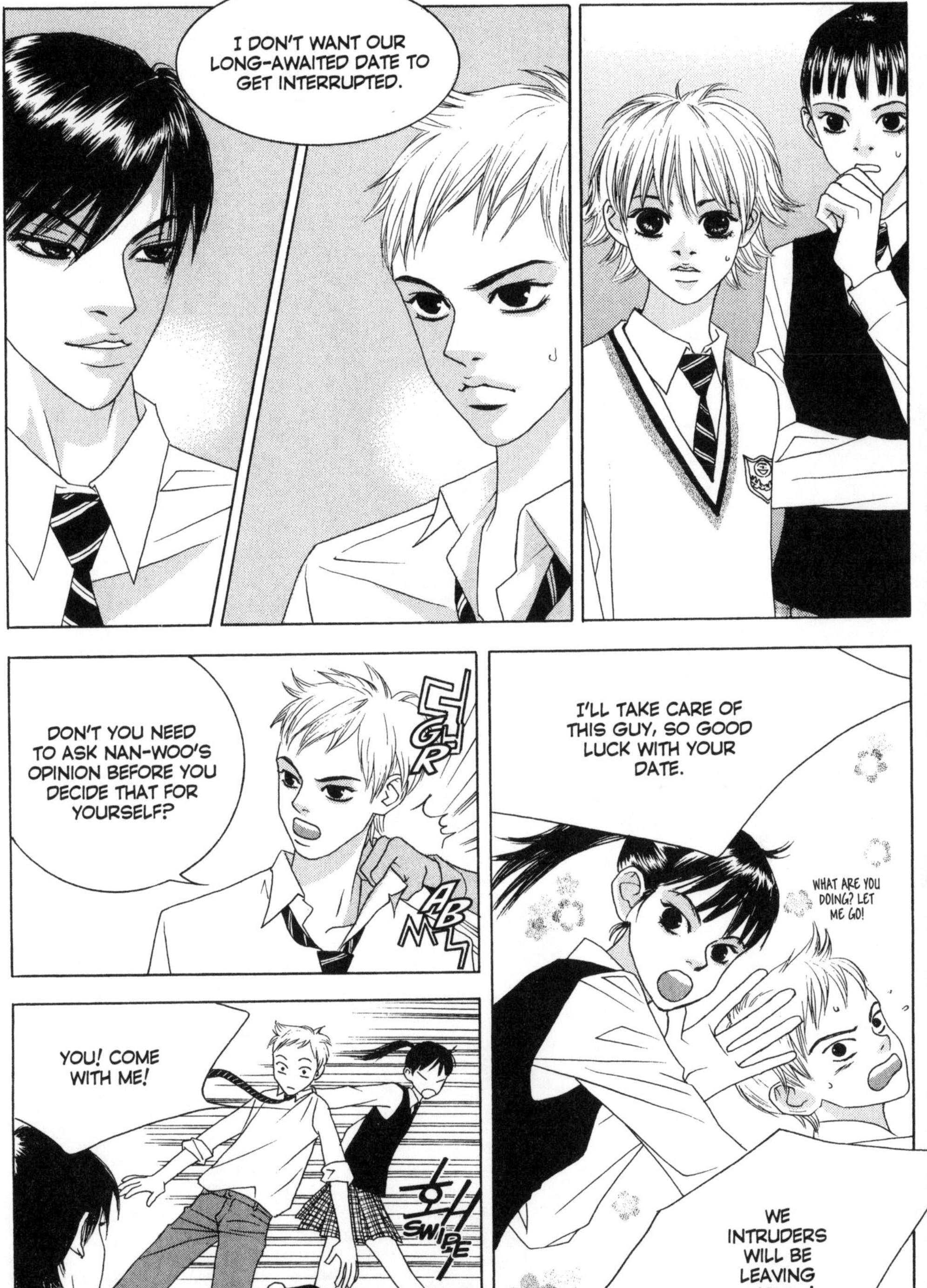
I DON'T WANT OUR LONG-AWAITED DATE TO GET INTERRUPTED.
DON'T YOU NEED TO ASK NAN-WOO'S OPINION BEFORE YOU DECIDE THAT FOR YOURSELF?
GR
AB
YOU! COME WITH ME!
SWIPE
I'LL TAKE CARE OF THIS GUY, SO GOOD LUCK WITH YOUR DATE.
WHAT ARE YOU DOING? LET ME GO!
WE INTRUDERS WILL BE LEAVING NOW~!

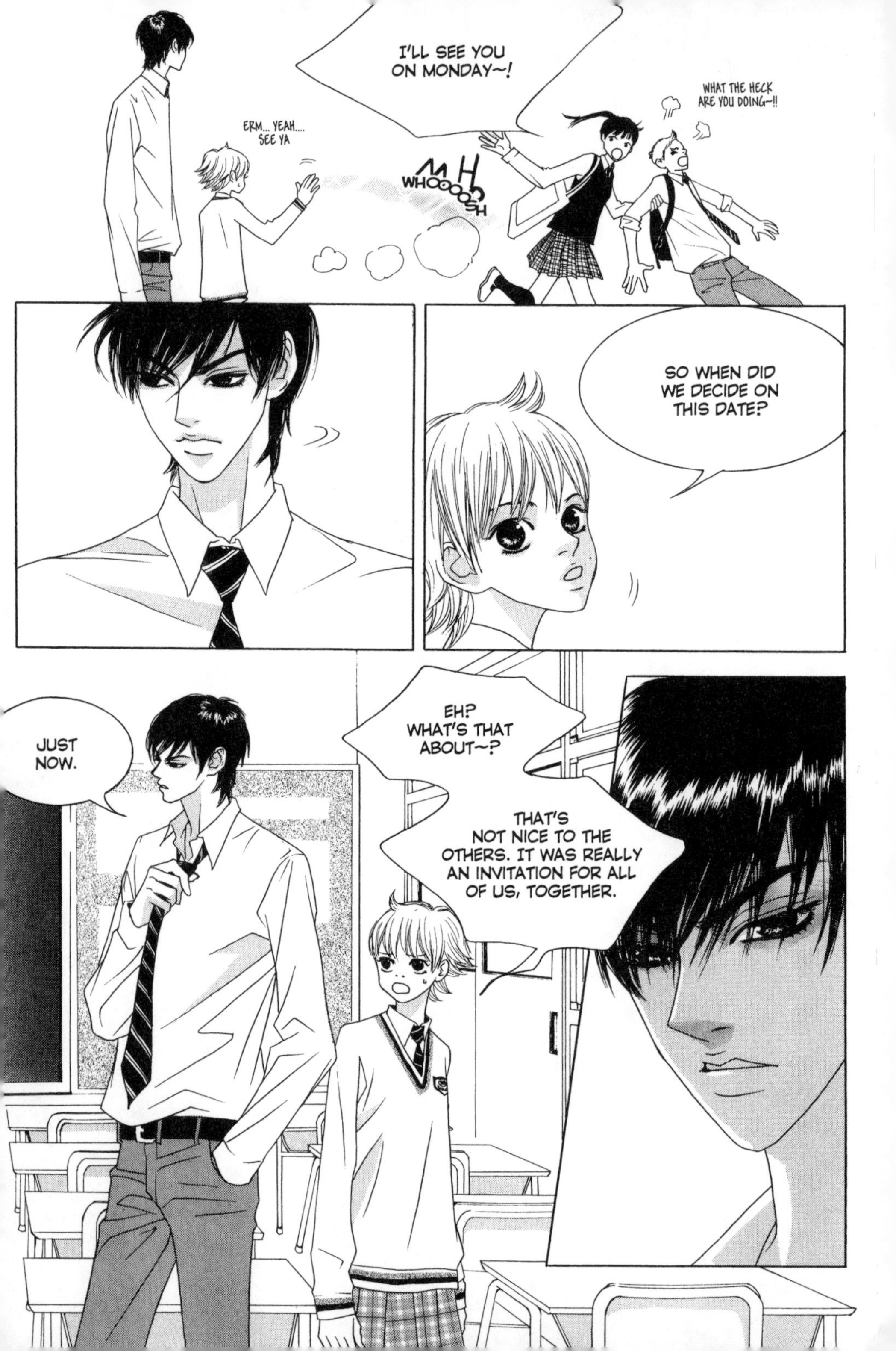
I'LL SEE YOU ON MONDAY~!
ERM... YEAH.... SEE YA
WHOOOOOSH
WHAT THE HECK ARE YOU DOING~!!
SO WHEN DID WE DECIDE ON THIS DATE?
JUST NOW.
EH? WHAT'S THAT ABOUT~?
THAT'S NOT NICE TO THE OTHERS. IT WAS REALLY AN INVITATION FOR ALL OF US, TOGETHER.

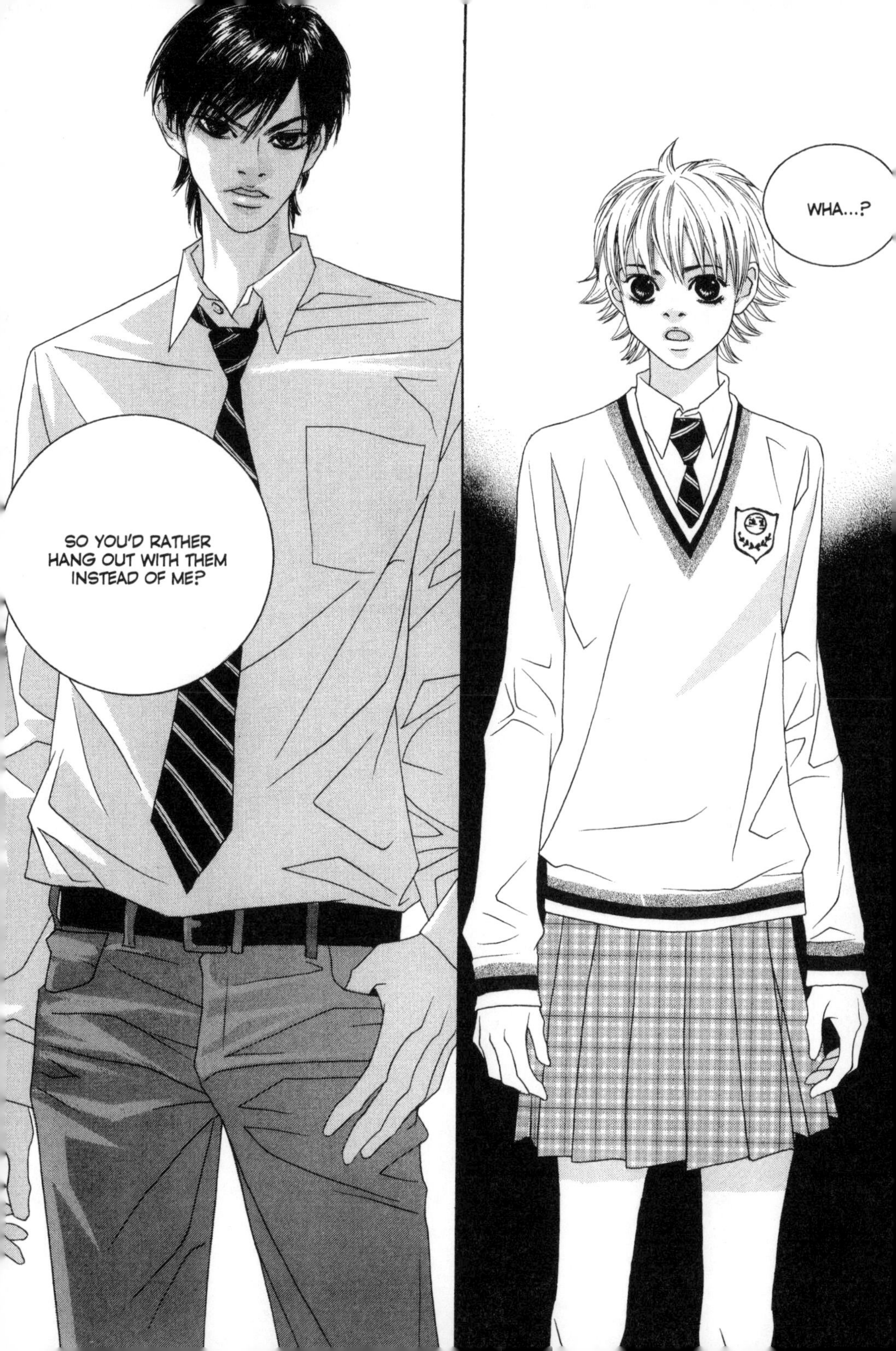
SO YOU'D RATHER HANG OUT WITH THEM INSTEAD OF ME?
WHA...?

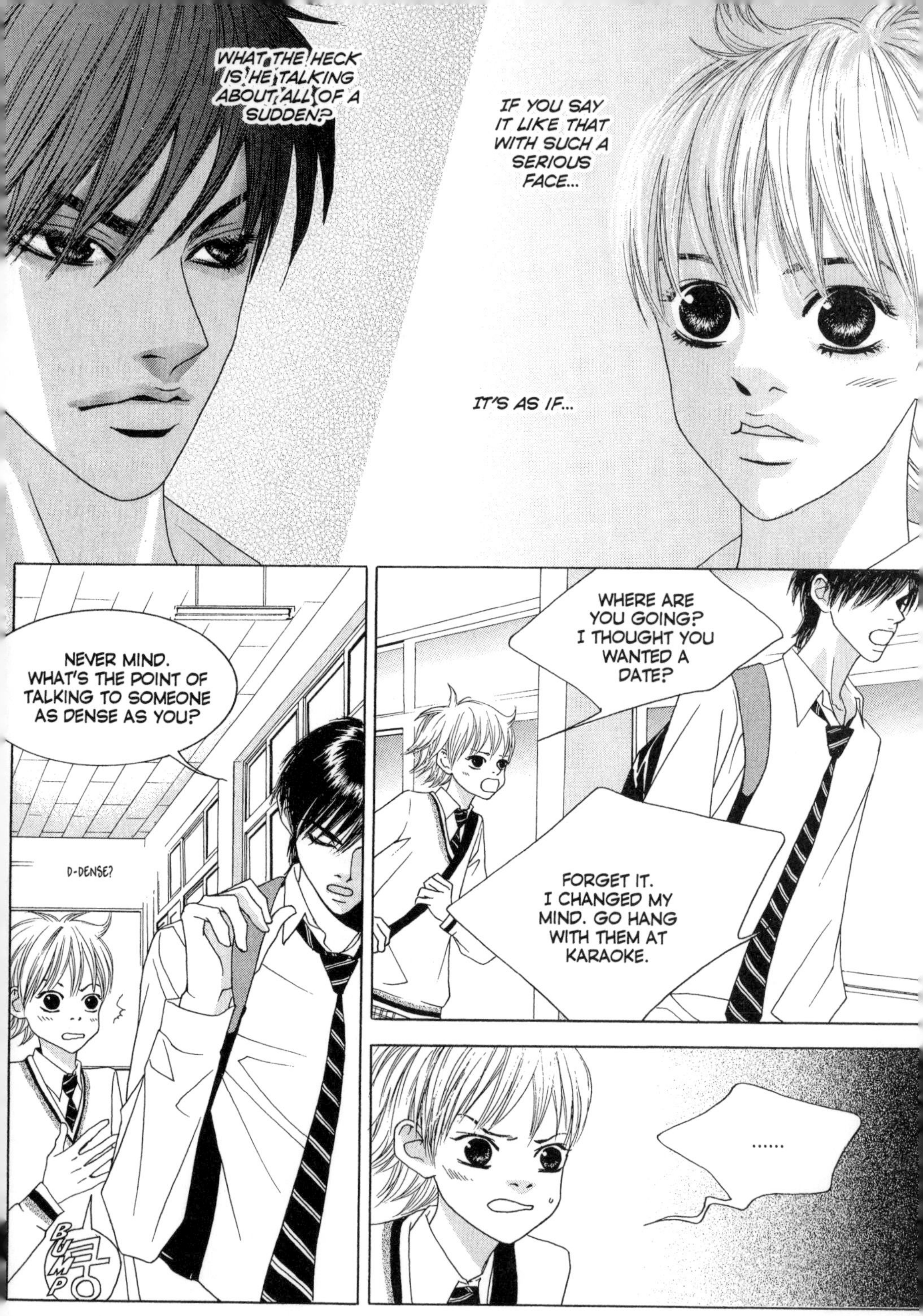
WHAT THE HECK IS HE TALKING ABOUT ALL OF A SUDDEN?
IF YOU SAY IT LIKE THAT WITH SUCH A SERIOUS FACE...
IT'S AS IF...
NEVER MIND. WHAT'S THE POINT OF TALKING TO SOMEONE AS DENSE AS YOU?
D-DENSE?
BUMP
WHERE ARE YOU GOING? I THOUGHT YOU WANTED A DATE?
FORGET IT. I CHANGED MY MIND. GO HANG WITH THEM AT KARAOKE.
......

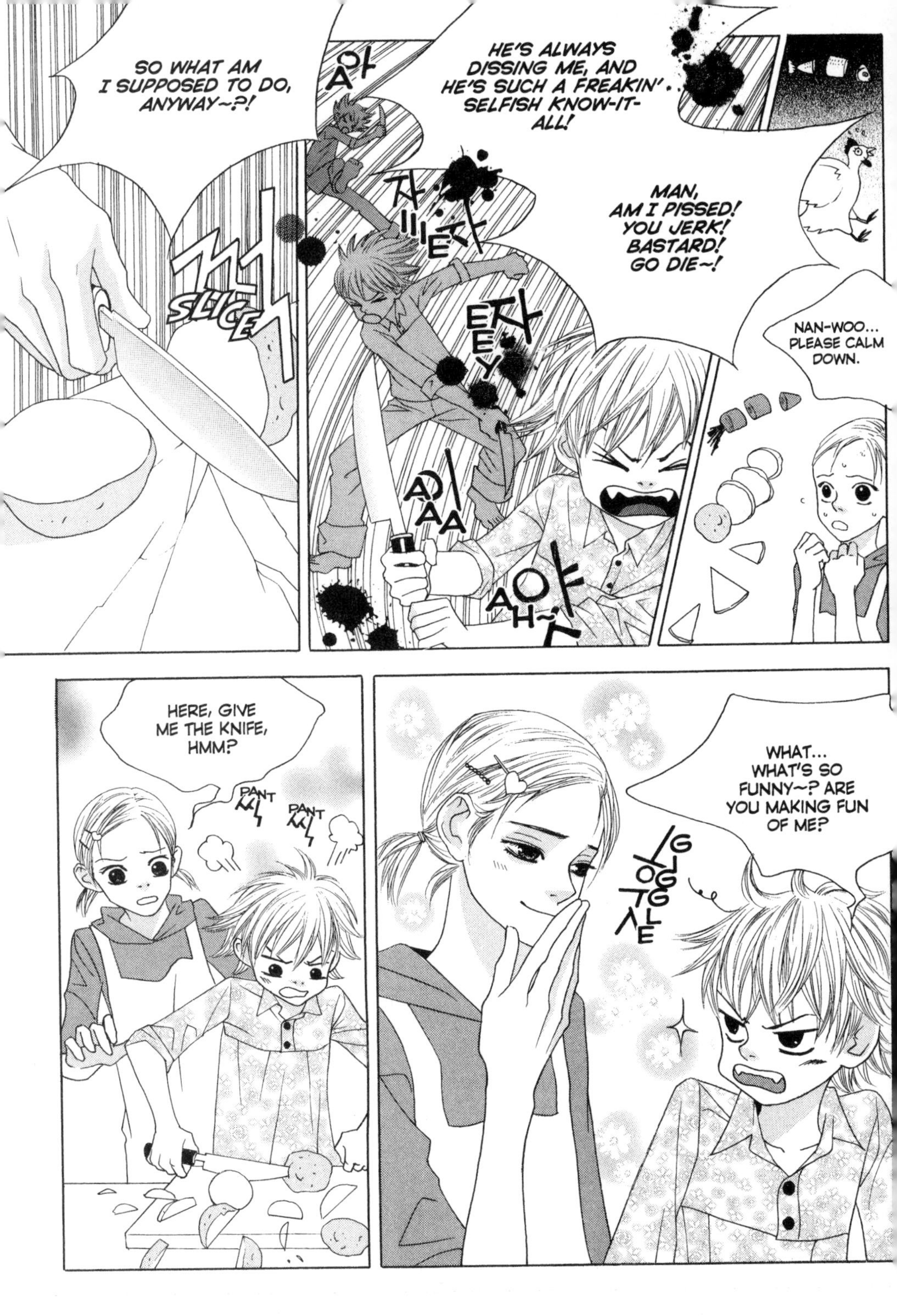
SO WHAT AM I SUPPOSED TO DO, ANYWAY~?!
SLICE
HE'S ALWAYS DISSING ME, AND HE'S SUCH A FREAKIN' SELFISH KNOW-IT-ALL!
MAN, AM I PISSED! YOU JERK! BASTARD! GO DIE~!
AH~
NAN-WOO... PLEASE CALM DOWN.
HERE, GIVE ME THE KNIFE, HMM?
PANT
PANT
WHAT... WHAT'S SO FUNNY~? ARE YOU MAKING FUN OF ME?

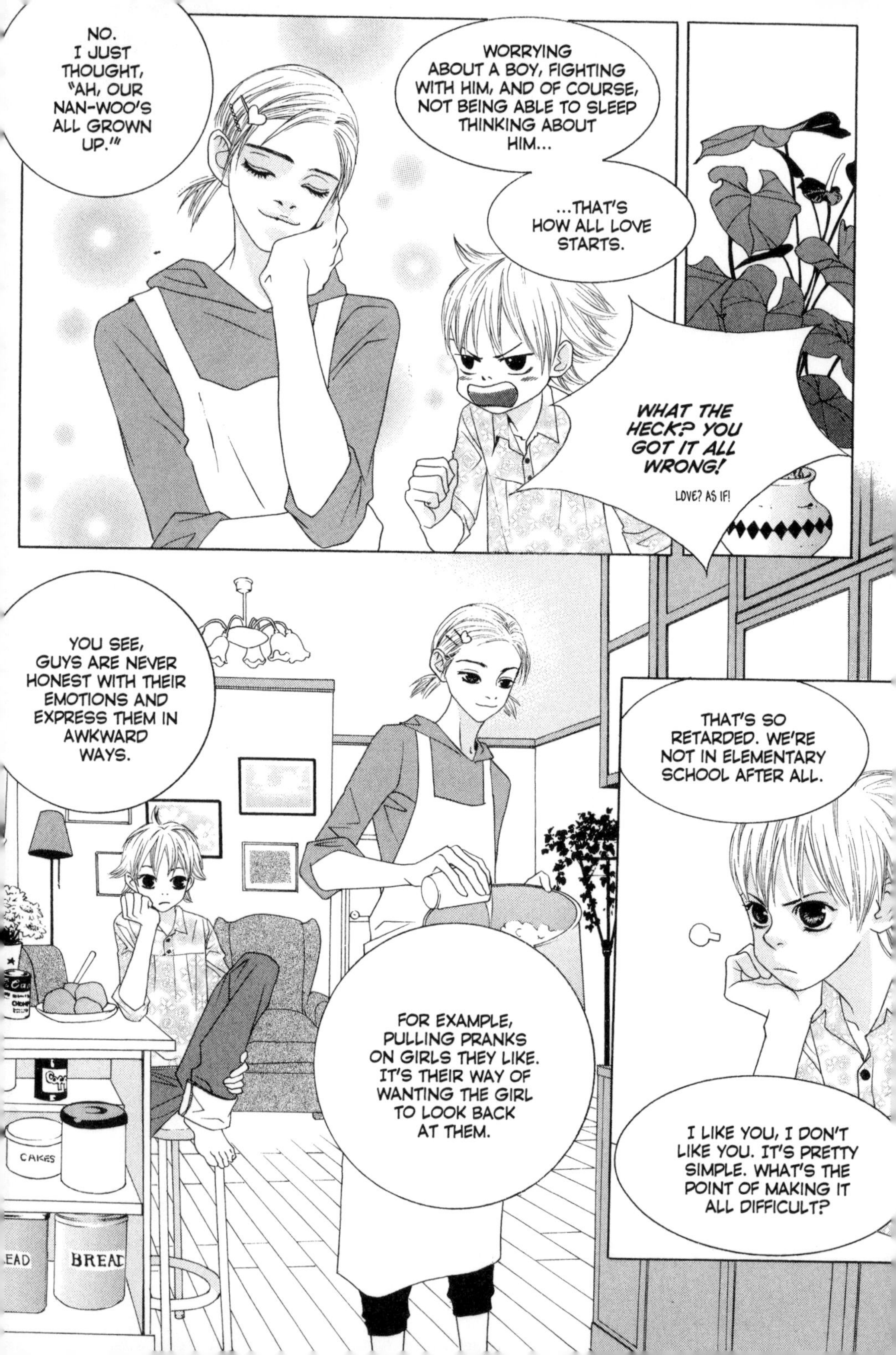
NO. I JUST THOUGHT, "AH, OUR NAN-WOO'S ALL GROWN UP."
WORRYING ABOUT A BOY, FIGHTING WITH HIM, AND OF COURSE, NOT BEING ABLE TO SLEEP THINKING ABOUT HIM...
...THAT'S HOW ALL LOVE STARTS.
WHAT THE HECK? YOU GOT IT ALL WRONG!
LOVE? AS IF!
YOU SEE, GUYS ARE NEVER HONEST WITH THEIR EMOTIONS AND EXPRESS THEM IN AWKWARD WAYS.
FOR EXAMPLE, PULLING PRANKS ON GIRLS THEY LIKE. IT'S THEIR WAY OF WANTING THE GIRL TO LOOK BACK AT THEM.
CAKES
BREAD
THAT'S SO RETARDED. WE'RE NOT IN ELEMENTARY SCHOOL AFTER ALL.
I LIKE YOU, I DON'T LIKE YOU. IT'S PRETTY SIMPLE. WHAT'S THE POINT OF MAKING IT ALL DIFFICULT?

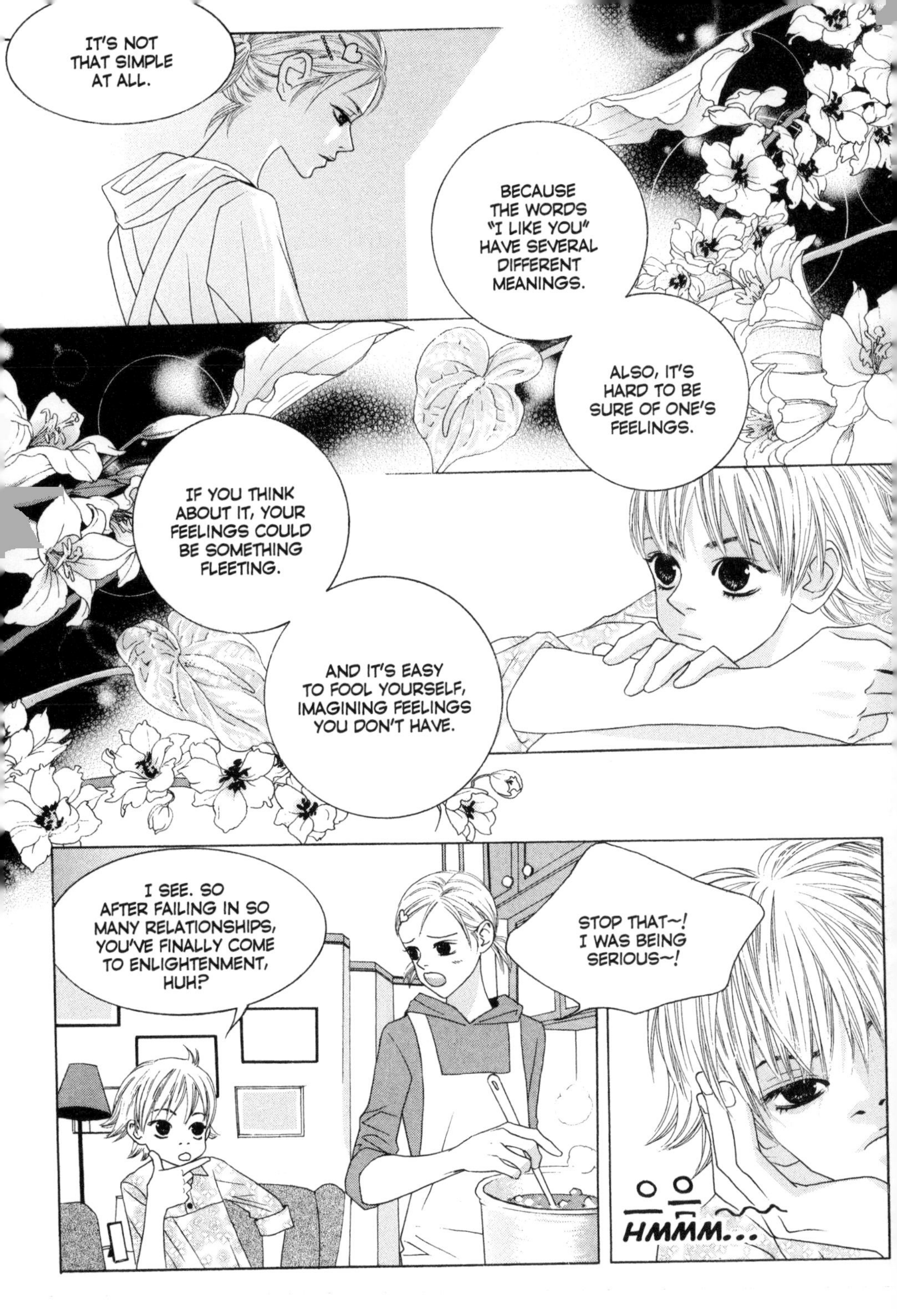
IT'S NOT THAT SIMPLE AT ALL.
BECAUSE THE WORDS "I LIKE YOU" HAVE SEVERAL DIFFERENT MEANINGS.
ALSO, IT'S HARD TO BE SURE OF ONE'S FEELINGS.
IF YOU THINK ABOUT IT, YOUR FEELINGS COULD BE SOMETHING FLEETING.
AND IT'S EASY TO FOOL YOURSELF, IMAGINING FEELINGS YOU DON'T HAVE.
I SEE. SO AFTER FAILING IN SO MANY RELATIONSHIPS, YOU'VE FINALLY COME TO ENLIGHTENMENT, HUH?
STOP THAT~! I WAS BEING SERIOUS~!
으응
HMMM...

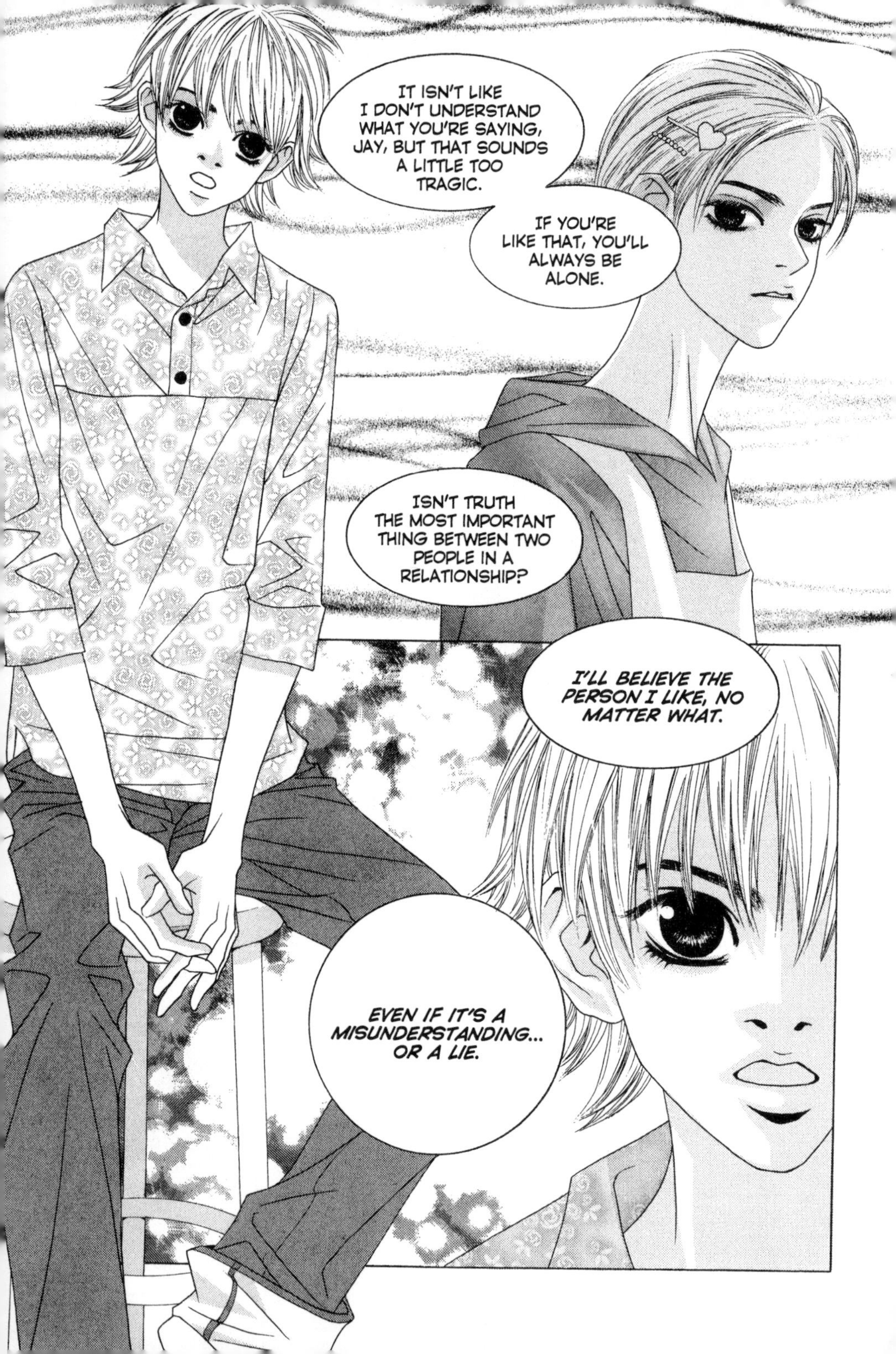
IT ISN'T LIKE I DON'T UNDERSTAND WHAT YOU'RE SAYING, JAY, BUT THAT SOUNDS A LITTLE TOO TRAGIC.
IF YOU'RE LIKE THAT, YOU'LL ALWAYS BE ALONE.
ISN'T TRUTH THE MOST IMPORTANT THING BETWEEN TWO PEOPLE IN A RELATIONSHIP?
I'LL BELIEVE THE PERSON I LIKE, NO MATTER WHAT.
EVEN IF IT'S A MISUNDERSTANDING... OR A LIE.

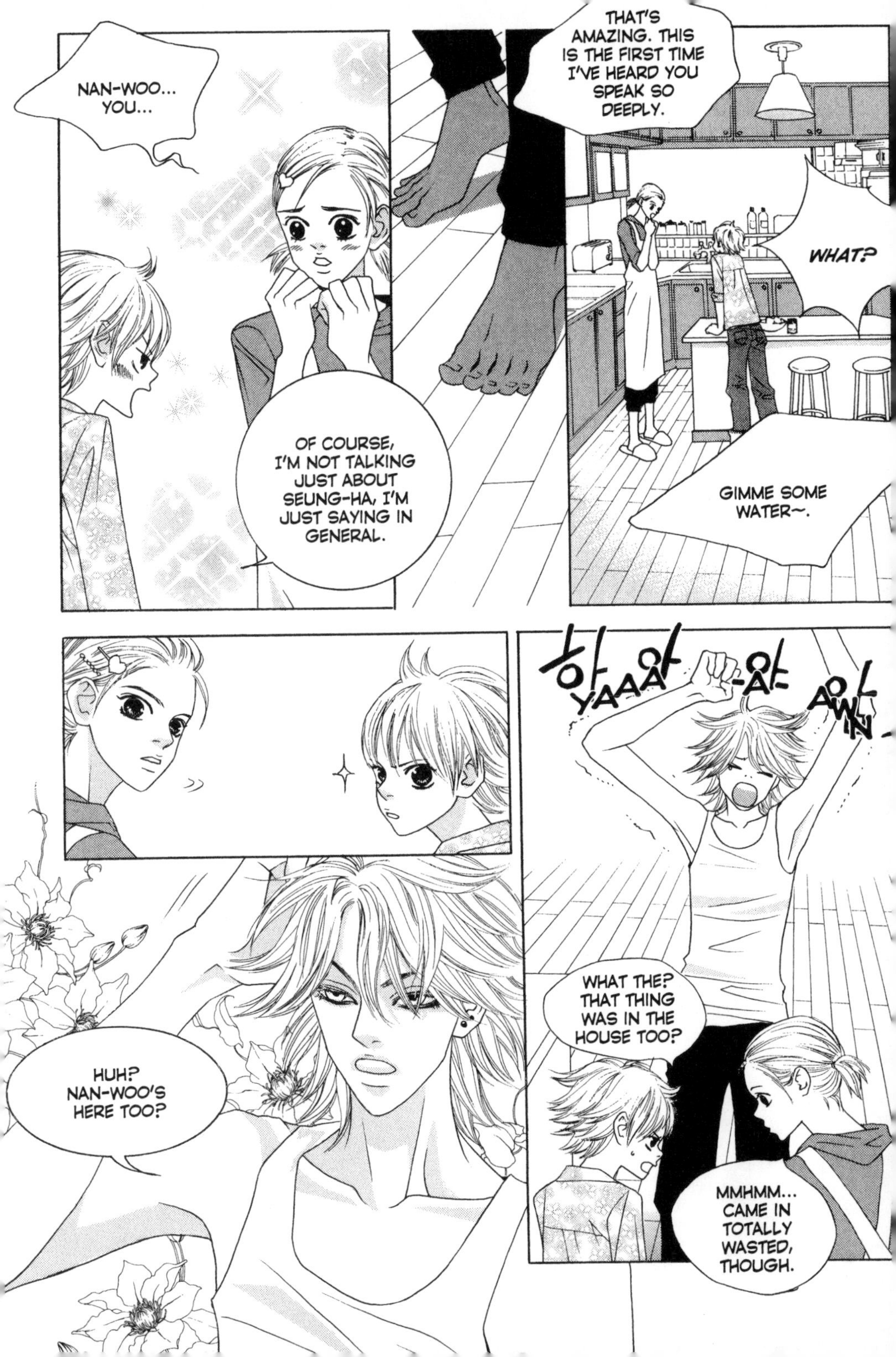
NAN-WOO... YOU...
OF COURSE, I'M NOT TALKING JUST ABOUT SEUNG-HA, I'M JUST SAYING IN GENERAL.
THAT'S AMAZING. THIS IS THE FIRST TIME I'VE HEARD YOU SPEAK SO DEEPLY.
WHAT?
GIMME SOME WATER~.
HUH? NAN-WOO'S HERE TOO?
YAAA-A-AWN
WHAT THE? THAT THING WAS IN THE HOUSE TOO?
MMHMM... CAME IN TOTALLY WASTED, THOUGH.

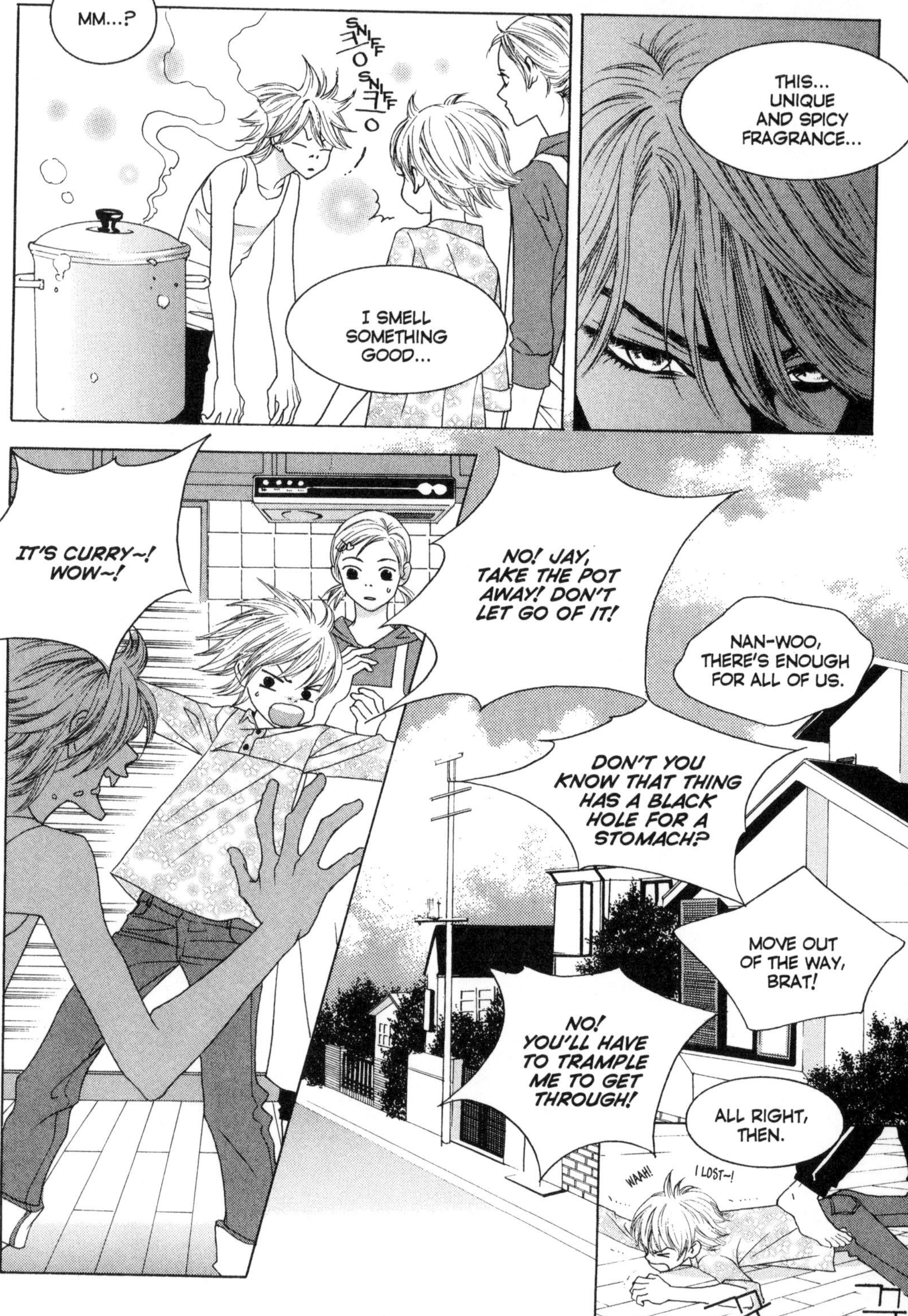
MM...?
SNIFF
SNIFF
I SMELL SOMETHING GOOD...
THIS... UNIQUE AND SPICY FRAGRANCE...
IT'S CURRY~! WOW~!
NO! JAY, TAKE THE POT AWAY! DON'T LET GO OF IT!
NAN-WOO, THERE'S ENOUGH FOR ALL OF US.
DON'T YOU KNOW THAT THING HAS A BLACK HOLE FOR A STOMACH?
MOVE OUT OF THE WAY, BRAT!
NO! YOU'LL HAVE TO TRAMPLE ME TO GET THROUGH!
ALL RIGHT, THEN.
WAAH!
I LOST~!

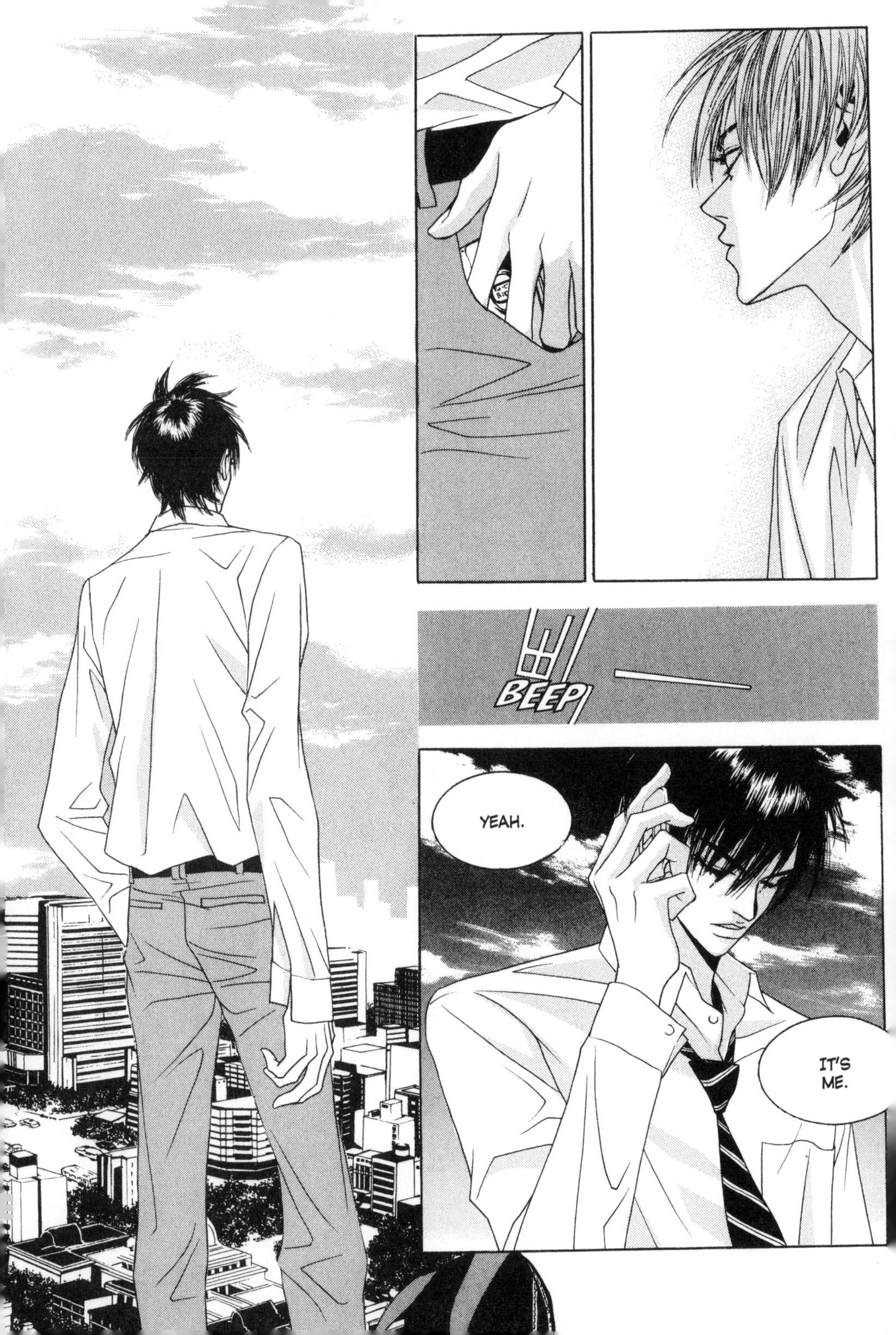
BEEP
YEAH.
IT'S ME.

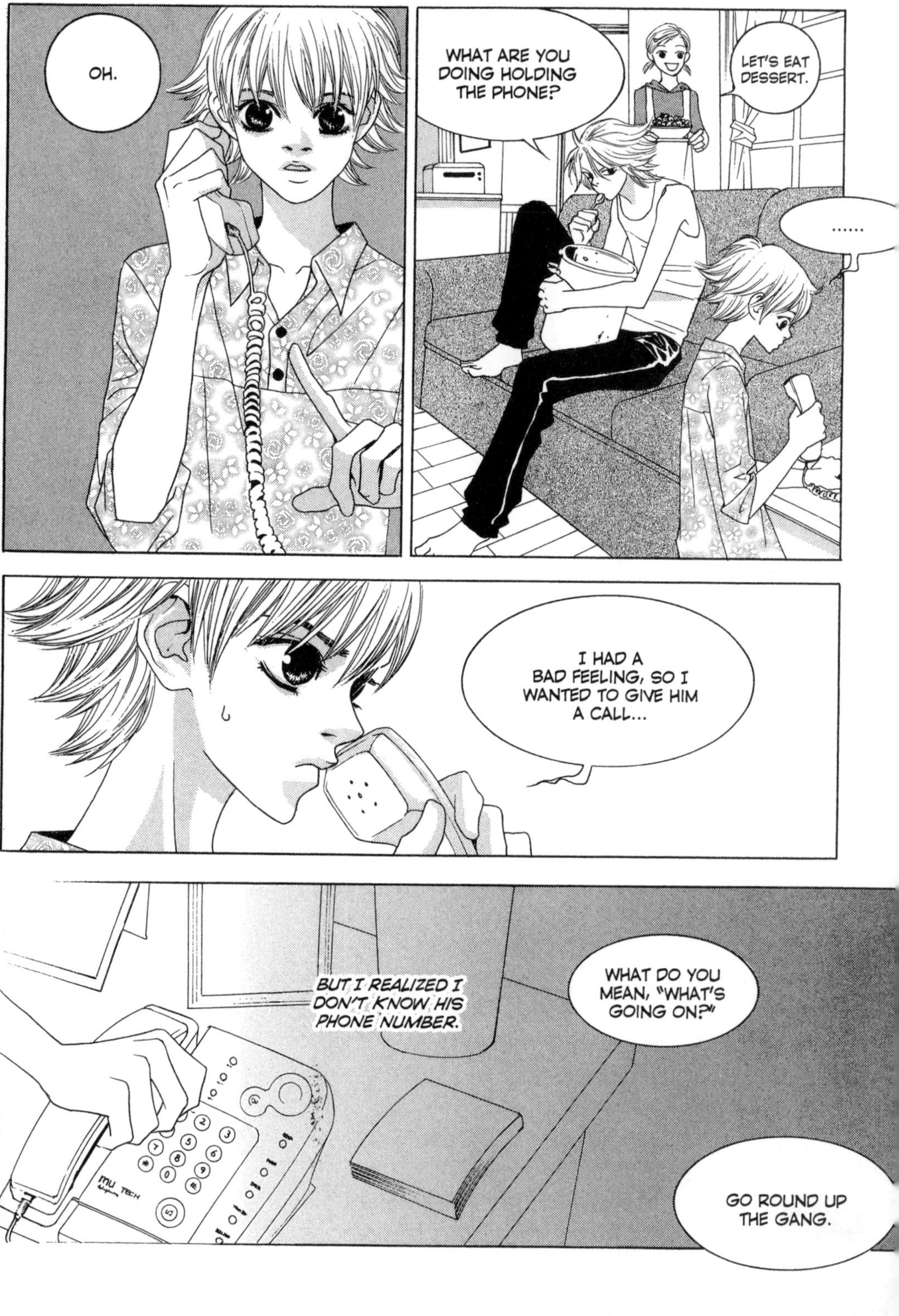

OH.
WHAT ARE YOU DOING HOLDING THE PHONE?
LET'S EAT DESSERT.
......
I HAD A BAD FEELING, SO I WANTED TO GIVE HIM A CALL...
BUT I REALIZED I DON'T KNOW HIS PHONE NUMBER.
WHAT DO YOU MEAN, "WHAT'S GOING ON?"
GO ROUND UP THE GANG.

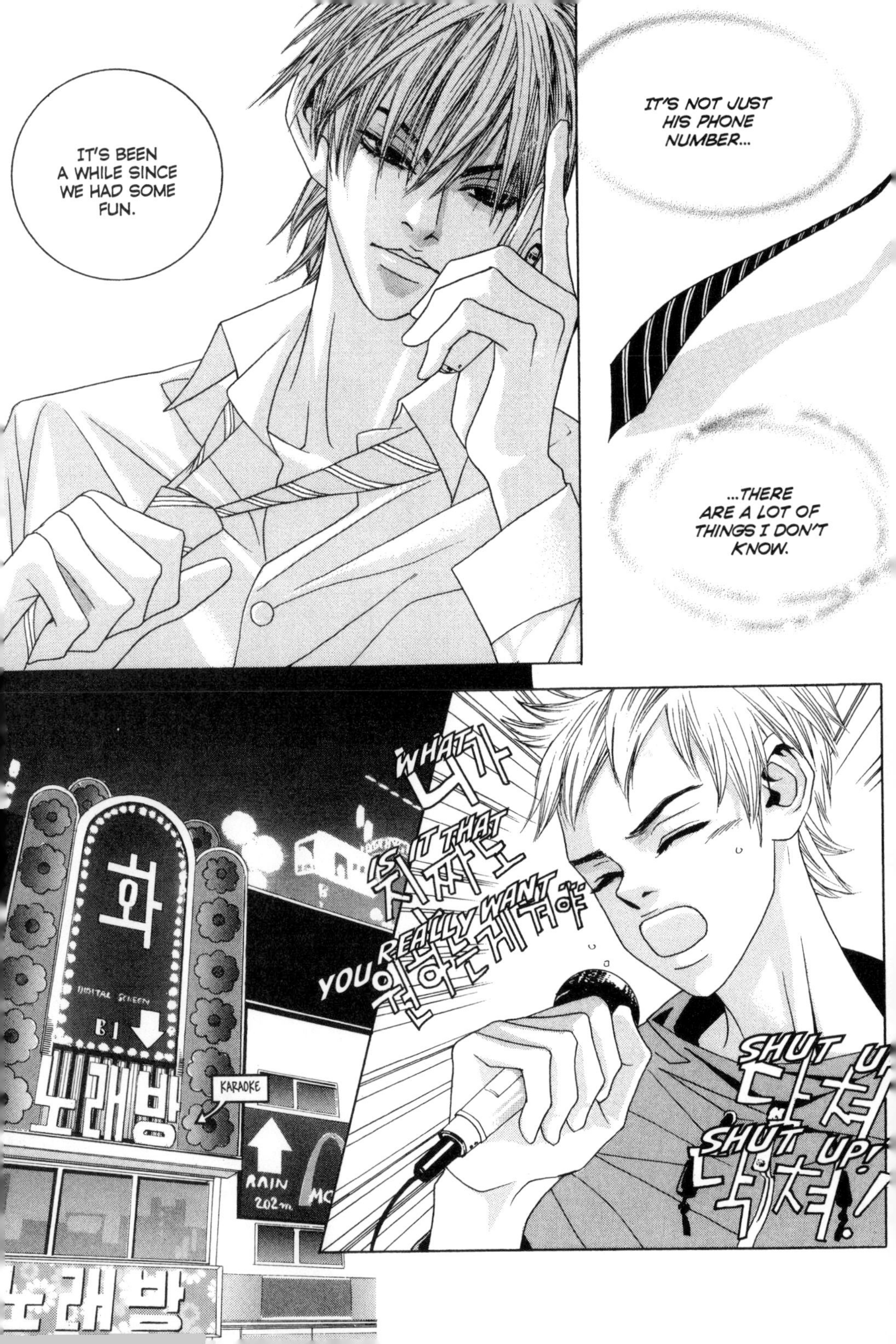
IT'S BEEN A WHILE SINCE WE HAD SOME FUN.
IT'S NOT JUST HIS PHONE NUMBER...
...THERE ARE A LOT OF THINGS I DON'T KNOW.
화
B1
노래방
KARAOKE
RAIN 202m.
노래방
WHAT
IS IT THAT
YOU REALLY WANT
SHUT UP
SHUT UP!

I'M ALL RIGHT!
난 괜찮아

ALL RIGHT
아야

I'M-AAA!
난 괜찮 낭

TODAY I'LL JUST HOLD IT IN!
오늘도 내가 참는다~~

AAAAAA

AAAH~

I'LL NEVER FALL~~~
절대로 쓰러지지 안아아~

That's pretty pathetic.

What's wrong with Chan-Gyu today?

He's not letting go of the mic!

Someone stop him.

Let us sing too, dammit.

STOP IT!

TT POW

WHO
와

-OOO-
와

GOOD JOB~♡

YOU'RE AMAZING!

-A~

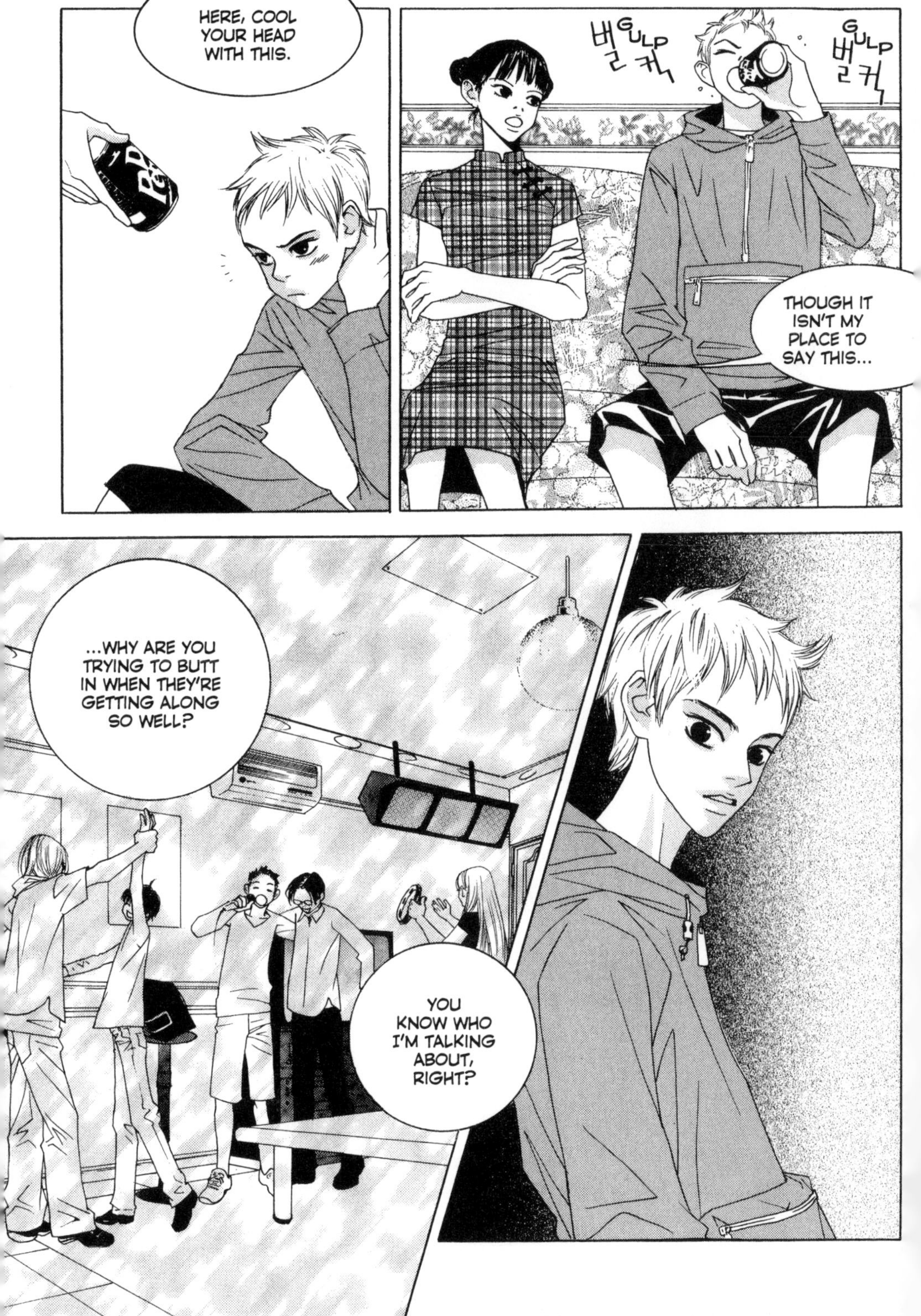
HERE, COOL YOUR HEAD WITH THIS.
벌컥 GULP
GULP 벌컥
THOUGH IT ISN'T MY PLACE TO SAY THIS...
...WHY ARE YOU TRYING TO BUTT IN WHEN THEY'RE GETTING ALONG SO WELL?
YOU KNOW WHO I'M TALKING ABOUT, RIGHT?

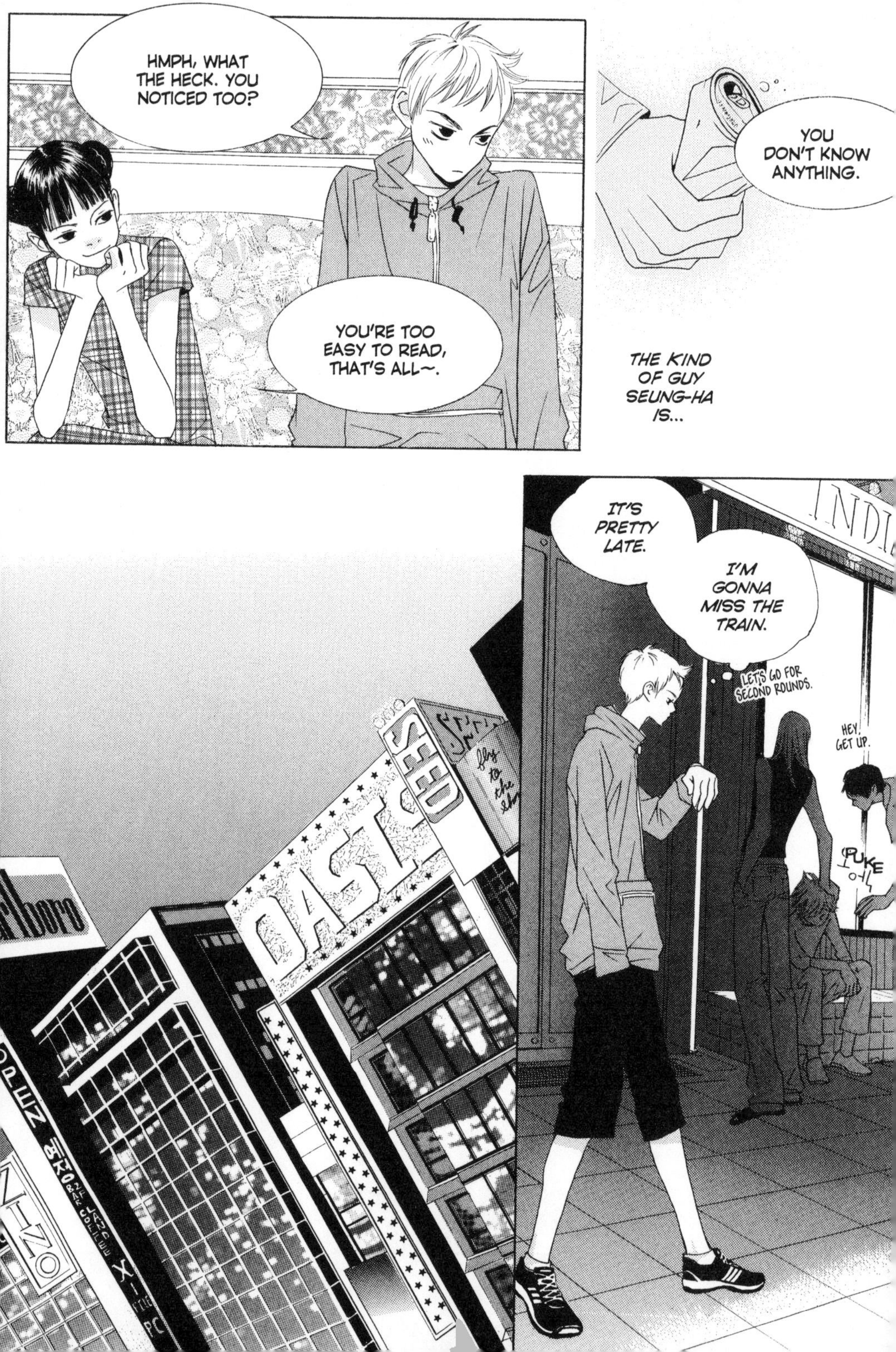
HMPH, WHAT THE HECK. YOU NOTICED TOO?
YOU'RE TOO EASY TO READ, THAT'S ALL~.
YOU DON'T KNOW ANYTHING.
THE KIND OF GUY SEUNG-HA IS...
SEED
IT'S PRETTY LATE.
I'M GONNA MISS THE TRAIN.
LET'S GO FOR SECOND ROUNDS.
HEY, GET UP.
PUKE

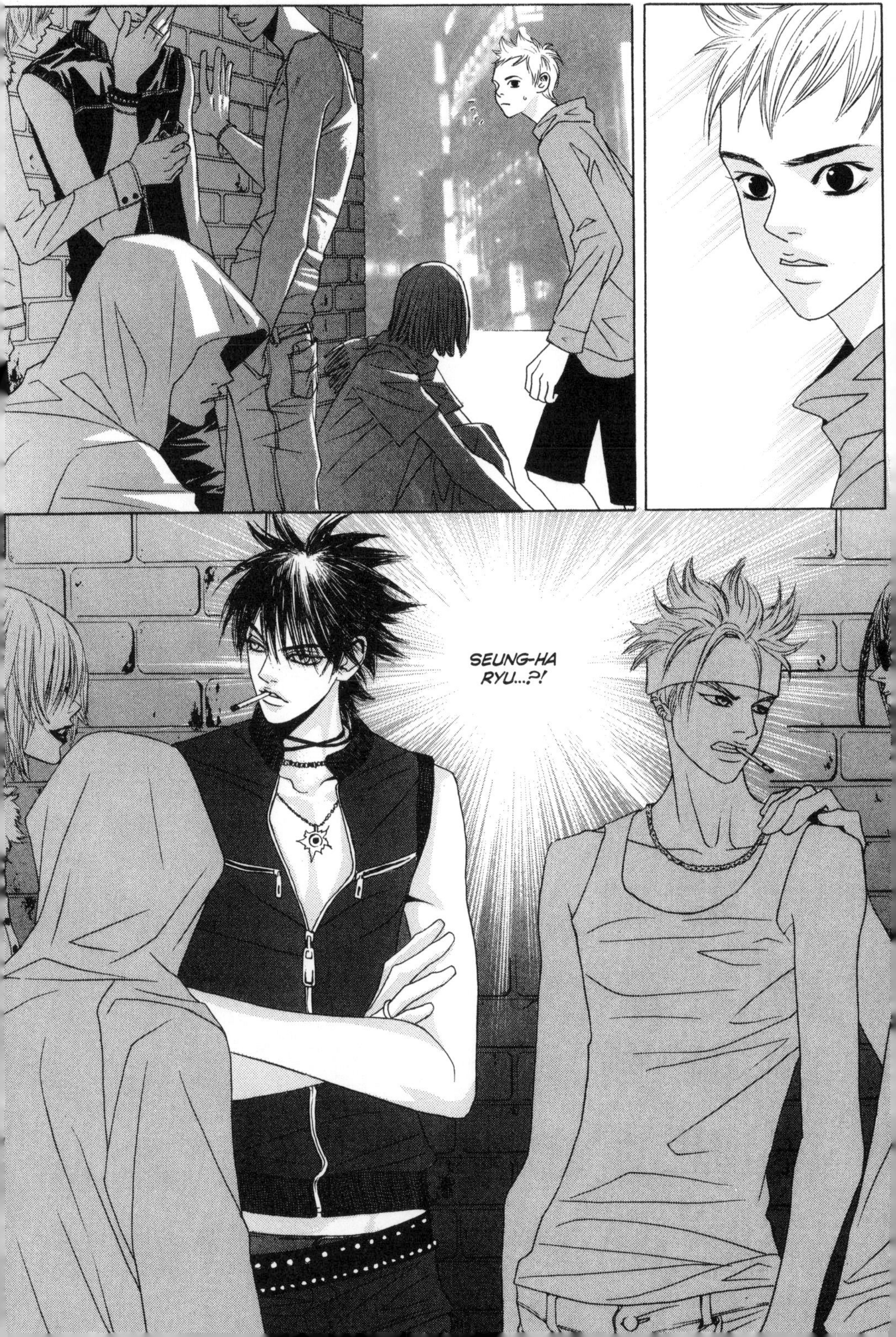
SEUNG-HA
RYU...?!

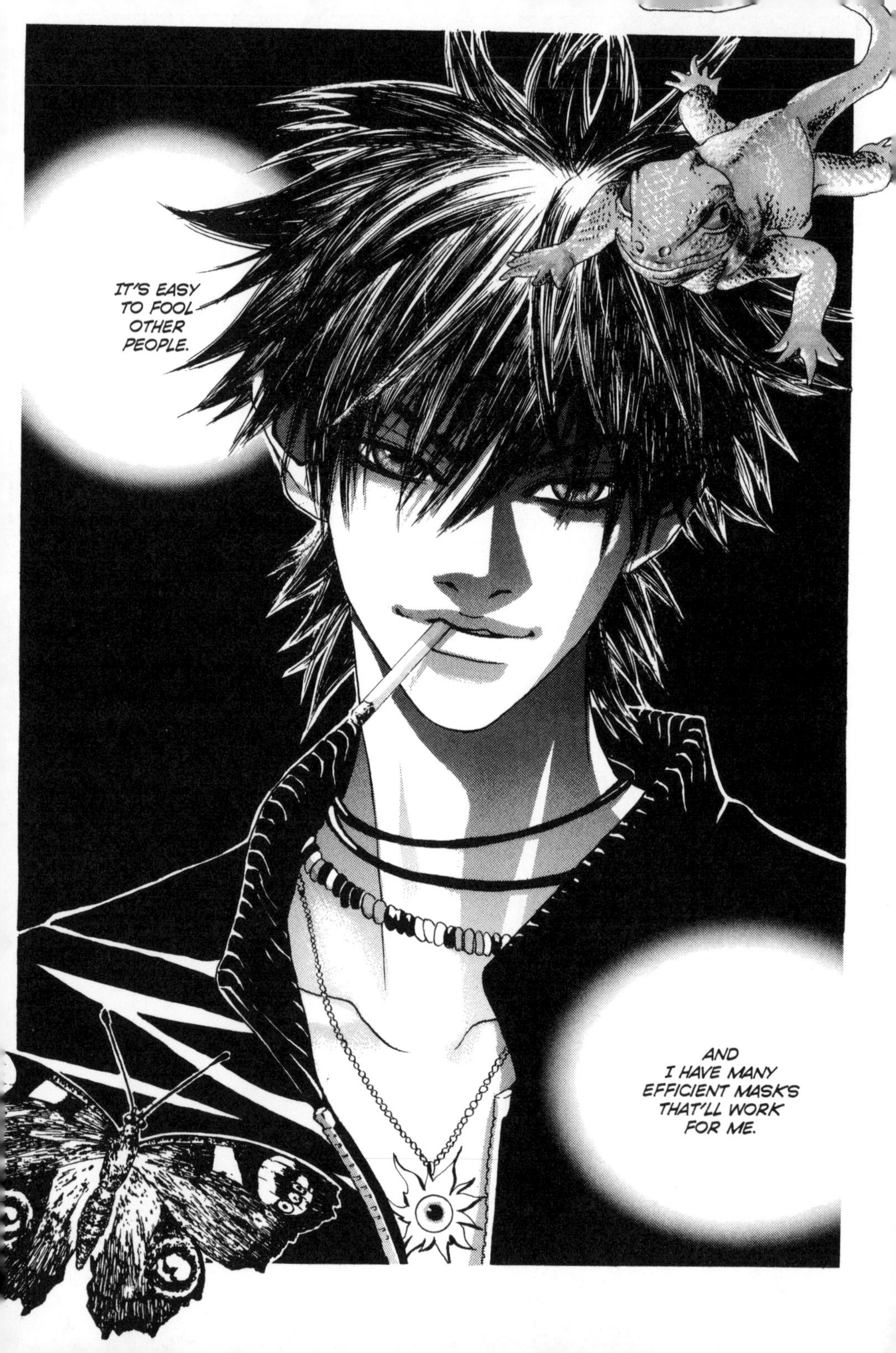
IT'S EASY TO FOOL OTHER PEOPLE.
AND I HAVE MANY EFFICIENT MASKS THAT'LL WORK FOR ME.

THEY ARE VERY DELICATE AND BEAUTIFUL, AND THEY FIT ME PERFECTLY.

AND IF I CONTINUE TO REPEAT MYSELF, IT'S EASY TO SWITCH FROM MASK TO MASK WITHOUT SO MUCH AS A THOUGHT.

I ALWAYS HAVE THE APPROPRIATE EXPRESSIONS AND A FLAWLESS ATTITUDE, PERFECT FOR ANY TEXTBOOK.

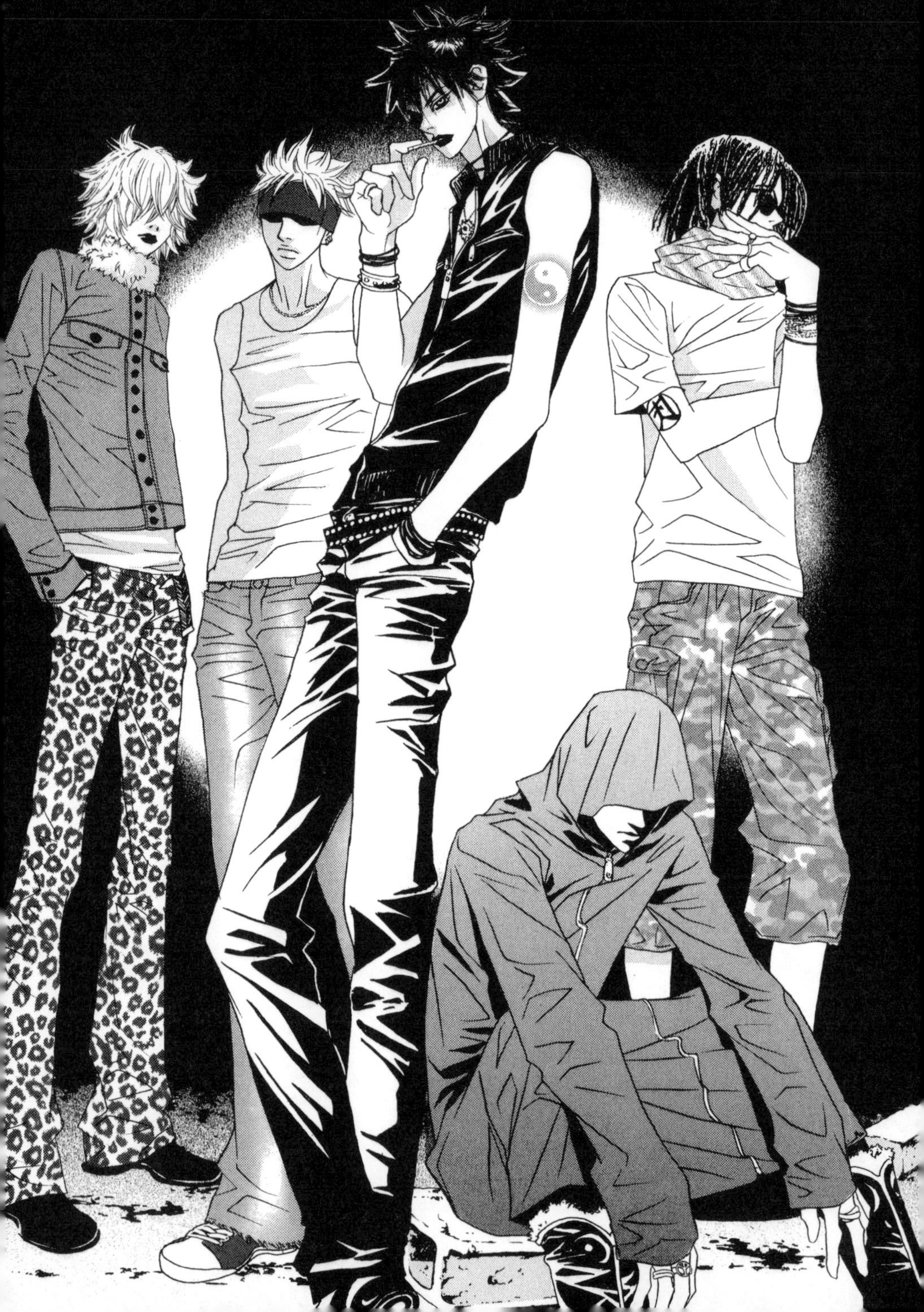

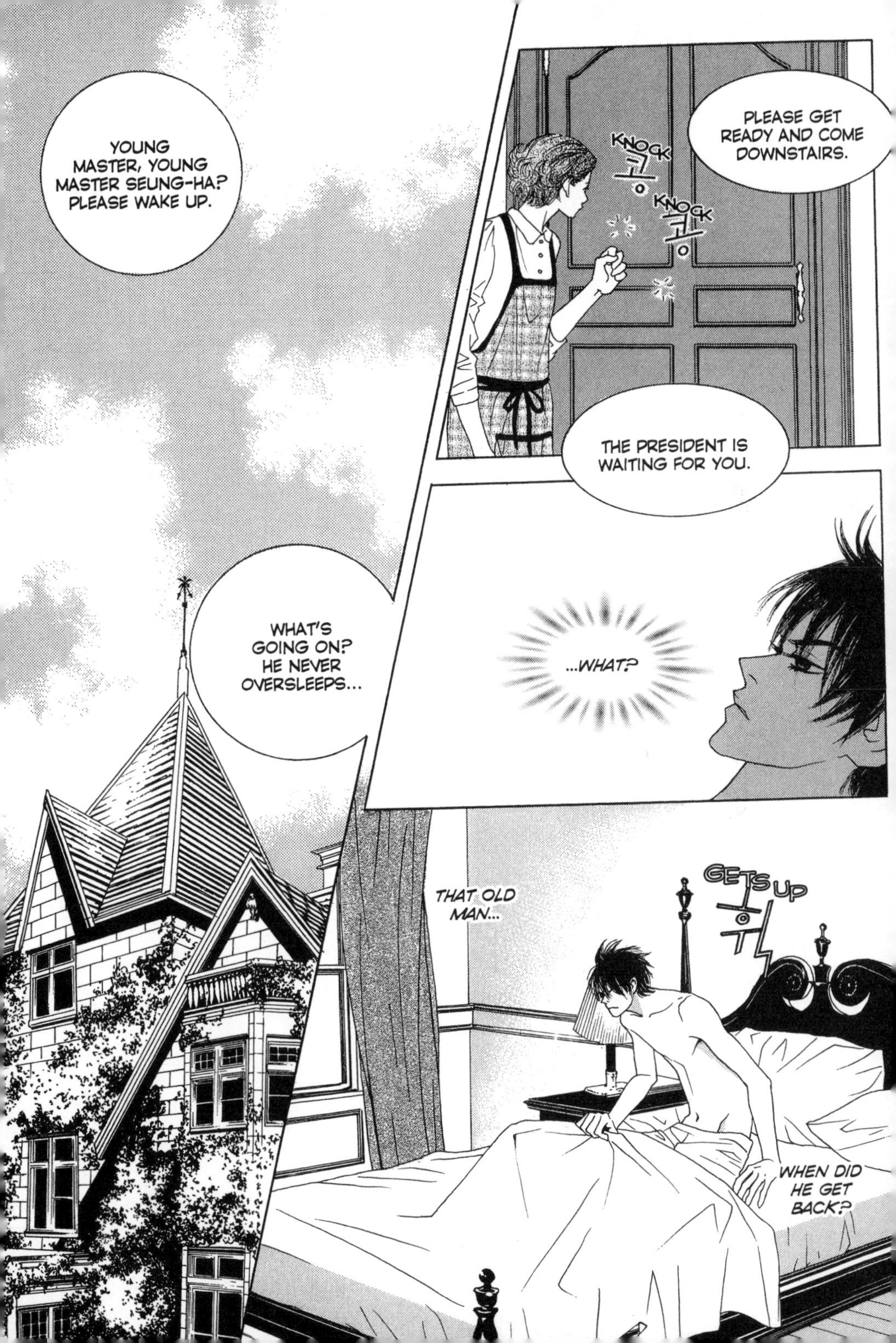

YOUNG MASTER, YOUNG MASTER SEUNG-HA? PLEASE WAKE UP.
WHAT'S GOING ON? HE NEVER OVERSLEEPS...
KNOCK
KNOCK
PLEASE GET READY AND COME DOWNSTAIRS.
THE PRESIDENT IS WAITING FOR YOU.
...WHAT?
THAT OLD MAN...
GETS UP
WHEN DID HE GET BACK?

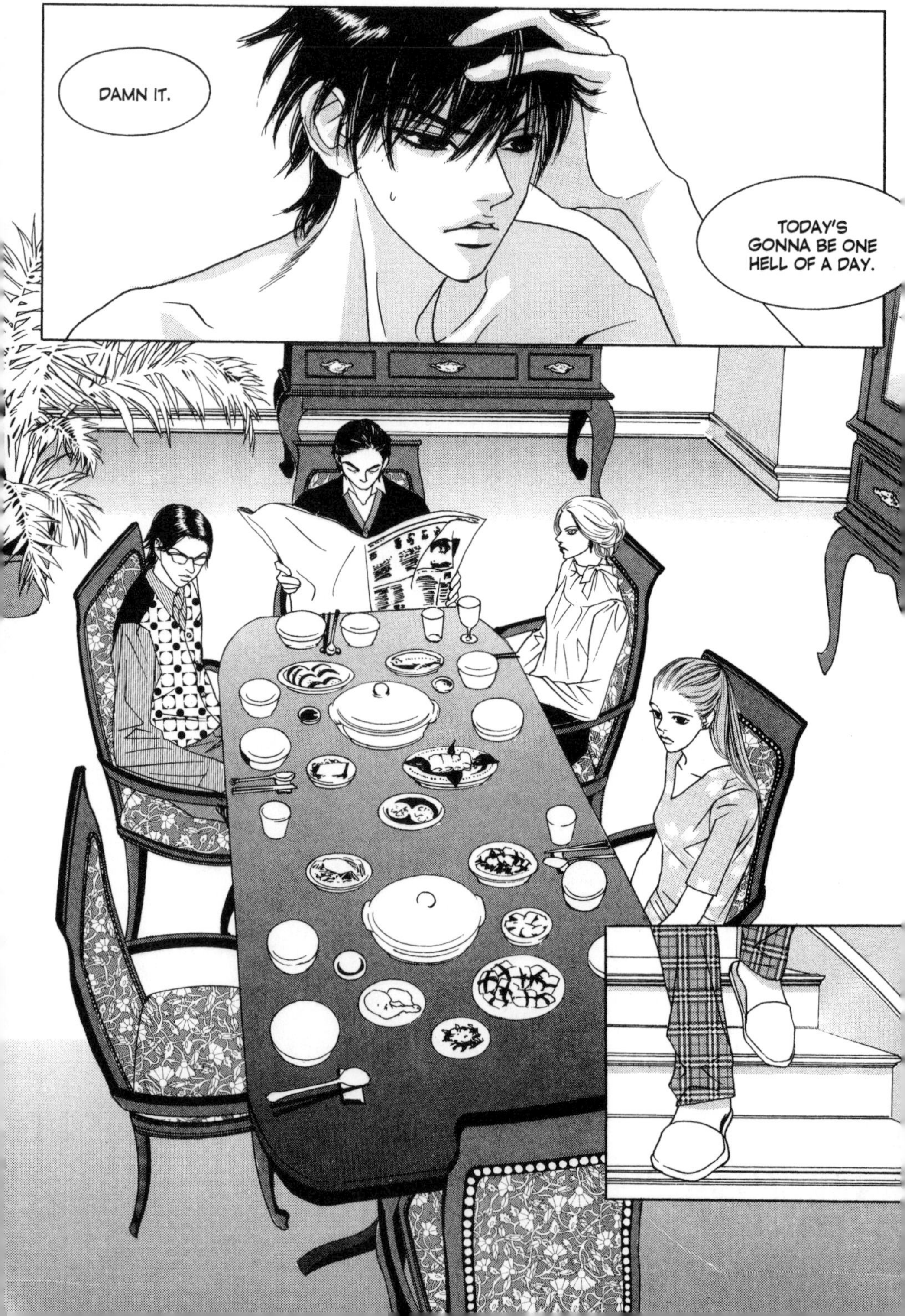
DAMN IT.
TODAY'S GONNA BE ONE HELL OF A DAY.

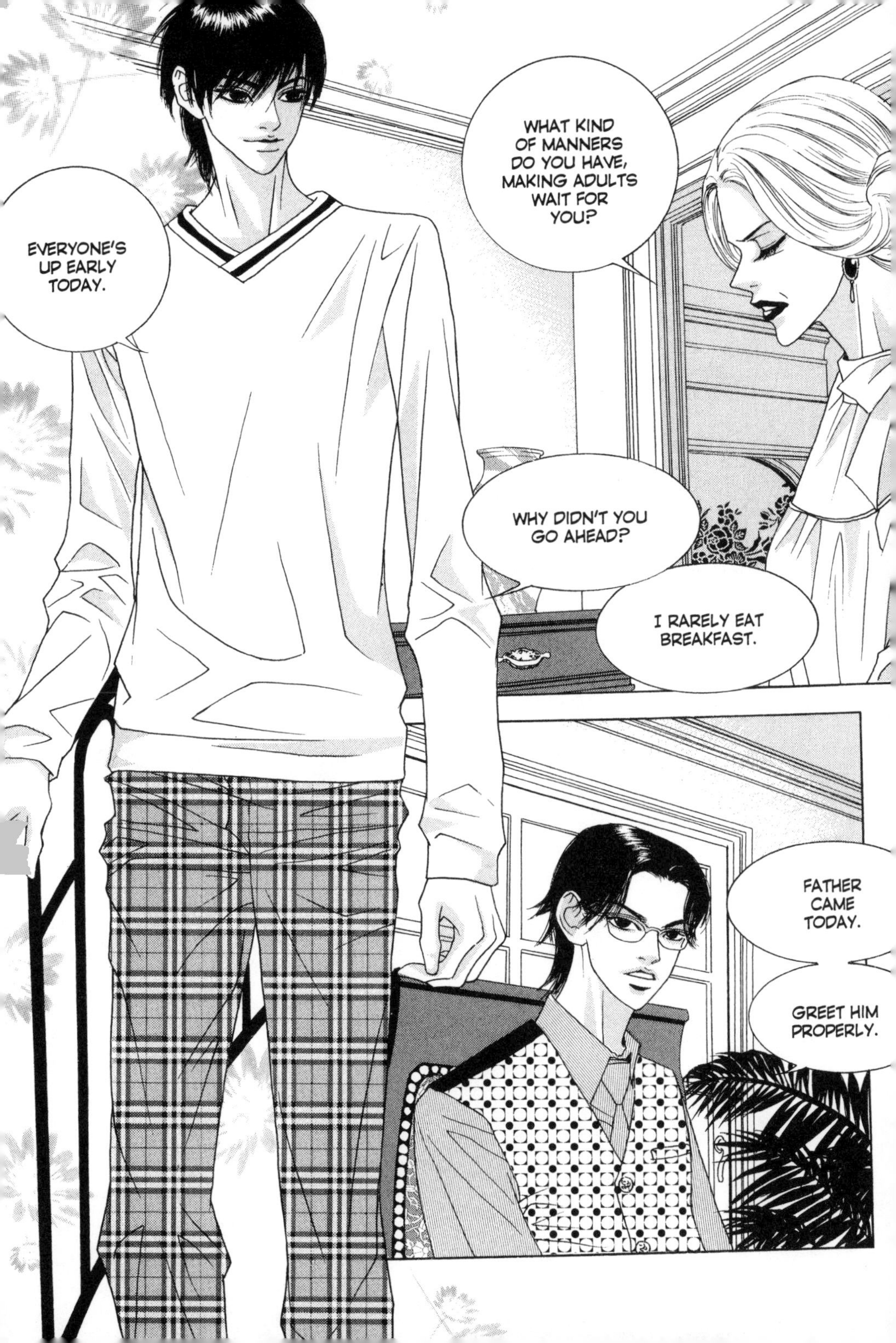
EVERYONE'S UP EARLY TODAY.
WHAT KIND OF MANNERS DO YOU HAVE, MAKING ADULTS WAIT FOR YOU?
WHY DIDN'T YOU GO AHEAD?
I RARELY EAT BREAKFAST.
FATHER CAME TODAY.
GREET HIM PROPERLY.

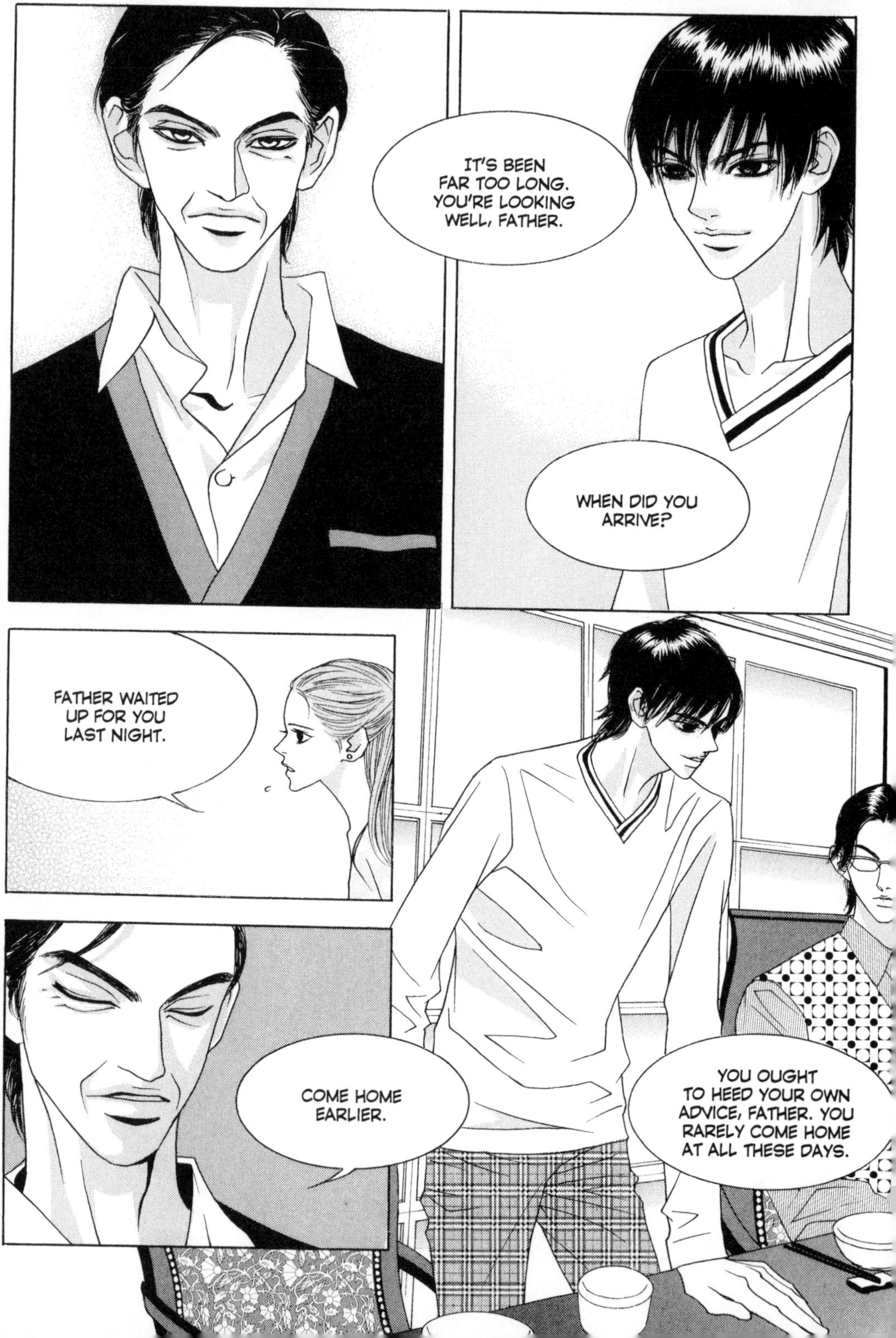
IT'S BEEN FAR TOO LONG. YOU'RE LOOKING WELL, FATHER.
WHEN DID YOU ARRIVE?
FATHER WAITED UP FOR YOU LAST NIGHT.
COME HOME EARLIER.
YOU OUGHT TO HEED YOUR OWN ADVICE, FATHER. YOU RARELY COME HOME AT ALL THESE DAYS.

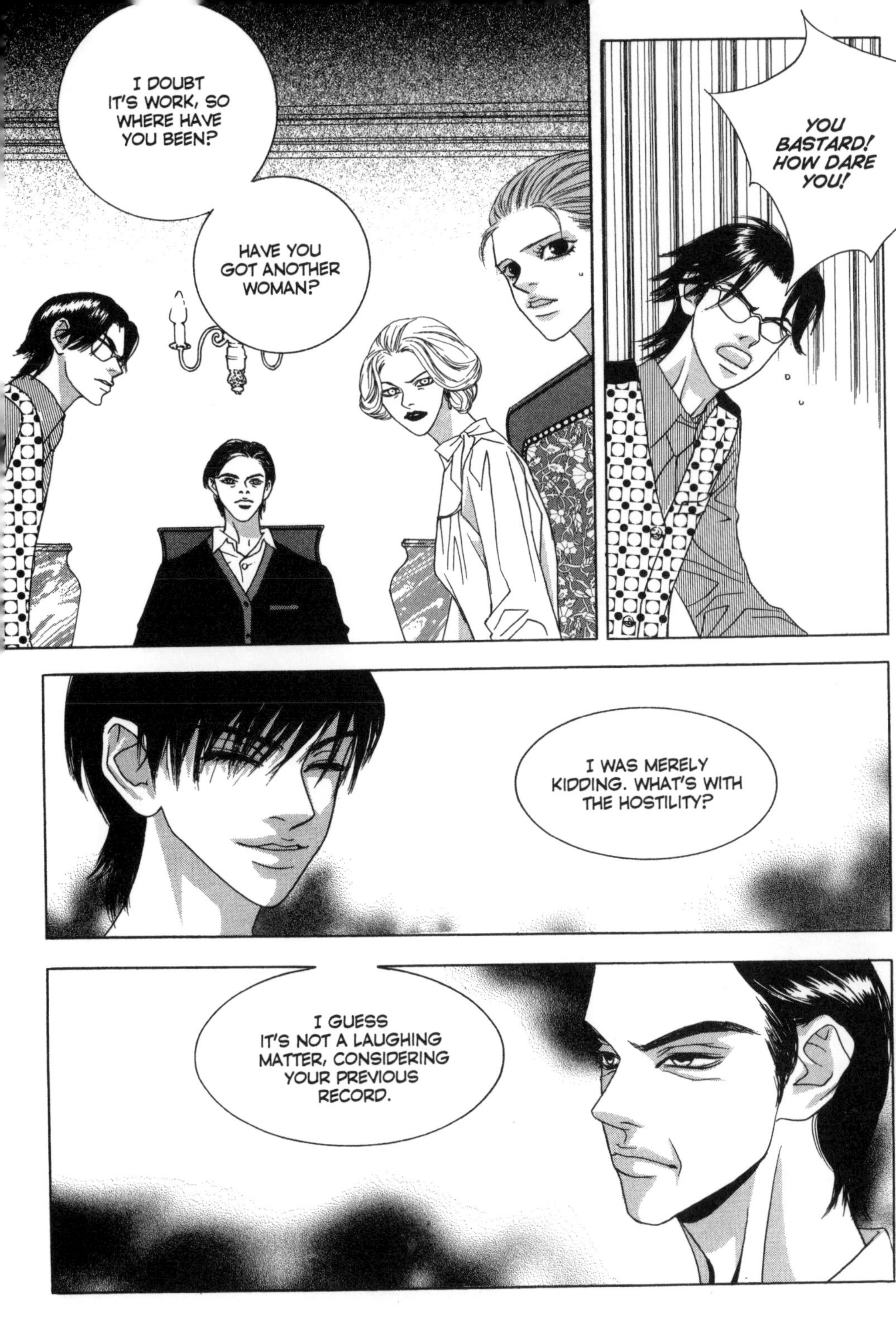
I DOUBT IT'S WORK, SO WHERE HAVE YOU BEEN?
HAVE YOU GOT ANOTHER WOMAN?
YOU BASTARD! HOW DARE YOU!
I WAS MERELY KIDDING. WHAT'S WITH THE HOSTILITY?
I GUESS IT'S NOT A LAUGHING MATTER, CONSIDERING YOUR PREVIOUS RECORD.

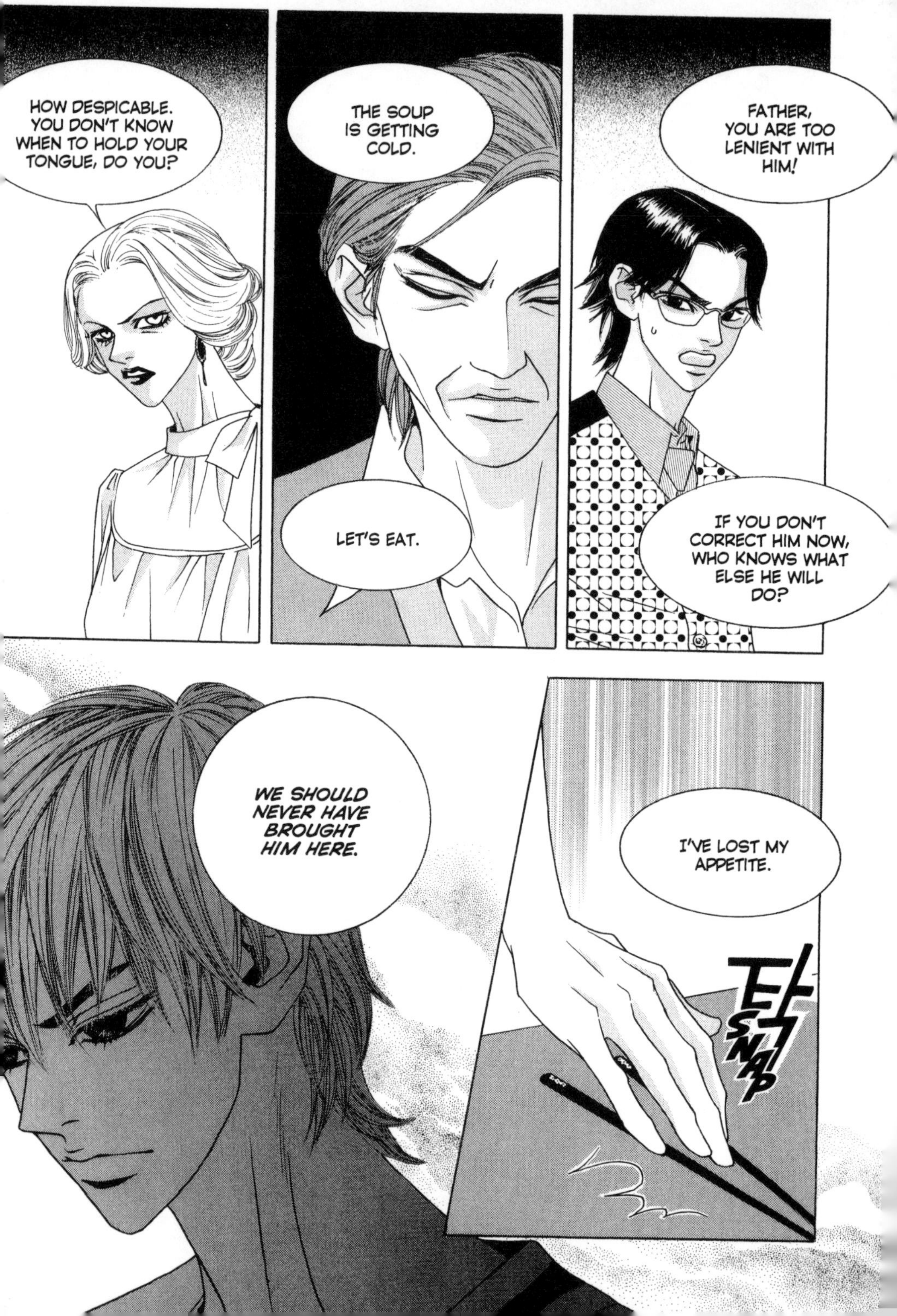
HOW DESPICABLE. YOU DON'T KNOW WHEN TO HOLD YOUR TONGUE, DO YOU?
THE SOUP IS GETTING COLD.
LET'S EAT.
FATHER, YOU ARE TOO LENIENT WITH HIM!
IF YOU DON'T CORRECT HIM NOW, WHO KNOWS WHAT ELSE HE WILL DO?
WE SHOULD NEVER HAVE BROUGHT HIM HERE.
I'VE LOST MY APPETITE.
탁 SNAP

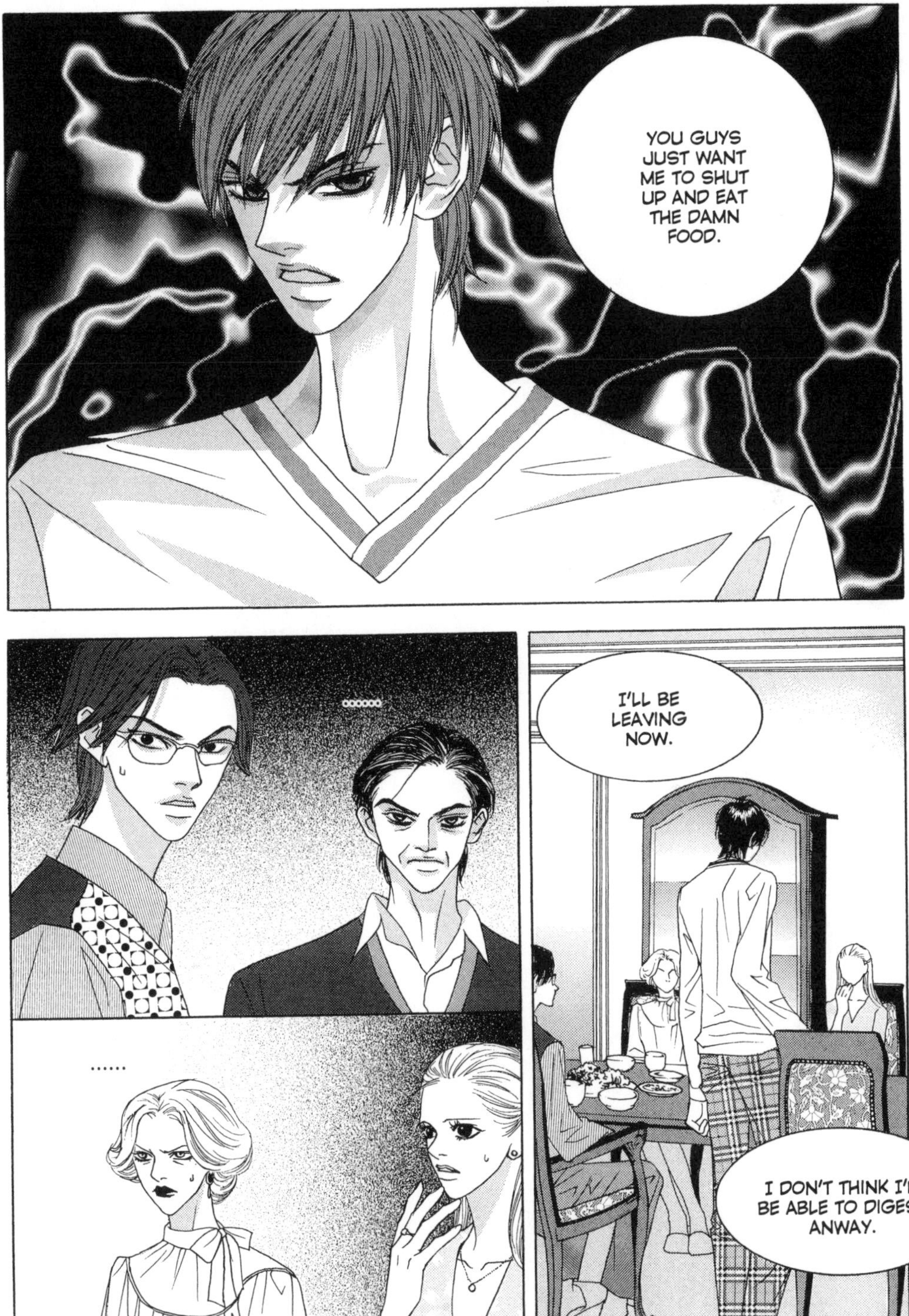
YOU GUYS JUST WANT ME TO SHUT UP AND EAT THE DAMN FOOD.
......
......
I'LL BE LEAVING NOW.
I DON'T THINK I'D BE ABLE TO DIGEST ANWAY.

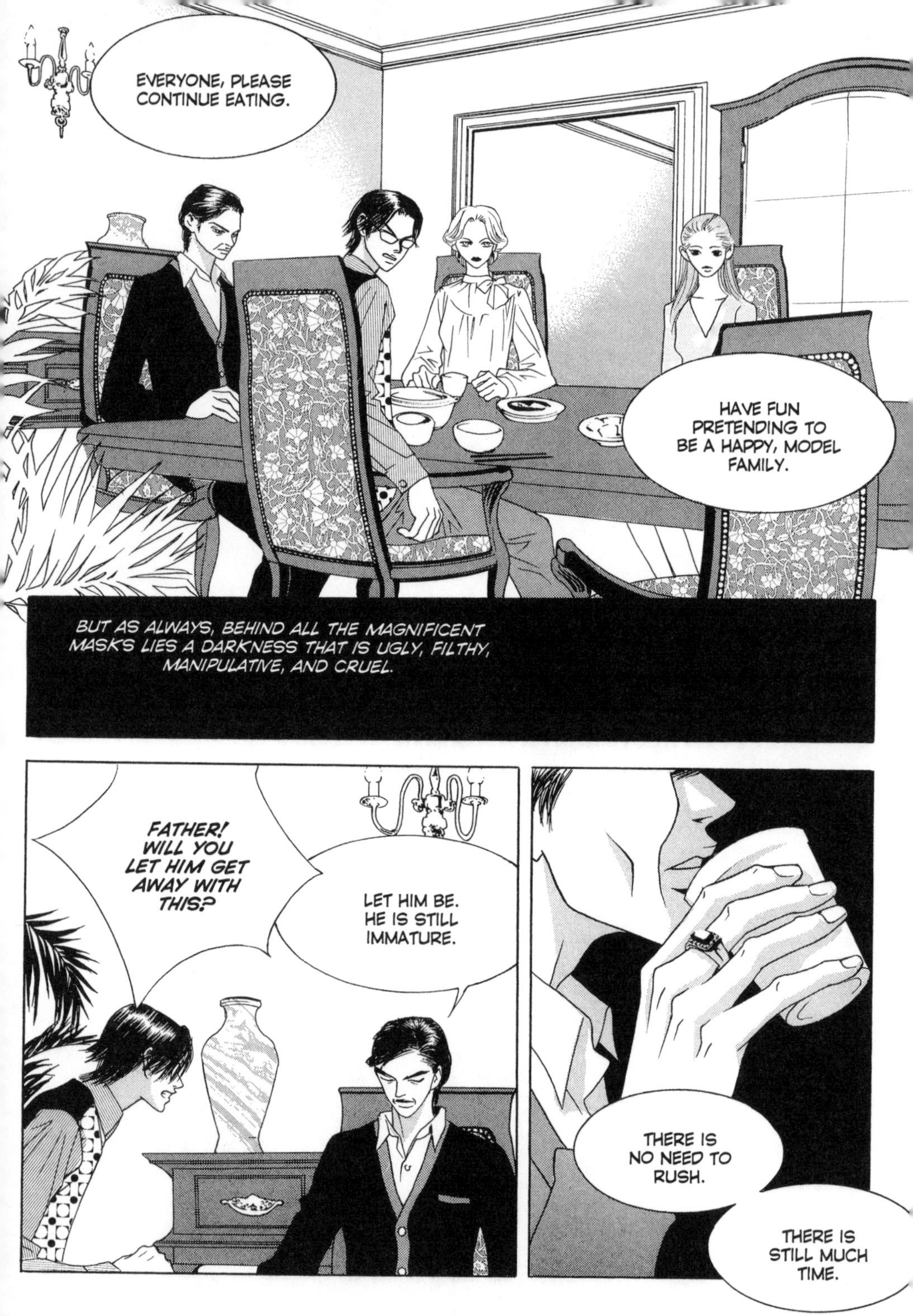
EVERYONE, PLEASE CONTINUE EATING.
HAVE FUN PRETENDING TO BE A HAPPY, MODEL FAMILY.
BUT AS ALWAYS, BEHIND ALL THE MAGNIFICENT MASKS LIES A DARKNESS THAT IS UGLY, FILTHY, MANIPULATIVE, AND CRUEL.
FATHER! WILL YOU LET HIM GET AWAY WITH THIS?
LET HIM BE. HE IS STILL IMMATURE.
THERE IS NO NEED TO RUSH.
THERE IS STILL MUCH TIME.

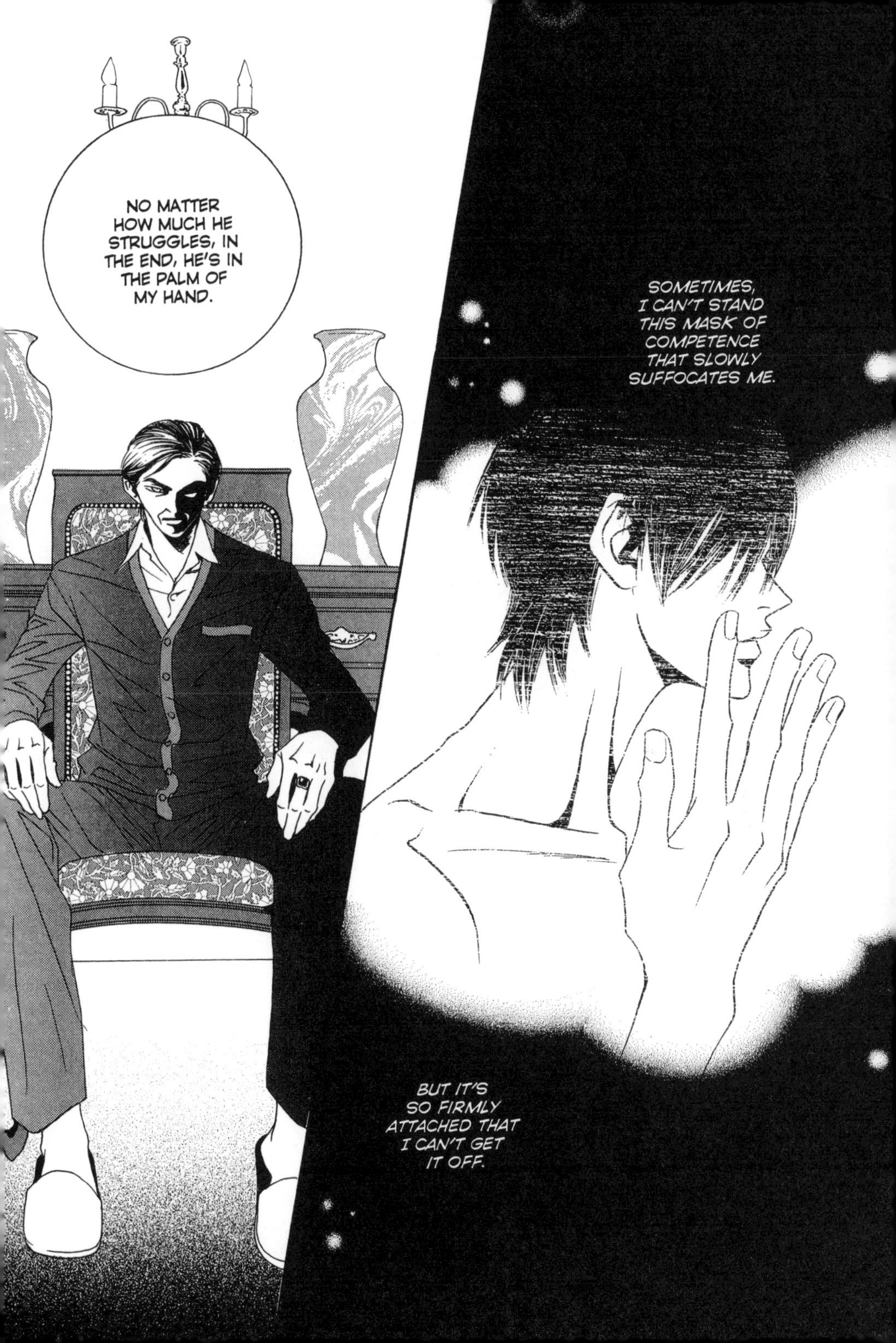
NO MATTER HOW MUCH HE STRUGGLES, IN THE END, HE'S IN THE PALM OF MY HAND.
SOMETIMES, I CAN'T STAND THIS MASK OF COMPETENCE THAT SLOWLY SUFFOCATES ME.
BUT IT'S SO FIRMLY ATTACHED THAT I CAN'T GET IT OFF.

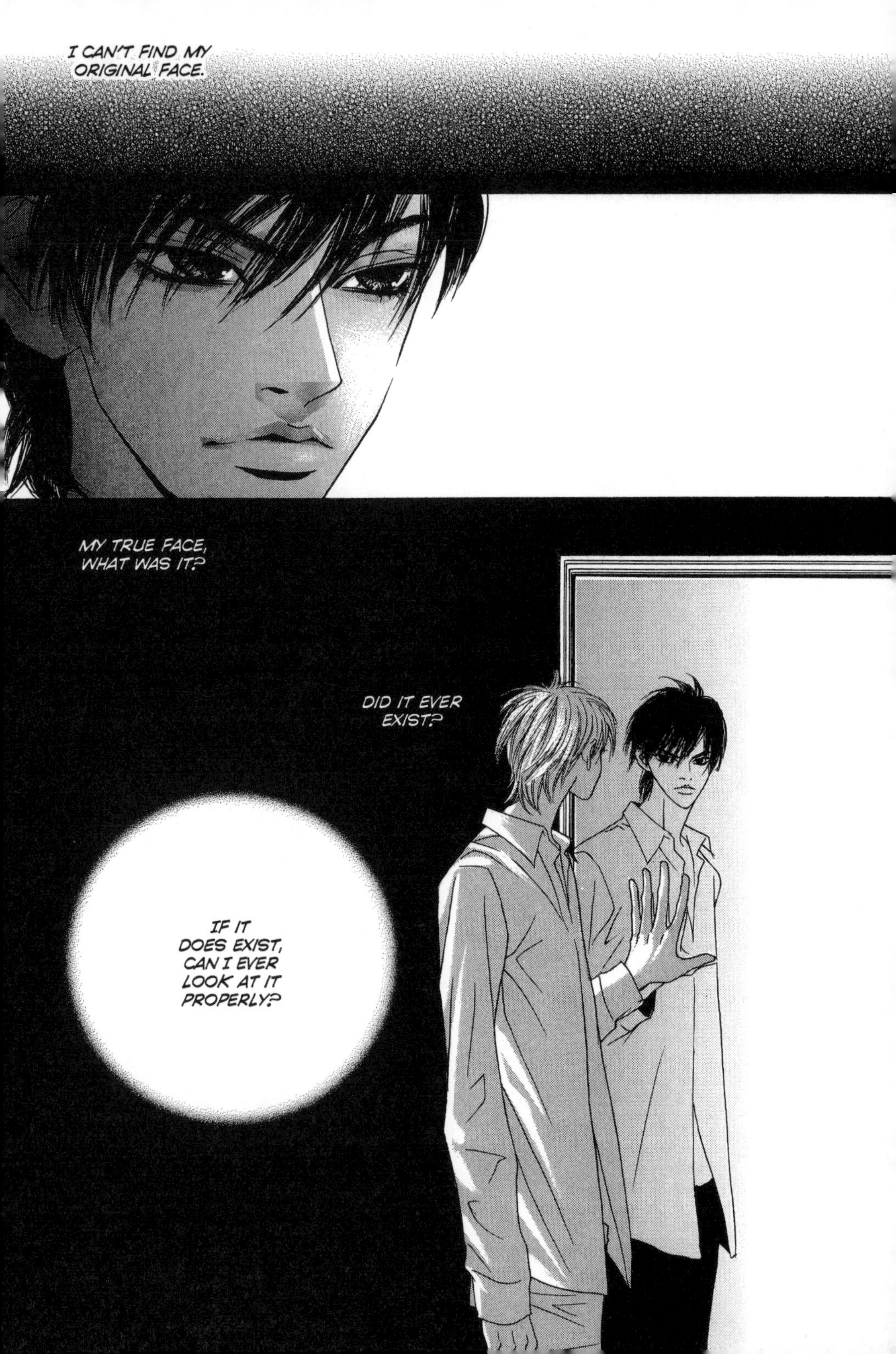
I CAN'T FIND MY ORIGINAL FACE.
MY TRUE FACE, WHAT WAS IT?
DID IT EVER EXIST?
IF IT DOES EXIST, CAN I EVER LOOK AT IT PROPERLY?

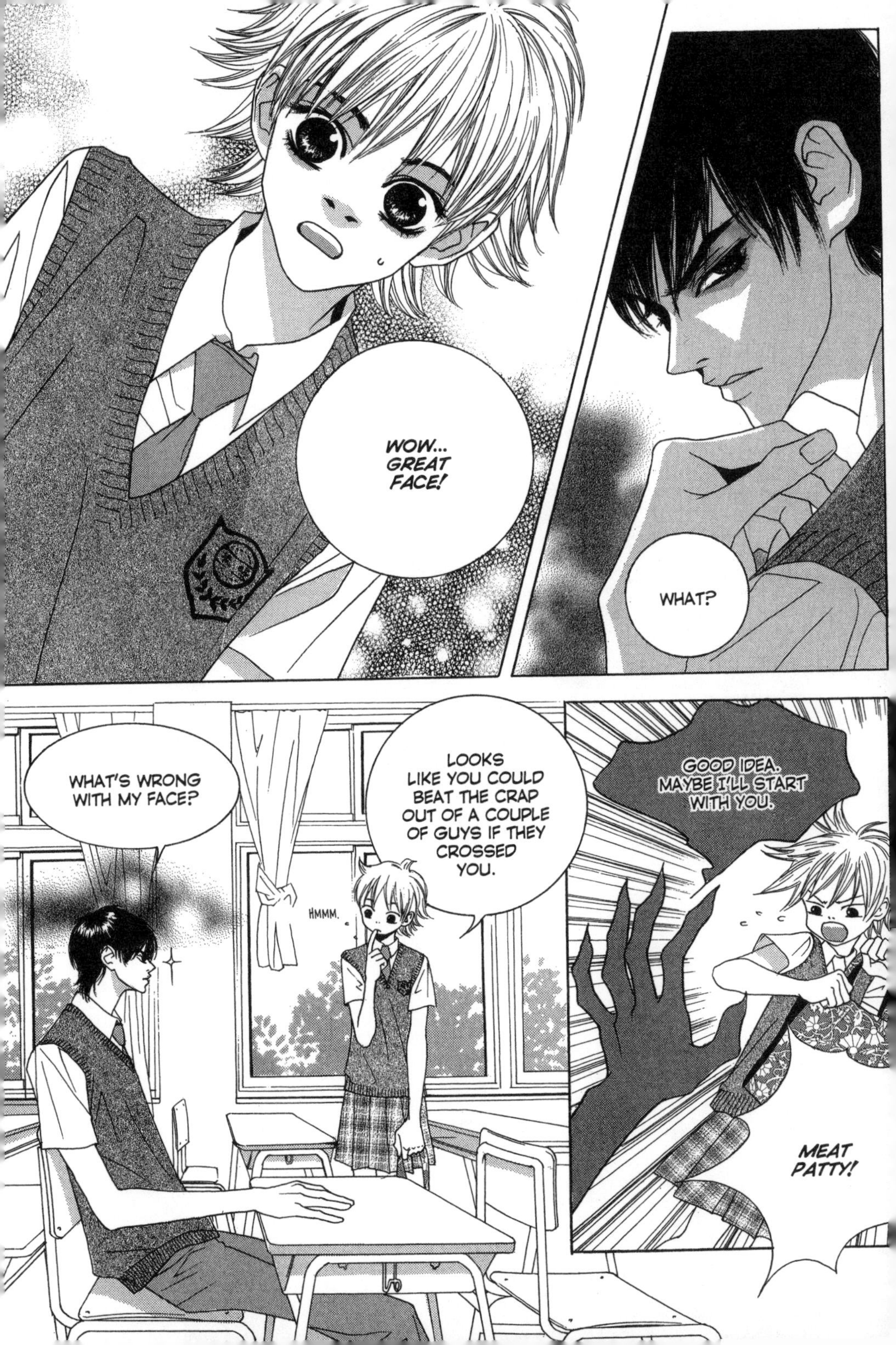
WOW... GREAT FACE!
WHAT?
WHAT'S WRONG WITH MY FACE?
HMMM.
LOOKS LIKE YOU COULD BEAT THE CRAP OUT OF A COUPLE OF GUYS IF THEY CROSSED YOU.
GOOD IDEA. MAYBE I'LL START WITH YOU.
MEAT PATTY!

WHAT?!

I BROUGHT A MEAT PATTY FOR LUNCH TODAY! IF I GO DOWN, THE FOOD GOES DOWN WITH ME! I'LL EAT IT ALL BEFORE I DIE!

SHE IS SO IMMATURE.

YOU AREN'T ANGRY ANYMORE?

WHY? DID YOU DO SOMETHING BEHIND MY BACK AGAIN?

WELL, IT'S JUST THAT...

WHY, YOU BASTARD.

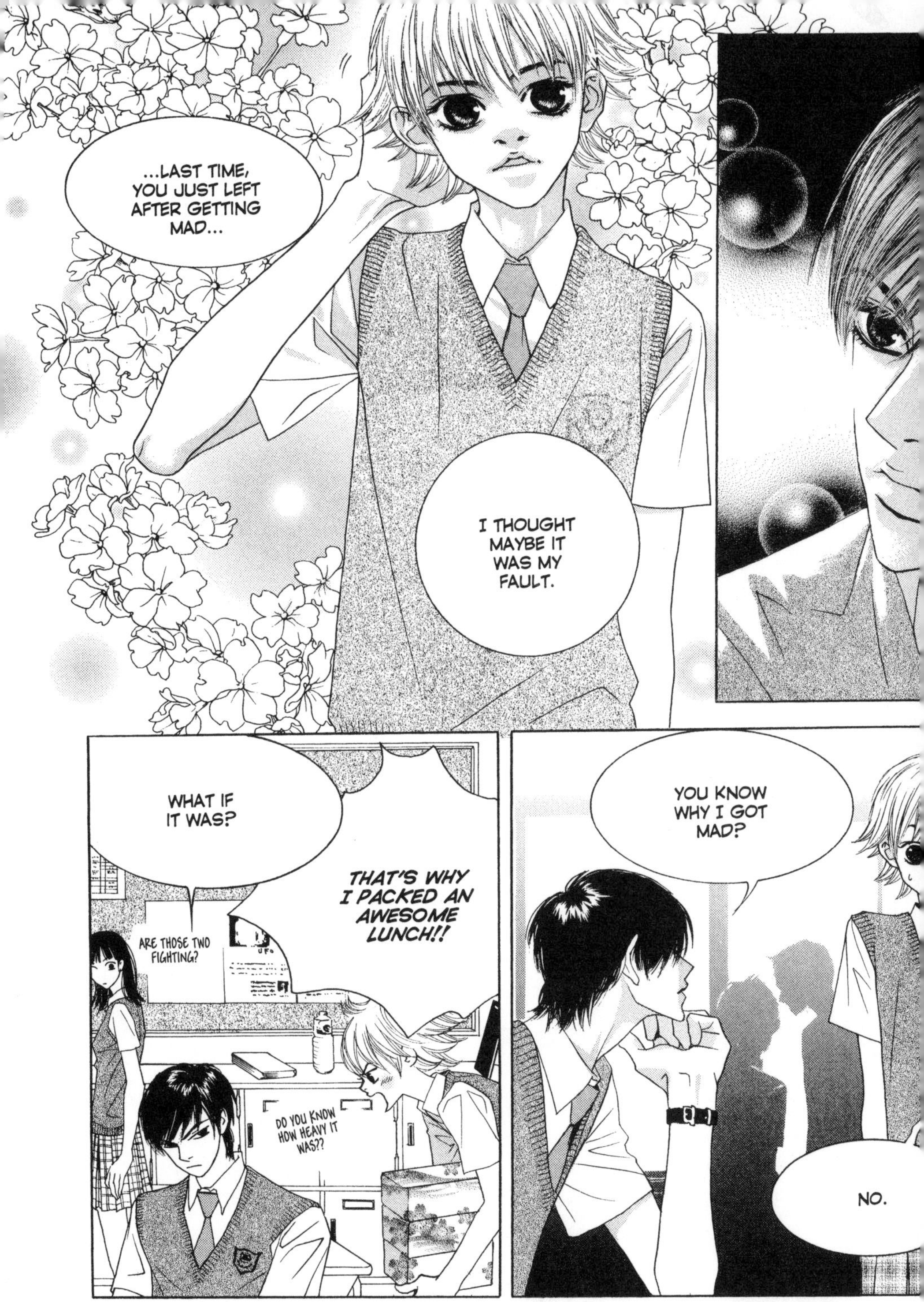
...LAST TIME, YOU JUST LEFT AFTER GETTING MAD...
I THOUGHT MAYBE IT WAS MY FAULT.
WHAT IF IT WAS?
THAT'S WHY I PACKED AN AWESOME LUNCH!!
ARE THOSE TWO FIGHTING?
DO YOU KNOW HOW HEAVY IT WAS??
YOU KNOW WHY I GOT MAD?
NO.

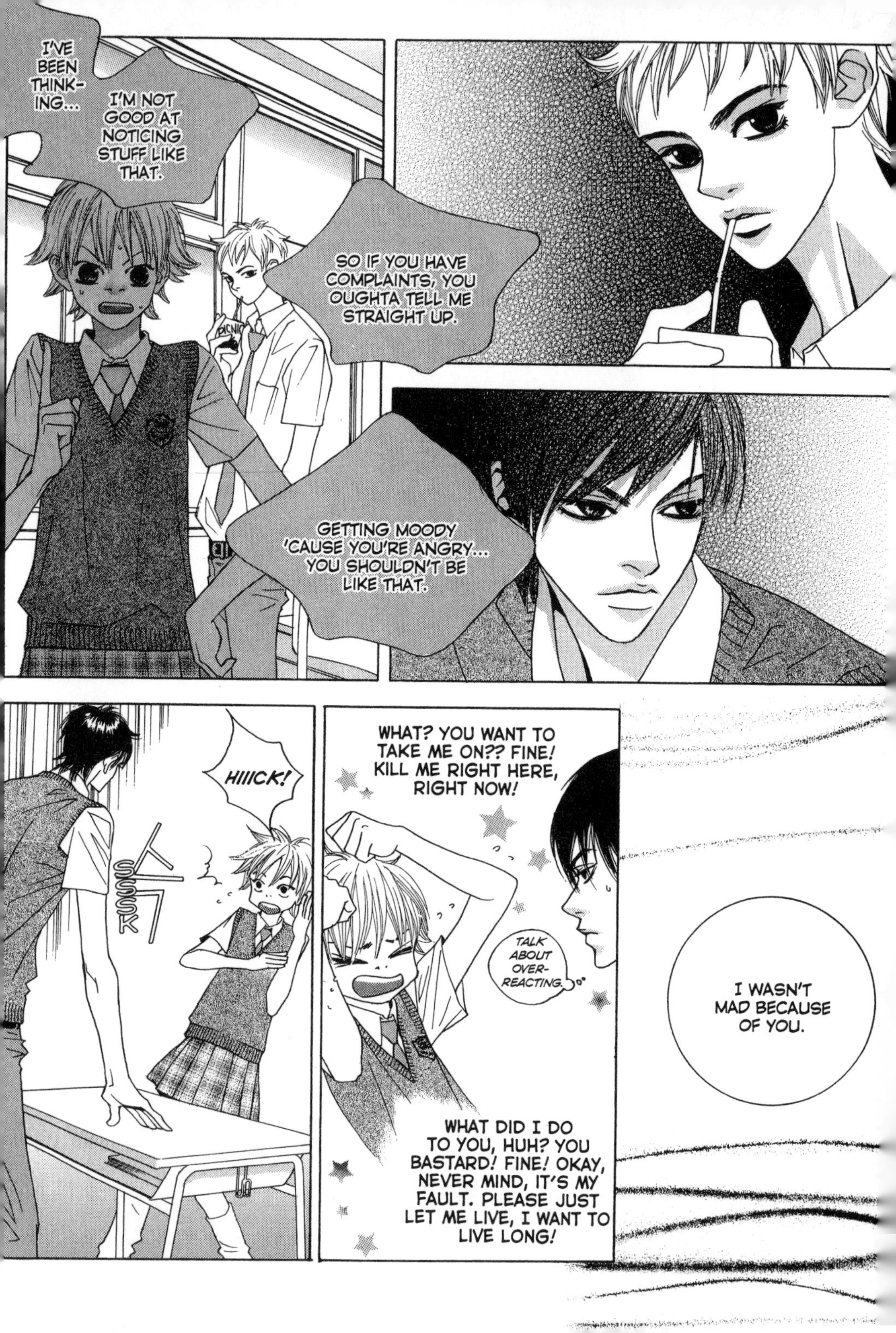
I'VE BEEN THINKING...
I'M NOT GOOD AT NOTICING STUFF LIKE THAT.
SO IF YOU HAVE COMPLAINTS, YOU OUGHTA TELL ME STRAIGHT UP.
PICNIC
GETTING MOODY 'CAUSE YOU'RE ANGRY... YOU SHOULDN'T BE LIKE THAT.
SSSK
HIIICK!
WHAT? YOU WANT TO TAKE ME ON?? FINE! KILL ME RIGHT HERE, RIGHT NOW!
TALK ABOUT OVER-REACTING.
WHAT DID I DO TO YOU, HUH? YOU BASTARD! FINE! OKAY, NEVER MIND, IT'S MY FAULT. PLEASE JUST LET ME LIVE, I WANT TO LIVE LONG!
I WASN'T MAD BECAUSE OF YOU.

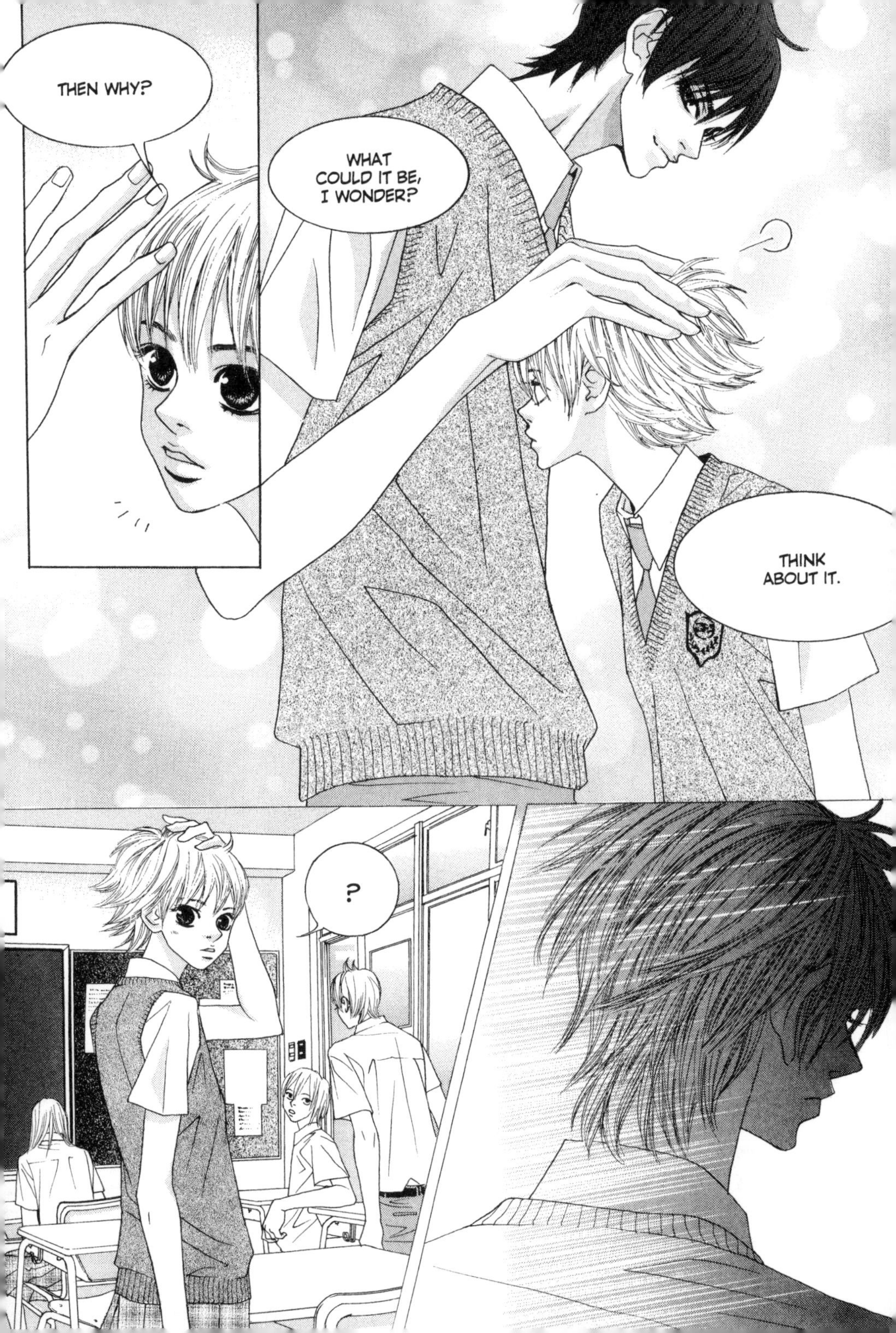
THEN WHY?
WHAT COULD IT BE, I WONDER?
THINK ABOUT IT.
?

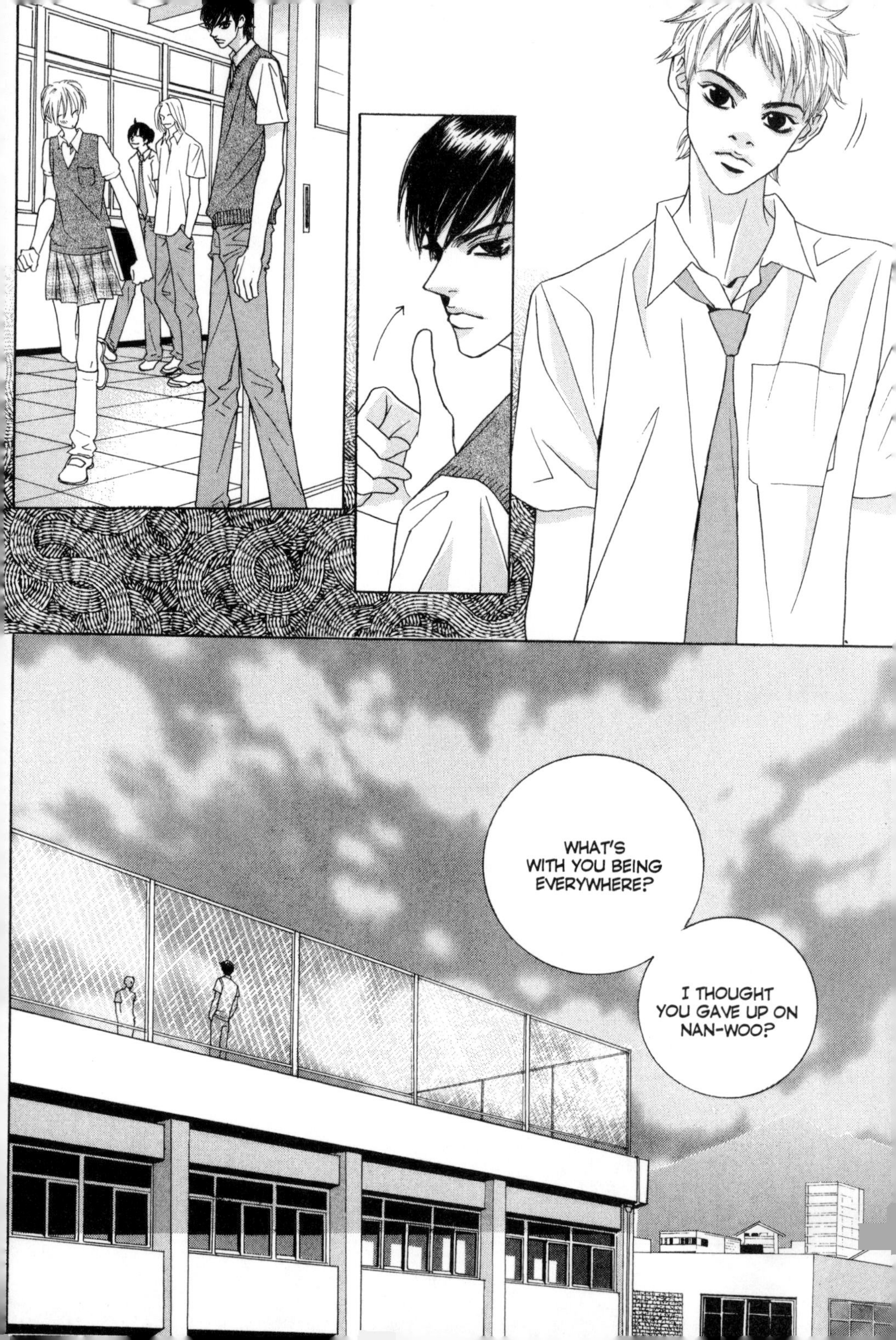
WHAT'S WITH YOU BEING EVERYWHERE?
I THOUGHT YOU GAVE UP ON NAN-WOO?

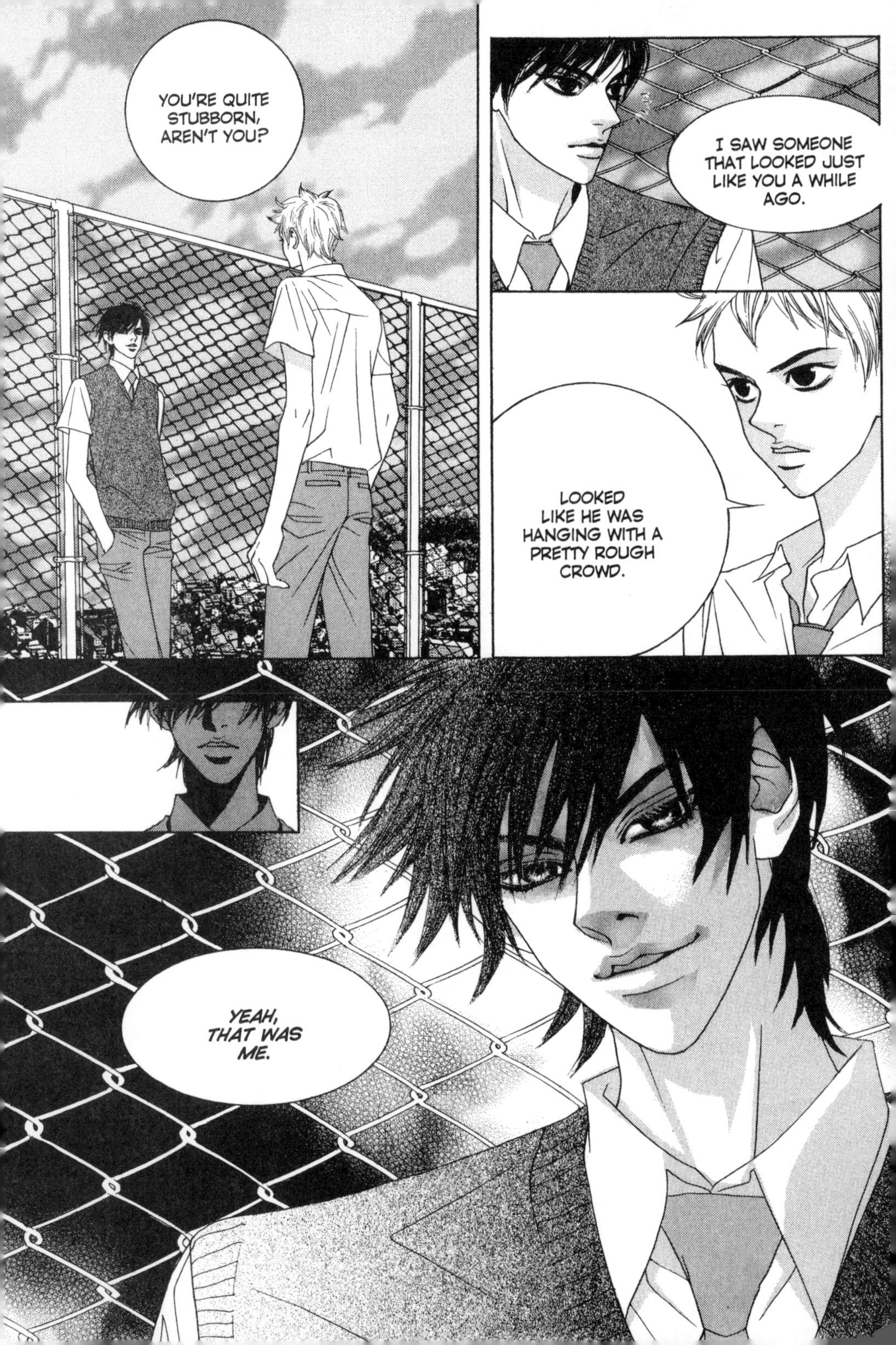
YOU'RE QUITE STUBBORN, AREN'T YOU?
I SAW SOMEONE THAT LOOKED JUST LIKE YOU A WHILE AGO.
LOOKED LIKE HE WAS HANGING WITH A PRETTY ROUGH CROWD.
YEAH, THAT WAS ME.

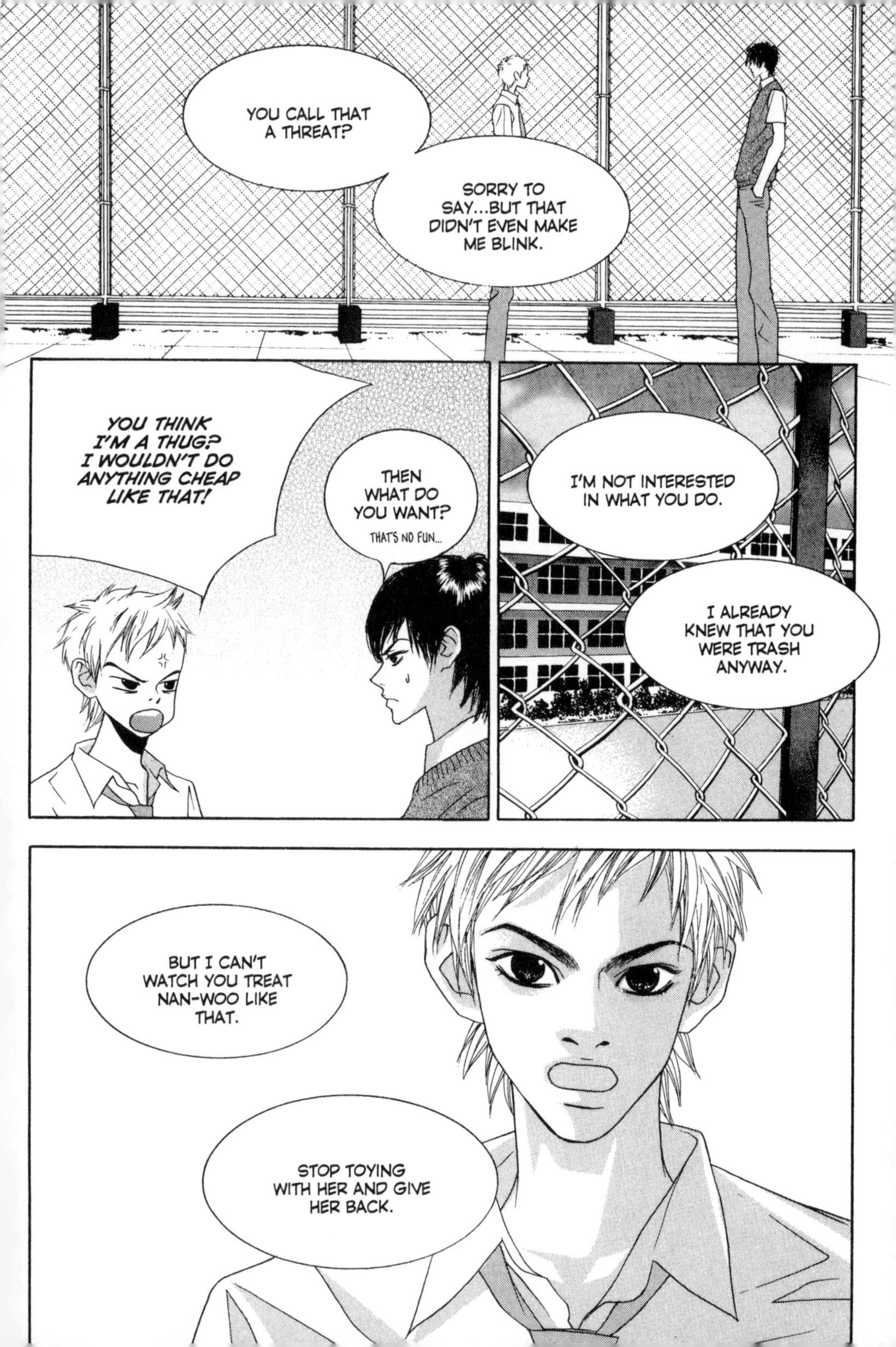
YOU CALL THAT A THREAT?
SORRY TO SAY...BUT THAT DIDN'T EVEN MAKE ME BLINK.
YOU THINK I'M A THUG? I WOULDN'T DO ANYTHING CHEAP LIKE THAT!
THEN WHAT DO YOU WANT?
THAT'S NO FUN...
I'M NOT INTERESTED IN WHAT YOU DO.
I ALREADY KNEW THAT YOU WERE TRASH ANYWAY.
BUT I CAN'T WATCH YOU TREAT NAN-WOO LIKE THAT.
STOP TOYING WITH HER AND GIVE HER BACK.

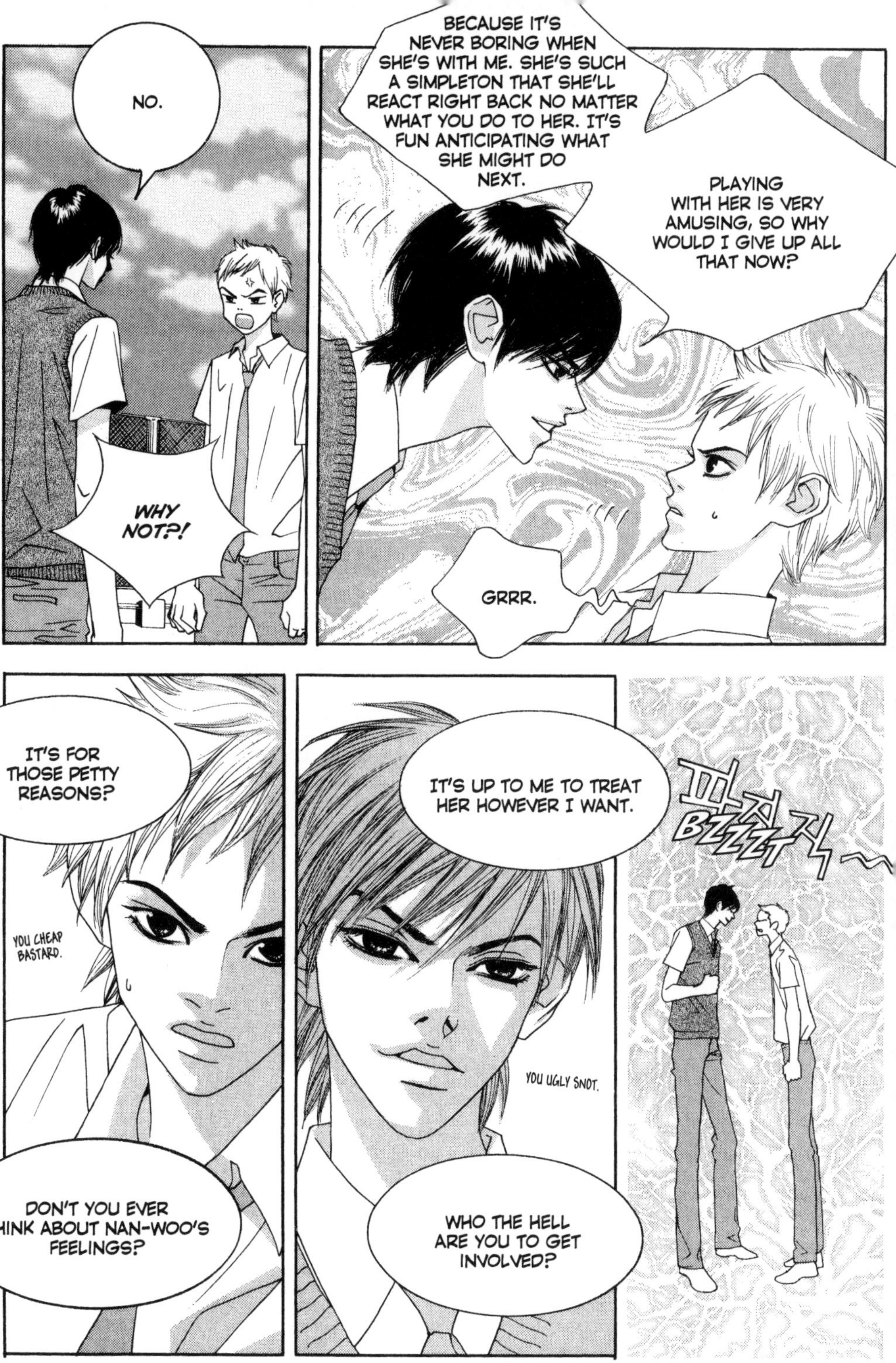
NO.
WHY NOT?!
BECAUSE IT'S NEVER BORING WHEN SHE'S WITH ME. SHE'S SUCH A SIMPLETON THAT SHE'LL REACT RIGHT BACK NO MATTER WHAT YOU DO TO HER. IT'S FUN ANTICIPATING WHAT SHE MIGHT DO NEXT.
PLAYING WITH HER IS VERY AMUSING, SO WHY WOULD I GIVE UP ALL THAT NOW?
GRRR.
IT'S FOR THOSE PETTY REASONS?
YOU CHEAP BASTARD.
DON'T YOU EVER THINK ABOUT NAN-WOO'S FEELINGS?
IT'S UP TO ME TO TREAT HER HOWEVER I WANT.
YOU UGLY SNOT.
WHO THE HELL ARE YOU TO GET INVOLVED?
파지직
BZZZT

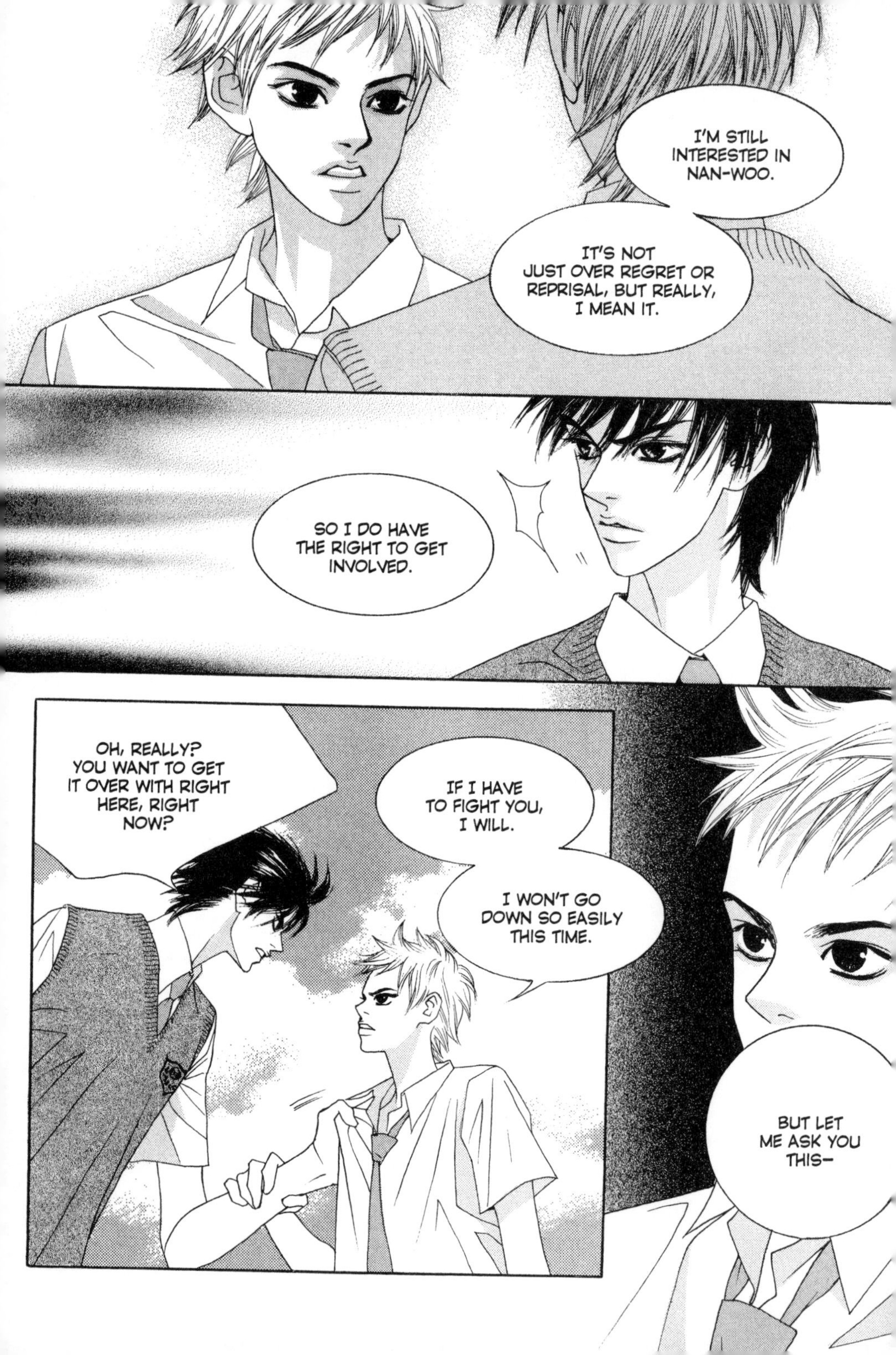
I'M STILL INTERESTED IN NAN-WOO.
IT'S NOT JUST OVER REGRET OR REPRISAL, BUT REALLY, I MEAN IT.
SO I DO HAVE THE RIGHT TO GET INVOLVED.
OH, REALLY? YOU WANT TO GET IT OVER WITH RIGHT HERE, RIGHT NOW?
IF I HAVE TO FIGHT YOU, I WILL.
I WON'T GO DOWN SO EASILY THIS TIME.
BUT LET ME ASK YOU THIS—

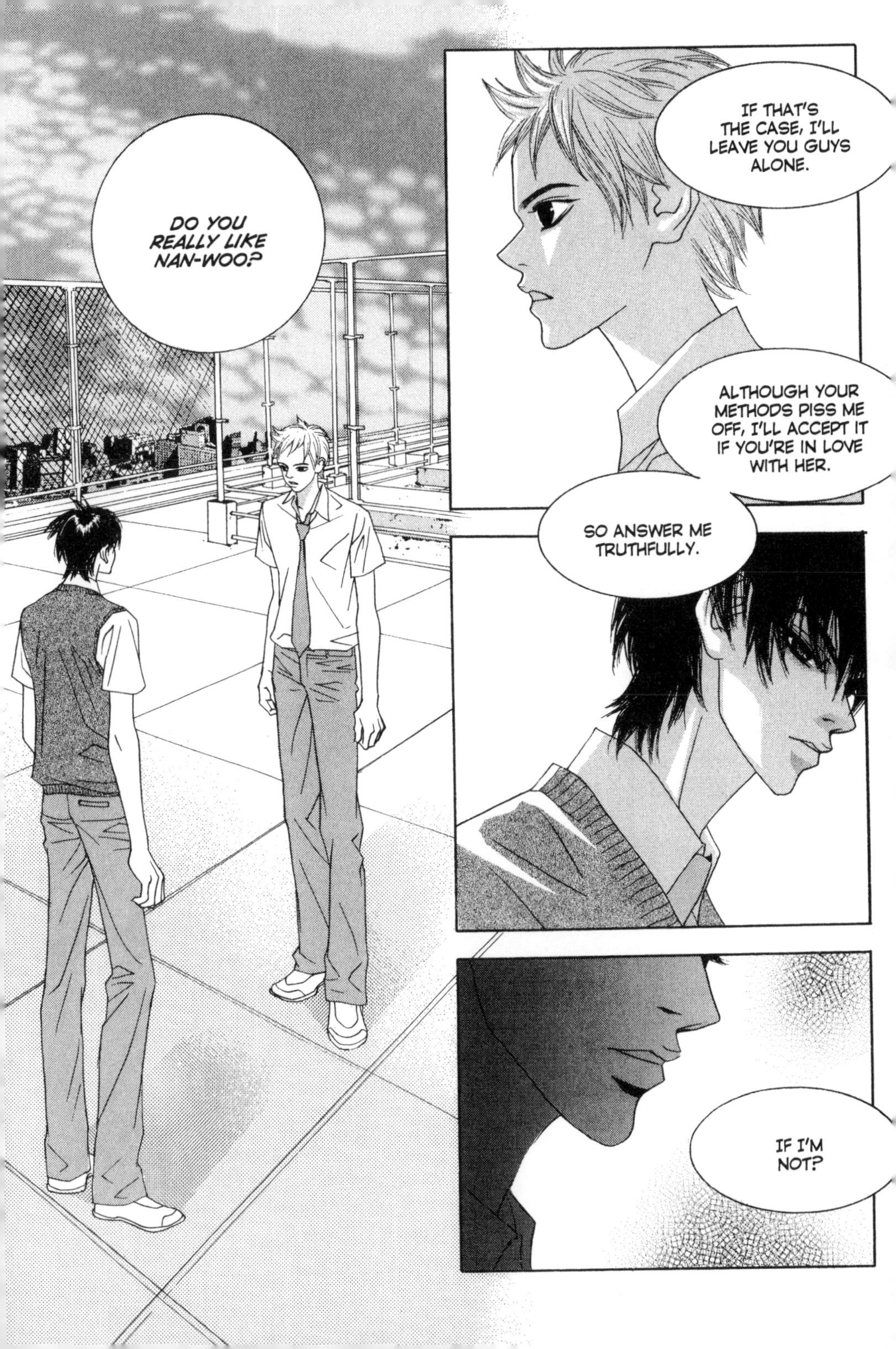
DO YOU REALLY LIKE NAN-WOO?
IF THAT'S THE CASE, I'LL LEAVE YOU GUYS ALONE.
ALTHOUGH YOUR METHODS PISS ME OFF, I'LL ACCEPT IT IF YOU'RE IN LOVE WITH HER.
SO ANSWER ME TRUTHFULLY.
IF I'M NOT?

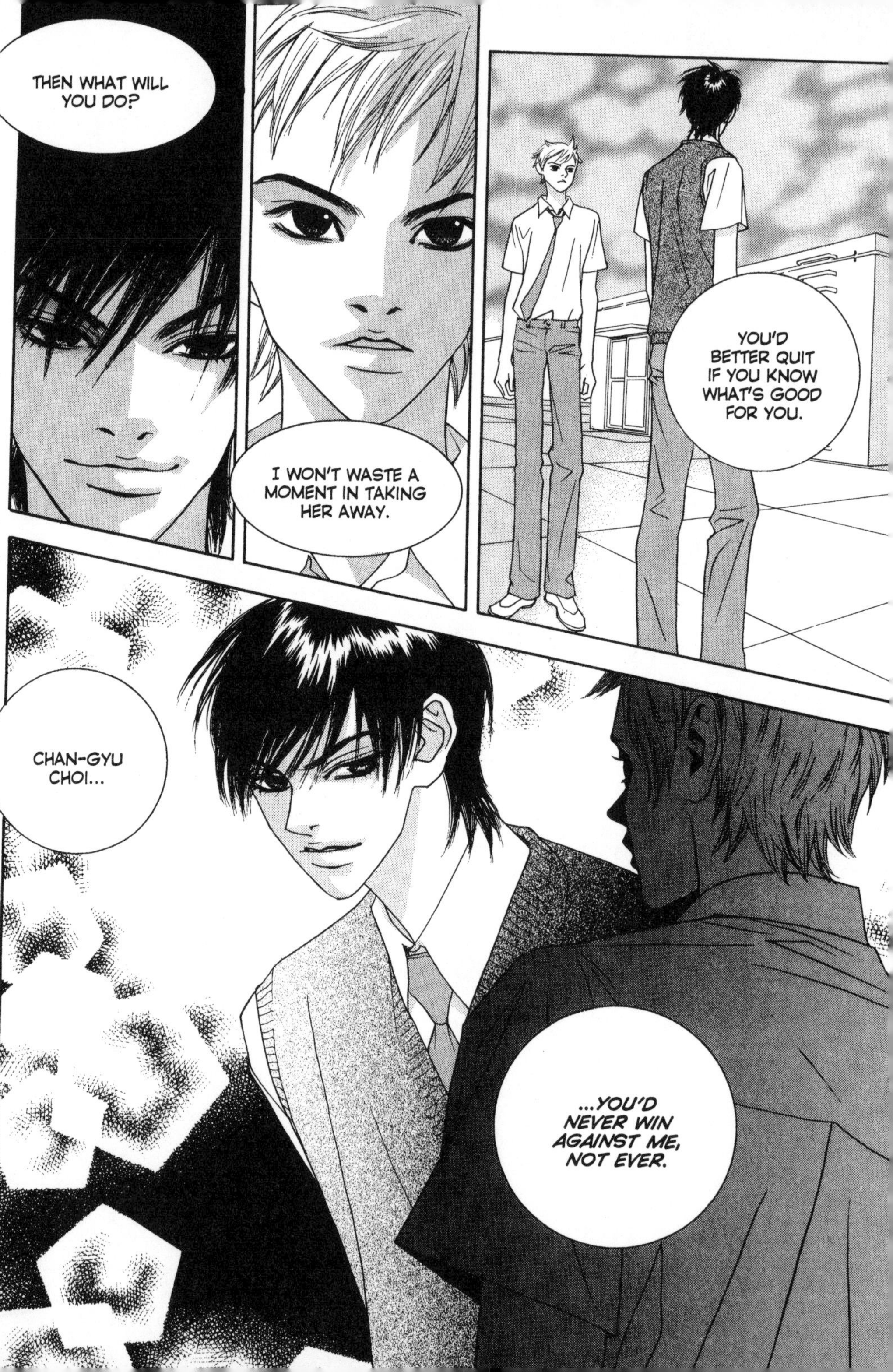
THEN WHAT WILL YOU DO?
I WON'T WASTE A MOMENT IN TAKING HER AWAY.
YOU'D BETTER QUIT IF YOU KNOW WHAT'S GOOD FOR YOU.
CHAN-GYU CHOI...
...YOU'D NEVER WIN AGAINST ME, NOT EVER.

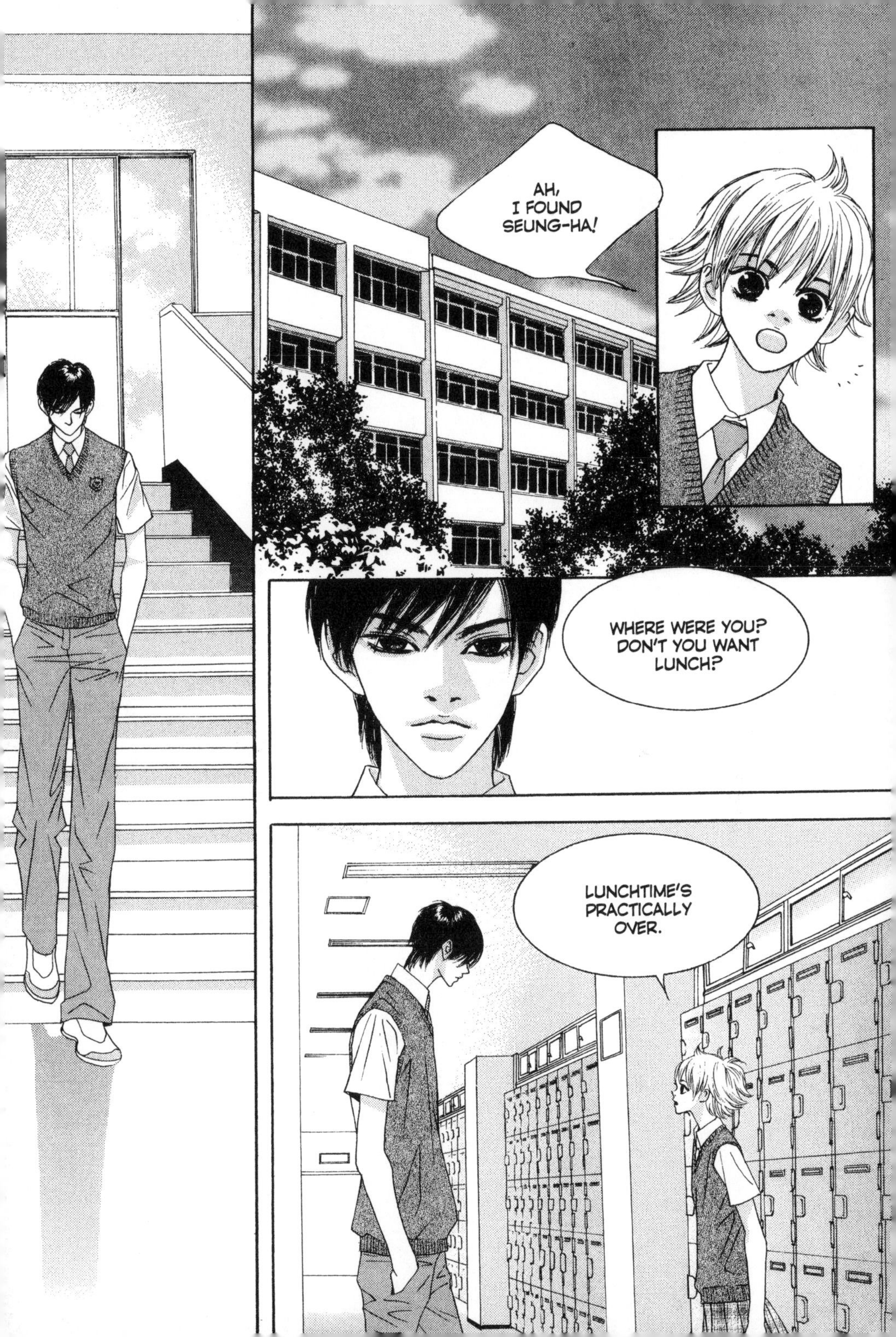
AH, I FOUND SEUNG-HA!
WHERE WERE YOU? DON'T YOU WANT LUNCH?
LUNCHTIME'S PRACTICALLY OVER.

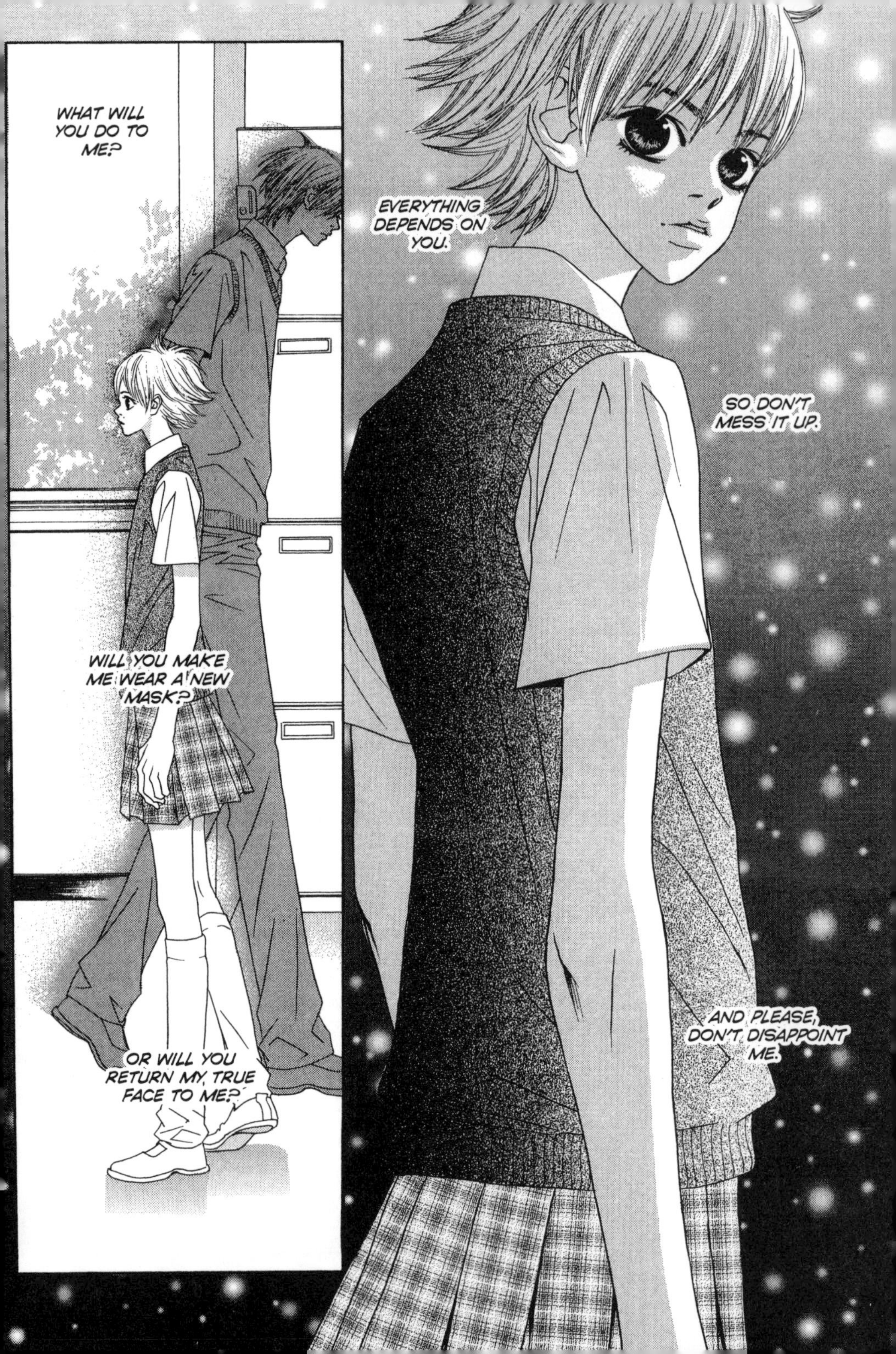
WHAT WILL YOU DO TO ME?
WILL YOU MAKE ME WEAR A NEW MASK?
OR WILL YOU RETURN MY TRUE FACE TO ME?
EVERYTHING DEPENDS ON YOU.
SO DON'T MESS IT UP.
AND PLEASE, DON'T DISAPPOINT ME.

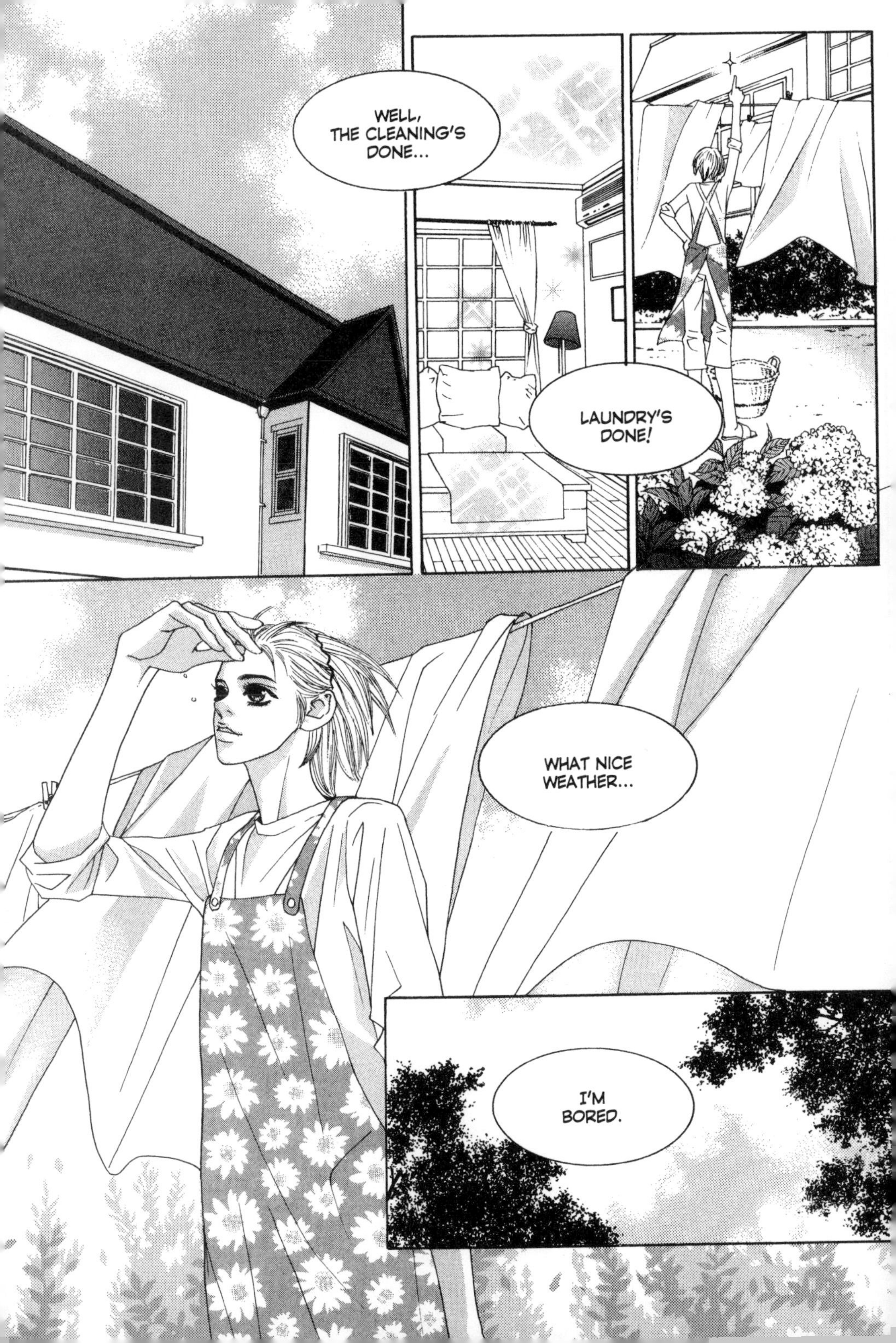
WELL, THE CLEANING'S DONE...
LAUNDRY'S DONE!
WHAT NICE WEATHER...
I'M BORED.

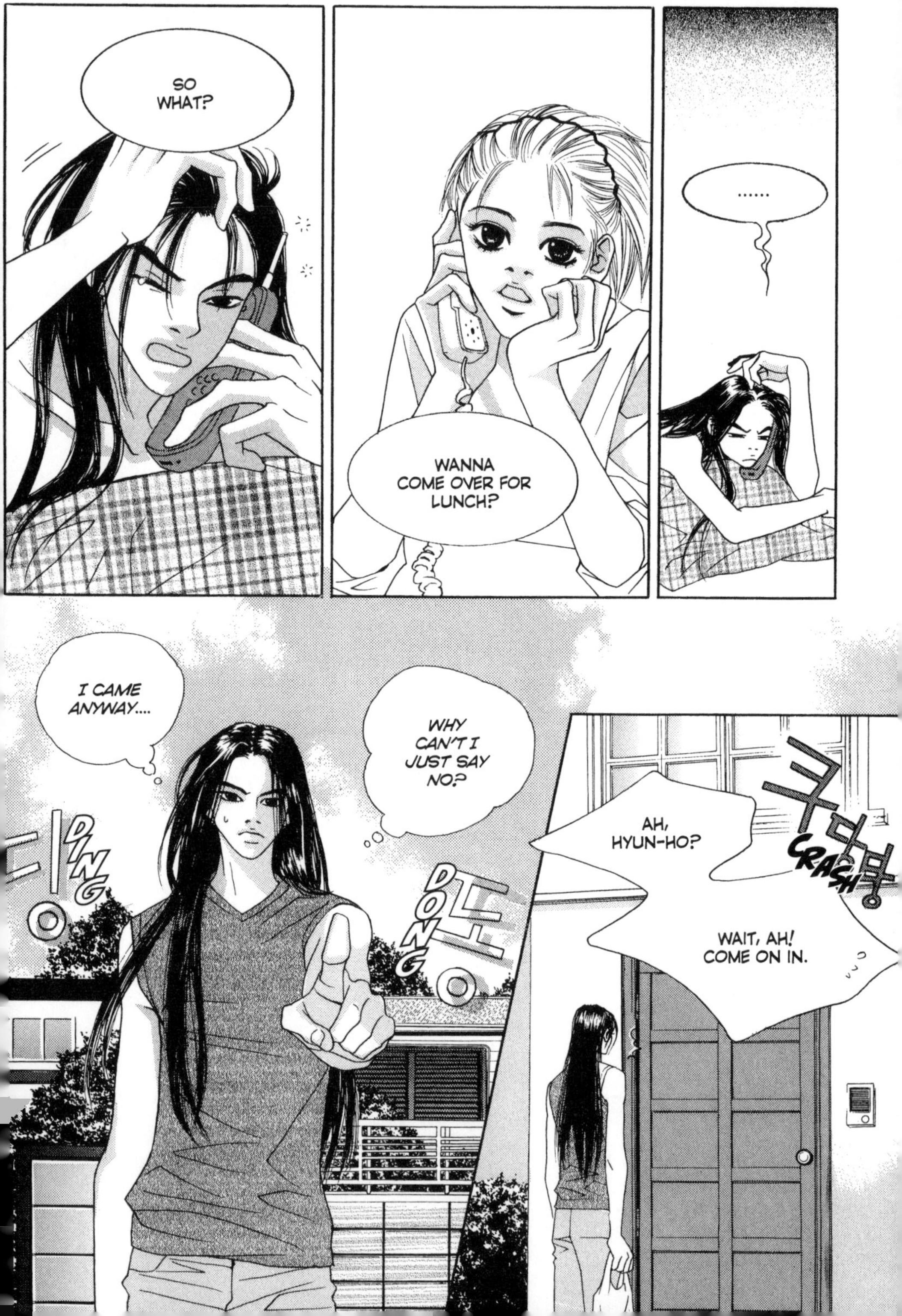
SO WHAT?
WANNA COME OVER FOR LUNCH?
......
I CAME ANYWAY....
DING
WHY CAN'T I JUST SAY NO?
DONG
AH, HYUN-HO?
CRASH
WAIT, AH! COME ON IN.

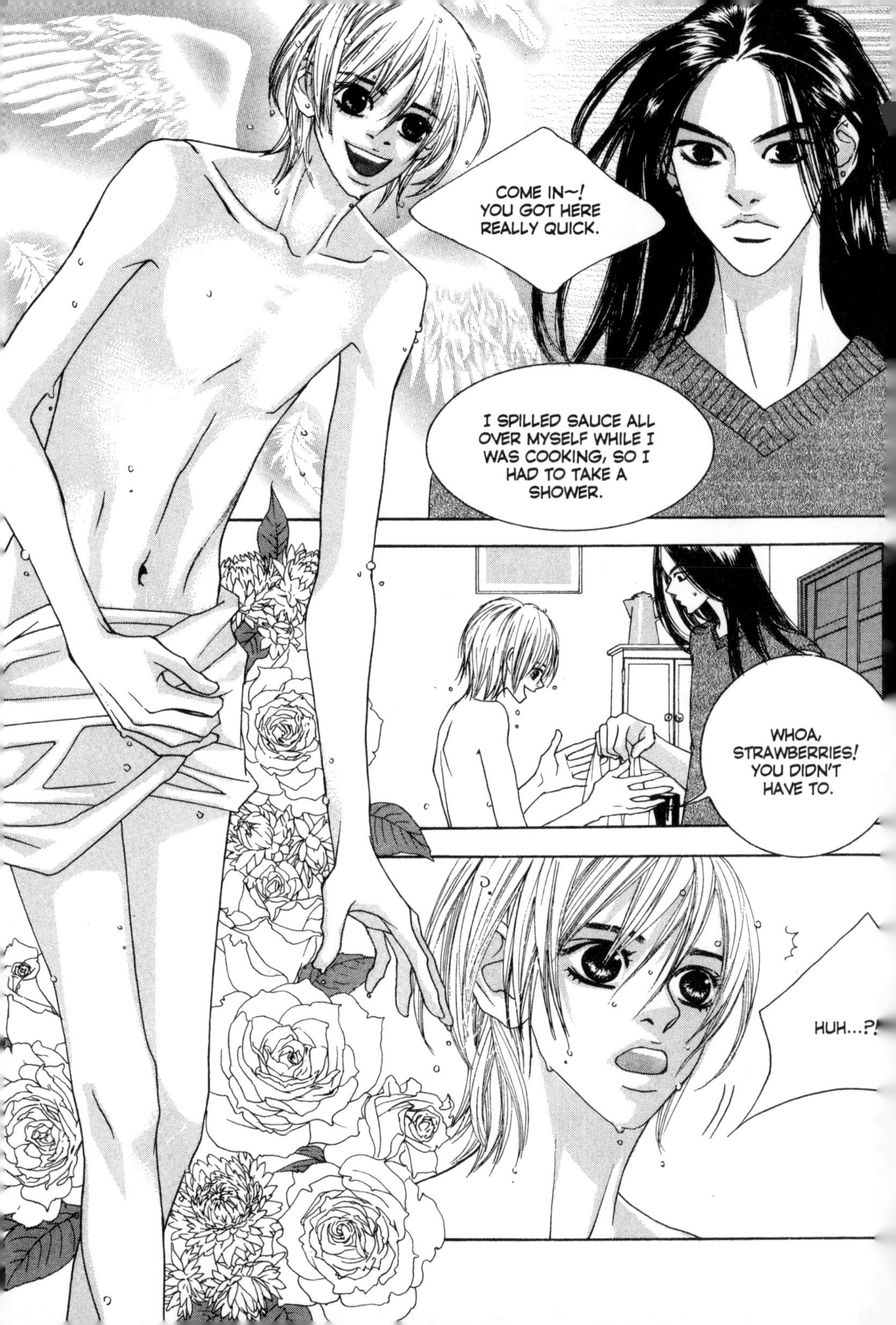
COME IN~! YOU GOT HERE REALLY QUICK.
I SPILLED SAUCE ALL OVER MYSELF WHILE I WAS COOKING, SO I HAD TO TAKE A SHOWER.
WHOA, STRAWBERRIES! YOU DIDN'T HAVE TO.
HUH...?!

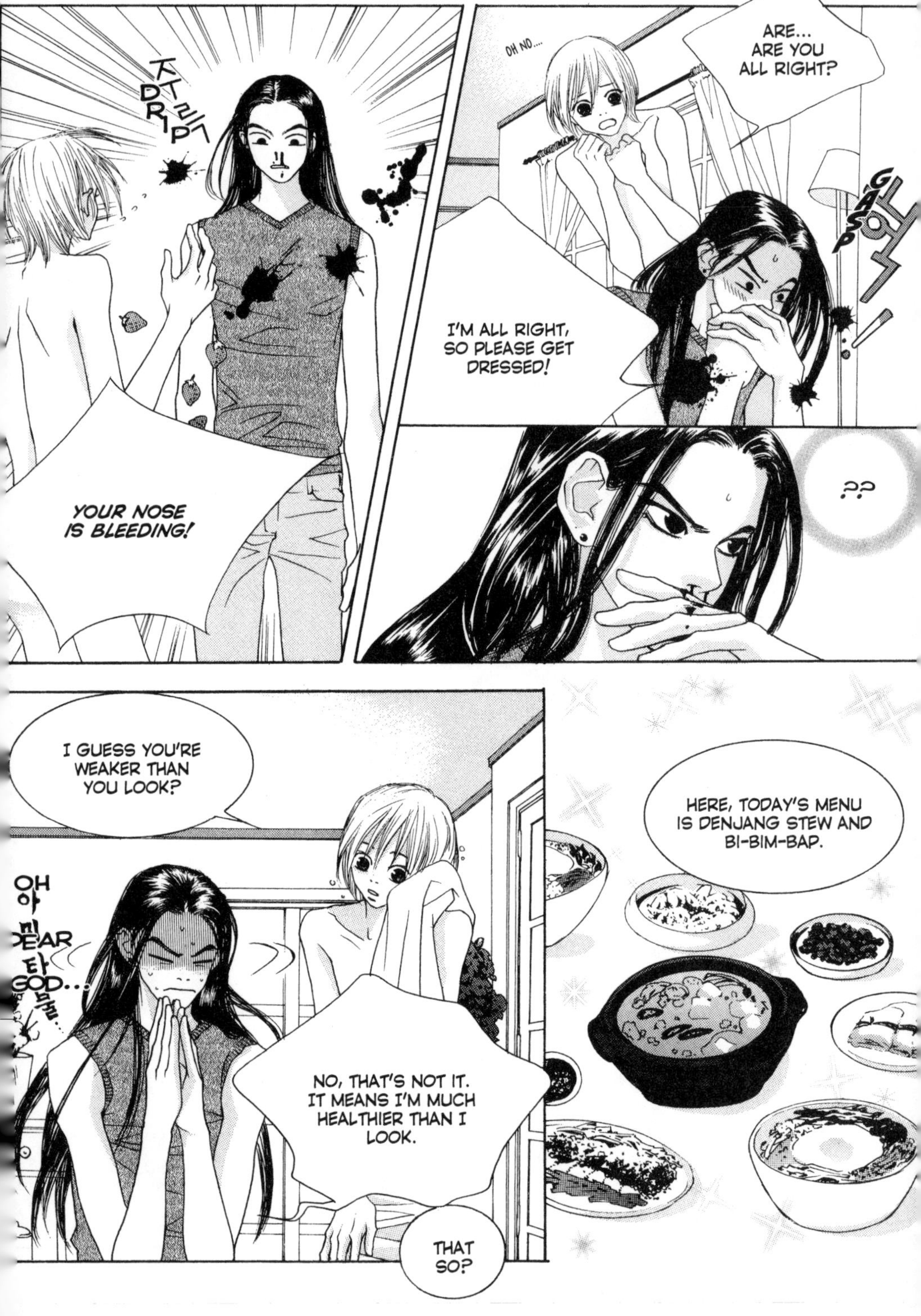
DRIP
YOUR NOSE IS BLEEDING!
OH NO....
ARE... ARE YOU ALL RIGHT?
I'M ALL RIGHT, SO PLEASE GET DRESSED!
GASP!
??
I GUESS YOU'RE WEAKER THAN YOU LOOK?
OH DEAR GOD...
NO, THAT'S NOT IT. IT MEANS I'M MUCH HEALTHIER THAN I LOOK.
THAT SO?
HERE, TODAY'S MENU IS DENJANG STEW AND BI-BIM-BAP.

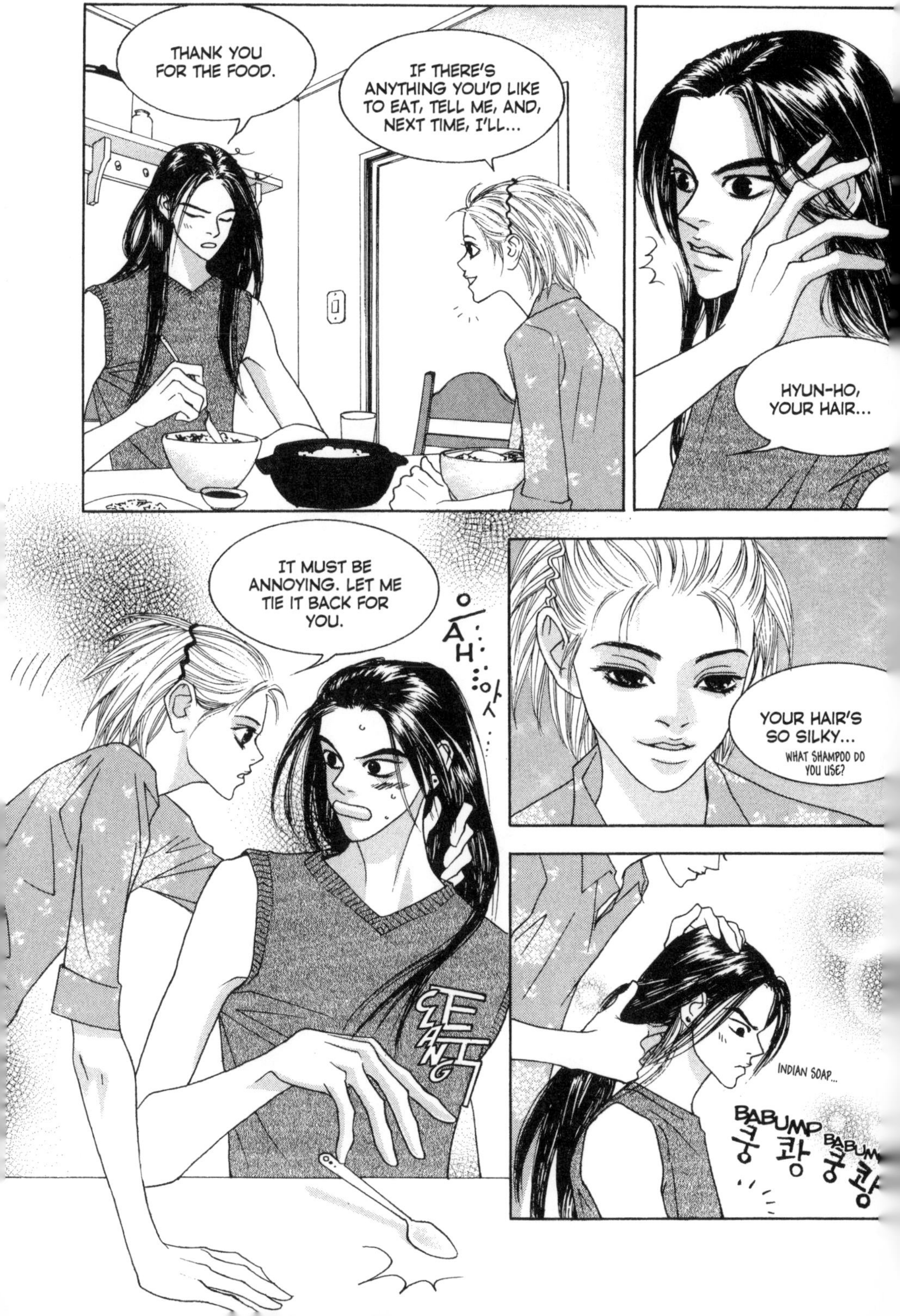
THANK YOU FOR THE FOOD.
IF THERE'S ANYTHING YOU'D LIKE TO EAT, TELL ME, AND, NEXT TIME, I'LL...
HYUN-HO, YOUR HAIR...
IT MUST BE ANNOYING. LET ME TIE IT BACK FOR YOU.
AH...
아...
앗...
YOUR HAIR'S SO SILKY...
WHAT SHAMPOO DO YOU USE?
INDIAN SOAP...
BABUMP BABUMP
쿵 쾅 쿵 쾅

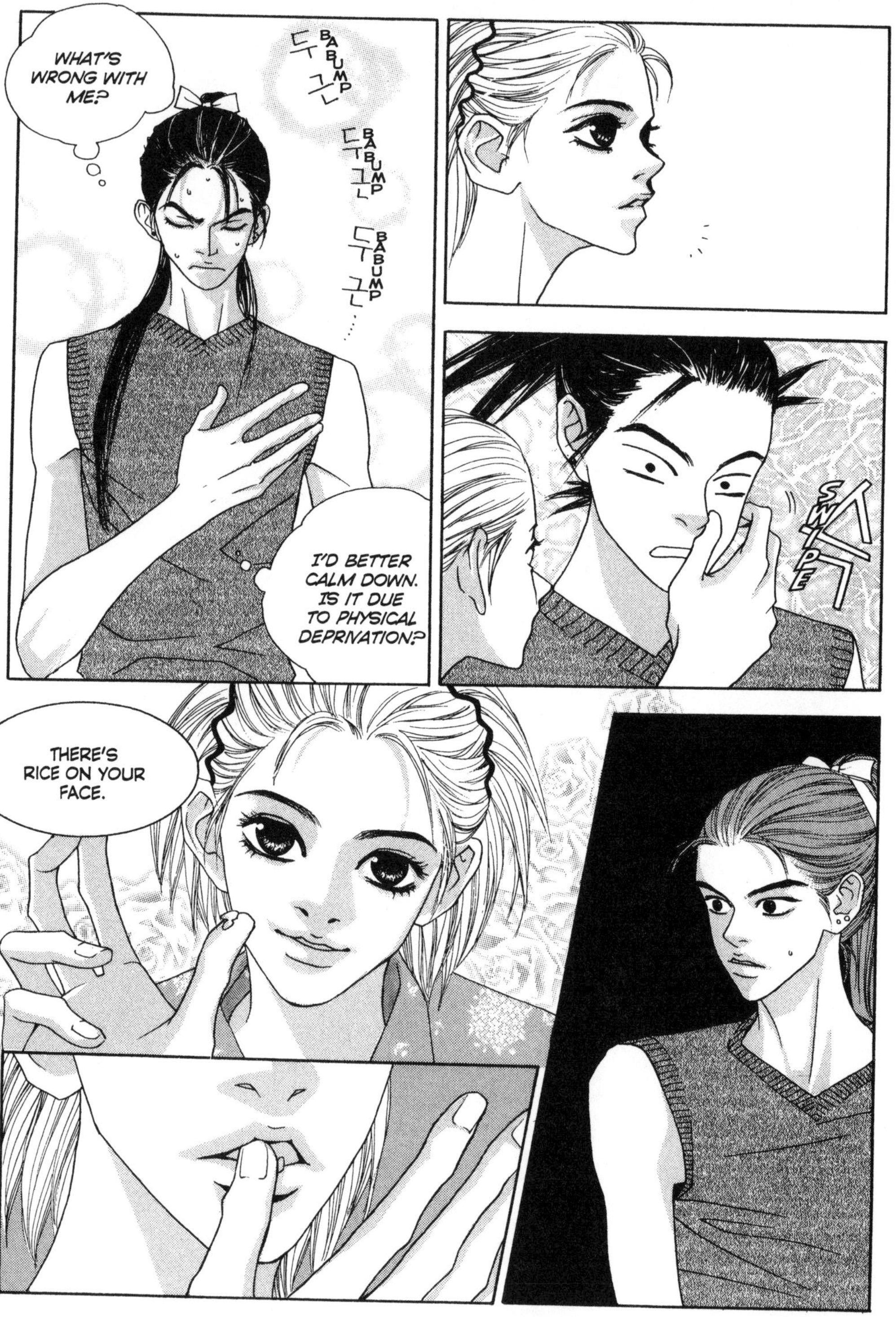
WHAT'S WRONG WITH ME?
두근 BABUMP
두근 BABUMP
두근 BABUMP
I'D BETTER CALM DOWN. IS IT DUE TO PHYSICAL DEPRIVATION?
슥 SWIPE
THERE'S RICE ON YOUR FACE.

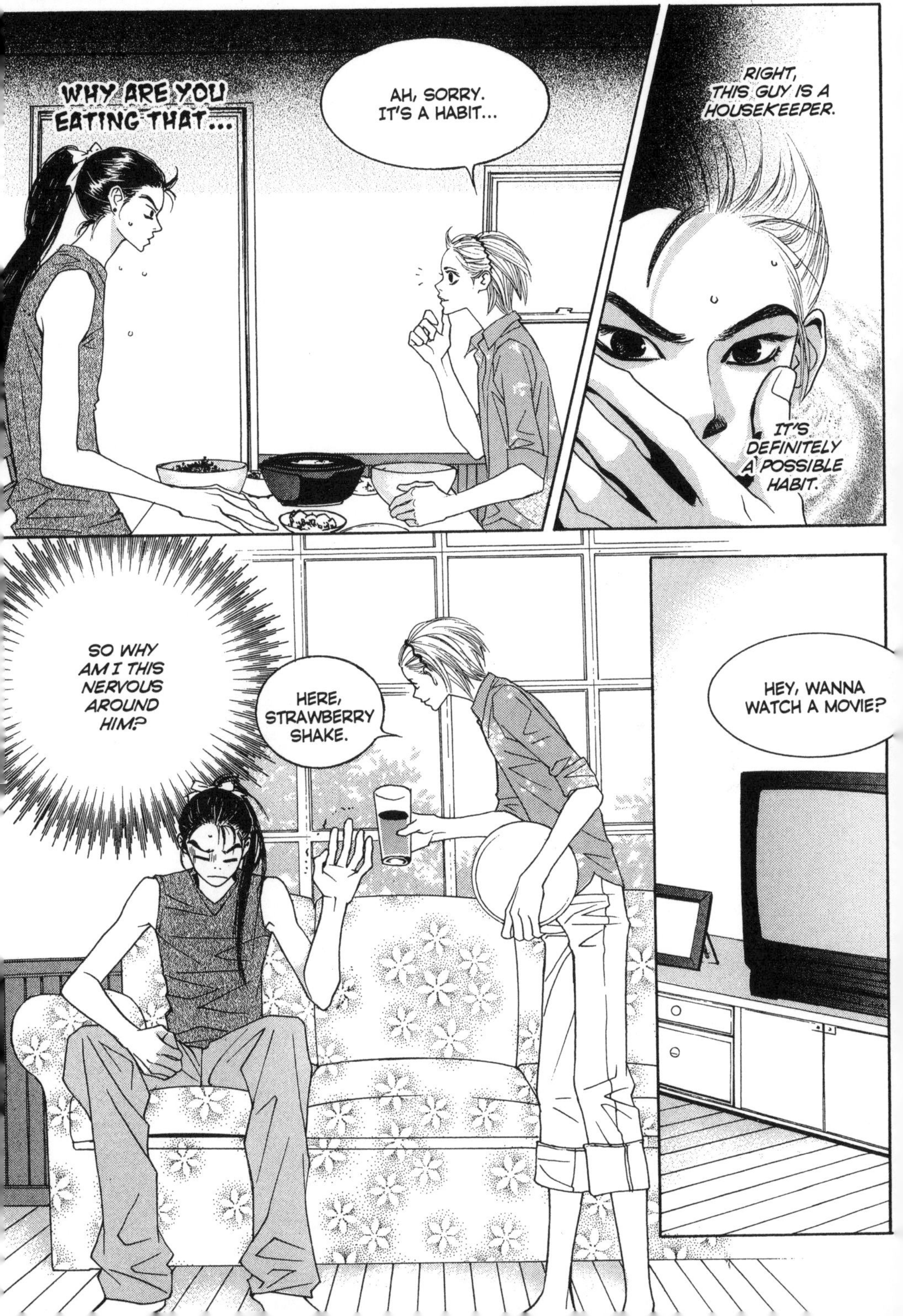
WHY ARE YOU EATING THAT...
AH, SORRY. IT'S A HABIT...
RIGHT, THIS GUY IS A HOUSEKEEPER.
IT'S DEFINITELY A POSSIBLE HABIT.
SO WHY AM I THIS NERVOUS AROUND HIM?
HERE, STRAWBERRY SHAKE.
HEY, WANNA WATCH A MOVIE?

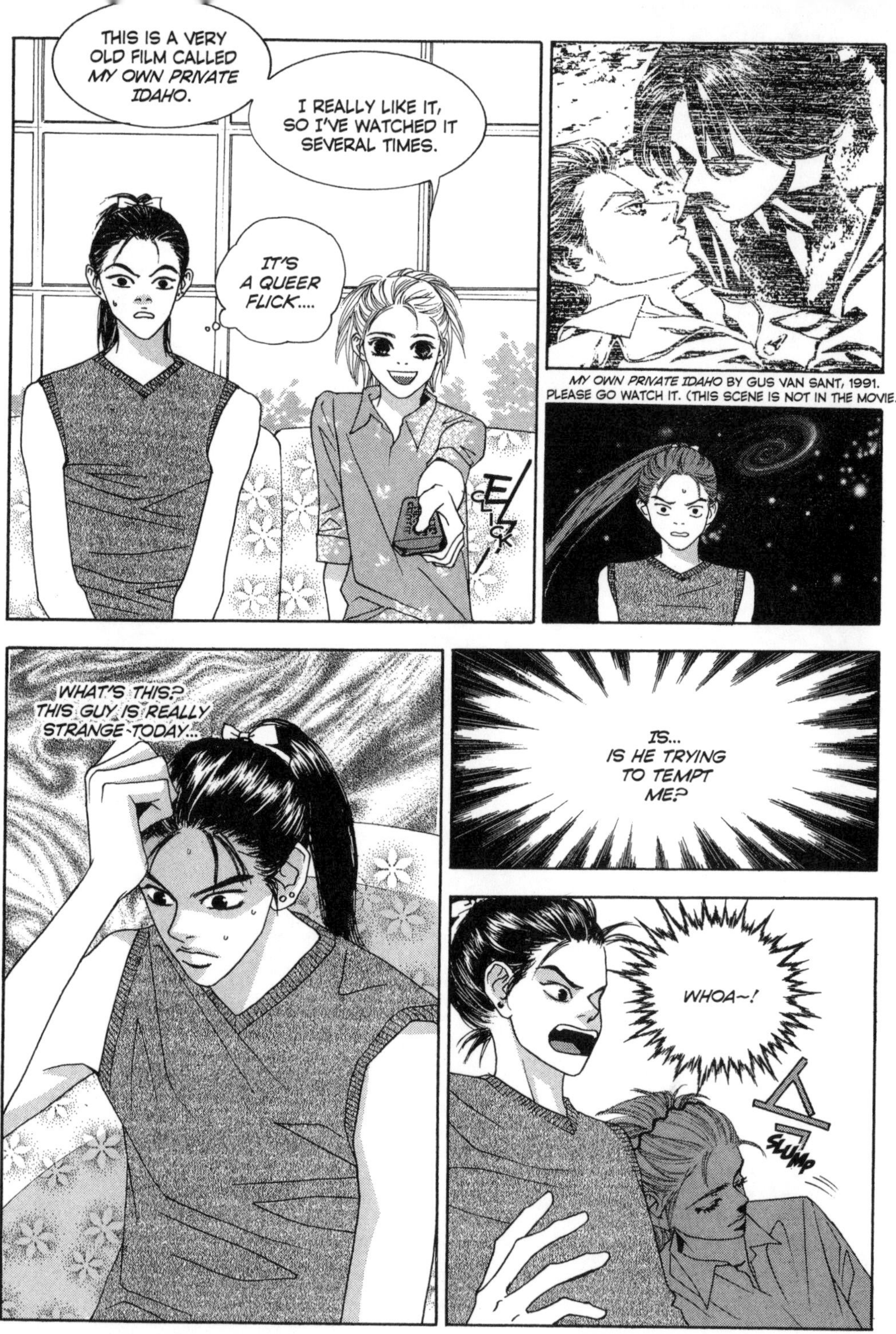
THIS IS A VERY OLD FILM CALLED *MY OWN PRIVATE IDAHO*.
I REALLY LIKE IT, SO I'VE WATCHED IT SEVERAL TIMES.
IT'S A QUEER FLICK....
CLICK
*MY OWN PRIVATE IDAHO* BY GUS VAN SANT, 1991. PLEASE GO WATCH IT. (THIS SCENE IS NOT IN THE MOVIE.)
WHAT'S THIS? THIS GUY IS REALLY STRANGE TODAY...
IS... IS HE TRYING TO TEMPT ME?
WHOA~!
SLUMP

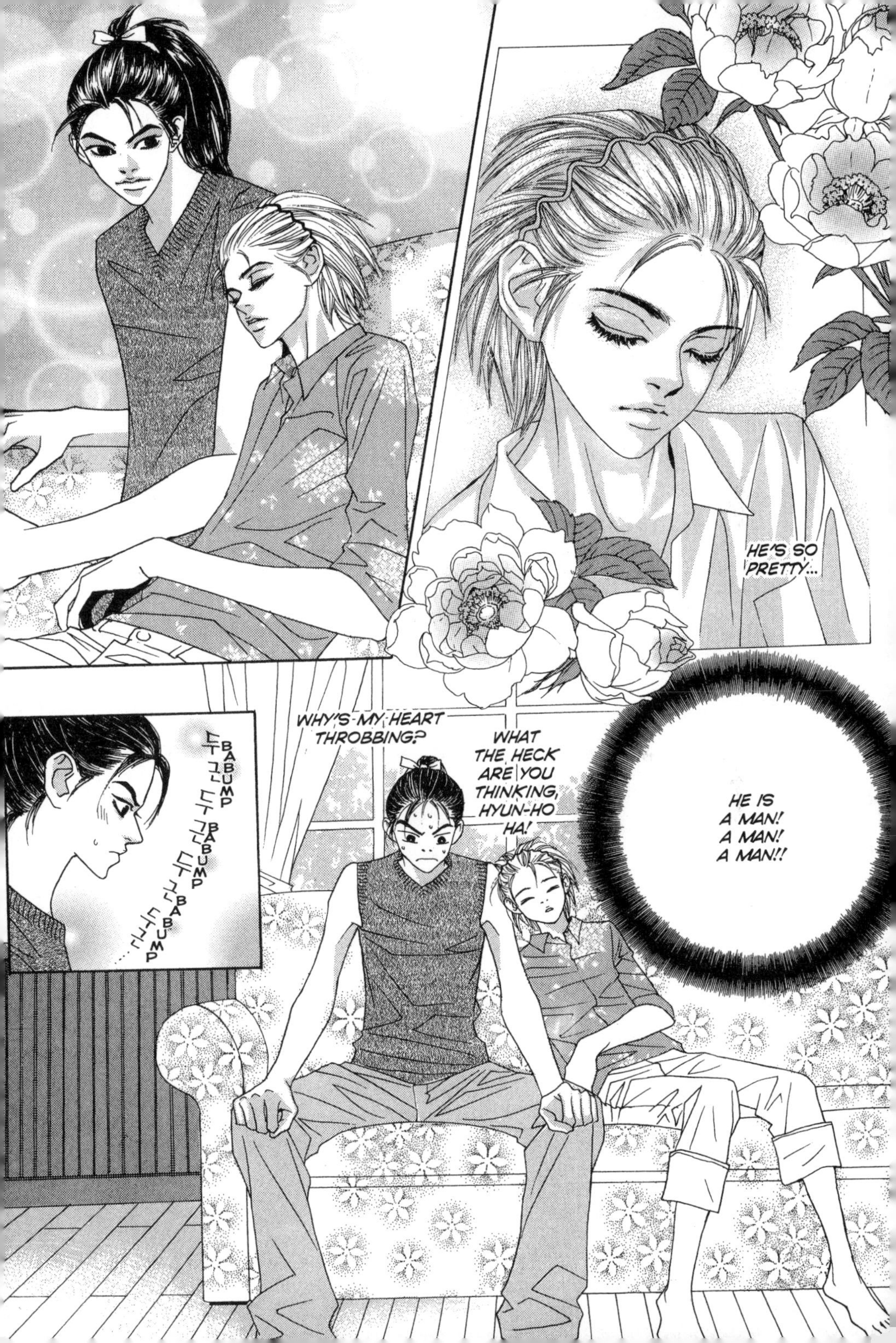
HE'S SO PRETTY...
BABUMP
BABUMP
BABUMP
BABUMP
WHY'S MY HEART THROBBING?
WHAT THE HECK ARE YOU THINKING, HYUN-HO HA!
HE IS A MAN! A MAN! A MAN!!

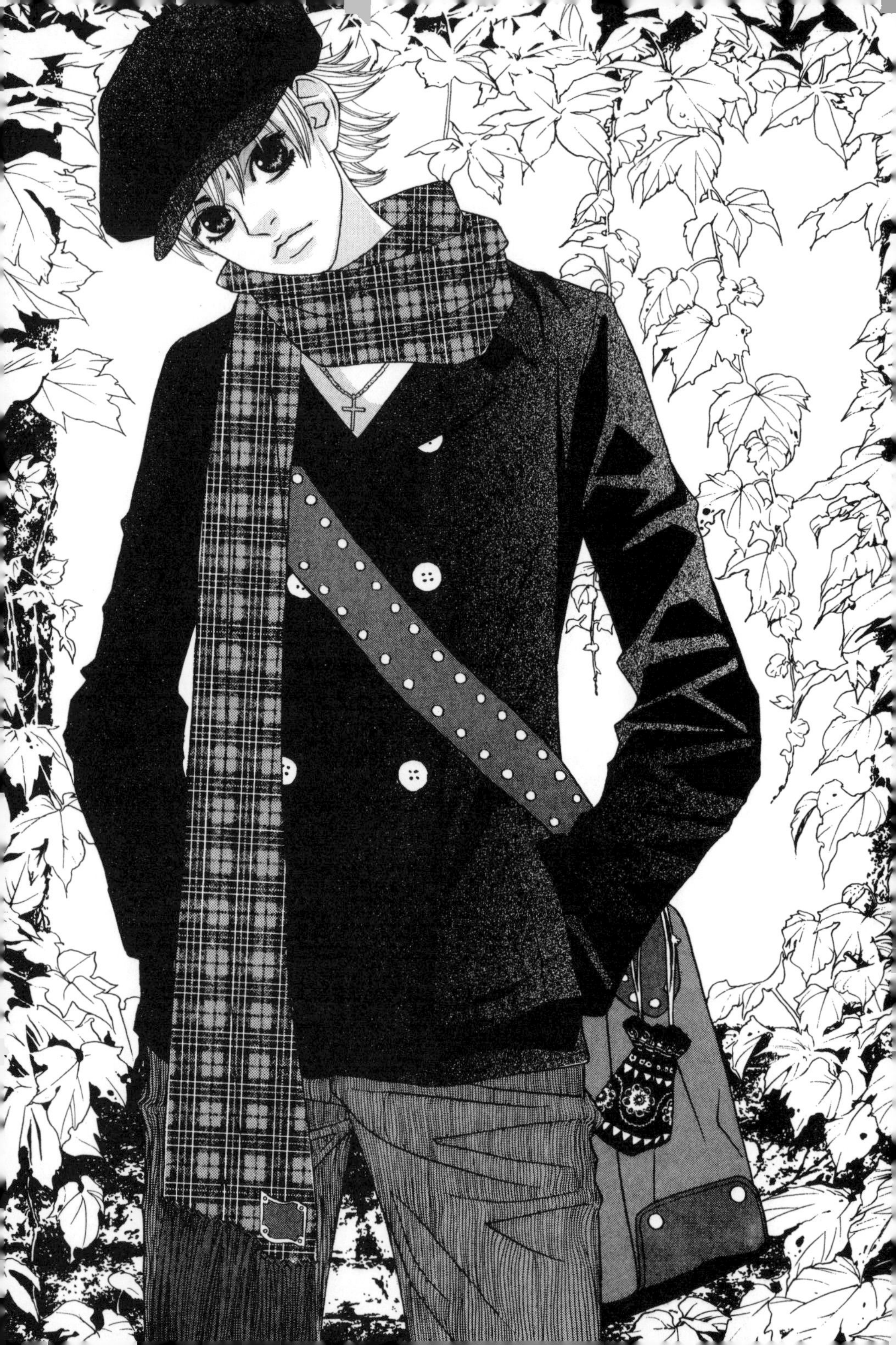

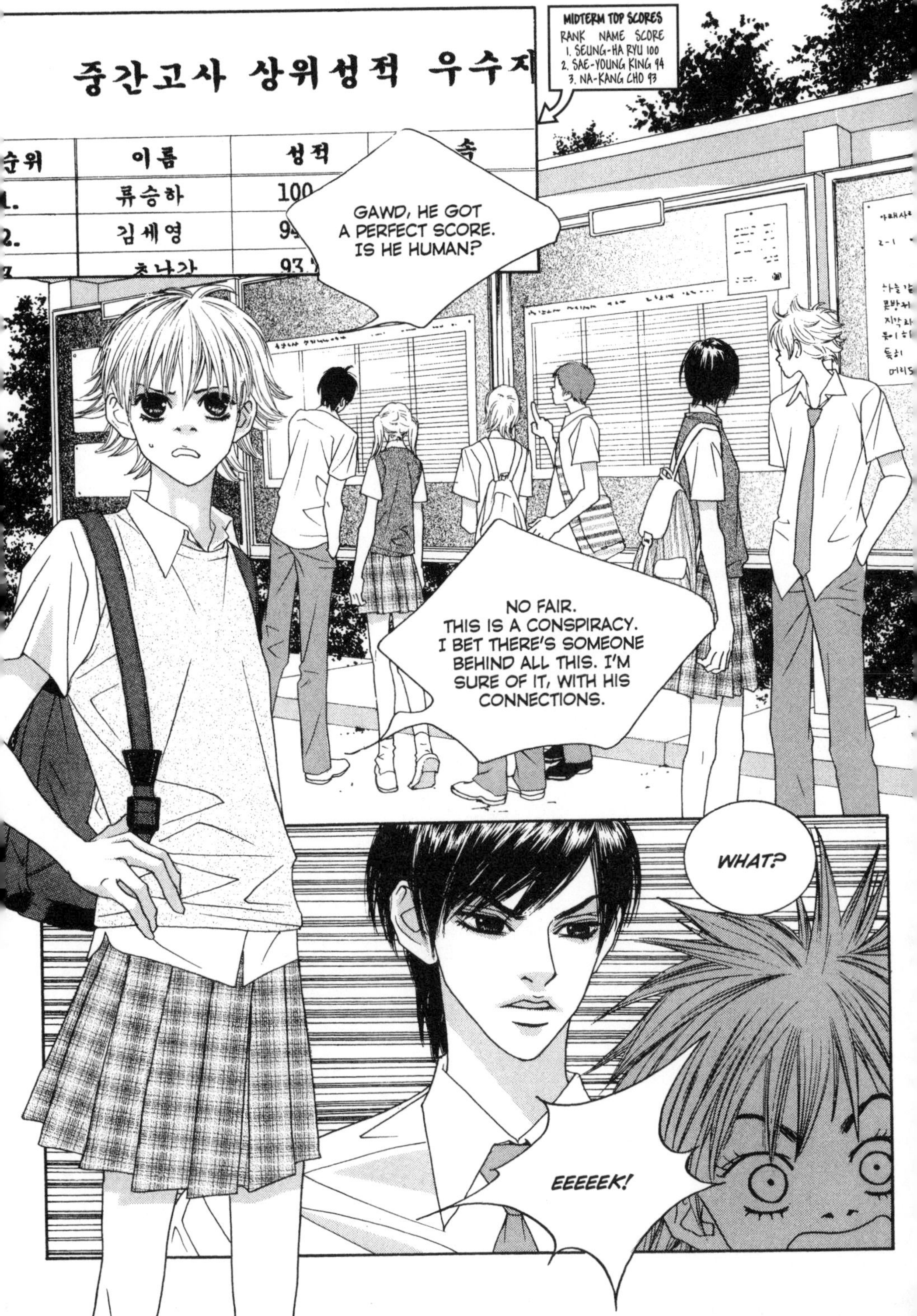
중간고사 상위성적 우수자
순위 이름 성적
1. 류승하 100
2. 김세영
MIDTERM TOP SCORES
RANK NAME SCORE
1. SEUNG-HA RYU 100
2. SAE-YOUNG KING 94
3. NA-KANG CHO 93
GAWD, HE GOT A PERFECT SCORE. IS HE HUMAN?
NO FAIR. THIS IS A CONSPIRACY. I BET THERE'S SOMEONE BEHIND ALL THIS. I'M SURE OF IT, WITH HIS CONNECTIONS.
WHAT?
EEEEEK!

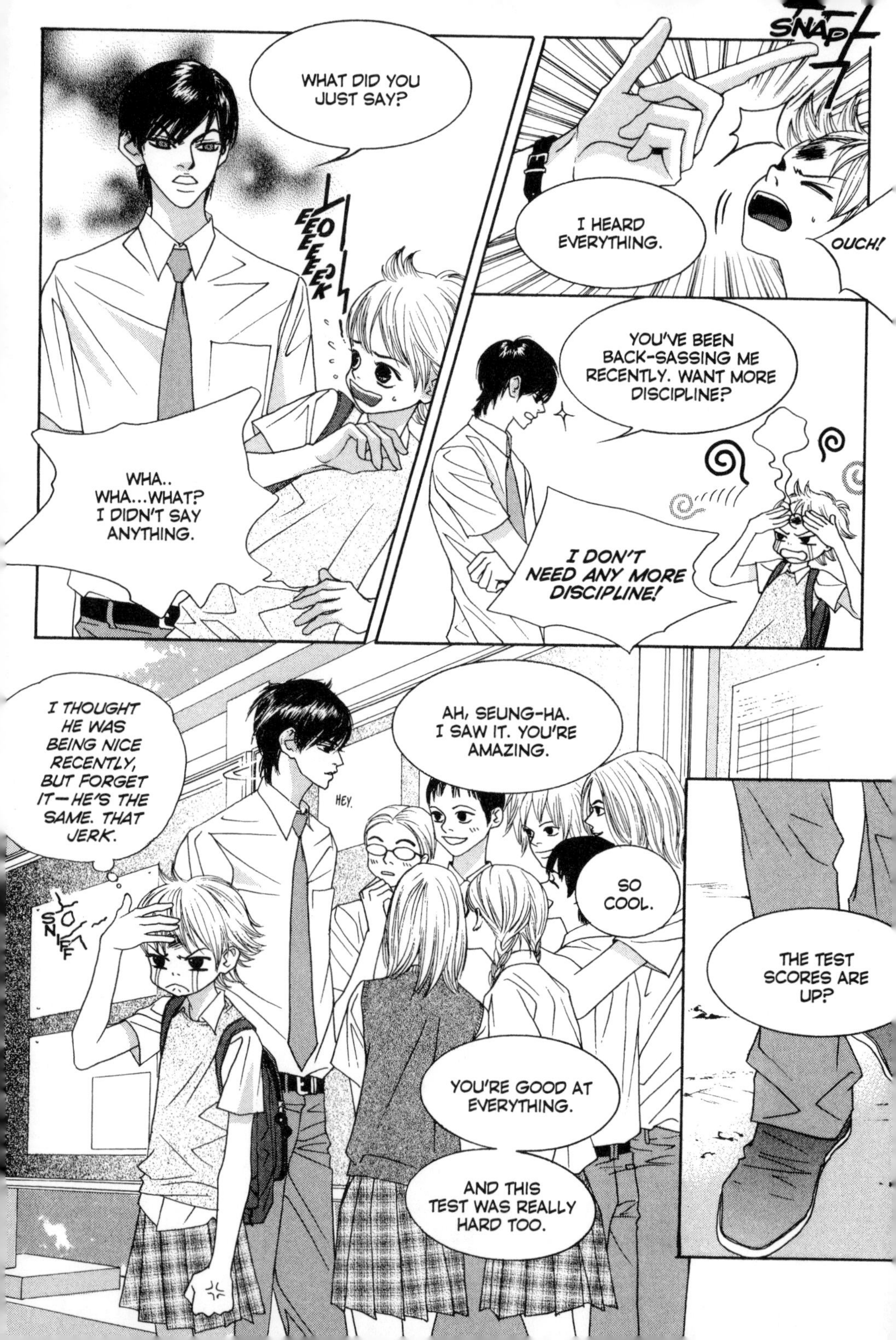
WHAT DID YOU JUST SAY?
WHA.. WHA...WHAT? I DIDN'T SAY ANYTHING.
SNAP
I HEARD EVERYTHING.
OUCH!
YOU'VE BEEN BACK-SASSING ME RECENTLY. WANT MORE DISCIPLINE?
*I DON'T NEED ANY MORE DISCIPLINE!*
*I THOUGHT HE WAS BEING NICE RECENTLY, BUT FORGET IT—HE'S THE SAME. THAT JERK.*
SNIFF
AH, SEUNG-HA. I SAW IT. YOU'RE AMAZING.
HEY.
SO COOL.
YOU'RE GOOD AT EVERYTHING.
AND THIS TEST WAS REALLY HARD TOO.
THE TEST SCORES ARE UP?

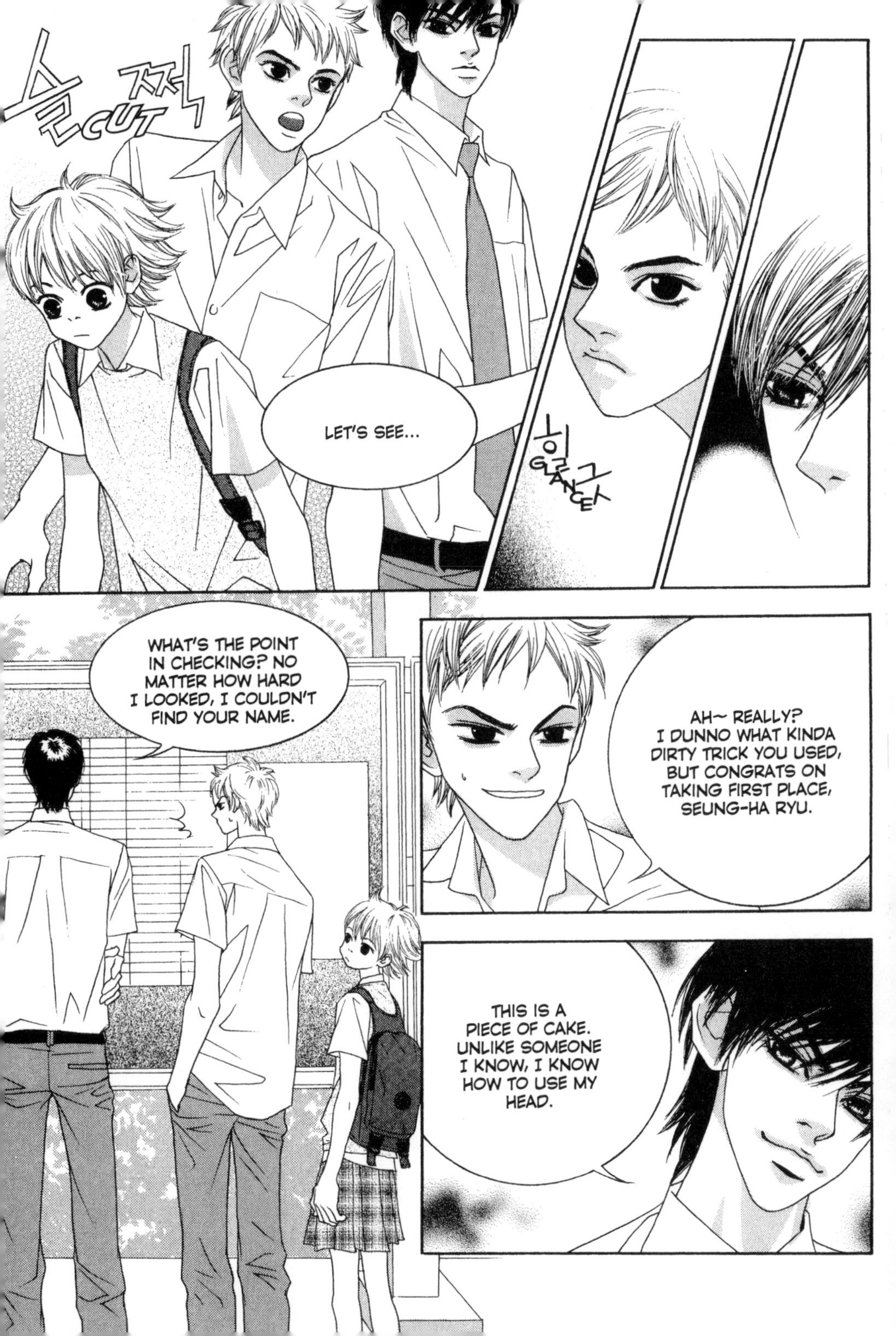

슬쩍
CUT
LET'S SEE...
힐긋
GLANCE
WHAT'S THE POINT IN CHECKING? NO MATTER HOW HARD I LOOKED, I COULDN'T FIND YOUR NAME.
AH~ REALLY? I DUNNO WHAT KINDA DIRTY TRICK YOU USED, BUT CONGRATS ON TAKING FIRST PLACE, SEUNG-HA RYU.
THIS IS A PIECE OF CAKE. UNLIKE SOMEONE I KNOW, I KNOW HOW TO USE MY HEAD.

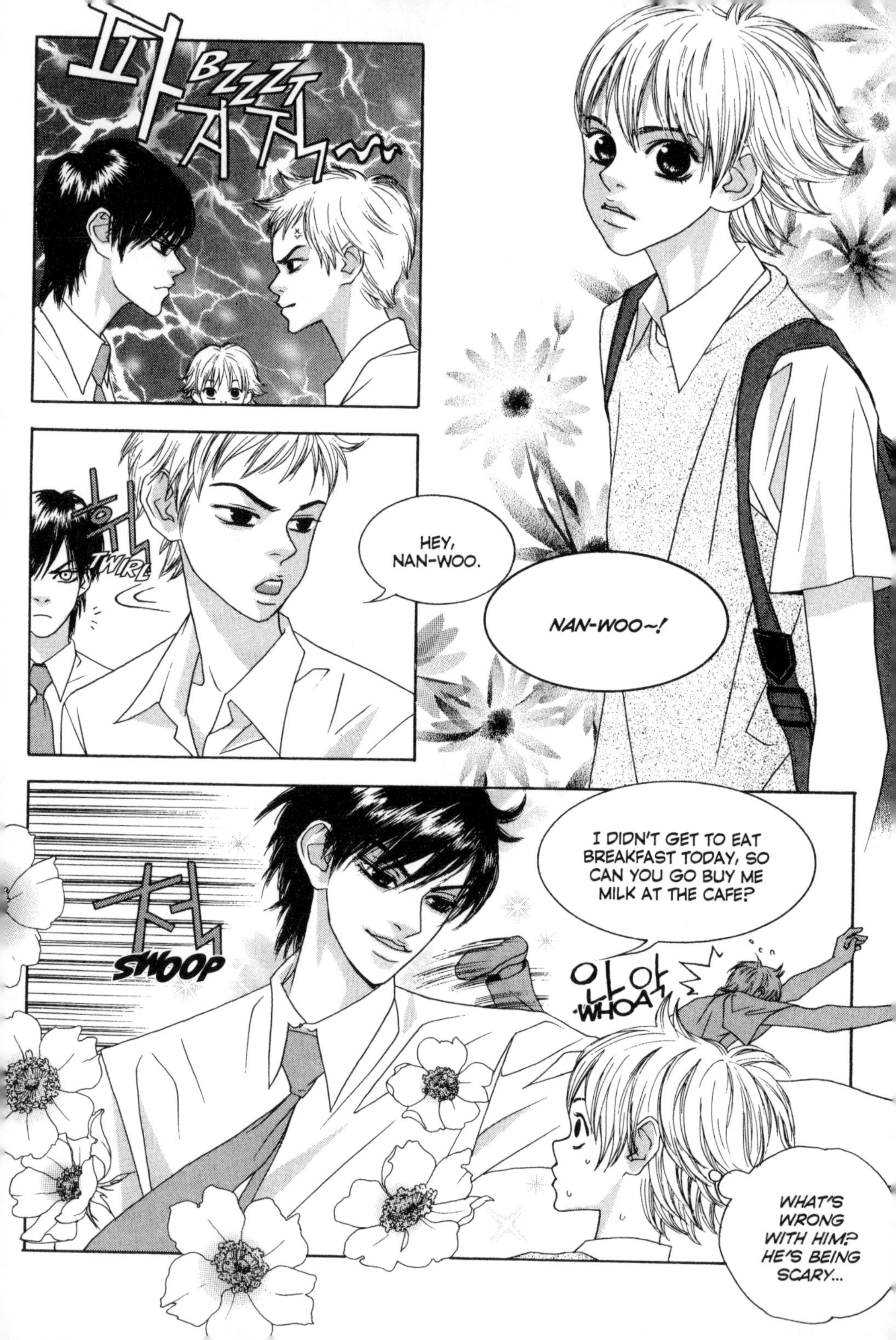
BZZZT
TWIRL
HEY, NAN-WOO.
NAN-WOO~!
SWOOP
I DIDN'T GET TO EAT BREAKFAST TODAY, SO CAN YOU GO BUY ME MILK AT THE CAFE?
WHOA
WHAT'S WRONG WITH HIM? HE'S BEING SCARY...

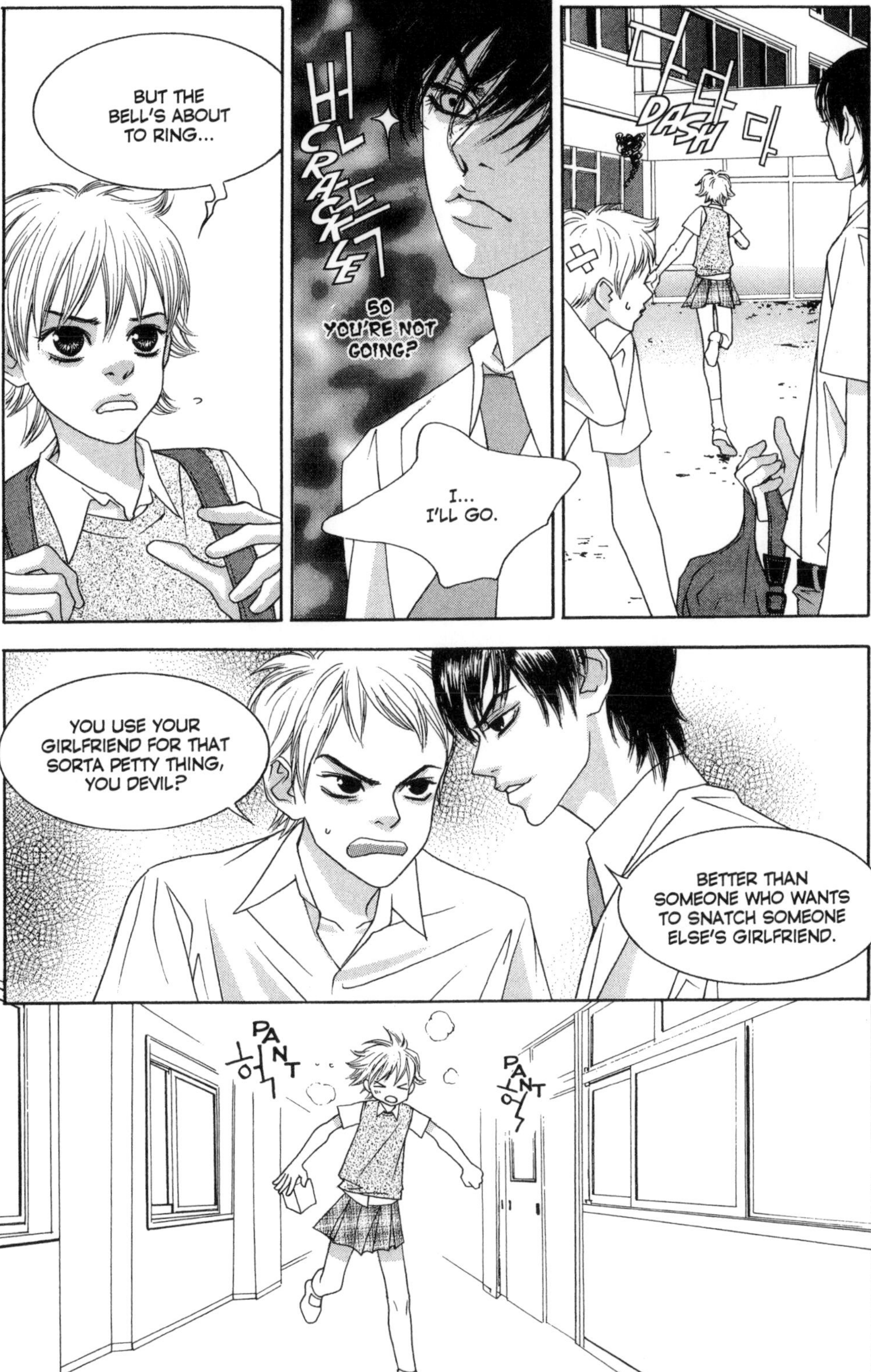
BUT THE BELL'S ABOUT TO RING...
CRACKLE
SO YOU'RE NOT GOING?
I... I'LL GO.
DASH
YOU USE YOUR GIRLFRIEND FOR THAT SORTA PETTY THING, YOU DEVIL?
BETTER THAN SOMEONE WHO WANTS TO SNATCH SOMEONE ELSE'S GIRLFRIEND.
PANT
PANT

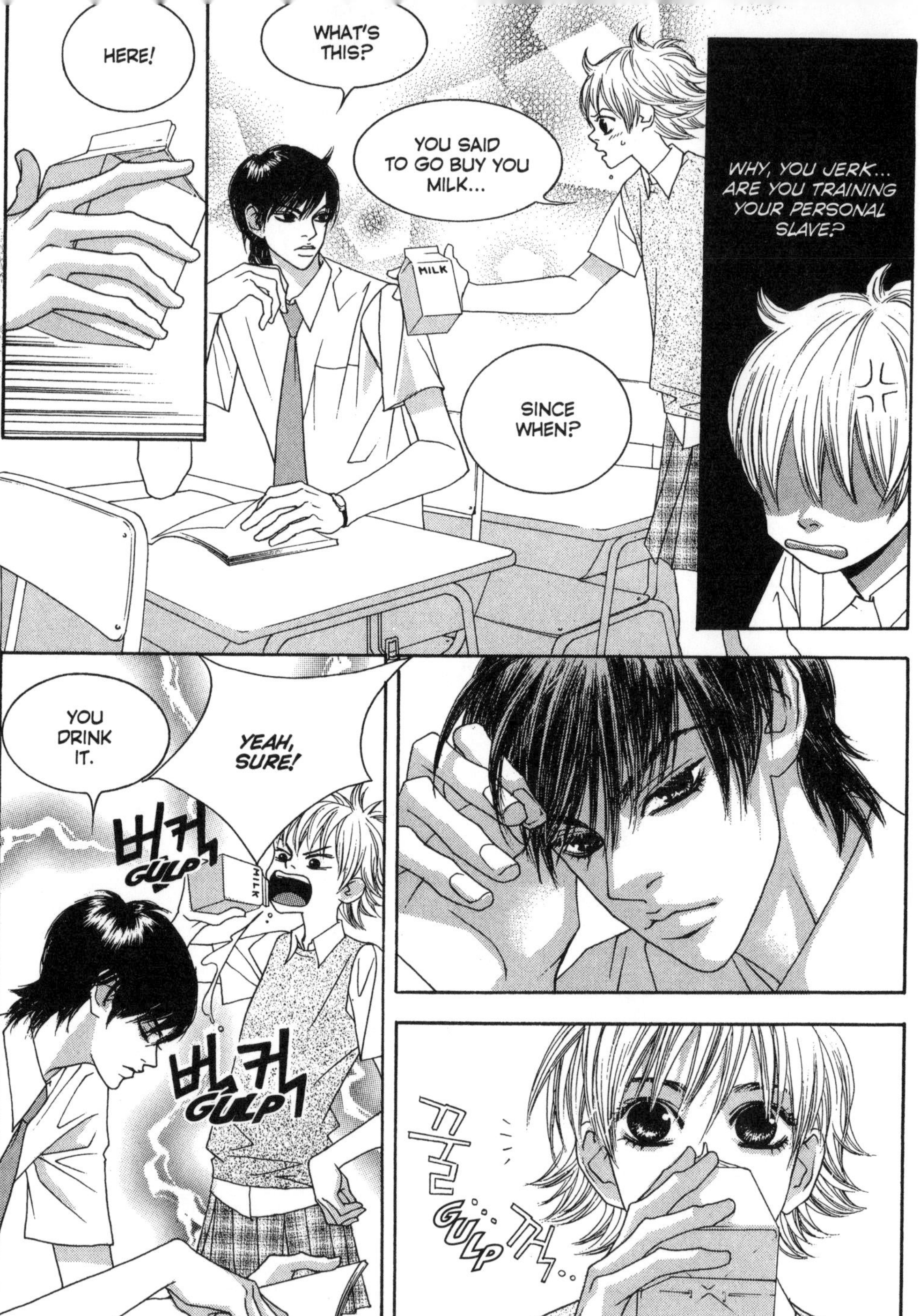
HERE!
WHAT'S THIS?
YOU SAID TO GO BUY YOU MILK...
MILK
SINCE WHEN?
WHY, YOU JERK... ARE YOU TRAINING YOUR PERSONAL SLAVE?
YOU DRINK IT.
YEAH, SURE!
벌컥
GULP
MILK
벌컥
GULP
꿀꺽
GULP

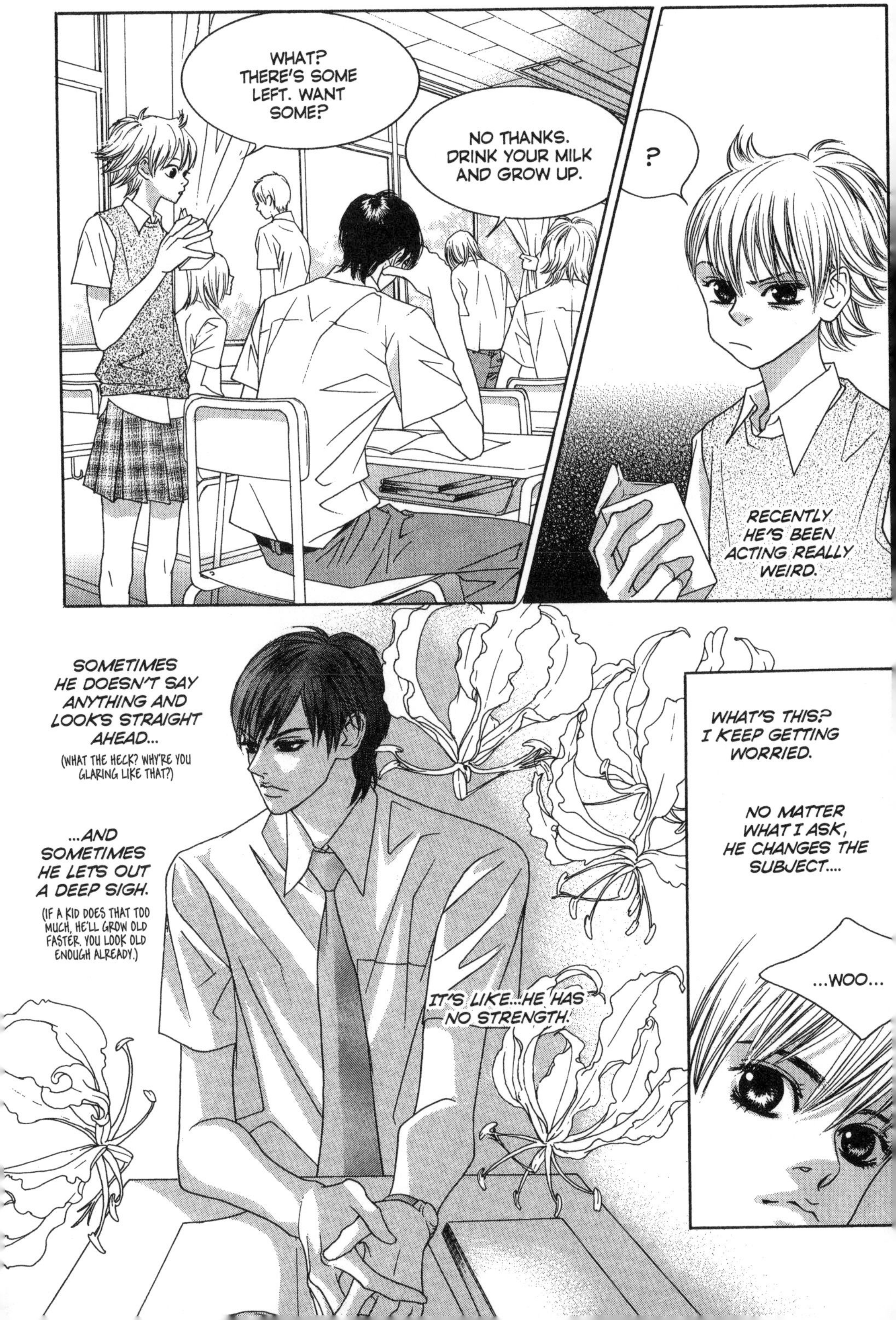
WHAT? THERE'S SOME LEFT. WANT SOME?
NO THANKS. DRINK YOUR MILK AND GROW UP.
?
RECENTLY HE'S BEEN ACTING REALLY WEIRD.
SOMETIMES HE DOESN'T SAY ANYTHING AND LOOKS STRAIGHT AHEAD...
(WHAT THE HECK? WHY'RE YOU GLARING LIKE THAT?)
...AND SOMETIMES HE LETS OUT A DEEP SIGH.
(IF A KID DOES THAT TOO MUCH, HE'LL GROW OLD FASTER. YOU LOOK OLD ENOUGH ALREADY.)
IT'S LIKE...HE HAS NO STRENGTH.
WHAT'S THIS? I KEEP GETTING WORRIED.
NO MATTER WHAT I ASK, HE CHANGES THE SUBJECT....
...WOO...

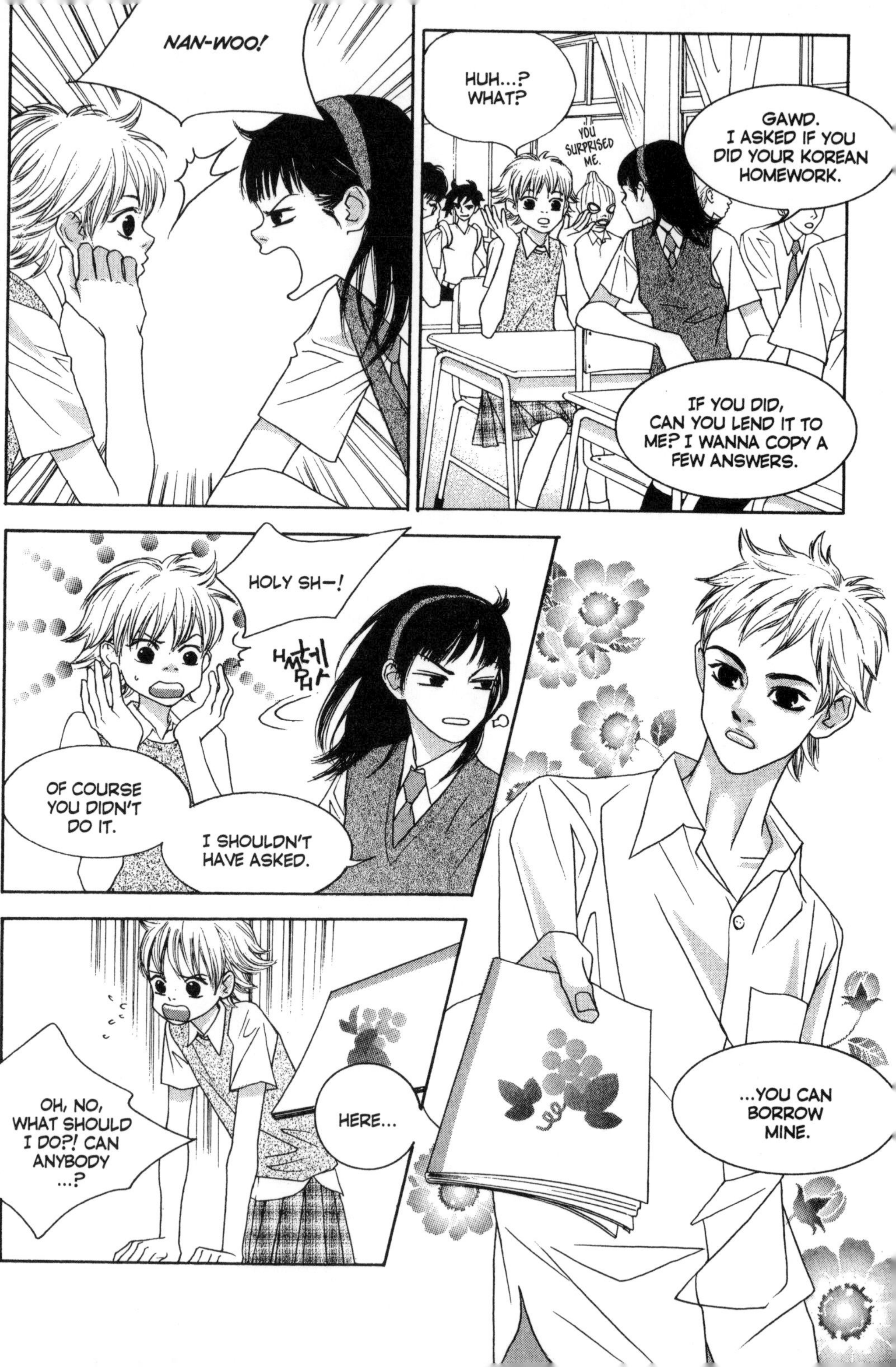
NAN-WOO!
HUH...? WHAT?
YOU SURPRISED ME.
GAWD. I ASKED IF YOU DID YOUR KOREAN HOMEWORK.
IF YOU DID, CAN YOU LEND IT TO ME? I WANNA COPY A FEW ANSWERS.
HOLY SH—!
OF COURSE YOU DIDN'T DO IT.
I SHOULDN'T HAVE ASKED.
OH, NO, WHAT SHOULD I DO?! CAN ANYBODY ...?
HERE...
...YOU CAN BORROW MINE.

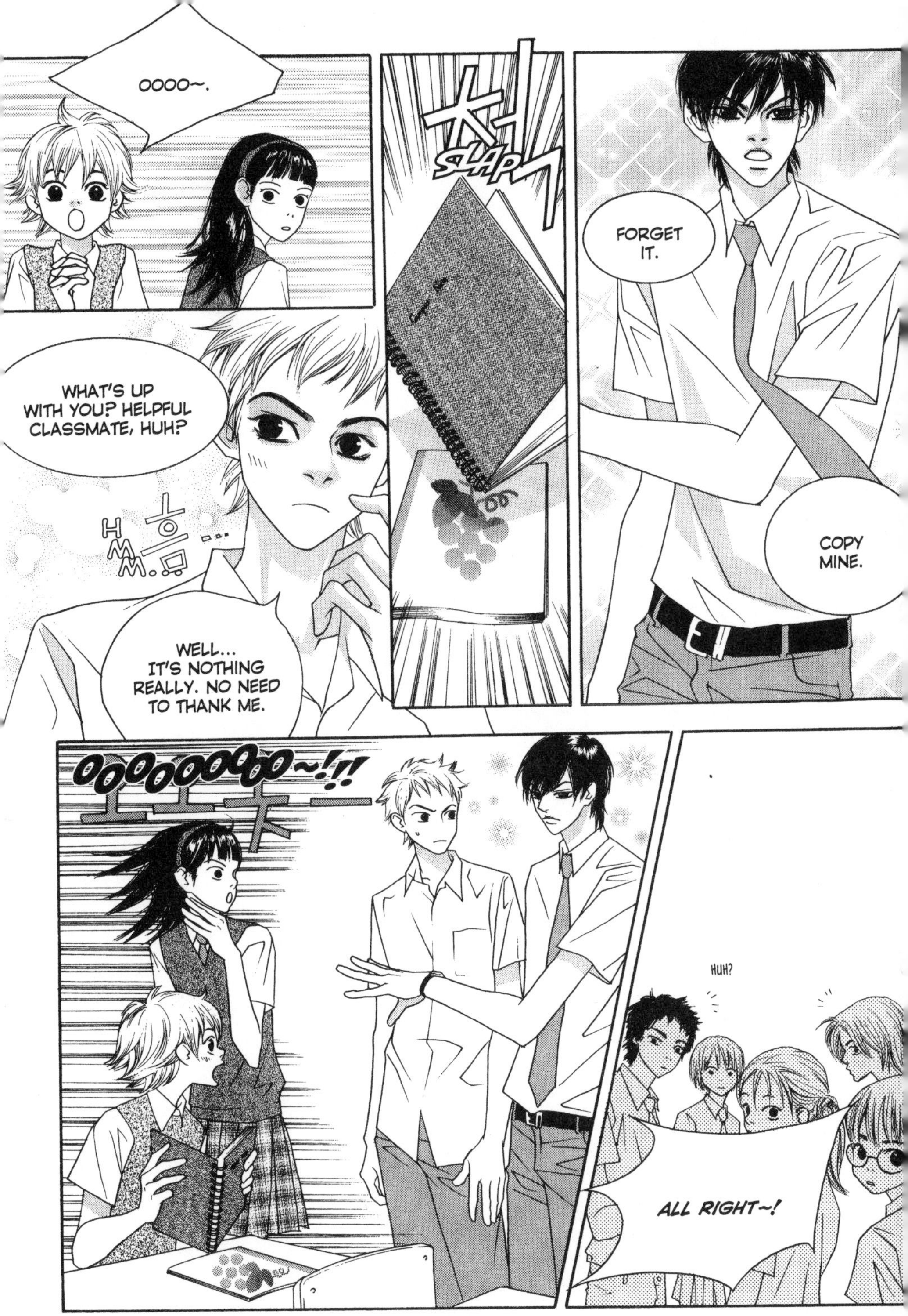
OOOO~.
WHAT'S UP WITH YOU? HELPFUL CLASSMATE, HUH?
HMM...
WELL... IT'S NOTHING REALLY. NO NEED TO THANK ME.
SLAP
FORGET IT.
COPY MINE.
OOOOOOOOO~!!!
HUH?
ALL RIGHT~!

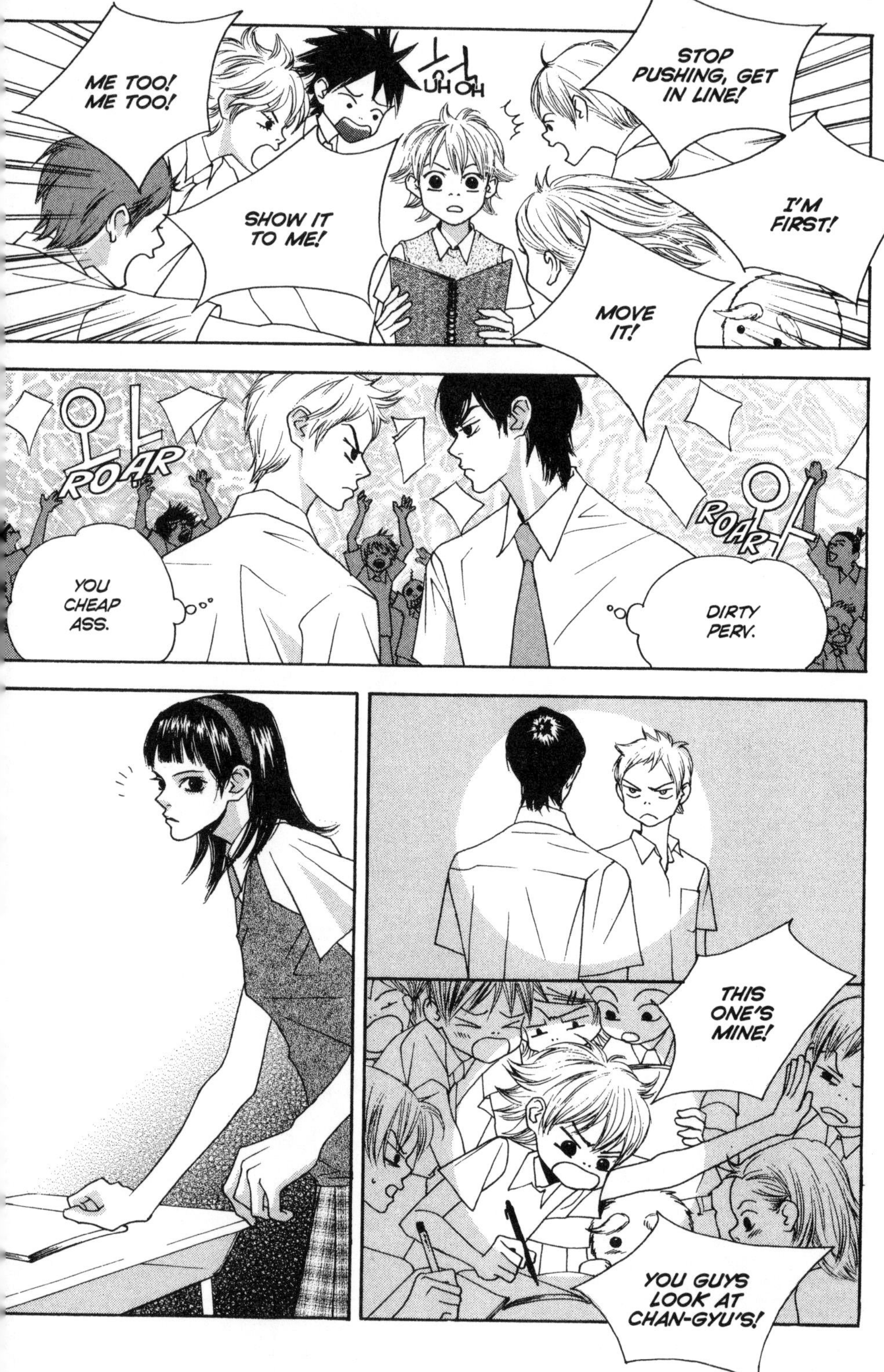
ME TOO! ME TOO!
UH OH
SHOW IT TO ME!
STOP PUSHING, GET IN LINE!
I'M FIRST!
MOVE IT!
ROAR
YOU CHEAP ASS.
ROAR
DIRTY PERV.
THIS ONE'S MINE!
YOU GUYS LOOK AT CHAN-GYU'S!

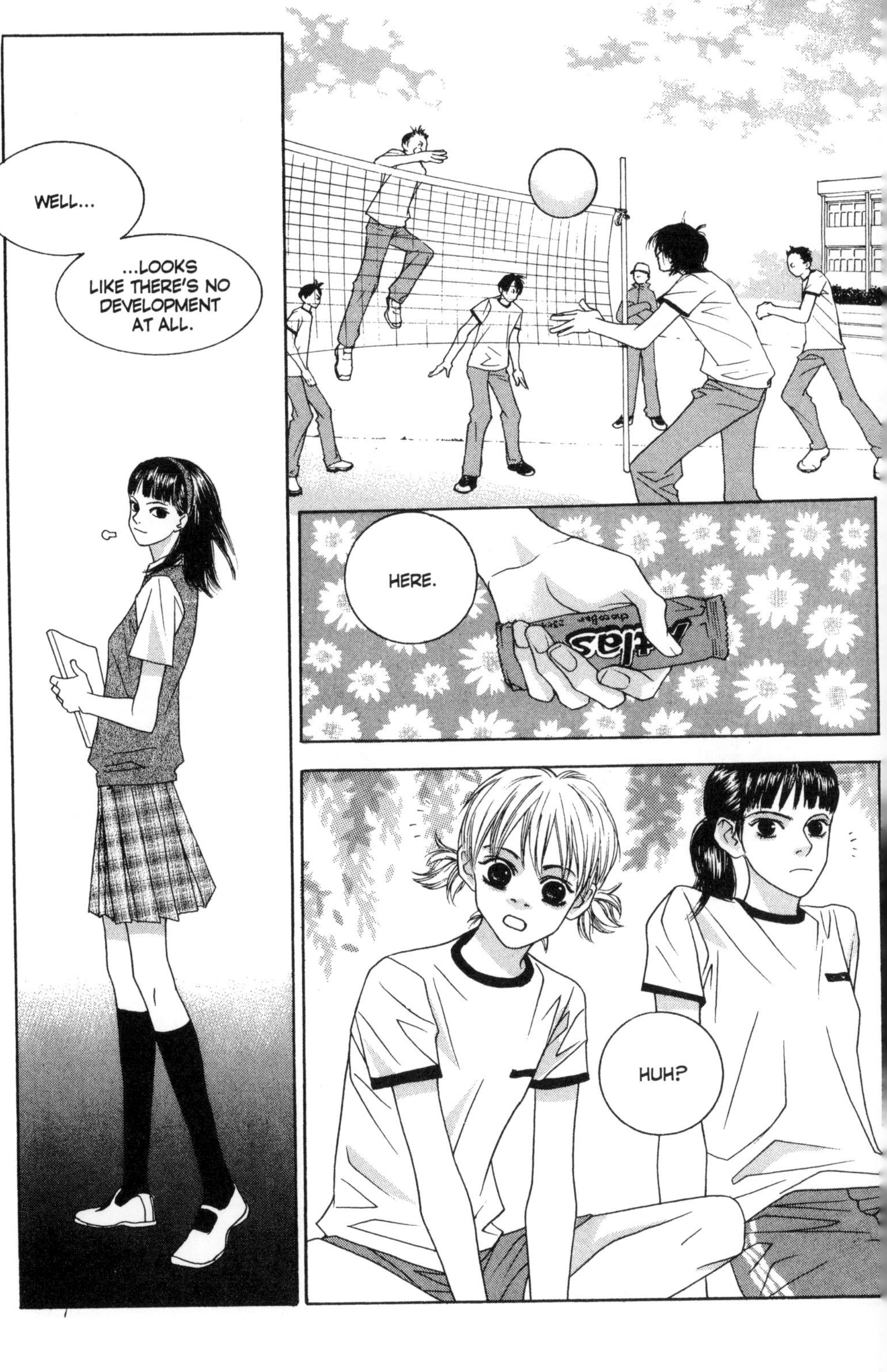
WELL...
...LOOKS LIKE THERE'S NO DEVELOPMENT AT ALL.
HERE.
HUH?

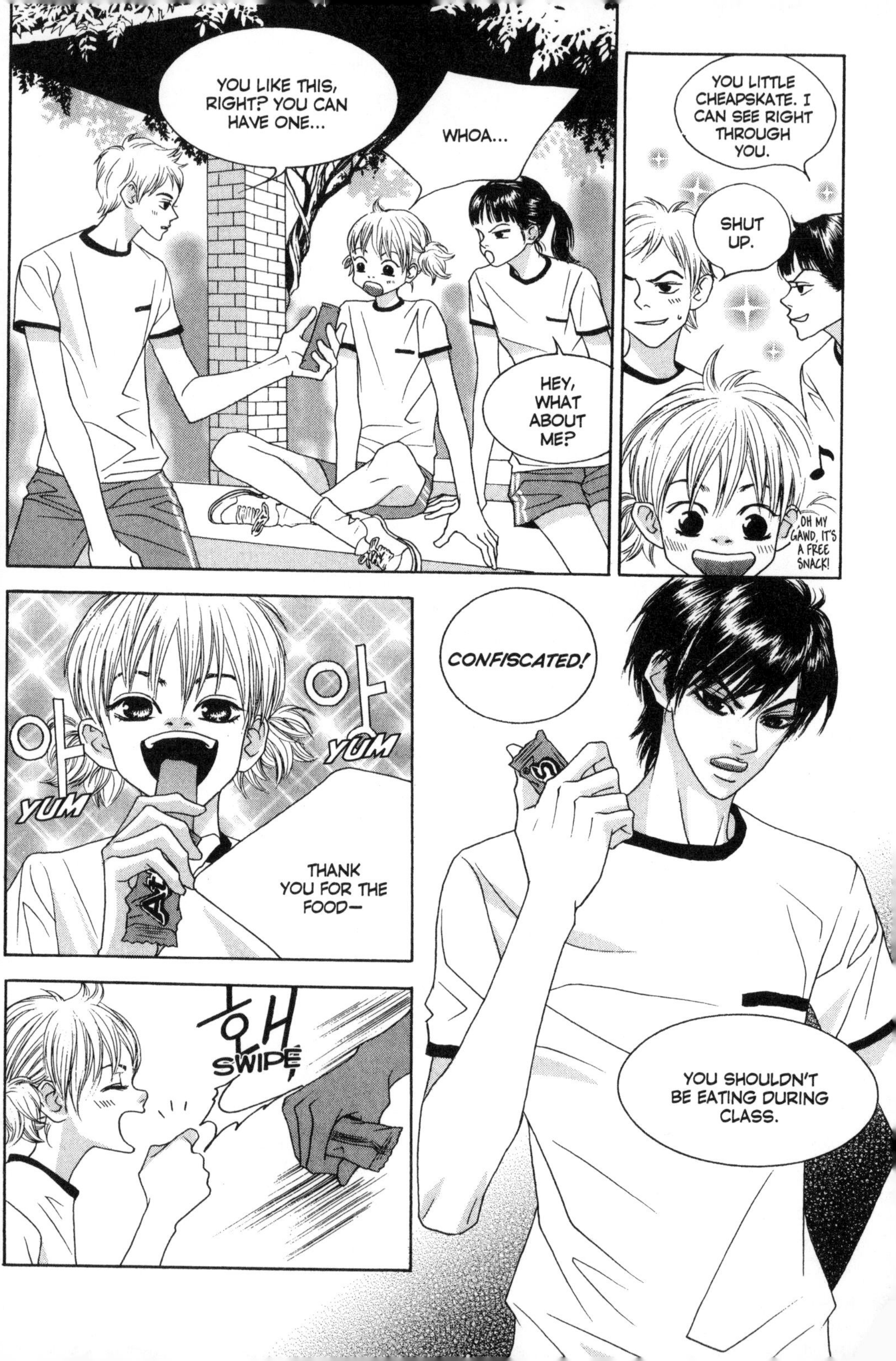
YOU LIKE THIS, RIGHT? YOU CAN HAVE ONE...
WHOA...
HEY, WHAT ABOUT ME?
YOU LITTLE CHEAPSKATE. I CAN SEE RIGHT THROUGH YOU.
SHUT UP.
OH MY GAWD, IT'S A FREE SNACK!
YUM
YUM
THANK YOU FOR THE FOOD—
SWIPE
CONFISCATED!
YOU SHOULDN'T BE EATING DURING CLASS.

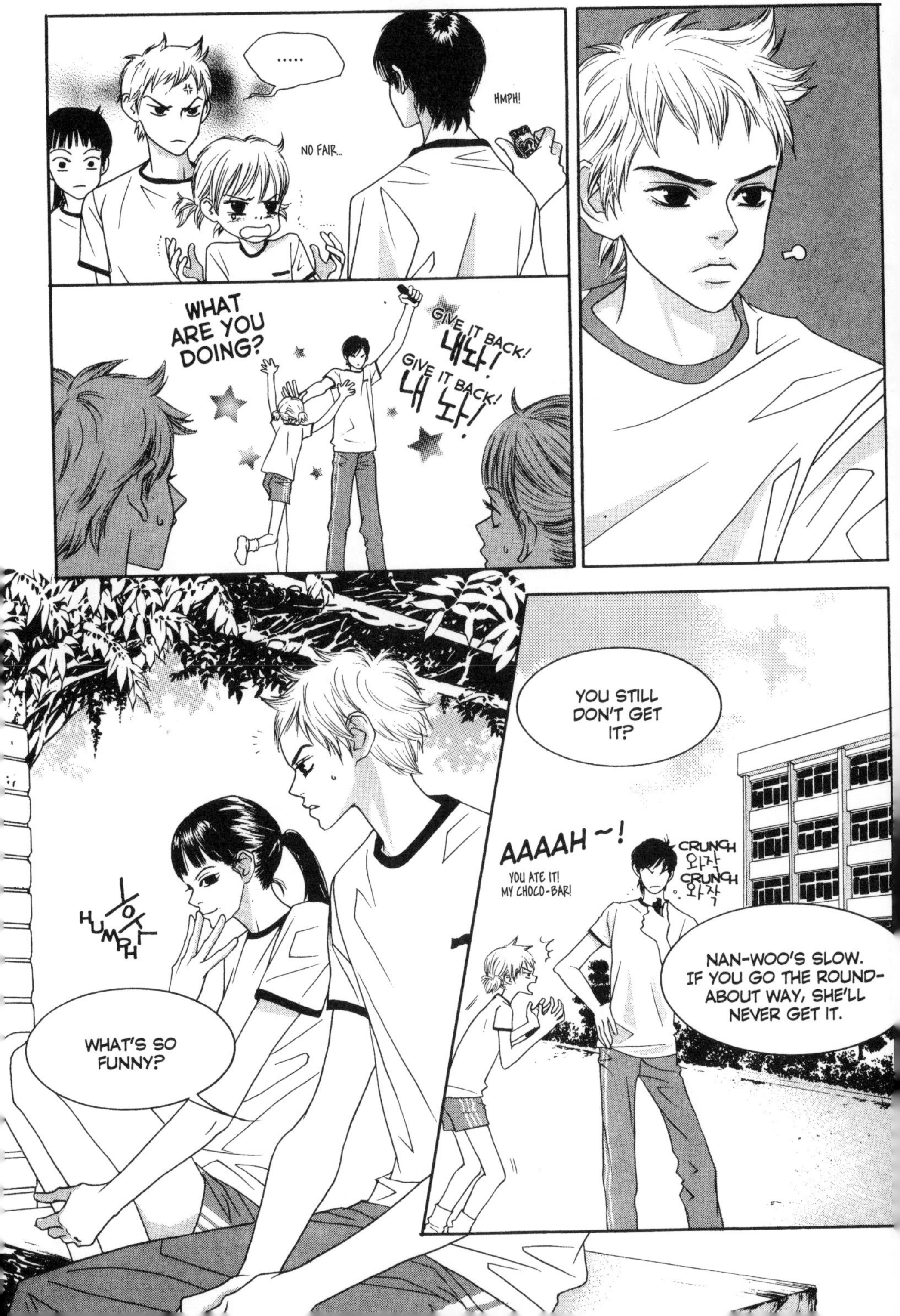

......
NO FAIR...
HMPH!
WHAT ARE YOU DOING?
GIVE IT BACK!
내놔!
GIVE IT BACK!
내 놔!
YOKI HUMPH
WHAT'S SO FUNNY?
YOU STILL DON'T GET IT?
AAAAH ~!
YOU ATE IT! MY CHOCO-BAR!
CRUNCH
와작
CRUNCH
와작
NAN-WOO'S SLOW. IF YOU GO THE ROUND-ABOUT WAY, SHE'LL NEVER GET IT.

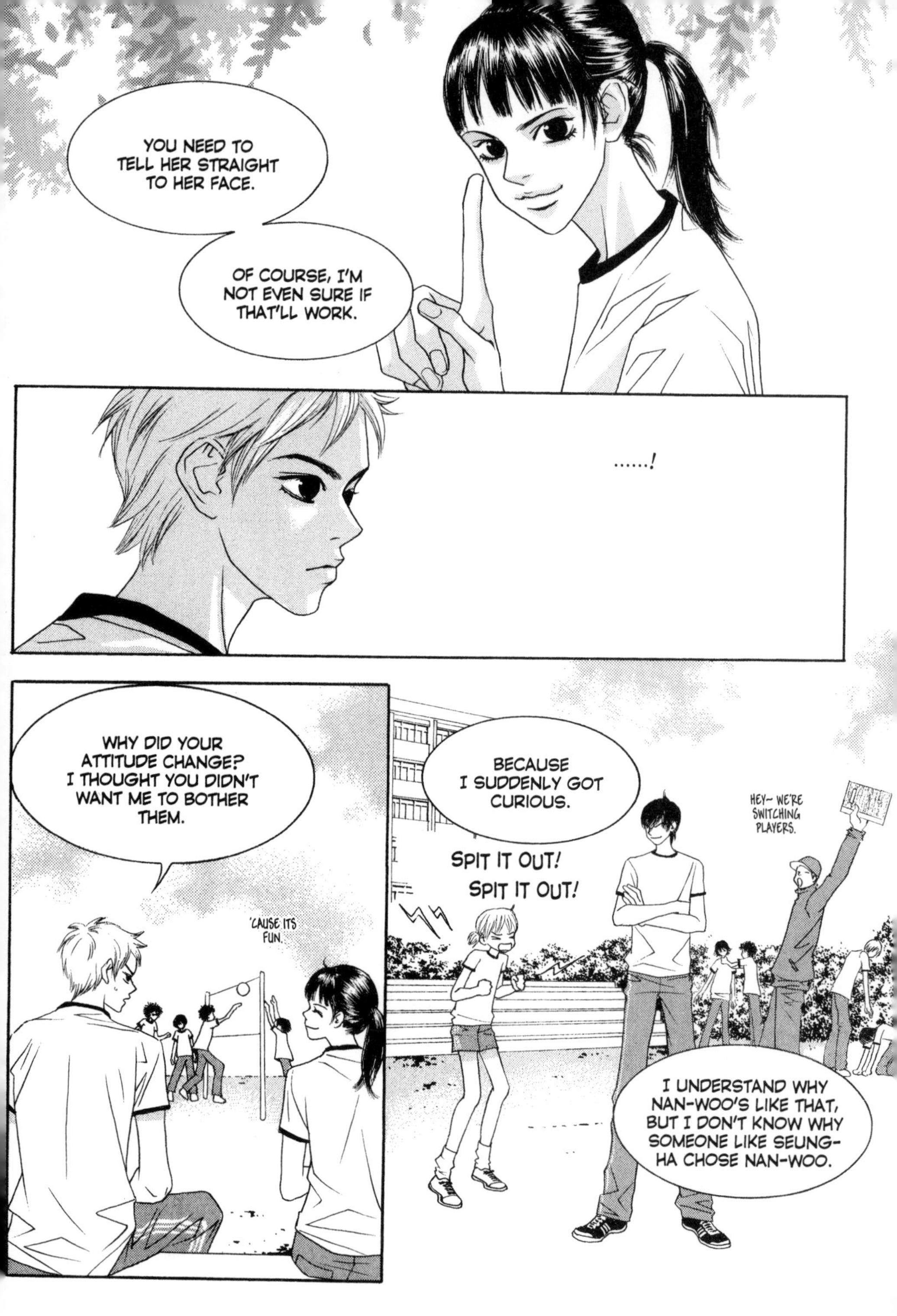
YOU NEED TO TELL HER STRAIGHT TO HER FACE.
OF COURSE, I'M NOT EVEN SURE IF THAT'LL WORK.
......!
WHY DID YOUR ATTITUDE CHANGE? I THOUGHT YOU DIDN'T WANT ME TO BOTHER THEM.
'CAUSE ITS FUN.
BECAUSE I SUDDENLY GOT CURIOUS.
SPIT IT OUT!
SPIT IT OUT!
HEY~ WE'RE SWITCHING PLAYERS.
I UNDERSTAND WHY NAN-WOO'S LIKE THAT, BUT I DON'T KNOW WHY SOMEONE LIKE SEUNG-HA CHOSE NAN-WOO.

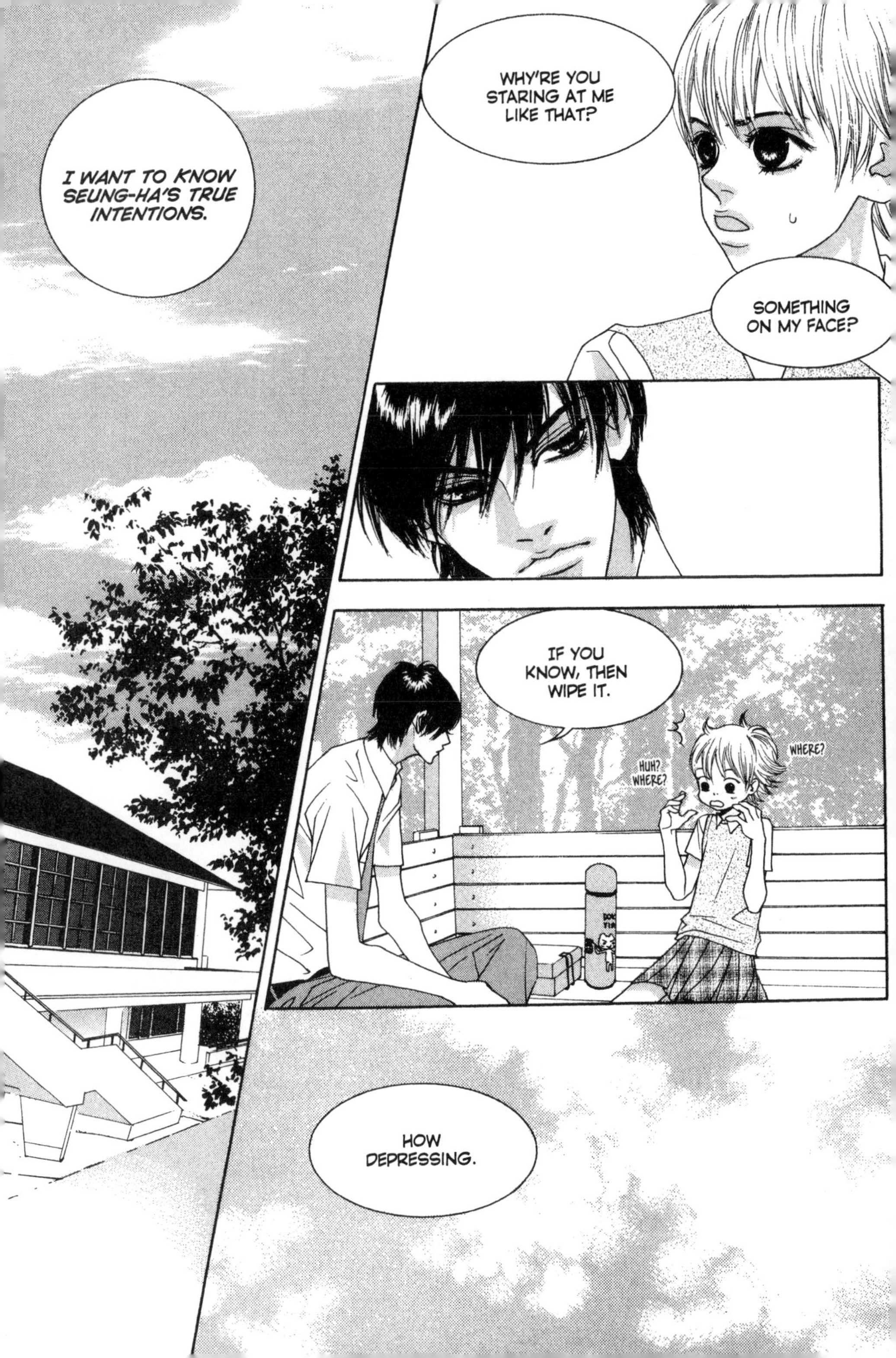

I WANT TO KNOW SEUNG-HA'S TRUE INTENTIONS.
WHY'RE YOU STARING AT ME LIKE THAT?
SOMETHING ON MY FACE?
IF YOU KNOW, THEN WIPE IT.
HUH? WHERE?
WHERE?
HOW DEPRESSING.

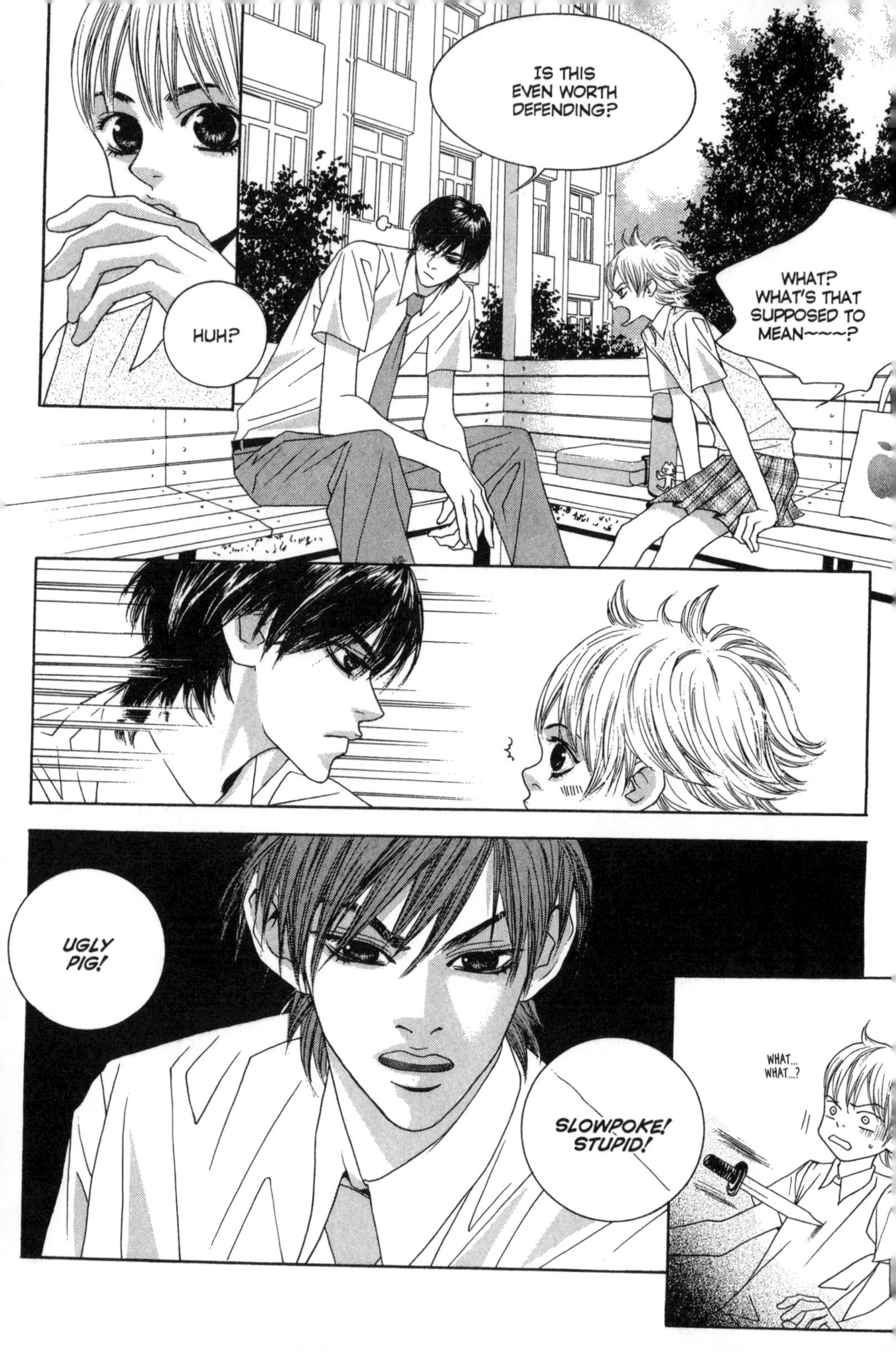
HUH?
IS THIS EVEN WORTH DEFENDING?
WHAT? WHAT'S THAT SUPPOSED TO MEAN~~~~?
UGLY PIG!
SLOWPOKE! STUPID!
WHAT... WHAT...?

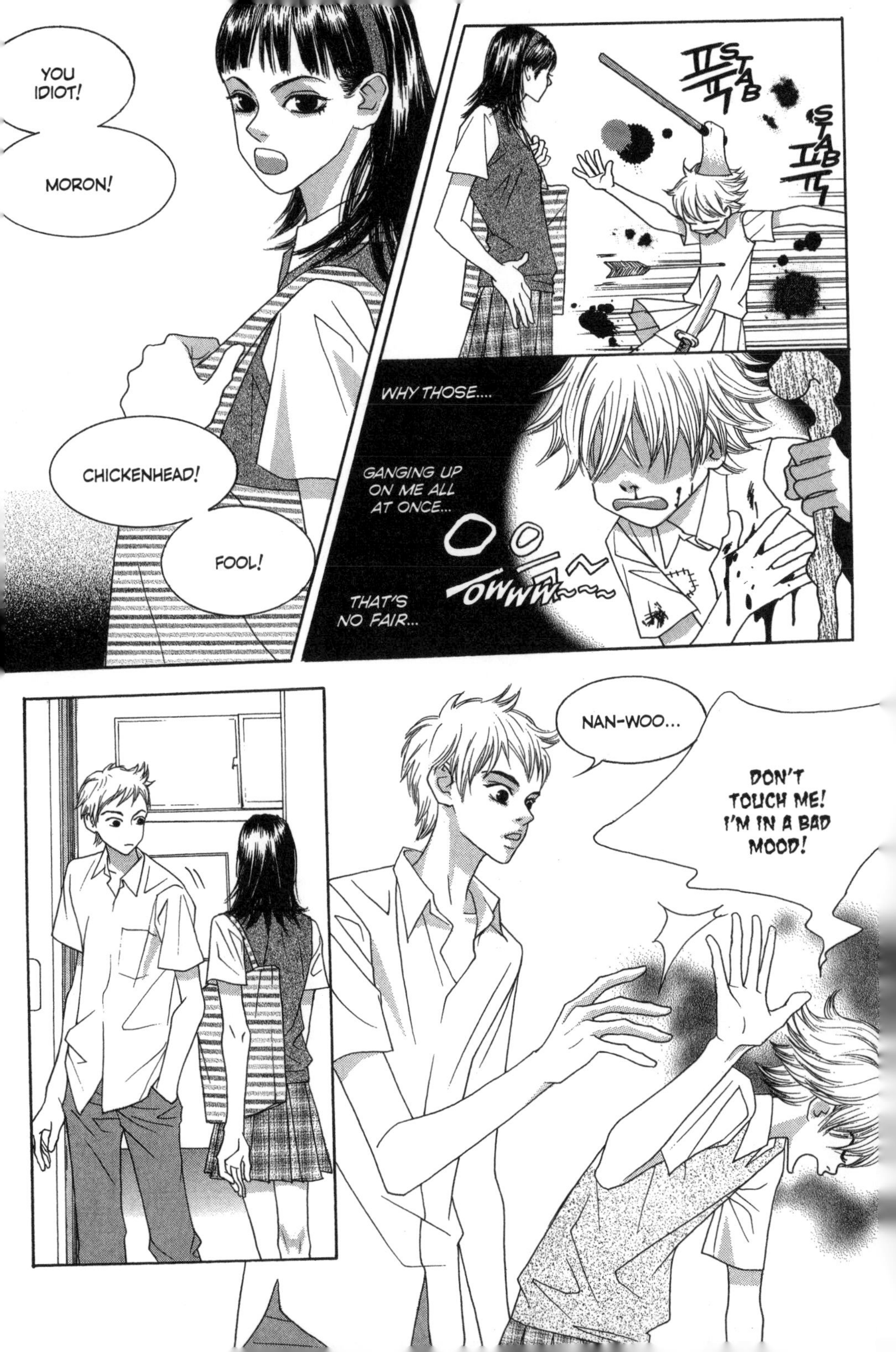
YOU IDIOT!
MORON!
CHICKENHEAD!
FOOL!
STAB
STAB
WHY THOSE....
GANGING UP ON ME ALL AT ONCE...
OWWW~~~
THAT'S NO FAIR...
NAN-WOO...
DON'T TOUCH ME! I'M IN A BAD MOOD!

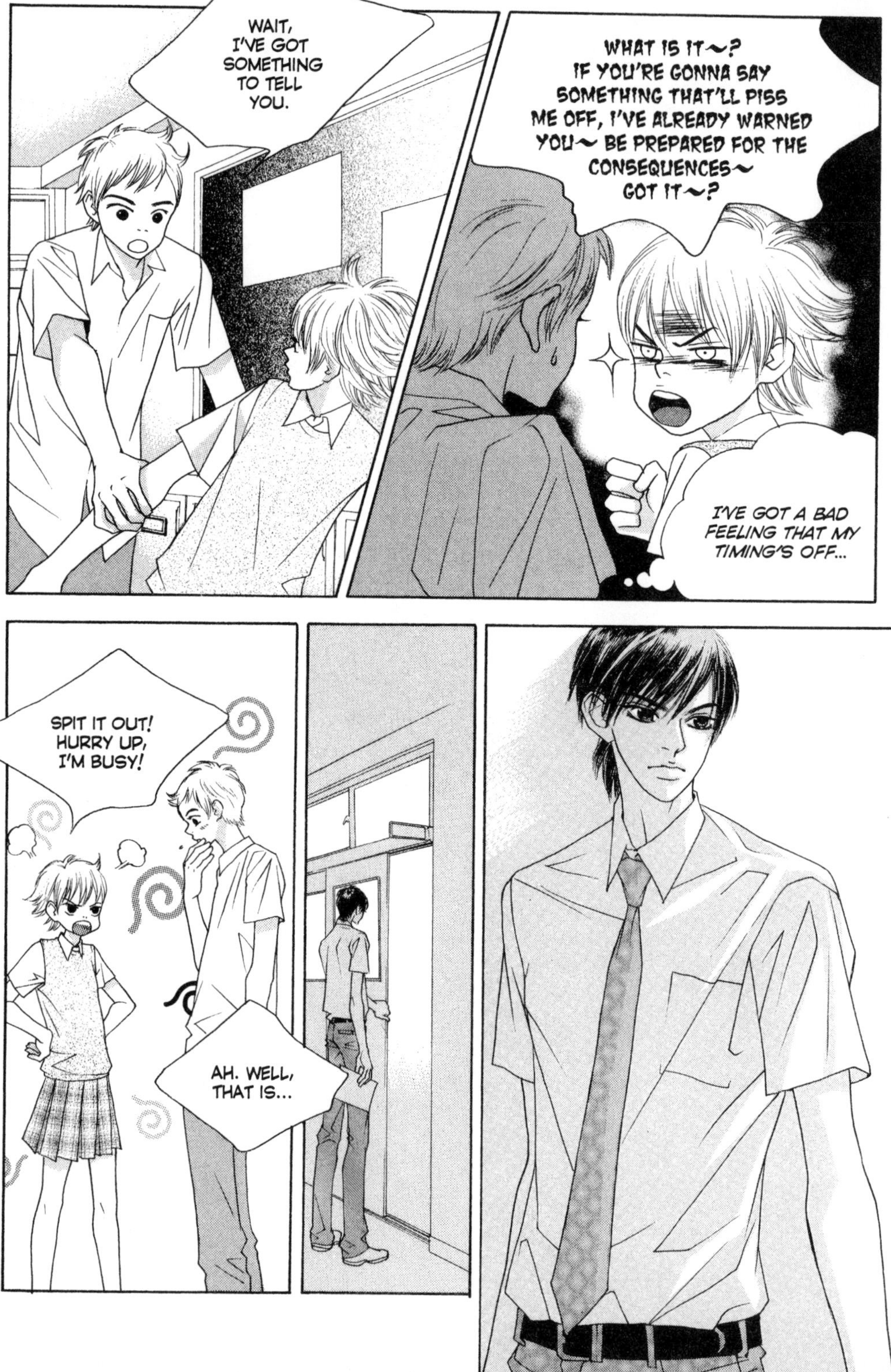
WAIT, I'VE GOT SOMETHING TO TELL YOU.
WHAT IS IT~? IF YOU'RE GONNA SAY SOMETHING THAT'LL PISS ME OFF, I'VE ALREADY WARNED YOU~ BE PREPARED FOR THE CONSEQUENCES~ GOT IT~?
I'VE GOT A BAD FEELING THAT MY TIMING'S OFF...
SPIT IT OUT! HURRY UP, I'M BUSY!
AH. WELL, THAT IS...

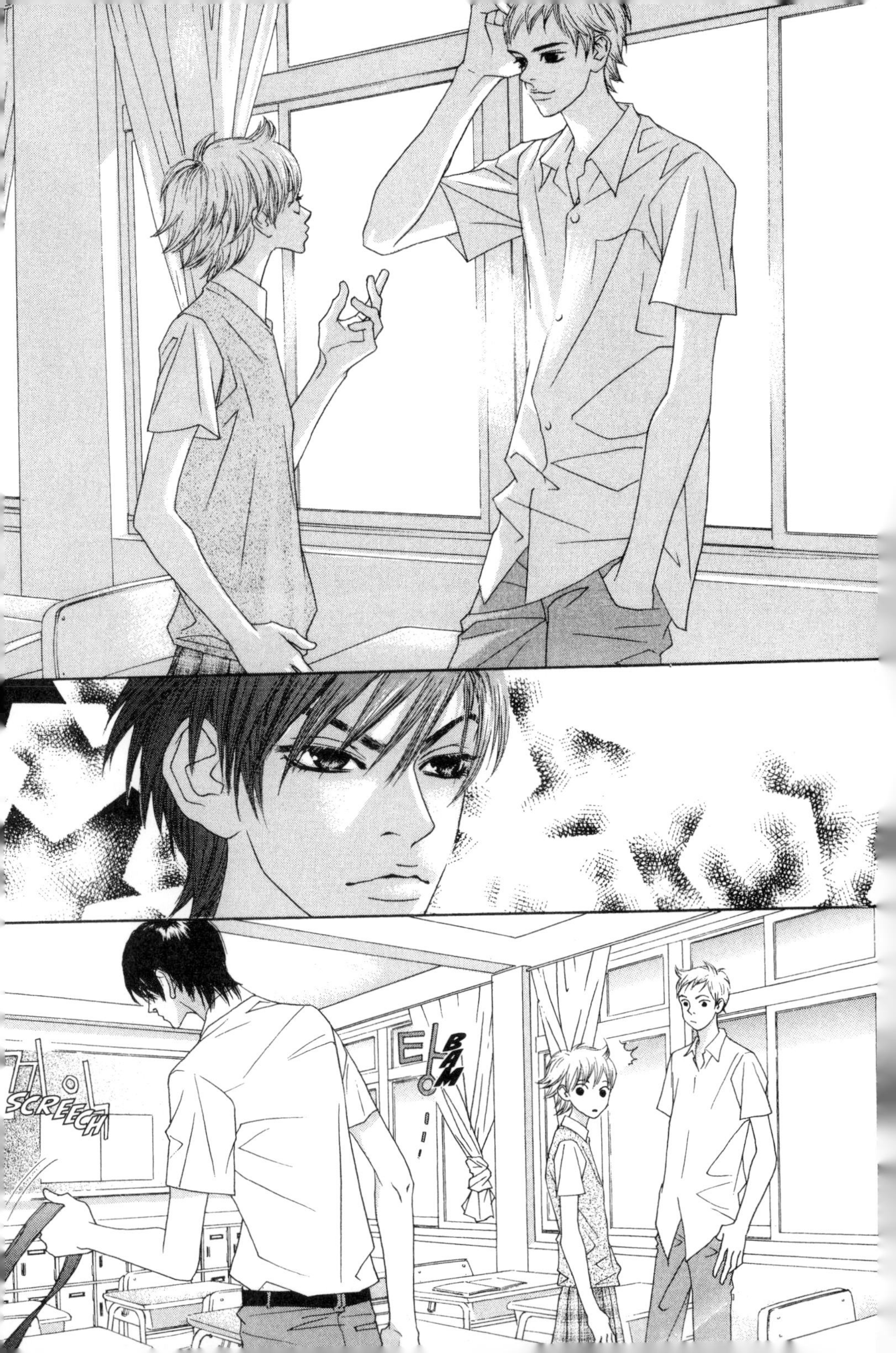
SCREECH
BAM

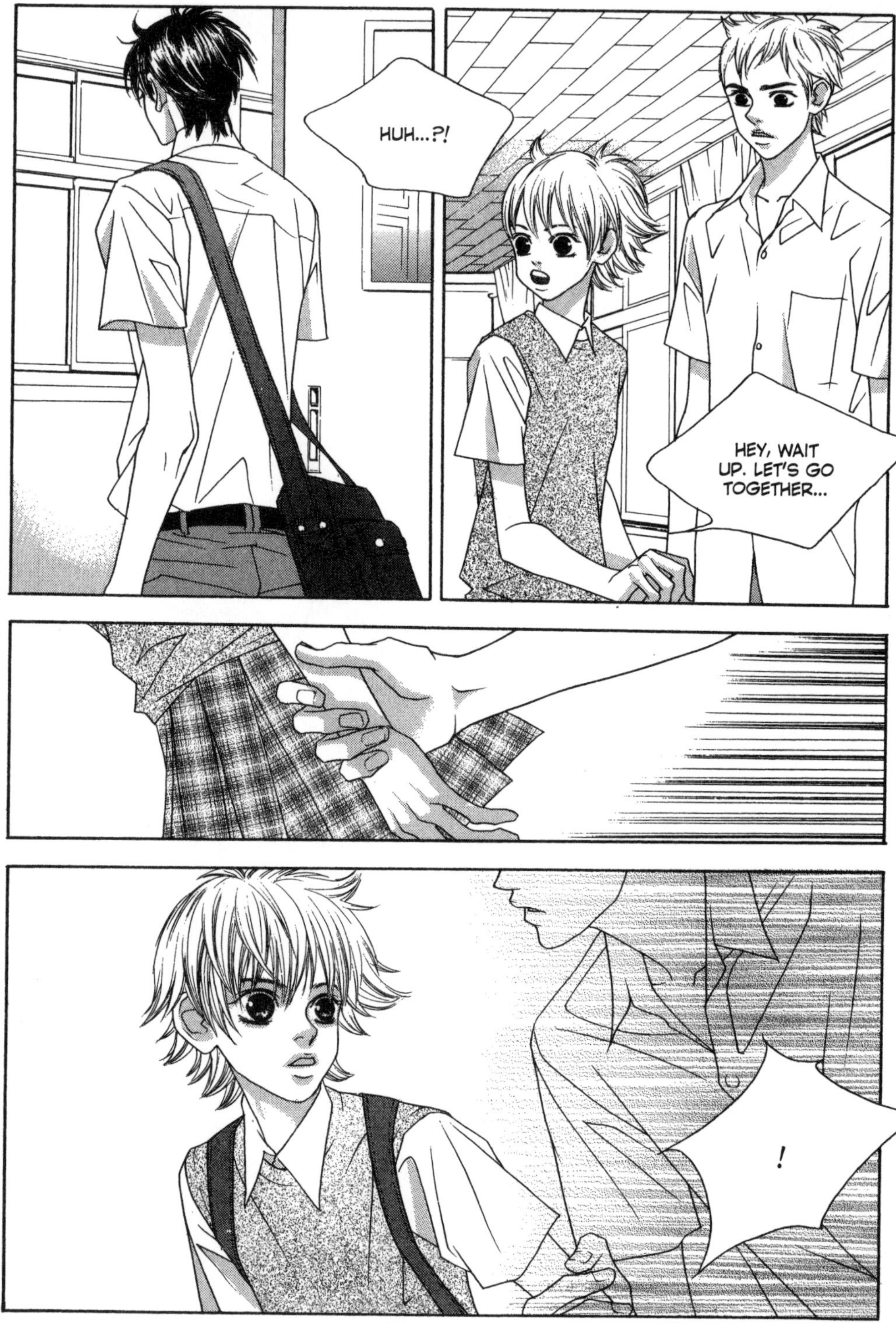
HUH...?!
HEY, WAIT UP. LET'S GO TOGETHER...
!

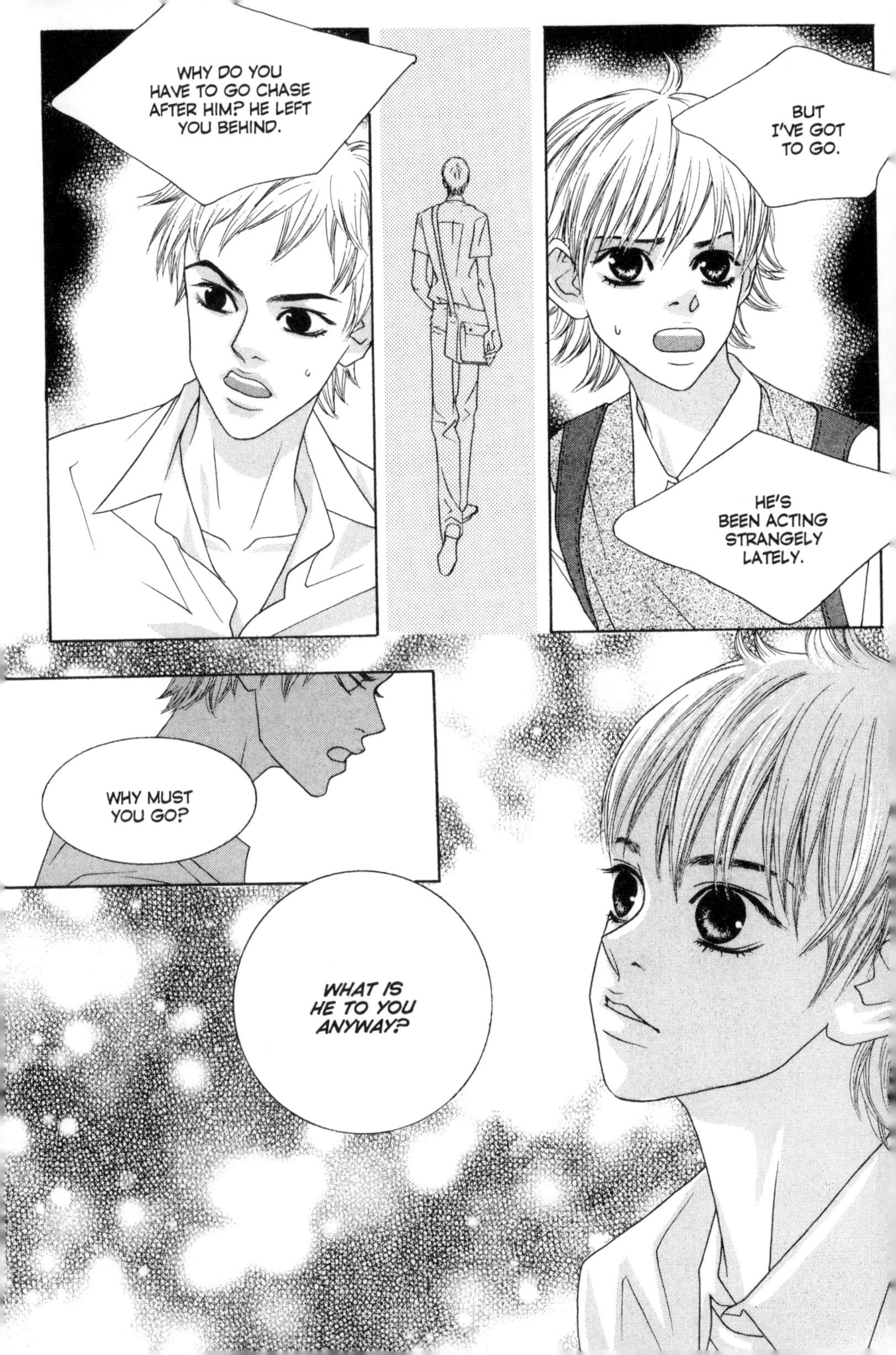
WHY DO YOU HAVE TO GO CHASE AFTER HIM? HE LEFT YOU BEHIND.
BUT I'VE GOT TO GO.
HE'S BEEN ACTING STRANGELY LATELY.
WHY MUST YOU GO?
WHAT IS HE TO YOU ANYWAY?

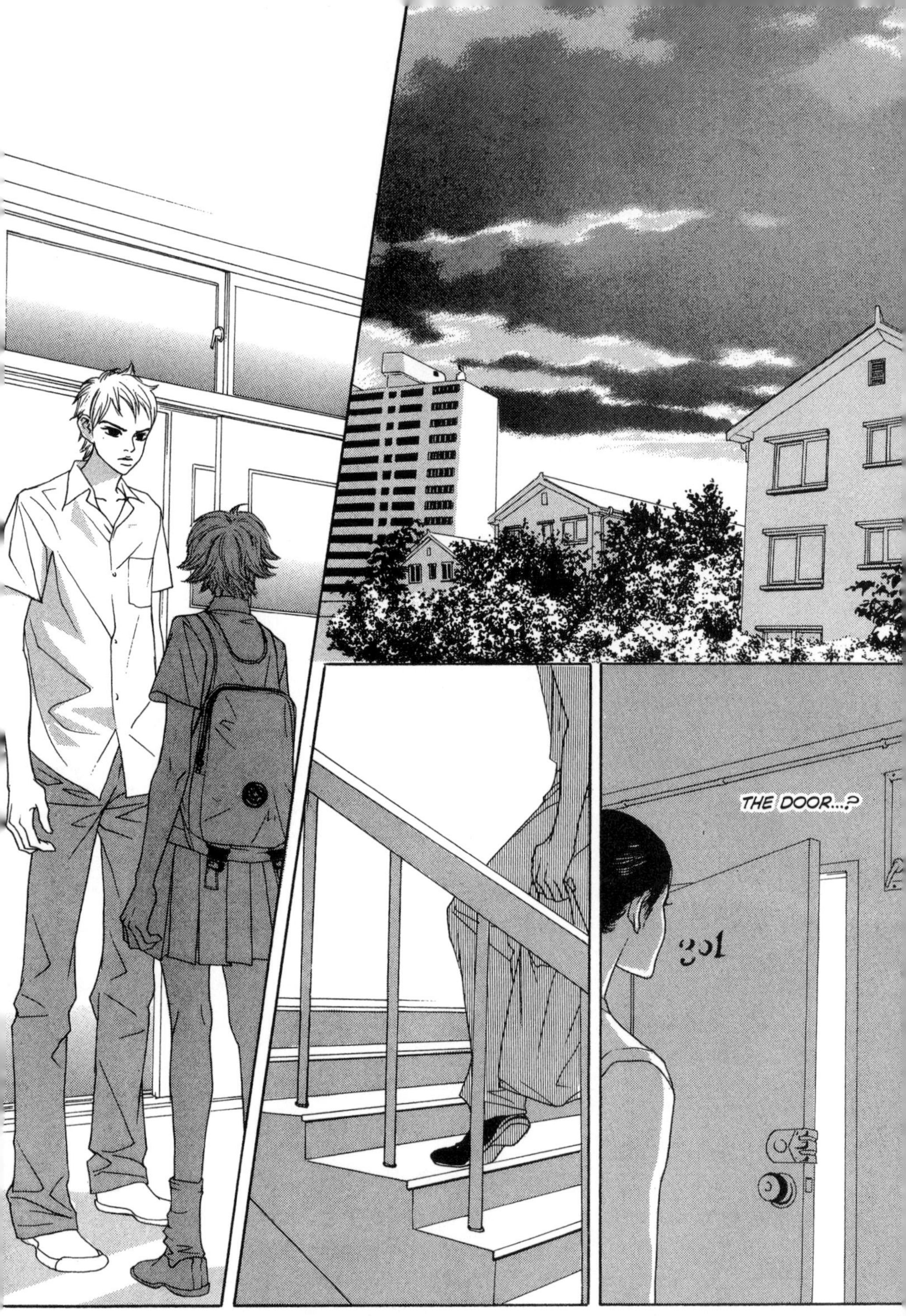
THE DOOR...?
301

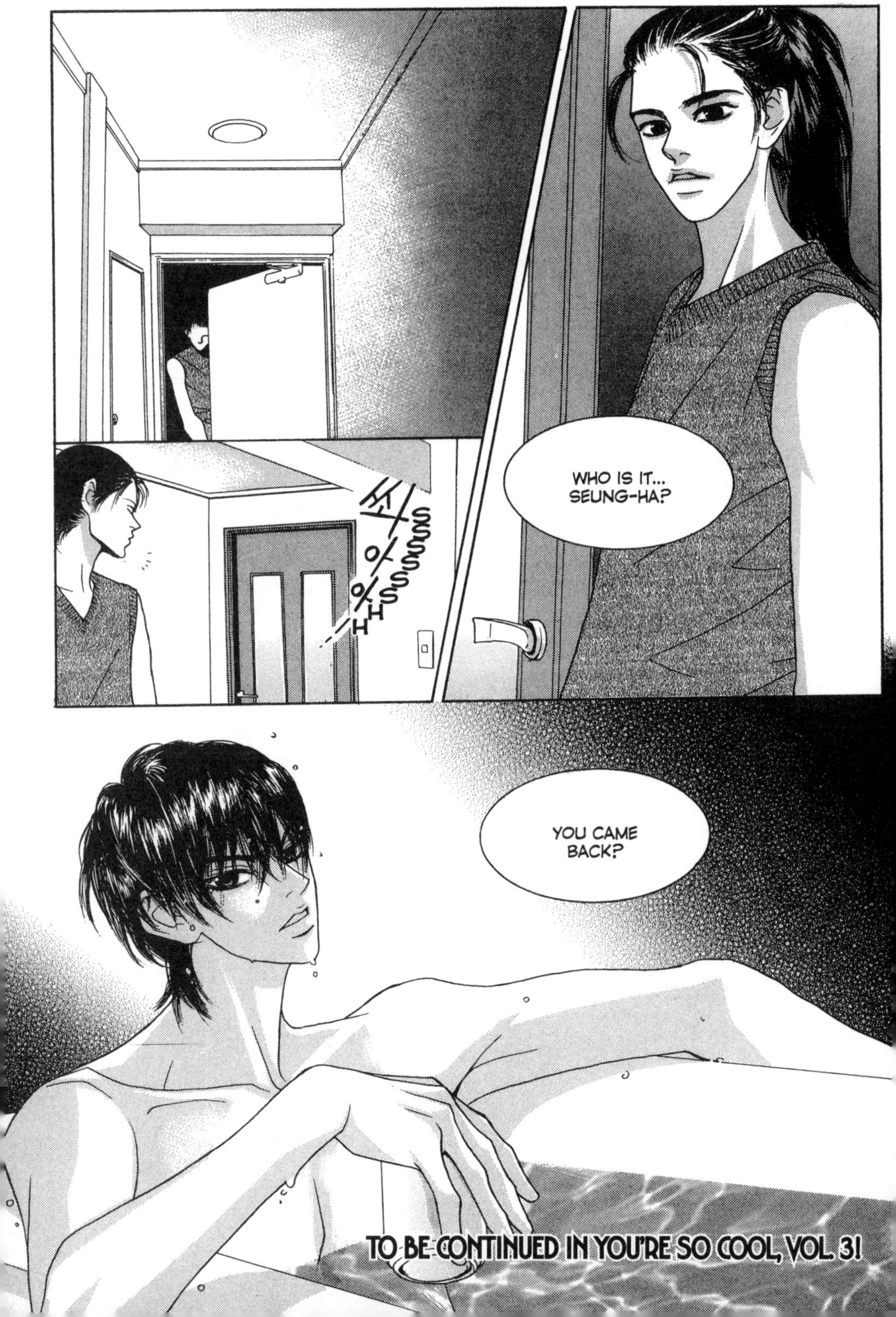
쏴아아
SSSSSSHH
WHO IS IT... SEUNG-HA?
YOU CAME BACK?
TO BE CONTINUED IN YOU'RE SO COOL, VOL. 3!

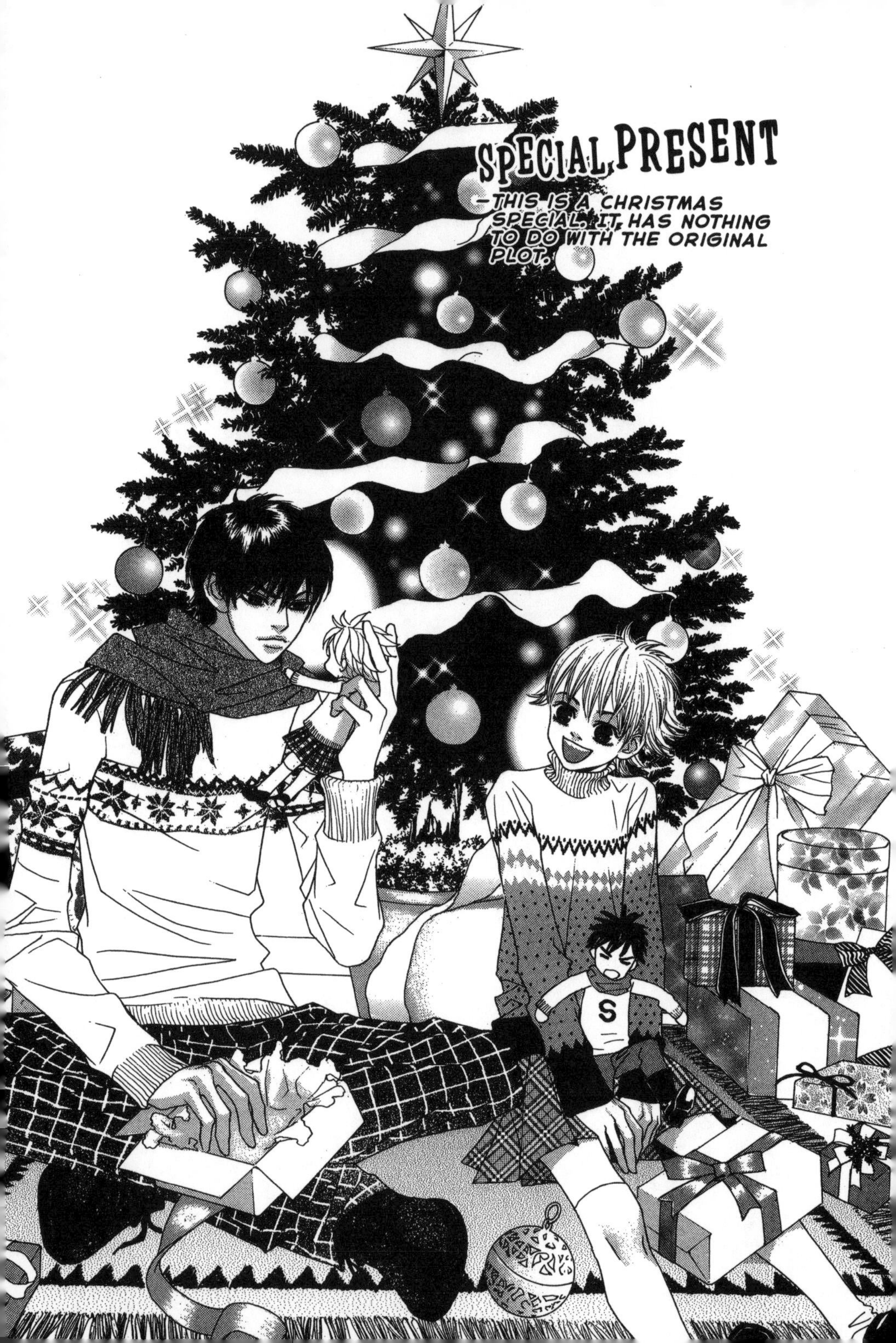
SPECIAL PRESENT
—THIS IS A CHRISTMAS SPECIAL. IT HAS NOTHING TO DO WITH THE ORIGINAL PLOT.
S

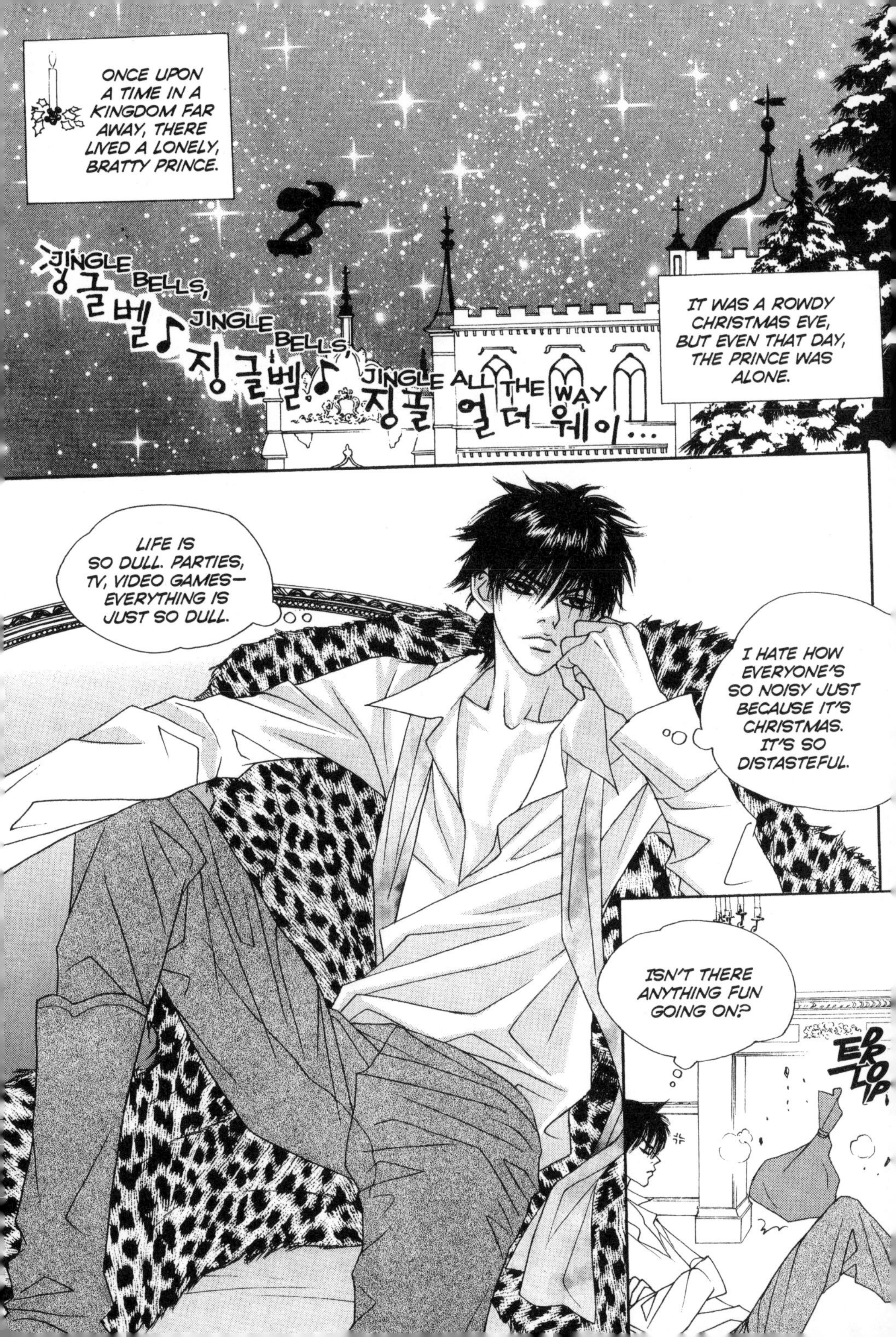

ONCE UPON A TIME IN A KINGDOM FAR AWAY, THERE LIVED A LONELY, BRATTY PRINCE.
징글벨♪ 징글벨♪ 징글 얼더 웨이…
JINGLE BELLS, JINGLE BELLS, JINGLE ALL THE WAY
IT WAS A ROWDY CHRISTMAS EVE, BUT EVEN THAT DAY, THE PRINCE WAS ALONE.
LIFE IS SO DULL. PARTIES, TV, VIDEO GAMES— EVERYTHING IS JUST SO DULL.
I HATE HOW EVERYONE'S SO NOISY JUST BECAUSE IT'S CHRISTMAS. IT'S SO DISTASTEFUL.
ISN'T THERE ANYTHING FUN GOING ON?

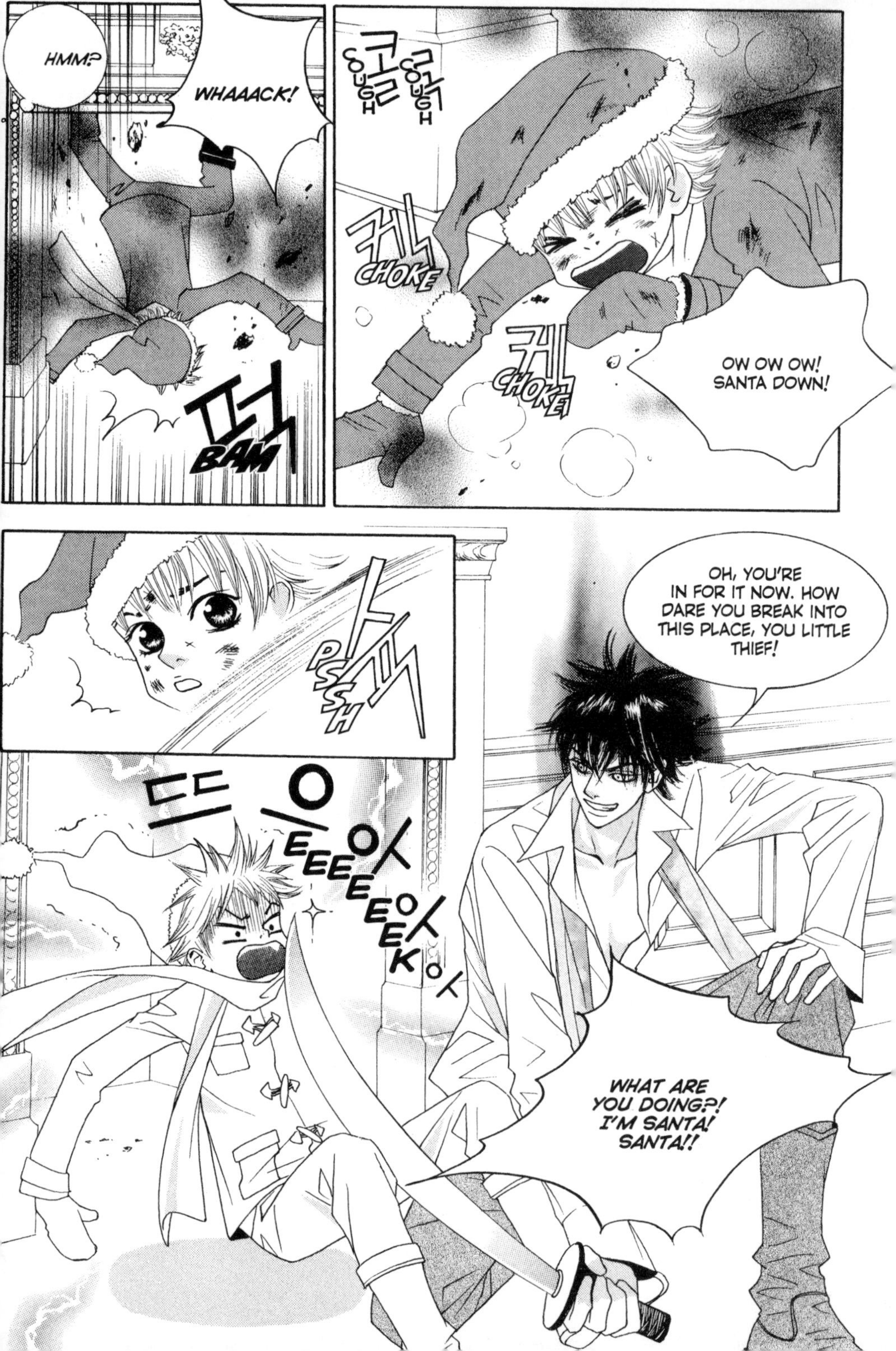

HMM?
WHAAACK!
BAM
COUGH COUGH
CHOKE
CHOKE
OW OW OW! SANTA DOWN!
PSSH
OH, YOU'RE IN FOR IT NOW. HOW DARE YOU BREAK INTO THIS PLACE, YOU LITTLE THIEF!
EEEEEEEK
WHAT ARE YOU DOING?! I'M SANTA! SANTA!!

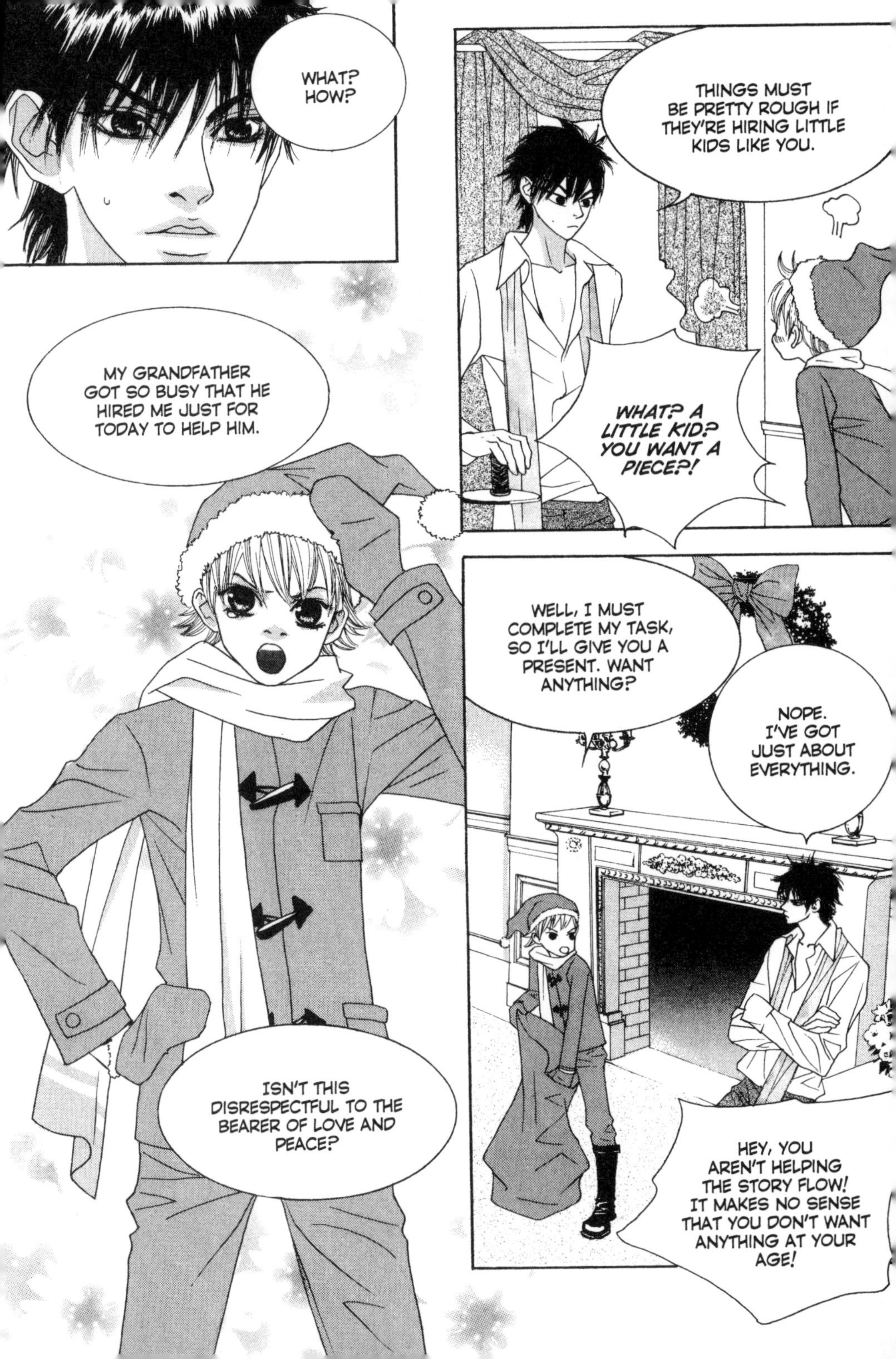
WHAT? HOW?
THINGS MUST BE PRETTY ROUGH IF THEY'RE HIRING LITTLE KIDS LIKE YOU.
WHAT? A LITTLE KID? YOU WANT A PIECE?!
MY GRANDFATHER GOT SO BUSY THAT HE HIRED ME JUST FOR TODAY TO HELP HIM.
ISN'T THIS DISRESPECTFUL TO THE BEARER OF LOVE AND PEACE?
WELL, I MUST COMPLETE MY TASK, SO I'LL GIVE YOU A PRESENT. WANT ANYTHING?
NOPE. I'VE GOT JUST ABOUT EVERYTHING.
HEY, YOU AREN'T HELPING THE STORY FLOW! IT MAKES NO SENSE THAT YOU DON'T WANT ANYTHING AT YOUR AGE!

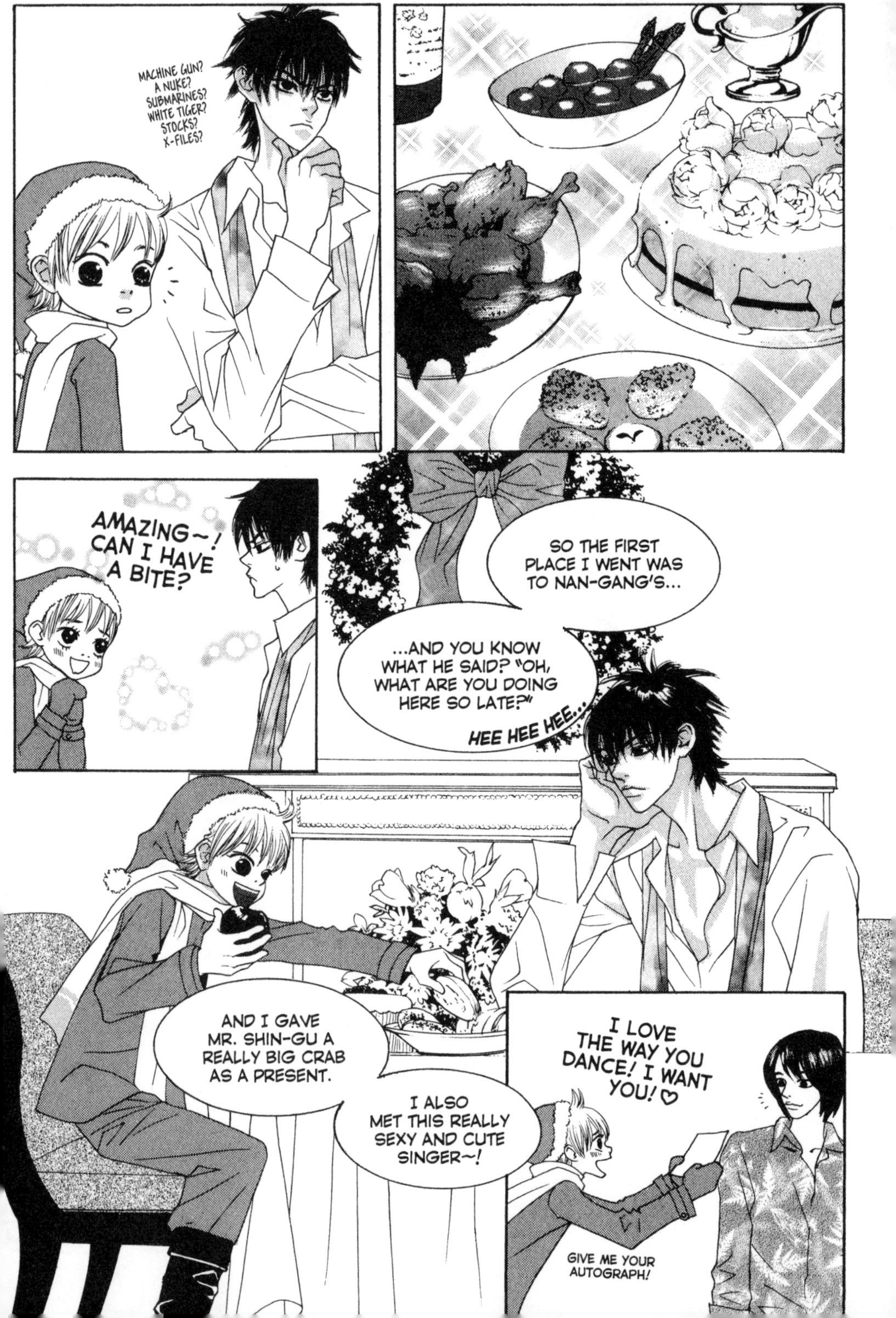
MACHINE GUN? A NUKE? SUBMARINES? WHITE TIGER? STOCKS? X-FILES?
AMAZING~! CAN I HAVE A BITE?
SO THE FIRST PLACE I WENT WAS TO NAN-GANG'S...
...AND YOU KNOW WHAT HE SAID? "OH, WHAT ARE YOU DOING HERE SO LATE?"
HEE HEE HEE...
AND I GAVE MR. SHIN-GU A REALLY BIG CRAB AS A PRESENT.
I ALSO MET THIS REALLY SEXY AND CUTE SINGER~!
I LOVE THE WAY YOU DANCE! I WANT YOU! ♡
GIVE ME YOUR AUTOGRAPH!

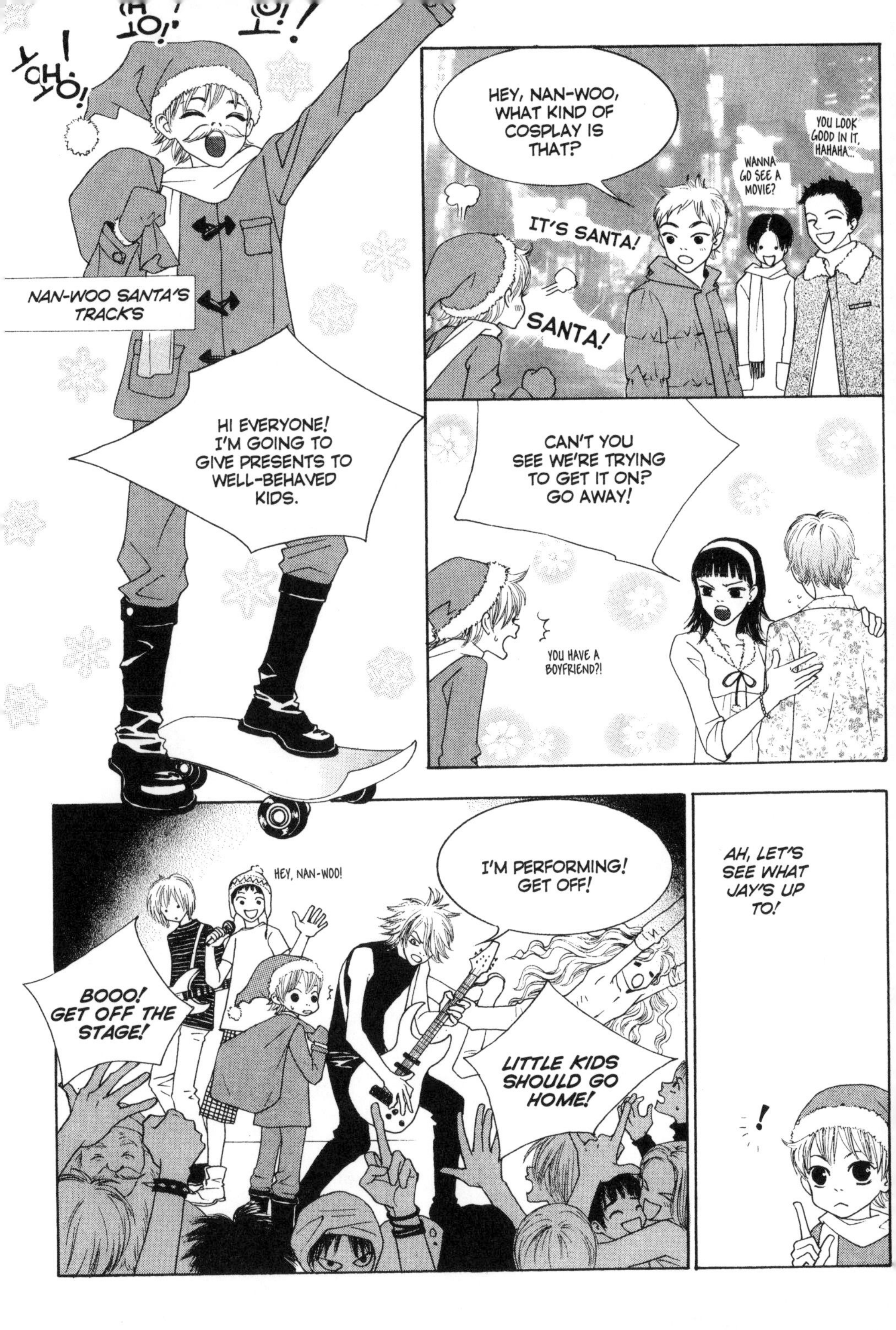
NAN-WOO SANTA'S TRACKS
HI EVERYONE! I'M GOING TO GIVE PRESENTS TO WELL-BEHAVED KIDS.
HEY, NAN-WOO, WHAT KIND OF COSPLAY IS THAT?
IT'S SANTA!
SANTA!
WANNA GO SEE A MOVIE?
YOU LOOK GOOD IN IT, HAHAHA...
CAN'T YOU SEE WE'RE TRYING TO GET IT ON? GO AWAY!
YOU HAVE A BOYFRIEND?!
HEY, NAN-WOO!
BOOO! GET OFF THE STAGE!
I'M PERFORMING! GET OFF!
LITTLE KIDS SHOULD GO HOME!
AH, LET'S SEE WHAT JAY'S UP TO!
!

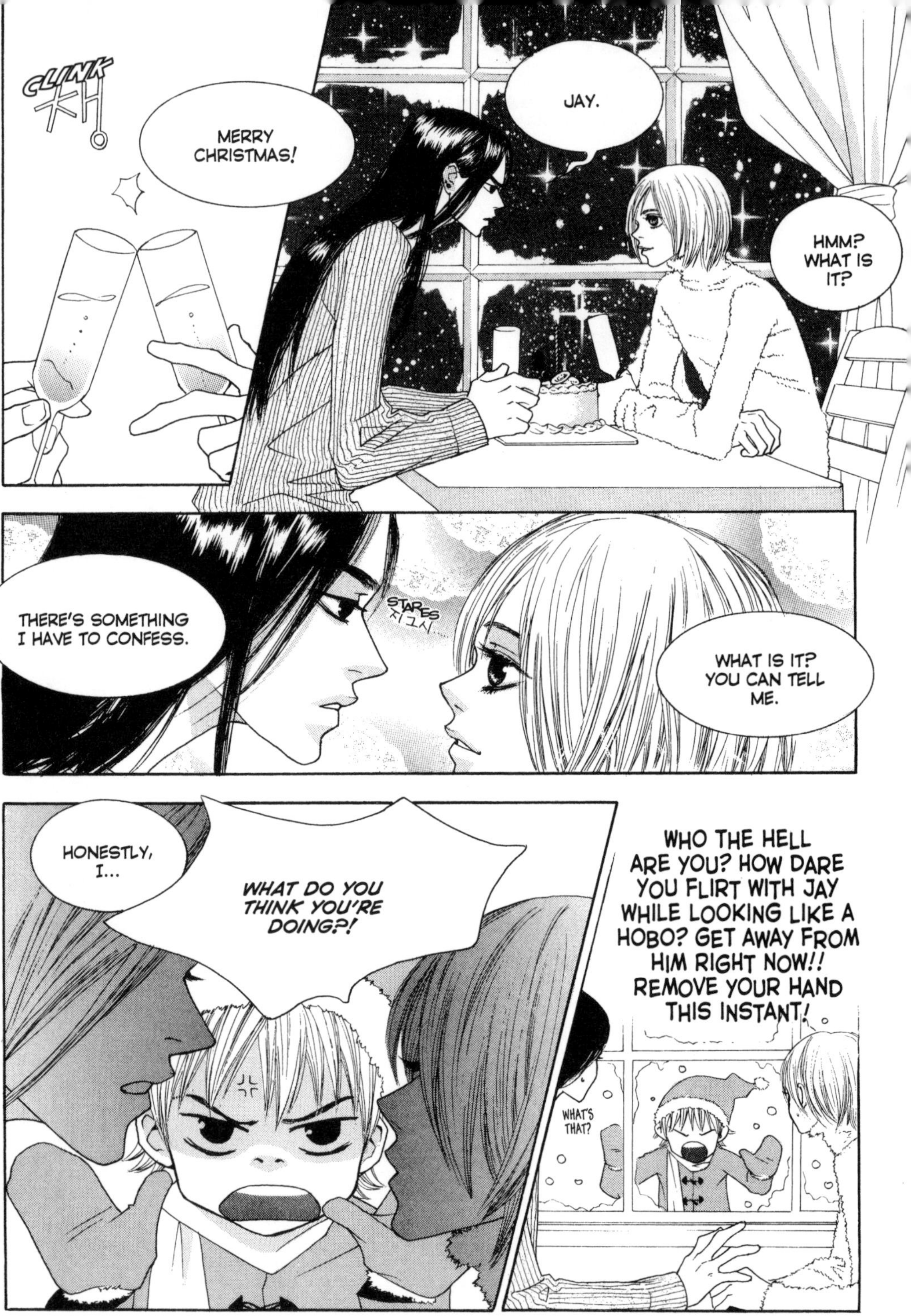
CLINK
MERRY CHRISTMAS!
JAY.
HMM? WHAT IS IT?
THERE'S SOMETHING I HAVE TO CONFESS.
STARES
지그시...
WHAT IS IT? YOU CAN TELL ME.
HONESTLY, I...
WHAT DO YOU THINK YOU'RE DOING?!
WHO THE HELL ARE YOU? HOW DARE YOU FLIRT WITH JAY WHILE LOOKING LIKE A HOBO? GET AWAY FROM HIM RIGHT NOW!! REMOVE YOUR HAND THIS INSTANT!
WHAT'S THAT?

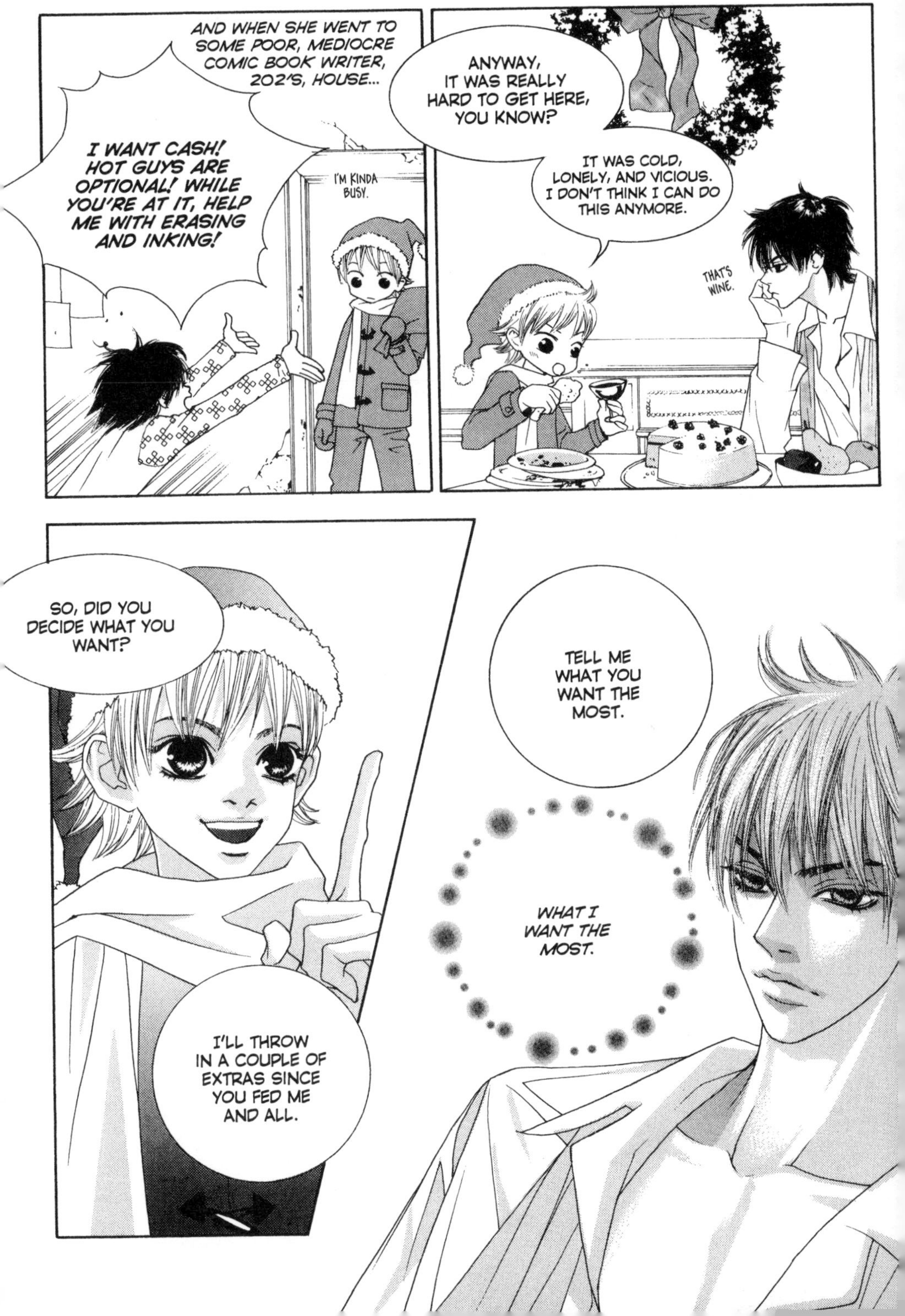
AND WHEN SHE WENT TO SOME POOR, MEDIOCRE COMIC BOOK WRITER, 202'S, HOUSE...
I WANT CASH! HOT GUYS ARE OPTIONAL! WHILE YOU'RE AT IT, HELP ME WITH ERASING AND INKING!
I'M KINDA BUSY.
ANYWAY, IT WAS REALLY HARD TO GET HERE, YOU KNOW?
IT WAS COLD, LONELY, AND VICIOUS. I DON'T THINK I CAN DO THIS ANYMORE.
THAT'S WINE.
SO, DID YOU DECIDE WHAT YOU WANT?
I'LL THROW IN A COUPLE OF EXTRAS SINCE YOU FED ME AND ALL.
TELL ME WHAT YOU WANT THE MOST.
WHAT I WANT THE MOST.

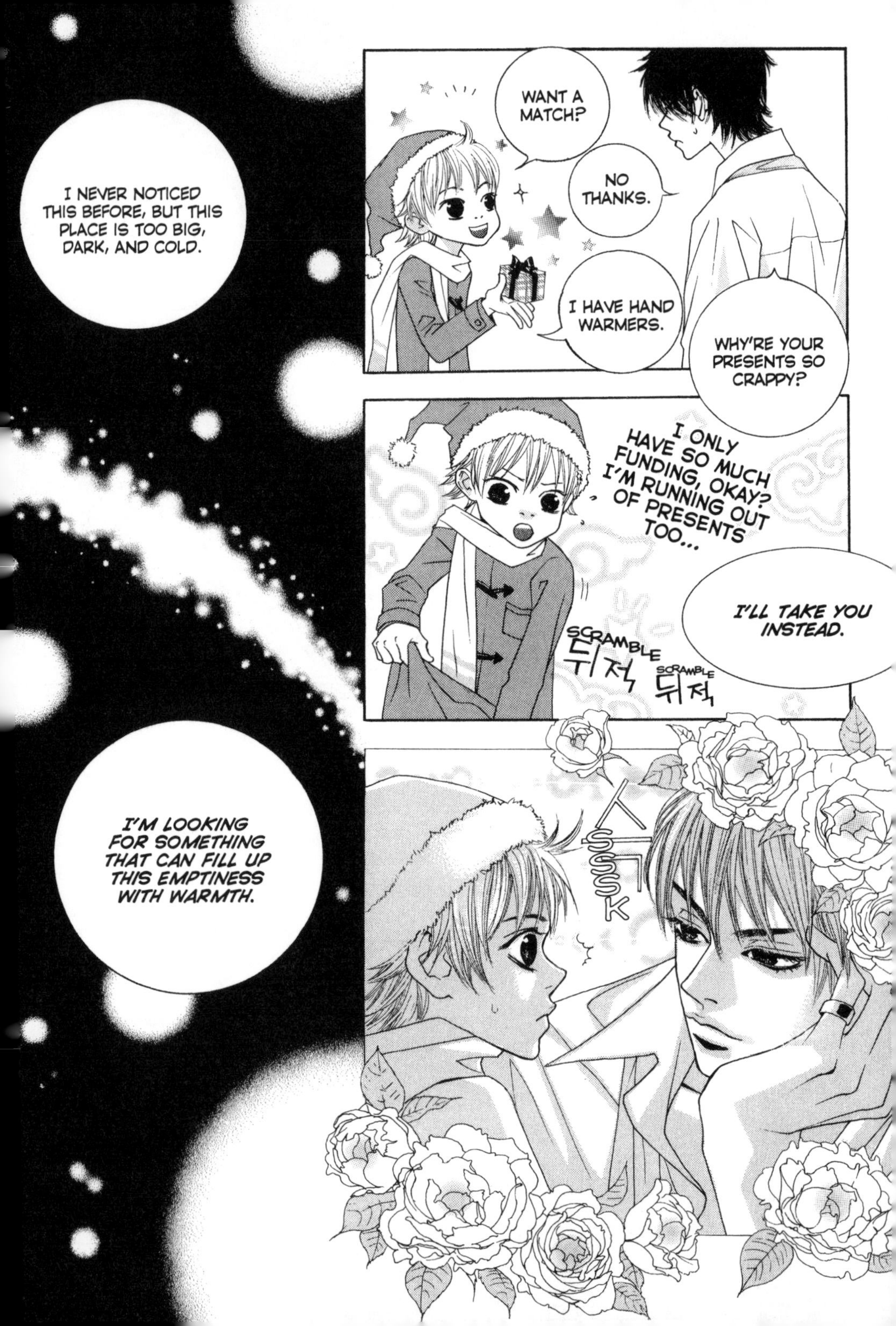
I NEVER NOTICED THIS BEFORE, BUT THIS PLACE IS TOO BIG, DARK, AND COLD.
I'M LOOKING FOR SOMETHING THAT CAN FILL UP THIS EMPTINESS WITH WARMTH.
WANT A MATCH?
NO THANKS.
I HAVE HAND WARMERS.
WHY'RE YOUR PRESENTS SO CRAPPY?
I ONLY HAVE SO MUCH FUNDING, OKAY? I'M RUNNING OUT OF PRESENTS TOO...
SCRAMBLE 뒤적
SCRAMBLE 뒤적
I'LL TAKE YOU INSTEAD.
SSSSK

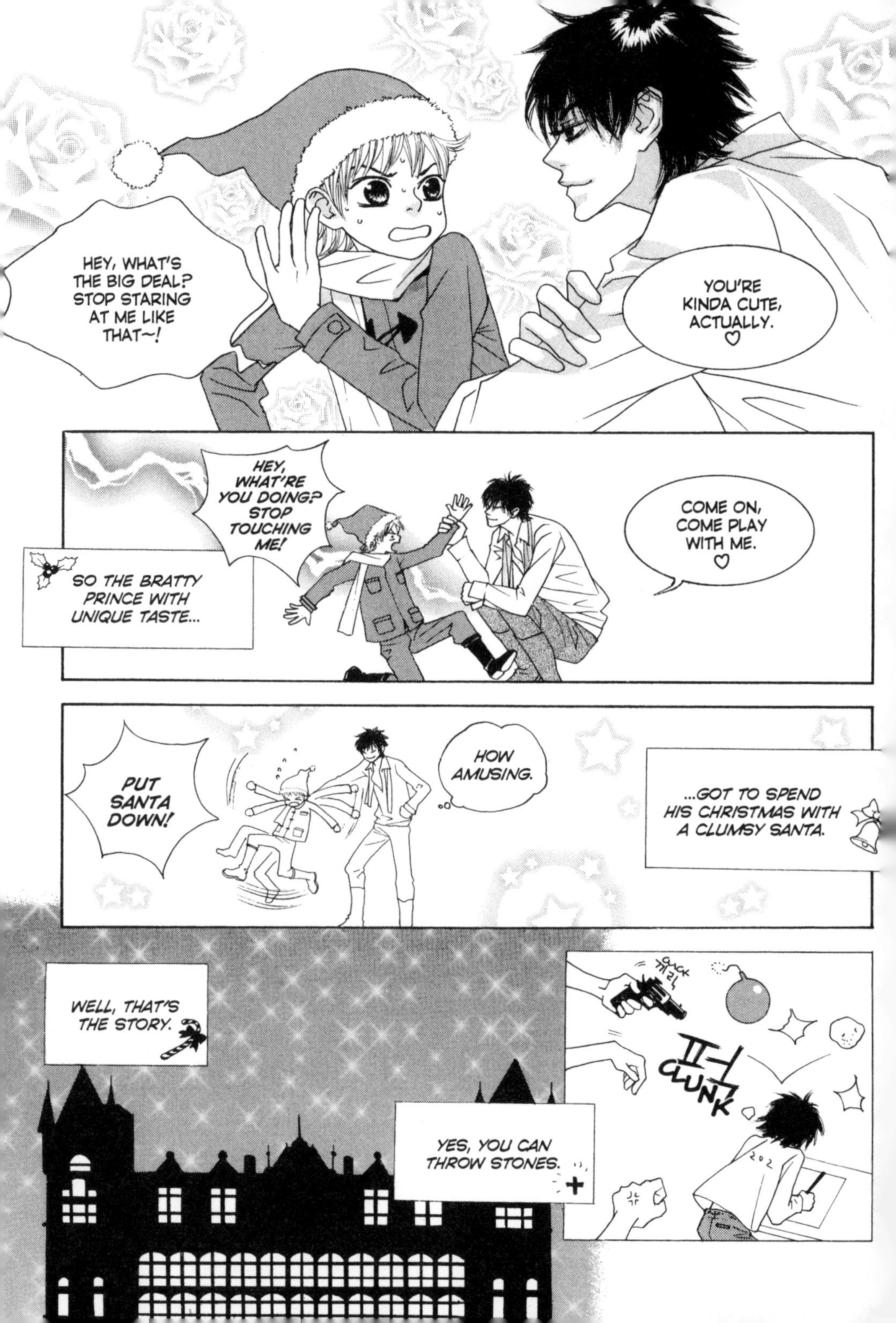
HEY, WHAT'S THE BIG DEAL? STOP STARING AT ME LIKE THAT~!
YOU'RE KINDA CUTE, ACTUALLY. ♡
SO THE BRATTY PRINCE WITH UNIQUE TASTE...
HEY, WHAT'RE YOU DOING? STOP TOUCHING ME!
COME ON, COME PLAY WITH ME. ♡
PUT SANTA DOWN!
HOW AMUSING.
...GOT TO SPEND HIS CHRISTMAS WITH A CLUMSY SANTA.
WELL, THAT'S THE STORY.
YES, YOU CAN THROW STONES.
CLACK
CLUNK
202

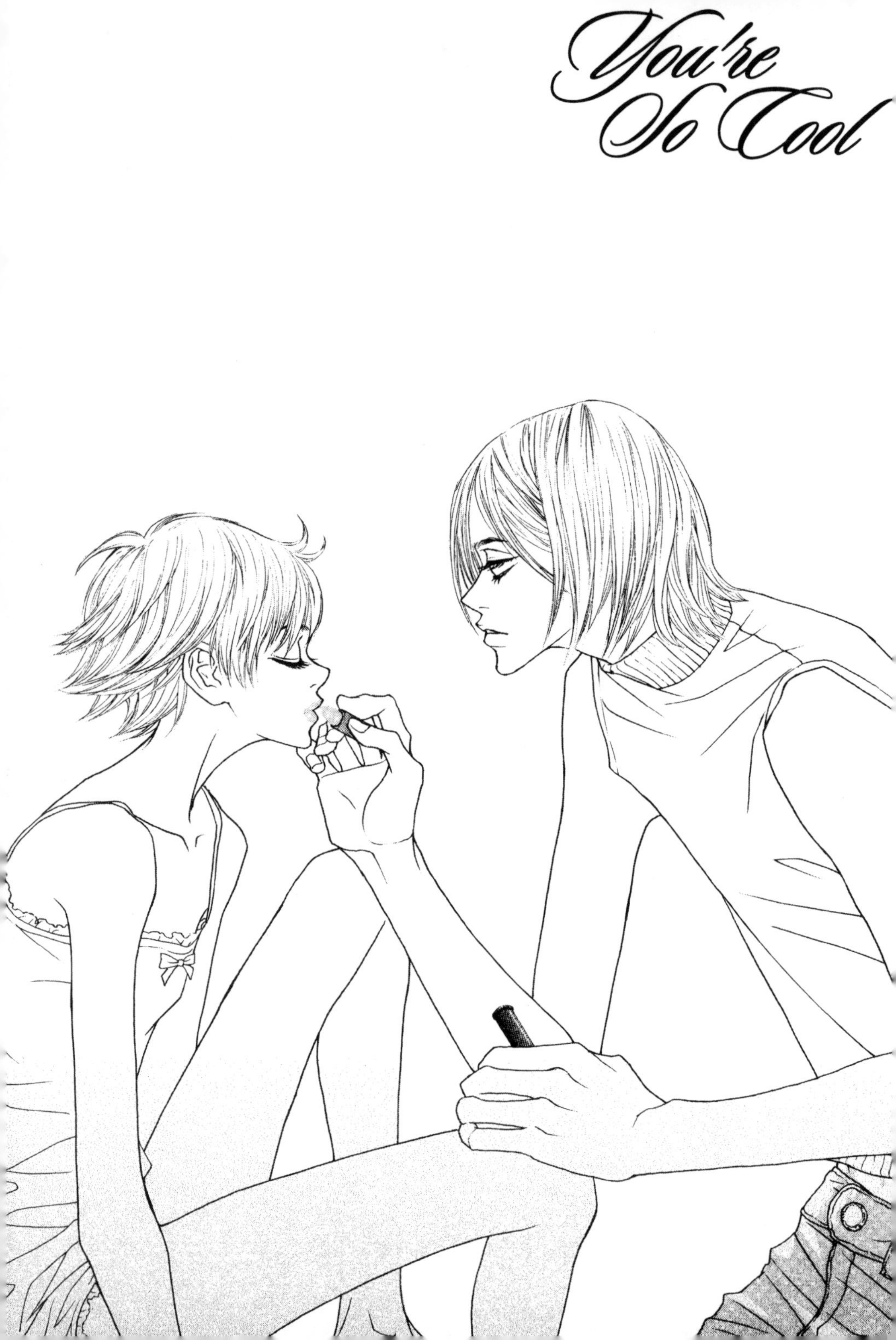
You're So Cool

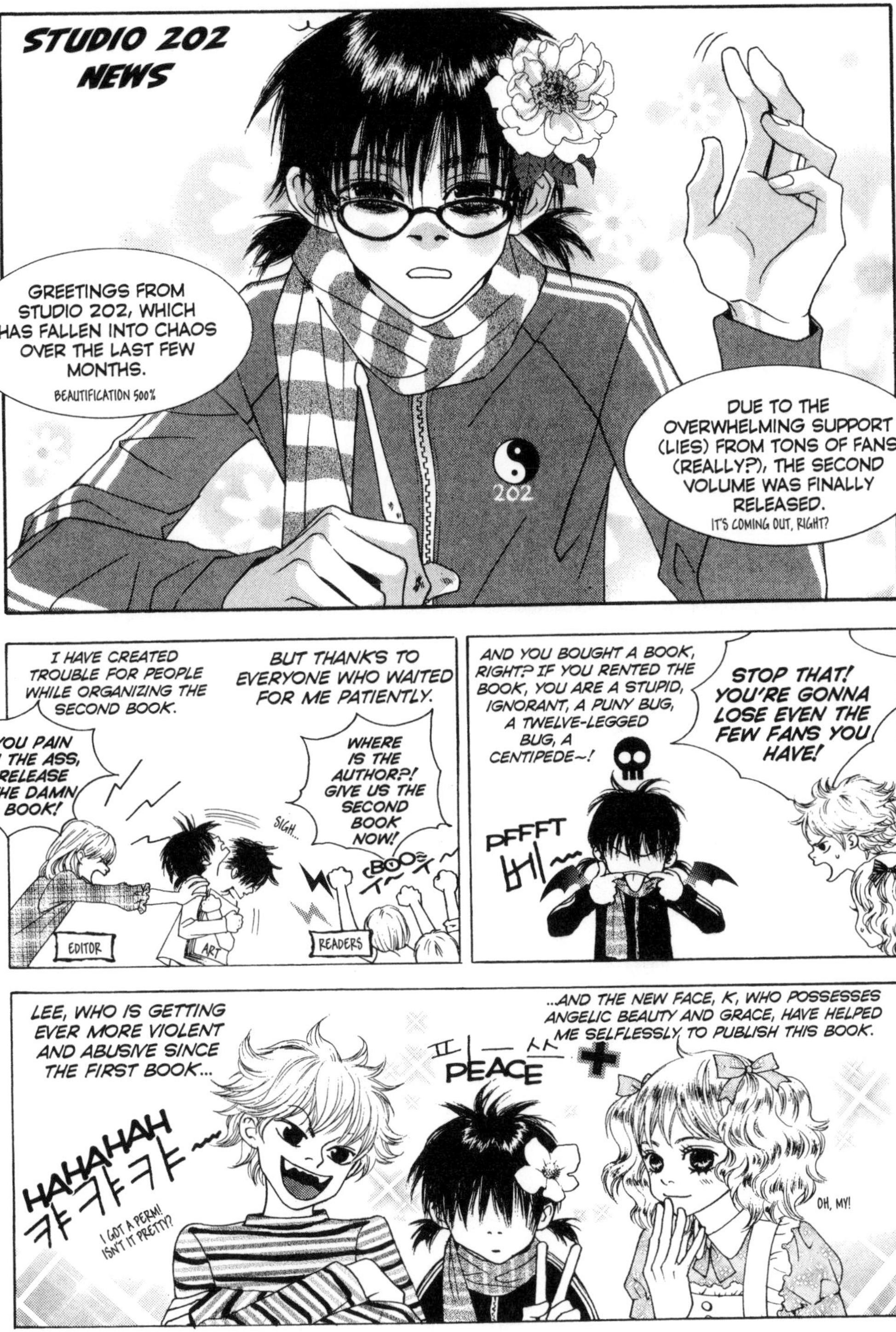
STUDIO 202 NEWS
GREETINGS FROM STUDIO 202, WHICH HAS FALLEN INTO CHAOS OVER THE LAST FEW MONTHS.
BEAUTIFICATION 500%
202
DUE TO THE OVERWHELMING SUPPORT (LIES) FROM TONS OF FANS (REALLY?), THE SECOND VOLUME WAS FINALLY RELEASED.
IT'S COMING OUT, RIGHT?
I HAVE CREATED TROUBLE FOR PEOPLE WHILE ORGANIZING THE SECOND BOOK.
BUT THANKS TO EVERYONE WHO WAITED FOR ME PATIENTLY.
YOU PAIN IN THE ASS, RELEASE THE DAMN BOOK!
WHERE IS THE AUTHOR?! GIVE US THE SECOND BOOK NOW!
SIGH...
BOO
EDITOR
ART
READERS
AND YOU BOUGHT A BOOK, RIGHT? IF YOU RENTED THE BOOK, YOU ARE A STUPID, IGNORANT, A PUNY BUG, A TWELVE-LEGGED BUG, A CENTIPEDE~!
STOP THAT! YOU'RE GONNA LOSE EVEN THE FEW FANS YOU HAVE!
PFFFT
LEE, WHO IS GETTING EVER MORE VIOLENT AND ABUSIVE SINCE THE FIRST BOOK...
...AND THE NEW FACE, K, WHO POSSESSES ANGELIC BEAUTY AND GRACE, HAVE HELPED ME SELFLESSLY TO PUBLISH THIS BOOK.
PEACE
HAHAHAH
I GOT A PERM! ISN'T IT PRETTY?
OH, MY!

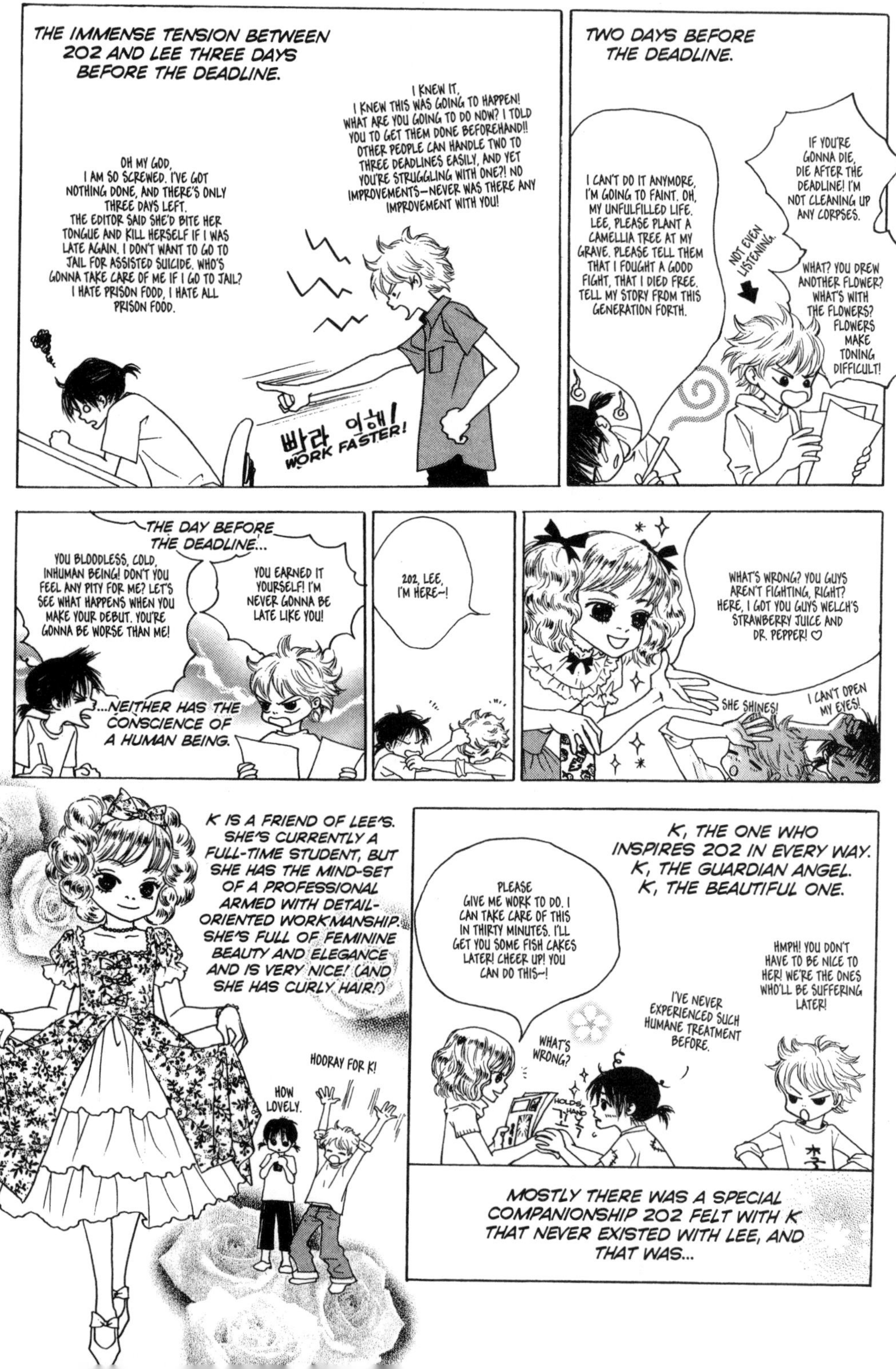
THE IMMENSE TENSION BETWEEN 202 AND LEE THREE DAYS BEFORE THE DEADLINE.
OH MY GOD, I AM SO SCREWED. I'VE GOT NOTHING DONE, AND THERE'S ONLY THREE DAYS LEFT. THE EDITOR SAID SHE'D BITE HER TONGUE AND KILL HERSELF IF I WAS LATE AGAIN. I DON'T WANT TO GO TO JAIL FOR ASSISTED SUICIDE. WHO'S GONNA TAKE CARE OF ME IF I GO TO JAIL? I HATE PRISON FOOD, I HATE ALL PRISON FOOD.
I KNEW IT, I KNEW THIS WAS GOING TO HAPPEN! WHAT ARE YOU GOING TO DO NOW? I TOLD YOU TO GET THEM DONE BEFOREHAND!! OTHER PEOPLE CAN HANDLE TWO TO THREE DEADLINES EASILY, AND YET YOU'RE STRUGGLING WITH ONE?! NO IMPROVEMENTS—NEVER WAS THERE ANY IMPROVEMENT WITH YOU!
WORK FASTER!
TWO DAYS BEFORE THE DEADLINE.
I CAN'T DO IT ANYMORE, I'M GOING TO FAINT. OH, MY UNFULFILLED LIFE. LEE, PLEASE PLANT A CAMELLIA TREE AT MY GRAVE. PLEASE TELL THEM THAT I FOUGHT A GOOD FIGHT, THAT I DIED FREE. TELL MY STORY FROM THIS GENERATION FORTH.
NOT EVEN LISTENING.
IF YOU'RE GONNA DIE, DIE AFTER THE DEADLINE! I'M NOT CLEANING UP ANY CORPSES.
WHAT? YOU DREW ANOTHER FLOWER? WHAT'S WITH THE FLOWERS? FLOWERS MAKE TONING DIFFICULT!
THE DAY BEFORE THE DEADLINE...
YOU BLOODLESS, COLD, INHUMAN BEING! DON'T YOU FEEL ANY PITY FOR ME? LET'S SEE WHAT HAPPENS WHEN YOU MAKE YOUR DEBUT. YOU'RE GONNA BE WORSE THAN ME!
YOU EARNED IT YOURSELF! I'M NEVER GONNA BE LATE LIKE YOU!
...NEITHER HAS THE CONSCIENCE OF A HUMAN BEING.
202, LEE, I'M HERE~!
WHAT'S WRONG? YOU GUYS AREN'T FIGHTING, RIGHT? HERE, I GOT YOU GUYS WELCH'S STRAWBERRY JUICE AND DR. PEPPER! ♡
SHE SHINES!
I CAN'T OPEN MY EYES!
K IS A FRIEND OF LEE'S. SHE'S CURRENTLY A FULL-TIME STUDENT, BUT SHE HAS THE MIND-SET OF A PROFESSIONAL ARMED WITH DETAIL-ORIENTED WORKMANSHIP. SHE'S FULL OF FEMININE BEAUTY AND ELEGANCE AND IS VERY NICE! (AND SHE HAS CURLY HAIR!)
HOW LOVELY.
HOORAY FOR K!
K, THE ONE WHO INSPIRES 202 IN EVERY WAY. K, THE GUARDIAN ANGEL. K, THE BEAUTIFUL ONE.
PLEASE GIVE ME WORK TO DO. I CAN TAKE CARE OF THIS IN THIRTY MINUTES. I'LL GET YOU SOME FISH CAKES LATER! CHEER UP! YOU CAN DO THIS~!
WHAT'S WRONG?
I'VE NEVER EXPERIENCED SUCH HUMANE TREATMENT BEFORE.
HOLDS HAND
HMPH! YOU DON'T HAVE TO BE NICE TO HER! WE'RE THE ONES WHO'LL BE SUFFERING LATER!
MOSTLY THERE WAS A SPECIAL COMPANIONSHIP 202 FELT WITH K THAT NEVER EXISTED WITH LEE, AND THAT WAS...

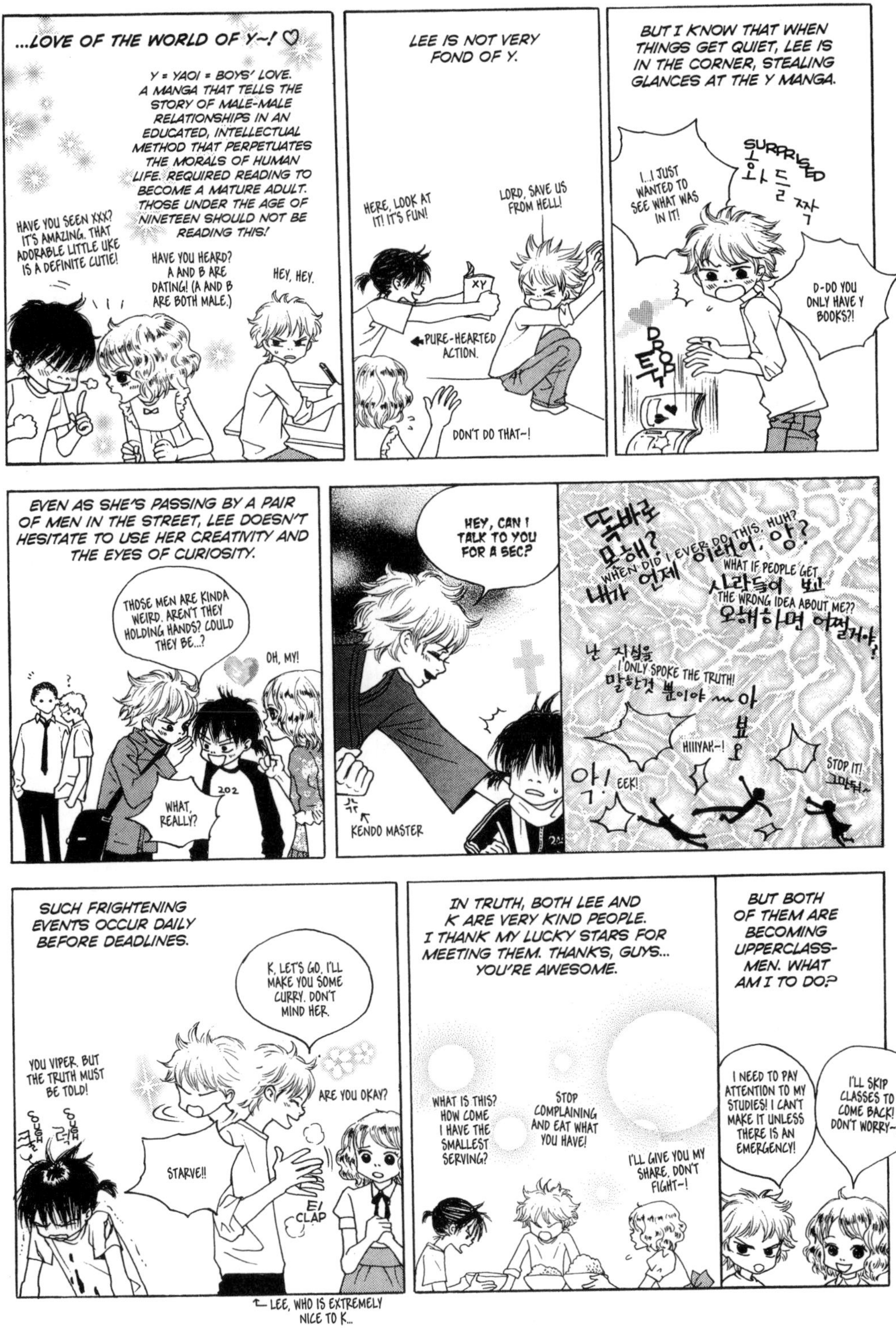
...LOVE OF THE WORLD OF Y~! ♡
Y = YAOI = BOYS' LOVE. A MANGA THAT TELLS THE STORY OF MALE-MALE RELATIONSHIPS IN AN EDUCATED, INTELLECTUAL METHOD THAT PERPETUATES THE MORALS OF HUMAN LIFE. REQUIRED READING TO BECOME A MATURE ADULT. THOSE UNDER THE AGE OF NINETEEN SHOULD NOT BE READING THIS!
HAVE YOU SEEN XXX? IT'S AMAZING. THAT ADORABLE LITTLE UKE IS A DEFINITE CUTIE!
HAVE YOU HEARD? A AND B ARE DATING! (A AND B ARE BOTH MALE.)
HEY, HEY.
LEE IS NOT VERY FOND OF Y.
HERE, LOOK AT IT! IT'S FUN!
XY
LORD, SAVE US FROM HELL!
PURE-HEARTED ACTION.
DON'T DO THAT~!
BUT I KNOW THAT WHEN THINGS GET QUIET, LEE IS IN THE CORNER, STEALING GLANCES AT THE Y MANGA.
I...I JUST WANTED TO SEE WHAT WAS IN IT!
SURPRISED
화들짝
D-DO YOU ONLY HAVE Y BOOKS?!
DROP
EVEN AS SHE'S PASSING BY A PAIR OF MEN IN THE STREET, LEE DOESN'T HESITATE TO USE HER CREATIVITY AND THE EYES OF CURIOSITY.
THOSE MEN ARE KINDA WEIRD. AREN'T THEY HOLDING HANDS? COULD THEY BE...?
OH, MY!
WHAT, REALLY?
202
HEY, CAN I TALK TO YOU FOR A SEC?
KENDO MASTER
WHEN DID I EVER DO THIS, HUH?
WHAT IF PEOPLE GET THE WRONG IDEA ABOUT ME??
I ONLY SPOKE THE TRUTH!
HIIIYAH~!
EEK!
STOP IT!
SUCH FRIGHTENING EVENTS OCCUR DAILY BEFORE DEADLINES.
K, LET'S GO. I'LL MAKE YOU SOME CURRY. DON'T MIND HER.
YOU VIPER. BUT THE TRUTH MUST BE TOLD!
COUGH
COUGH
ARE YOU OKAY?
STARVE!!
CLAP
LEE, WHO IS EXTREMELY NICE TO K...
IN TRUTH, BOTH LEE AND K ARE VERY KIND PEOPLE. I THANK MY LUCKY STARS FOR MEETING THEM. THANKS, GUYS... YOU'RE AWESOME.
WHAT IS THIS? HOW COME I HAVE THE SMALLEST SERVING?
STOP COMPLAINING AND EAT WHAT YOU HAVE!
I'LL GIVE YOU MY SHARE, DON'T FIGHT~!
BUT BOTH OF THEM ARE BECOMING UPPERCLASSMEN. WHAT AM I TO DO?
I NEED TO PAY ATTENTION TO MY STUDIES! I CAN'T MAKE IT UNLESS THERE IS AN EMERGENCY!
I'LL SKIP CLASSES TO COME BACK! DON'T WORRY~!

# SPECIAL AFTERWORDS BY THE REBEL ASSISTANT, LEE

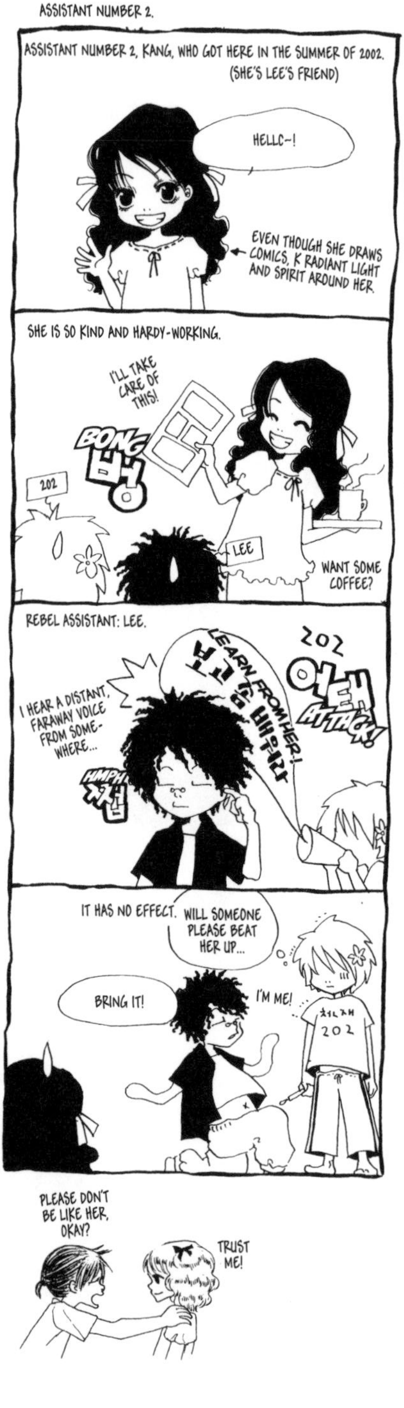
ASSISTANT NUMBER 2.
ASSISTANT NUMBER 2, KANG, WHO GOT HERE IN THE SUMMER OF 2002.
(SHE'S LEE'S FRIEND)
HELLC~!
EVEN THOUGH SHE DRAWS COMICS, K RADIANT LIGHT AND SPIRIT AROUND HER.
SHE IS SO KIND AND HARDY-WORKING.
I'LL TAKE CARE OF THIS!
BONG
202
LEE
WANT SOME COFFEE?
REBEL ASSISTANT: LEE.
I HEAR A DISTANT, FARAWAY VOICE FROM SOMEWHERE...
HMPH
LEARN FROM HER!
202
ATTACK!
IT HAS NO EFFECT.
WILL SOMEONE PLEASE BEAT HER UP...
BRING IT!
I'M ME!
202
PLEASE DON'T BE LIKE HER, OKAY?
TRUST ME!

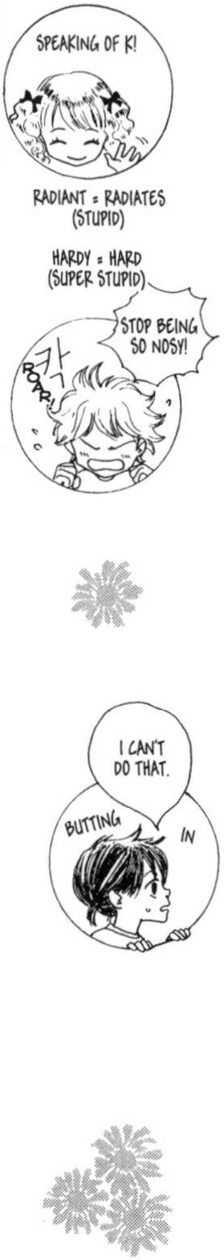
SPEAKING OF K!
RADIANT = RADIATES (STUPID)
HARDY = HARD (SUPER STUPID)
STOP BEING SO NOSY!
ROAR!
I CAN'T DO THAT.
BUTTING IN

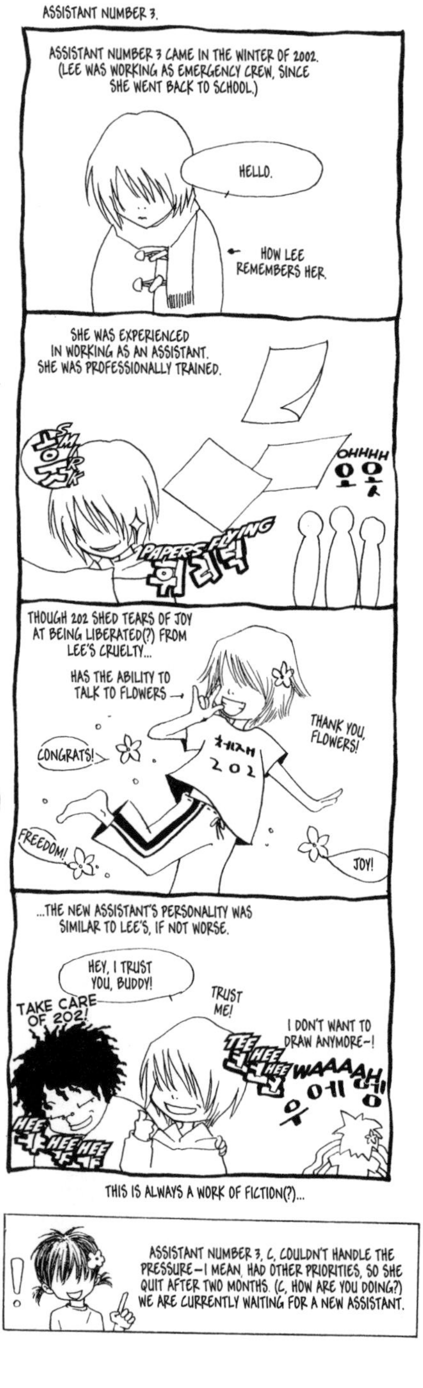
ASSISTANT NUMBER 3.
ASSISTANT NUMBER 3 CAME IN THE WINTER OF 2002. (LEE WAS WORKING AS EMERGENCY CREW, SINCE SHE WENT BACK TO SCHOOL.)
HELLO.
HOW LEE REMEMBERS HER.
SHE WAS EXPERIENCED IN WORKING AS AN ASSISTANT. SHE WAS PROFESSIONALLY TRAINED.
SMIRK
OHHHH
PAPERS FLYING
THOUGH 202 SHED TEARS OF JOY AT BEING LIBERATED(?) FROM LEE'S CRUELTY...
HAS THE ABILITY TO TALK TO FLOWERS
THANK YOU, FLOWERS!
CONGRATS!
202
FREEDOM!
JOY!
...THE NEW ASSISTANT'S PERSONALITY WAS SIMILAR TO LEE'S, IF NOT WORSE.
HEY, I TRUST YOU, BUDDY!
TAKE CARE OF 202!
TRUST ME!
I DON'T WANT TO DRAW ANYMORE~!
TEE HEE HEE
WAAAAH
HEE HEE HEE
THIS IS ALWAYS A WORK OF FICTION(?)...
ASSISTANT NUMBER 3, C, COULDN'T HANDLE THE PRESSURE—I MEAN, HAD OTHER PRIORITIES, SO SHE QUIT AFTER TWO MONTHS. (C, HOW ARE YOU DOING?) WE ARE CURRENTLY WAITING FOR A NEW ASSISTANT.

# MESSAGE...

THE WORK ON VOLUME TWO WAS DONE DURING SUMMER THROUGH LATE AUTUMN. BY NATURE, 202 IS VERY INACTIVE, BUT THE SEASONS WENT BY SO FAST AS I CONCENTRATED FULLY ON THE WORK. ALWAYS BACKING OUT OF PROMISES TO HANG WITH FRIENDS, NOT BEING ABLE TO SEE THE SEASHORE THAT WAS ONLY TEN MINUTES AWAY, AND BREAKING PROMISES TO THOSE AROUND ME DUE TO THE SHORTAGE OF TIME LEFT ME FEELING EMPTY AND DRIED UP.
I APOLOGIZE TO EVERYONE WHO HAD TO DEAL WITH THIS.
ESPECIALLY TO MY HEAD EDITOR WHO HAD TO DEAL WITH MY SLOW HAND AND MY LIES.
(I HOPE YOUR BABY GROWS HEALTHY!)
AND TO LEE AND K, FOR WHOM I FEEL BAD THAT THEY HAD TO MEET SUCH CLUMSY MANHWAGA, THANKS AGAIN FOR WORKING SO HARD—YOU GUYS ARE TERRIFIC!
AND TO MY FRIENDS, WHOM I DITCHED EVERY TIME DUE TO DEADLINE CRUNCHES, ALWAYS KNOW THAT I'M THERE WITH YOU IN SPIRIT. THANKS FOR CHEERING ME UP THROUGH YOUR CALLS AND MESSAGES.

I WANT TO ESPECIALLY THANK THE DAUM CAFÉ FAN CLUB, "WHA" (FLOWER), WHICH CONSTANTLY OVERWHELMS ME WITH GIGANTIC SUPPORT AND CARING. I CANNOT THANK YOU GUYS ENOUGH FOR IT.
PARTICULARLY TO MISS SOO-JEUNG OF "WHA," YOU ARE SO AMAZING!
TO THOSE WHO READ MY WORK IN SILENCE, EVEN THOUGH I AM LACKING, I'LL DO MY BEST TO CONSTANTLY IMPROVE MYSELF.
PLEASE LOVE THE THIRD BOOK AS WELL!

3.4.2003, 202.

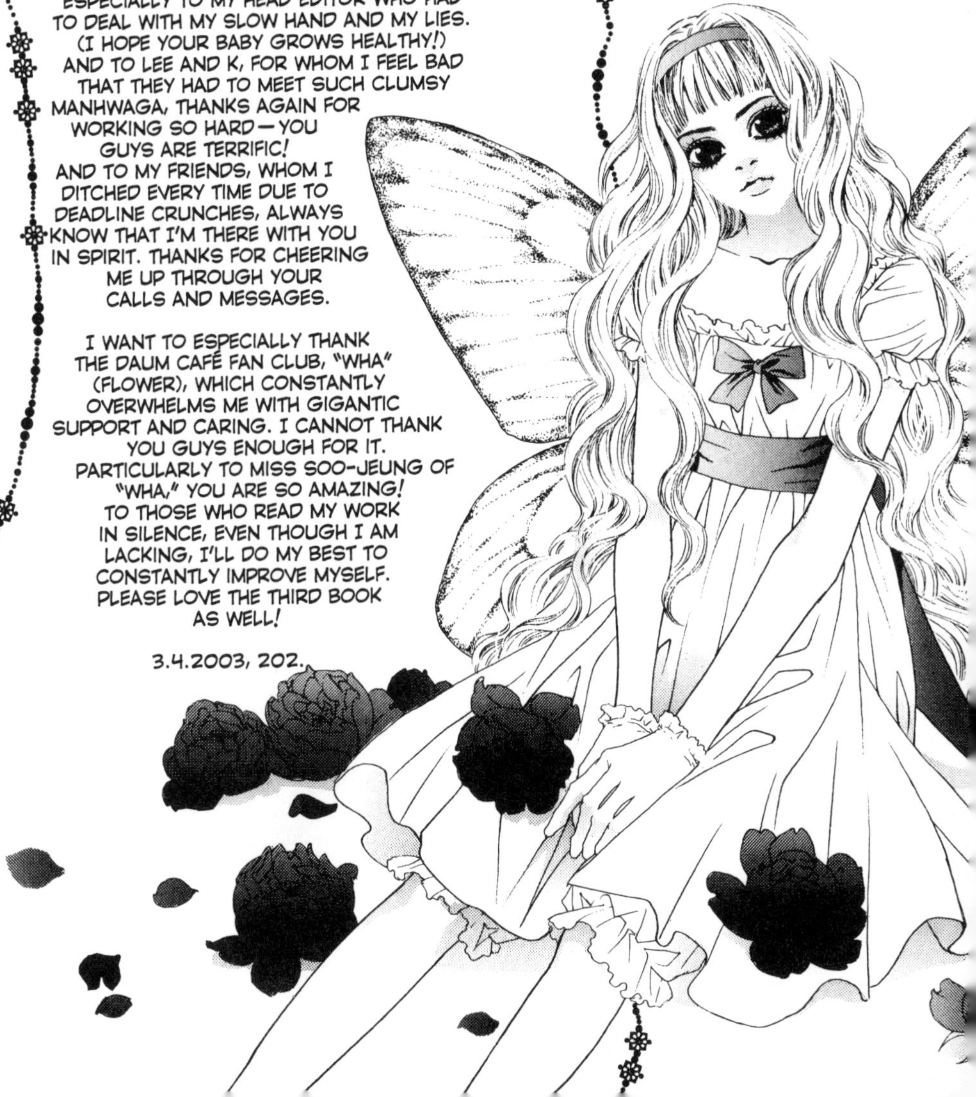

Yen Press
www.yenpress.com

# Becoming the princess... Isn't that every girl's dream?!

Monarchy rule ended long ago in Korea, but there are still other countries with kings, queens, princes and princesses. What if Korea had continued monarchism? What if all the beautiful palaces, which are now only historical relics, were actually filled with people? What if the glamorous royal family still maintained the palace customs? Welcome to a world where Korea still has the royal family living in their everyday lives! Only for this one high school girl, Chae-Kyung, is this a tragedy, since she has to marry the prince — who apparently is a total bastard!

## THE ROYAL PALACE
# Goong
### vol.1~2

## Park SoHee

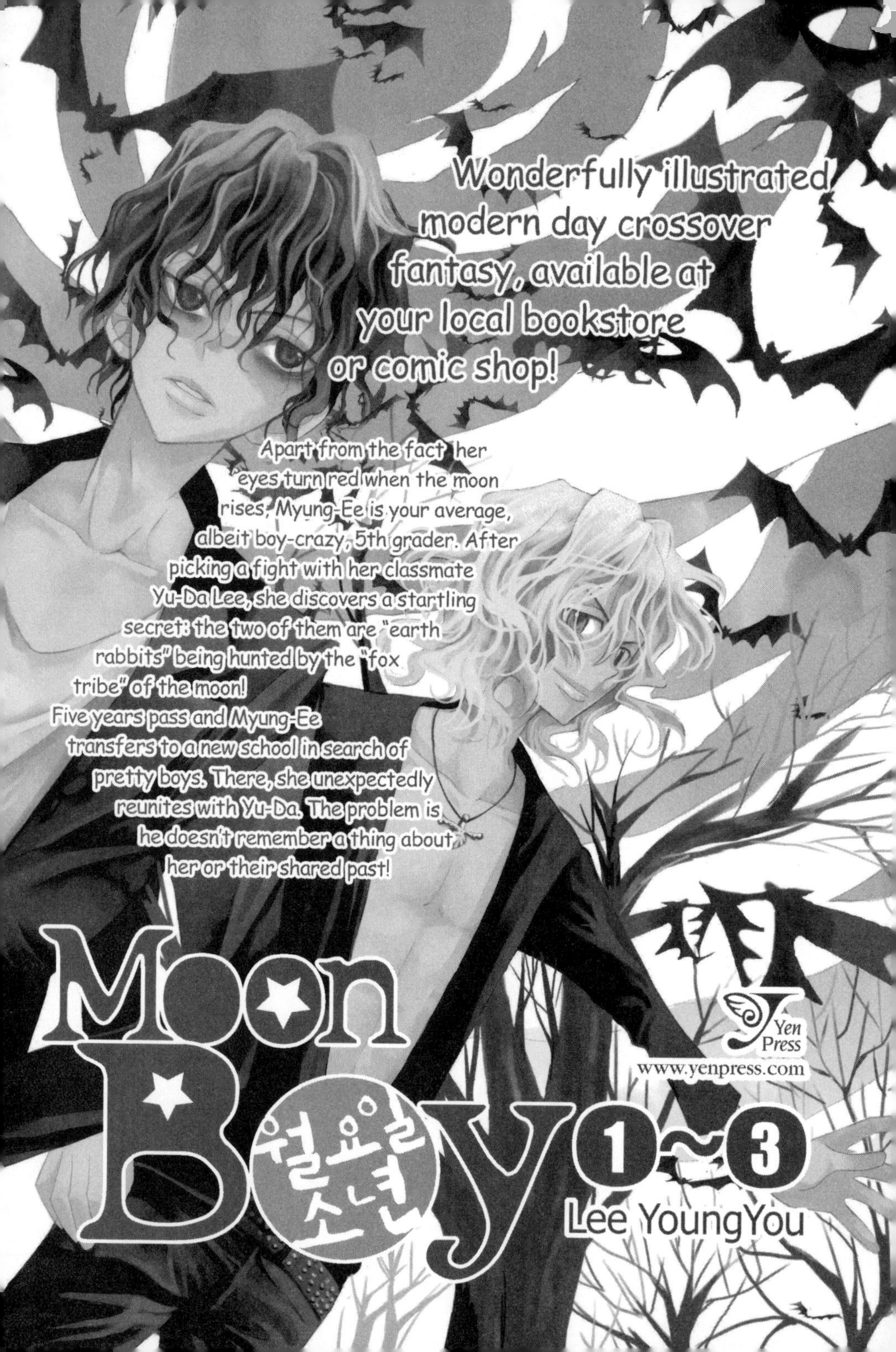

Wonderfully illustrated modern day crossover fantasy, available at your local bookstore or comic shop!
Apart from the fact her eyes turn red when the moon rises, Myung-Ee is your average, albeit boy-crazy, 5th grader. After picking a fight with her classmate Yu-Da Lee, she discovers a startling secret: the two of them are "earth rabbits" being hunted by the "fox tribe" of the moon!
Five years pass and Myung-Ee transfers to a new school in search of pretty boys. There, she unexpectedly reunites with Yu-Da. The problem is, he doesn't remember a thing about her or their shared past!
Moon Boy
월요일 소년
1~3
Lee YoungYou
Yen Press
www.yenpress.com

# Totally new Arabian nights, where Shahrazad is a guy!

Everyone knows the story of Shahrazad and her wonderful tales from the Arabian Nights. For one thousand and one nights, the stories that she created entertained the mad Sultan and eventually saved her life. In this version, Shahrazad is a guy who wanted to save his sister from the mad Sultan by disguising himself as a woman. When he puts his life on the line, what kind of strange and unique stories would he tell? This new twist on one of the greatest classical tales might just keep you awake for another ONE THOUSAND AND ONE NIGHTS.

Yen Press
www.yenpress.com

Available at bookstores near you!

# One thousand and one nights 1~4

## Han SeungHee · Jeon JinSeok